SUPERSTITION WILDERNESS
TRAILS WEST
HIKES, HORSE RIDES, AND HISTORY

JACK CARLSON

ELIZABETH STEWART

CLEAR CREEK PUBLISHING, TEMPE, ARIZONA

SUPERSTITION WILDERNESS TRAILS WEST
HIKES, HORSE RIDES, AND HISTORY

JACK CARLSON AND ELIZABETH STEWART

Clear Creek Publishing
P.O. Box 24666, Tempe, Arizona 85285 U.S.A.
www.ClearCreekPublishing.com

Copyright © 2012, 2013, 2015, 2017, 2022 by Jack Carlson and Elizabeth Stewart
First Edition 2012. Second Edition 2022.
Printed and bound in the United States of America.

Cover and book design by Ron Short, Santa Fe, New Mexico, www.ronshortstudios.com.

Cover photograph of Superstition Mountain by the authors.

Back cover photographs: La Barge Creek between Music Canyon and La Barge Spring; Jesse Feldman of OK Corral Stables riding Doc, leading Molly (white horse), and Virgil on the Bull Pass Trail in Needle Canyon; Superstition Mountain; Inscribed rock on Black Top Mesa.

Images of the boots, book and pen, spur, and horseshoe are courtesy of the Grand Canyon National Park Museum.

Photographs not otherwise credited were taken by the authors.

Publishers Cataloging-in-Publication Data
Carlson, Jack
Superstition Wilderness trails west : hikes, horse rides, and history/ by Jack Carlson and Elizabeth Stewart.
2nd ed.
416 p. : ill., maps ; 22 cm.
Bibliography: p. 399
Includes index.
1. Hiking—Arizona—Superstition Wilderness—Guidebooks. 2. Superstition Wilderness (Ariz.)—Guidebooks. 3. Lost Dutchman Mine—Arizona—History.
I. Stewart, Elizabeth (Elizabeth J.) II. Title.

917.9175 dc23   Library of Congress Control Number: 2021931229
978-1-884224-12-6

10 9 8 7 6 5 4 3 2 1

Two roads diverge in a wood, and I—

I took the one less traveled by,

And that has made all the difference.

Robert Frost, 1874–1963

ACKNOWLEDGMENTS

Many people contributed to this guidebook. We appreciate the assistance and encouragement that each person has provided. We are indebted to the other authors who have documented their Superstition Mountain travels and experiences. We acknowledge their books, photographs, and contributions throughout *Superstition Wilderness Trails West*.

The newspaper and historical records of Greg Davis and *The Chronological History of the Superstition Wilderness Area* by the late Tom Kollenborn were essential for our research. John Fritz, Dave Cameron, Todd Gartman, Joe Bartels, Irv Kanode, Wally Farak, Mike Stivers, Kent Struble, and all the folks who wrote comments on www.hikearizona.com and www.arizonahikers.com provided us with trail updates. Discussions of current research on the former www.thelostduchman.net site were useful and helped us with sources for our own research. Howard Horinek taught Jack how to ride a horse and wrangle a packhorse, which gave us a better appreciation of the hazards facing stockmen. Exploratory hikes and discussions of historical events with Jack San Felice, Greg Davis, Steve Bowser, and Dick Walp anchored the dialogue to the physical locations in the mountains.

The ranching history was revealed to us by late Nancy McCollough, the late Ken McCollough, the late Bill Martin, the late Helen Martin, George and Lynn Martin, the late Jim Herron, the late Phyllis Herron, Frank Herron, Chuck and Judy Backus, Howard Horinek, Peter Busnack, Betty Jean Schahrer, the late Harry Smith, the late Gladys Walker, the late John Olson, Manny Ruiz, and Louis Ruiz.

For their advice and assistance, we thank Bob and the late Helen Corbin, Tom Glover, Clay Worst, the late George Johnston, Brian Lickman, Larry Hedrick, Ron and Jayne Feldman, Jesse Feldman, Josh Feldman, Ken Nelssen, Scotty McBride, Greg Hansen, Russ Orr, Don Van Driel, Connie Lane, the late Pete Weinel, Michael Sullivan, Steve Germick, Scott Wood, Martin McAllister, Brad Orr, the late Stu Herkenhoff, Anthony Miller, Helen Thompson, Hazel Clark, the late Bill Sewrey, the late Tom Clary, John Wilburn, the late Ray Ruiz, Dave Hughes, the late Rick Gwynne, the late Joe Ribaudo, Chris Coleman, Rosemary and Larry Shearer, Anne Coe, the late Don Wells, Tony Backus, the late Merlin Yeager, Mike and Amy Doyle, Beth Roth, the late Susan Yarina and Joe Yarina, the late Bill Smith, George Harbin, Ted Tenny, Bob and Lou Ann Schoose, Shelly Dudley, Ileen Snoddy, the late Bob and Kay Stewart, Kathy Winston, Barbara Stewart, Robert Stewart, the late Bill McKenzie and Gini McKenzie, Jan Hancock, John Stanley, Rogil Schroeter, Dave Cameron, Deborah Shelton, Melanie Sturgeon, Nancy Sawyer, Wendi Goen, Don Langlois, Julie Hoff, Tony Smith, K. C. Nash, Margaret T. Baker, Bill and Lynn Haak, the late Donna Anderson, Chris Reid, John Tanner, John Langellier, Susan Lintelmann, Neal Berg, Robert Mason, Dave Leach, Bob Pugh, Clay Workman, Art Christiansen, the late Lynn Heglie, John Shaw, the late John Swearengin, Roelof Velthuis, Paul Blanc, Wendy Howe, John Rosenstock, Ed Stevens, Bill Pool, Lon McAdam, Joe Monaco, Ti Ayers, Sandie Buto, Monika Wood, Bill Wood, Ken Olum, and Peg Primak.

The organizations that helped us are Superstition Mountain Historical Society; Tonto National Forest—Phoenix Office, Mesa District, Tonto Basin District, and Globe District; Bureau of Land Management, Phoenix Office; Reevis Mountain School; Salt River Project Research Archives; Arizona Book Publishing Association; Tempe Public Library; Arizona Department of Library and Archives; Arizona Historical Society; Arizona Historical Foundation; Gila County Historical Society; Gila County Recorder and Treasurer; Pinal County Historical Society; Pinal County Recorder and Treasurer; Superior Historical Society; Superstition Area Land Trust; University of Arizona Library and Special Collections; Arizona State University Library and Special Collections; Grand Canyon National Park Museum; Sharlot Hall Museum and Archives; Arizona Game and Fish Department; Arizona State Land Department; Mesa Library; Mesa Family History Center; Impression Makers; Costco Photo, Tempe; Image Craft; Thomson-Shore, Inc.; United States Military Academy Library; National Archives, Washington, DC; National Archives, College Park, Maryland; National Archives, Riverside, California; National Geodetic Survey, Silver Spring, Maryland; USGS, Denver; Arizona Geological Survey, Tucson; Arizona Department of Mines and Mineral Resources; and University of Nevada, Reno—Mackay School of Mines and Getchell Library.

We wish to give a special thanks to three people that helped a great deal on the project: book and cover designer Ron Short of Ron Short Studios, Santa Fe, New Mexico; editor Gwen Henson of Sagebrush Publications, Tempe, Arizona; and editor Kathy Winston of Robstown, Texas.

For the 2022 edition, we thank Wally Farak and Steve Bowser for field checking and documenting the extent of the June 2019 Woodbury Fire, the June 2020 Sawtooth Fire, and the August 2020 Superstition Fire. They documented the corrals, buildings, signs, and other landmarks that were burned or spared in the wildfire. We used their findings in making our revisions.

Table of Contents

Warning and Disclaimer

Warning and Disclaimer: Hiking, climbing, horse riding, and all outdoor activities are inherently dangerous.

Trail and route conditions continually change due to flash floods, erosion, and other natural or man-made events. Although every effort has been made to check the accuracy of the information in this book, errors and omissions may still occur. You must decide whether the trail and weather conditions are safe and satisfactory for you to initiate or continue your trip.

In addition, you must determine whether your own skill, knowledge, and physical conditioning is commensurate with the requirements of a particular trip. You are on your own, and your decisions are entirely your responsibility.

The authors, publisher, and those associated with this publication, directly or indirectly, assume no responsibility for any accident, injury, damage, or loss that may result from participating in any of the activities described in this book.

George "Brownie" Holmes and his dog Music with Adolph Ruth's skull at the junction [9-UU] of the Bull Pass Trail and the Dutchman's Trail. Photo by E. D. Newcomer in December 1931. Courtesy of Superstition Mountain Historical Society, Adolph Ruth Collection.

PREFACE

This second edition of *Superstition Wilderness Trails West* includes updated directions to several trailheads due to locked gates and new highways, updated GPS coordinates, additions to the History and Legends, and updated trail maps. The trip, map, and page numbers remain the same.

This book, *Superstition Wilderness Trails West*, covers the trails in the western Superstition Wilderness, including the JF Trail and all the country going west to the Lost Dutchman State Park. Our companion book, *Superstition Wilderness Trails East*, covers the Reavis Ranch Trail, Rogers Canyon Trail, and all trails east from there to Roosevelt Lake. Each book includes all trailhead descriptions for the east and west halves of the Wilderness with a brief explanation of the trails from each trailhead.

Our books provide an in-depth look at the primary source material behind the events and stories of the late 1800s and early 1900s. City, county, state, and federal documents furnished dates, names, and sometimes reflections of the times. We tried to wrap the individual events into a larger story to show that the Superstition Mountains and the surrounding communities were closely connected. Historical photographs help portray the way that men and women lived in and around the Superstition Mountains.

With more horse riders on the trails and having participated in horse pack trips ourselves, we have included potential trail hazards and trail difficulty ratings for horses and riders that may be useful to stockmen. We talked with outfitters and other riders to supplement our knowledge of riding and packing. We hope our comments are helpful.

The widespread use of the Global Positioning System (GPS) makes accurate coordinates important, so all of our data was taken on site in the field. Be sure to set your GPS unit to map datum NAD27 to match our readings. We included GPS coordinates for trailheads and some points of interest to make travel in the mountains more precise. We did not give the exact locations for petroglyphs and other sensitive sites, but those with a persistent desire will be able to locate them with a little thought and research.

The June 2019 Woodbury Fire, the June 2020 Sawtooth Fire, and the August 2020 Superstition Fire all took a toll on the Wilderness, but it is still a great place to visit.

We hope you have many fine trips in the Superstition Wilderness. See you on the trails.

Trip Summary Chart

Trip Number and Name	Historic Areas	Prehistoric Areas	Scenic Trip	Easy Trip	Challenging Trip	Day Trip	Multi-day Trip	Hike Difficulty Rating	Ride Difficulty Rating
1 Rogers Canyon Cliff Dwellings	•	•	•			•	•	3	3
2 Dripping Spring		•	•			•		2	3
3 Whetrock Canyon Loop	•		•		•	•		3	X
4 Randolph Canyon Loop			•			•		2	X
5 Red Tanks Divide Loop			•		•	•	•	4	X
6 Fremont Saddle			•			•		2	X
7 Cave Trail			•			•		2	X
8 Bluff Spring Loop	•		•			•		2	3
9 Bluff Spring Trail	•		•			•		2	X
10 East Boulder—Needle Canyon Loop	•		•			•		3	X
11 Middle Trail	•		•			•		2	X
12 Barks Canyon Trail	•		•			•		2	X
13 Weavers Needle Crosscut	•		•			•		2	X
14 Charlebois Spring—Loop 1	•		•			•	•	3	3
15 Charlebois Spring—Loop 2	•		•		•	•	•	3	3
16 Charlebois Spring—Loop 3	•		•			•	•	2	X
17 Reeds Water	•		•	•		•		2	2
18 Upper La Barge Box Loop			•		•	•	•	4	X
19 Ely-Anderson Trail	•		•			•		2	X
20 Southwest Route			•		•	•		3	X
21 Hidden Valley Loop	•		•		•	•		4	X
22 Northeast Route			•		•	•		3	X

Trip Summary Chart

Trip Number and Name	Historic Areas	Prehistoric Areas	Scenic Trip	Easy Trip	Challenging Trip	Day Trip	Multi-day Trip	Hike Difficulty Rating	Ride Difficulty Rating
23 Whiskey Spring Trail	•		•	•		•		1	2
24 Trap Canyon			•	•		•	•	1	X
25 Music Canyon			•			•	•	2	X
26 Lost Goldmine Trail from Dons Camp TH			•	•		•		1	2
27 West Boulder Saddle			•			•		2	X
28 Superstition Mountain Ridgeline			•		•	•		4	X
29 Dacite Mesa Loop			•		•	•		3	X
30 Lost Goldmine Trail from Carney Springs TH			•	•		•		1	2
31 Hieroglyphic Trail		•	•			•		1	2
32 Superstition Mountain Peak 5057			•		•	•		4	X
33 Lost Goldmine Trail from Hieroglyphic TH			•	•		•		1	2
34 Jacob's Crosscut Trail from Broadway TH			•	•		•		1	2
35 Broadway Cave Trail			•			•		1	X
36 Lost Goldmine Trail from Broadway TH			•	•		•		1	2
37 Siphon Draw Trail			•	•		•		1	X
38 Jacob's Crosscut Trail Loop			•			•		1	X
39 Treasure Loop Trail to Green Boulder			•			•		1	X
40 Jacob's Crosscut Trail from Crosscut TH			•	•		•		1	2
41 Silverlock Prospect	•		•			•		1	2
42 Massacre Grounds Trail	•		•	•		•		1	2
43 Windmill	•		•	•		•		1	2
44 Hackberry Spring			•	•		•		1	2

Trip Summary Chart

Trip Number and Name	Historic Areas	Prehistoric Areas	Scenic Trip	Easy Trip	Challenging Trip	Day Trip	Multi-day Trip	Hike Difficulty Rating	Ride Difficulty Rating
45 Garden Valley Loop		•	•	•		•		1	2
46 Hackberry Valley			•			•		2	2
47 West Fork First Water Creek			•			•		2	X
48 Upper First Water Creek	•		•			•		2	X
49 Willow Spring	•		•			•		2	2
50 Second Water Spring			•			•		2	2
51 Black Mesa Loop			•			•		2	2
52 Marsh Valley Loop	•		•			•	•	3	3
53 Lower First Water Creek			•			•		3	X
54 First Water Creek Overlook Trail			•	•		•		1	X
55 First Water Creek Canyon	•		•			•		2	X
56 Boulder Canyon Trail to Marsh Valley			•			•	•	3	3
57 Lower La Barge Creek			•			•		2	X
58 Lower Tortilla Creek Loop	•		•		•	•		4	X
59 Peters Canyon Loop	•		•		•	•	•	4	X
60 Squaw Canyon	•		•		•	•		4	X
61 Spanish Trail and Malapais Mountain	•		•		•	•	•	4	X
62 Fish Creek Loop			•		•	•		3	X
63 Hoolie Bacon Trail—Peters Trail Loop			•			•		3	3
64 Peters Trail to Charlebois Spring			•			•	•	3	4
65 JF Trail to Woodbury Trailhead	•		•			•	•	2	3
66 Music Mountain			•					3	X
67 Tortilla Creek Waterfall	•		•		•	•		3	X

INTRODUCTION

This book, *Superstition Wilderness Trails West*, describes the trails in the western half of the Superstition Wilderness. The Reavis Ranch, Rogers Canyon, and Frog Tanks Trails form the approximate dividing line between this book and our companion volume, *Superstition Wilderness Trails East*. The map on the last page of this book shows the area contained in each book. GPS coordinates for trailheads, important trail junctions such as the Weavers Needle Crosscut, and many points of interest are provided.

On the western end of the Superstition Wilderness, we write about the early years of land settlement and mining near the present-day towns of Apache Junction, Gold Canyon, Queen Valley, and Superior.

Because trans-wilderness trips between trailheads are becoming more popular, we included all the trailheads surrounding the Superstition Wilderness. In the section on trans-wilderness trips, we provide the trail mileage, shuttle mileage, and a brief trip outline.

HOW TO USE THIS BOOK

Trailheads

Trailhead defines a point normally accessed by vehicle. Trips are organized in the Table of Contents according to the nearest *Trailhead*. This arrangement will help you quickly find all the trips available for each starting point.

Itinerary

This section gives a summary of the trip noting the main trails used. Alternate routes and trails to or from the destination may be listed.

Difficulty

The *hiker's boot* symbol, for hikers, and the *horseshoe* symbol, for stockmen, are printed on the first page of each trip for a quick reference to the trip's difficulty. The trips are rated *easy*, *moderate*, *difficult*, and *very difficult*.

Hiker ratings are established on the premise that a hiker can complete the hike in the time suggested under the Length and Time heading. The rating considers both physical and mental abilities needed to complete the hike. Hikes covering a short distance with a long hiking time indicate extremely rough terrain or a large elevation gain.

Experienced riders and horses are required on all riding trips. Beginning and intermediate riders supervised by an outfitter company or by experienced friends should be able to ride the moderate trails. Stockman ratings reflect only the trail conditions and hazards since we have not attached mileage criteria to those ratings. An X horseshoe symbol is displayed on some trip descriptions because either the entire trip or a portion of the trip may not be appropriate for horses. We sometimes provide a turnaround point for riders so they can at least travel on part of that trek. Each trip has a description of the unusual hazards so riders can decide for themselves if the trip is suitable for them and their horses.

Easy Hike

Moderate Hike

Difficult Hike

Very Difficult Hike

No Stock Animals

Moderate Ride

Difficult Ride

Very Difficult Ride

Bouldering is a term used in the text to describe a type of climbing familiar to most hikers who explore canyons blocked by large rocks. The highest point of this climbing is usually within jumping distance to the ground; therefore, this technique requires no climbing equipment. The hiker should be skilled in balance and have a knowledge of foot and handhold techniques. Do not try any of the trips requiring *bouldering* unless you have the necessary skills. Join a climbing club, or take a class to learn how to boulder.

Hikers and riders need not complete the entire trip to have an enjoyable outing. They may enjoy the first part of a more difficult trip by selecting a turnaround point, such as a stream crossing, pass, ridgeline, or a trail intersection as their destination. Having fun and traveling at a comfortable pace is more important than completing the entire trip.

Easy Trip

An *easy* hike usually follows established trails with a trip length less than 5 miles and a time less than 3 hours. A few *easy* trips follow the creek bed through a canyon. Some beginning hikers may find the elevation gain or length of the hike more strenuous than they expected.

For riders, none of the Superstition Wilderness trails are considered *easy* due to the hazards of the desert and mountains. All trips require riders and horses to be experienced with travel on mountain, desert, and rough terrain.

Moderate Trip

A *moderate* hike usually involves some off-trail hiking and may require basic route-finding skills. The trip length is less than 10 miles and less than 6 hours hiking time. The abilities to follow rock cairns, use a compass, and read a map are necessary. These treks are for experienced hikers only.

For riders, a *moderate* ride includes trips with stream crossings, narrow trails, and some slick rock sections of trail. The trip usually follows the main Forest Service trail system and does not require off-trail riding.

Difficult Trip

A *difficult* hike requires extensive off-trail hiking over rough terrain. The trip length is less than 15 miles, with hiking time less than 12 hours. Hikers will often need excellent route-finding skills and basic *rock-bouldering* techniques. These treks are for very experienced hikers only.

For riders, a *difficult* ride covers portions of non-maintained trails with steep sections, extensive slick rock, loose rocks or dirt, and small drops in trail contour. Thick vegetation and lack of use may make the trail difficult to follow.

Very Difficult Trip

A *very difficult* hike has all the characteristics of the *difficult* hike along with the distinct possibility that the hiker may not be able to complete the entire hike in one day. The trip length is less than 18 miles with hiking times less than 14 hours. On a *very difficult* trip, hikers may find the challenge rewarding and inspiring upon completion of a successful hike. On the other hand, hikers may find themselves stranded overnight due to errors in route finding or underestimation of hiking times. Hikers must be familiar with *rock-bouldering* skills. None of the hikes require technical rock climbing equipment. Hikers can extend the *very difficult* hikes to make enjoyable and leisurely overnight hikes. These treks are for expert hikers only.

A *very difficult* trip for riders includes cross-country travel where route conditions are often unknown. Those conditions may make the trip unsafe.

Length and Time

The round-trip or one-way distance and time are based on hiking times. Some loop trips, which have alternate return routes, list only the one-way distance. The length of the trips has been derived from USGS maps using the computer program Terrain Navigator Pro by MyTopo (formerly Maptech). We cross-checked those mileages with various sources including the U.S. Forest Service trail mileages, other hiking books, and maps.

Use the distances for off-trail trips as a guideline, since your route may differ slightly from ours. Time is a more useful measurement for off-trail travel. Our hiking times include short rest stops and time to enjoy the scenic highlights of the trip. Backpackers carrying heavier packs should expect longer hiking times. Faster and slower hikers will need to adjust the times for their style of hiking. Riders usually travel faster than hikers, but time for saddling up and stops for tightening cinches and adjusting pack animal loads may reduce that advantage.

For each trip, we provide the uphill elevation change (indicated by a plus sign, +) and the downhill elevation change (indicated by a minus sign, -). For loop trips, the uphill and downhill elevation change is the same. On one-way trips, the uphill and downhill elevation change is usually different. Elevation change is not the same as the difference between the high and low points of the trip. For example, if you go up and down two hills, one 1,500 feet high and another 2,000 feet high, the total elevation change is +3,500 and -3,500, expressed in the book as ±3,500 feet. Small fluctuations in trail elevation may create up to a 10 percent error in our elevation change.

A trail profile of elevation is included with each trip. The profile shows where the major ups and downs occur along the trail.

On one-way trans-wilderness trips, the shuttle distance is the one-way road distance you need to drive to place a vehicle at the destination of your trip. You need two vehicles to arrange a shuttle trip or a good friend who is willing to wait for you at your destination. Another way to make a one-way trip is to arrange for two groups to start from opposite trailheads and travel to the other group's vehicle. Be sure both groups have keys to each vehicle. Don't try to exchange keys during the trip.

Maps

In this section, we list the USGS 7.5 minute topographic (topo) maps used for each trip. The scale for the USGS maps is about 2.5 inches per mile. On trips covering more than one map, such as the corners of four maps, you may wish to make or purchase a composite copy of the four USGS maps for a handy area reference. USGS maps are available online from the U.S. Geological Survey at www.usgs.gov.

The 7.5 minute USGS topographic maps in this book are annotated with the trails or route for each trip. We show numbered Forest Service trails as dashed lines with the trail number in parentheses. Non-maintained trails and trails-of-use are dashed lines without a number. Trails-of-use are trails that have been established by repetitive travel to popular destinations. Off-trail routes are shown as dotted lines. Main roads open to vehicles are shown as solid lines, but some roads behind locked gates are shown as trails.

The *Tonto National Forest* map issued by the Forest Service is good for viewing the big picture and the access roads, but is not very useful as a trail guide. The scale is about 0.5 inch per mile.

In addition to the USGS topo maps, we carry two other maps on all trips: *Superstition Wilderness* by Beartooth Maps with a scale of about 1.4 inches per mile, which is based on the USGS topo maps; and *Superstition Wilderness, Tonto National Forest* map issued by the Forest Service with a 1.0 inch per mile scale.

We use GPS coordinates (NAD27) in the degree, minute, and second format (dd mm ss) because we find the format easier to plot on a paper USGS topo map when we are on the trail and back at the office. Data plotting is easy with the *Waypointer Map Scale* from Wide World of Maps & More or another Internet store. If you prefer to use a different coordinate system, change our numbers by entering them as a waypoint (dd mm ss) in your GPS unit, and then change the GPS unit to read out the waypoint in your desired position format. When you are online, you can use the *Geodetic Tool Kit,* which is described below, for interactive conversion between the UTM format and Latitude/Longitude format.

		Theodore Roosevelt Dam	Windy Hill	
		1964	1964	
Mormon Flat Dam	Horse Mesa Dam	Pinyon Mountain	Two Bar Mountain	
1964	1964	1964	1964	
Goldfield	Weavers Needle	Iron Mountain	Haunted Canyon	Inspiration
1956	1966	1948	1948	1945
		Picketpost Mountain		
		1948		

The 7.5 minute USGS topographic maps with the North American Datum 1927 (NAD27) used in this book are shown above. Set your GPS to NAD27.

Over the years, we have noticed that the repeatability of our older field GPS measurements is only good to plus or minus one second. The newer GPS units give better results, but we will have to live with a few old numbers until we verify them in the field again. The GPS coordinates will get you close to your destination, but you will need to complete the route visually.

The 2004 series USGS topo maps modified by the Tonto National Forest were first issued in 2008. Those maps are designed with the NAD83 map datum, which creates an offset when compared to the maps that we use—1940s to 1960s series with NAD27. The longitude offset is about 2 seconds and

▬▬▬	Main Road (both paved and dirt)
▬▬▬	Secondary Road (dirt)
– – – –	Maintained Trail or Major Trail-of-Use
••••••••	Off-Trail Route or Abandoned Trail
A	Point of Interest (letters from A to ZZZ)
⊙	Point of Interest Location
TH	Trailhead
(109)	U.S. Forest Service Trail Number
FR212	U.S. Forest Road Number (dirt)
↦	Locked gate or road closed
60	U.S. Highway Route Number (paved)
88	State Highway Route Number (mostly paved)

Map legend for the annotated topographic maps in this book.

the latitude offset is about 0.2 second. For exact coordinate conversion, NAD83 to NAD27 or NAD27 to NAD83, use the online converter at www.ngs.noaa. gov—select *Geodetic Tool Kit*, NADCON, *Access Tool . . .* enter your coordinates and select *Submit*. Select the *Converted Coordinate* tab to view the result. UTM conversions can also be made.

Be sure to set the *map datum* on your GPS to the type of map you are using—NAD27 or NAD83. We estimate that our latitude coordinates (NAD27), shown in this book, will result in a tenth-inch offset (about 200 feet on the ground) to the east of your desired location if plotted on the 2004 series NAD83 maps. If you are using our GPS coordinates to locate your position on the ground, set your GPS map datum to NAD27.

Finding the Trail

Looking for the start of the trail is sometimes the hardest part of a trip. This section helps the hiker and rider get out of the parking lot and onto the correct trail. For trips not starting from a parking lot, a narrative is provided describing the terrain and local landmarks near the beginning of the trip. The trailhead GPS coordinates identify the start of the trail.

The Trip

Here we describe the trip, water availability, and other information necessary to complete the trek. The topographic maps in this book contain point of interest notations identifying the major landmarks. For example, [1-X, 3.2, 4400] indicates point of interest X on Map 1, 3.2 miles from the beginning of the trip, at an elevation of 4,400 feet. Mileage is rounded to the nearest tenth of a mile. For some points of interest, the mileage and/or elevation are not included. We indicate the U.S. Forest Service official trail numbers in parentheses, for example, Reavis Ranch Trail (109). Non-official trails are identified on the maps by the traditional name or a name we have assigned.

History and Legends

We include stories associated with each trip to help you experience the past. In some cases, it is impossible to separate history from legend, but we tried to correct misconceptions where we found more reliable information. In many cases, the facts are still being uncovered by dedicated researchers such as Greg Davis of the Superstition Mountain Historical Society. Current research is often discussed on the Internet. Since domain names change, you should search the web for an active discussion forum. Our reference notes, which will guide you to more in-depth reading and research, are shown as superscript numbers in the text. Notes are listed in the back of the book in the section titled Reference Notes to help you find the source of our information.

HOW TO GET THERE

The boundary of the Superstition Mountains is roughly defined by US60 on the southern side, SR88 in the western and northern regions, and SR188 on the eastern edge. The edges of the Superstition Wilderness are 40 miles east of Phoenix, Arizona, 100 miles north of Tucson, Arizona, and 18 miles west of Globe and Miami, Arizona.

Pauline Weaver's headstone for his grave at Sharlot Hall Museum, Prescott, Arizona. September 2008 photo.

Apache Junction, Arizona, is the closest town on the western side of the mountains. Apache Junction is located next to the southwest corner of the Wilderness where the prominent Superstition Mountains rise from the desert floor to 5,057 feet.

The Superstition Freeway, US60, provides easy access to the Superstition Wilderness from the metropolitan areas of Phoenix, Tempe, Mesa, and Apache Junction. At the eastern end of the Superstition Freeway, US60 continues east as a divided four-lane highway. Stay on US60 to the turnoffs for Hieroglyphic, Peralta, Woodbury, Rogers Trough, Pinto Creek, Haunted Canyon, and Miles Ranch Trailheads. For the Roosevelt Lake area north of Globe, leave US60 in Globe and Miami, and turn north on SR188 for Campaign, Tule, Frazier, and Roosevelt Cemetery Trailheads.

For the trailheads north of Apache Junction on SR88—Lost Dutchman State Park, Massacre Grounds, First Water, Canyon Lake, Tortilla Flat, Peters Mesa, Tortilla, Reavis, and Pine Creek Trailheads—use Idaho Road exit 196 on the Superstition Freeway, and drive north on Idaho Road into Apache Junction to connect with SR88. Allow extra driving time on SR88 north of Apache Junction for slow traffic on the winding two-lane road. SR88 is unpaved from the Tortilla Trailhead junction to Roosevelt Dam.

Several Superstition Wilderness trailheads are a short distance from the towns of Globe, Miami, and Roosevelt. For the Miles Ranch Trailhead, drive west on US60 from the towns of Globe and Miami, and use the access on Pinto Valley Mine Road. For trailheads near Roosevelt Lake, go north from Globe and Miami on SR188 to Roosevelt, Arizona, for the Tule, Campaign, Frazier, Roosevelt Cemetery, Reavis, and Pine Creek Trailheads. Roosevelt Lake has very nice camping facilities.

The routes to the popular Rogers Trough and Woodbury Trailheads begin on US60 several miles west of the town of Superior. Forest Service road FR172 to these trailheads offers spectacular views of rugged cliffs and the surrounding Sonoran Desert. Flat areas along FR172 provide easy car camping if you need to rest before your Wilderness trip.

Most trailheads described in this book are accessible by automobile. Some trailheads start next to the paved SR88 and SR188. The trailhead directions indicate when four-wheel-drive or high-clearance vehicles are required.

SUPERSTITION WILDERNESS

According to the book *Geology, Historical Events, Legends and Lore of Superstition Mountain*, by the Superstition Mountain Historical Society, the Indians considered the Superstition Mountains dangerous and a place to avoid. One of the names they gave the mountain was Superstitious Mountain—later the Anglos changed the name to Superstition Mountain.

In 1908, the federal government set aside the Superstition Mountains as a Forest Reserve. The Superstition Primitive Area was established in February 1939 and later upgraded to a Wilderness classification in April 1940. Finally, on September 3, 1964, Congress designated the mountains as the Superstition Wilderness in the National Wilderness Preservation System.

The present size of the Wilderness is 158,345 acres. The north-south distance varies from 9 to 12 miles while the east-west length stretches across 24 miles. Most of the Wilderness is surrounded by the Tonto National Forest except for thirteen sections of Arizona State Trust land along the southwest boundary. One section of private land lies adjacent to the Wilderness near Hieroglyphic Canyon.

The Tonto National Forest, U.S. Forest Service, Department of Agriculture manages the Superstition Wilderness. One of the management objectives for the Wilderness is to perpetuate a long-lasting system of high-quality wilderness that represents a natural ecosystem. Other objectives are to provide public enjoyment of the resource, to allow for the development of indigenous plants and animals, and to maintain the primitive character of the Wilderness as a benchmark for ecological studies.

High use and human influence on our wilderness lands require the Forest Service to manage the Wilderness by providing wilderness-value education; by prohibiting permanent structures such as campgrounds, buildings, and antennas; by regulating trail use and party size; and by allowing fires to burn only under preplanned conditions.

Superstition Wilderness sign on JF Trail near Woodbury windmill [1-C]. The JF Trail goes over Tortilla Pass [1-J], which is the dip in the horizon above the sign. May 2010 photo.

Hunting, fishing, and trapping in the Superstition Wilderness are managed under state and federal laws. Outfitting and guide services are managed under special use permits with the Tonto National Forest. Livestock grazing is still permitted where grazing existed prior to designation as a Wilderness, but the number of animals is prescribed by the Forest Service.

The Wilderness Act prohibits motorized equipment and mechanical transport in the Superstition Wilderness. The prohibited equipment includes motorcycles, chain saws, generators, mountain bikes, and wagons. Hiking, camping, and horseback riding permits are not required for individuals.

Group size is limited to fifteen people and fifteen head of stock. This rule may limit the number of riders to fewer than fifteen if you have pack animals. Larger groups must be divided into groups of fifteen people or fewer, and they must be separated on the trail by at least thirty minutes. The separated groups must camp out of sight of each other. The length of stay is limited to fourteen days.

Current information and publications on the Superstition Wilderness are available from the Tonto National Forest Supervisor's Office in Phoenix, Arizona, and the Mesa Ranger District in Mesa, Arizona. The Mesa Ranger District is the lead district under a consolidated management system with the Globe Ranger District and the Tonto Basin Ranger District. The Tonto National Forest map shows the boundaries for these three districts. Addresses and telephone numbers for these offices are listed in the back of this book under Useful Addresses.

WILDERNESS ETHICS

Take Pictures and Memories—Leave Nothing says it all. *No trace* hiking, riding, and camping are necessary to preserve the Wilderness for future enjoyment. Please join us in preserving the natural and historical heritage of our beautiful Superstition Wilderness.

Large groups of hikers and riders have a greater impact on the Superstition Wilderness than small groups. If you have a large group (more than five hikers or riders), stay on the trails—avoid off-trail and cross-country route travel. Riparian zones are the most fragile. Large groups should use previously occupied campsites and avoid establishing new camps. Restoring a campsite to its natural condition is nearly impossible for a large group of campers. Small groups of campers should be able to return a camp to its natural state if they avoid digging holes, cutting vegetation, and building fires. Every attempt should be made to restore the ground cover so the area will look visually appealing to the next group of campers.

Campfires are permitted, and enjoyable on occasion, but we have found that the use of a lightweight backpacker stove is a convenient alternative. Many areas have almost no fuel wood, so a stove is often a necessity. If you need to build a fire, use an existing fire site. Do not use a fire ring (a ring of rocks), do not try to burn the unburnable (foil, plastics, metal, etc.), and keep the fire away from cliffs and boulders to avoid coating them with black soot. If firewood is scarce, do not pick the ground clean. Put out campfires with water, not dirt, so they are cold to the touch of your hand.

Pack it in—Pack it out. Everything that you take into the Wilderness must be taken out. If you take food items that don't generate a lot of waste and take only the amount you will consume on the trip, you will lighten your load and also reduce the amount of trash that needs to be packed out. Don't bury trash, because animals will dig up the trash and scatter it. Remember that cigarette butts, orange peels, apple cores, and candy wrappers are litter. Unpacking after a day trip or overnight trip is much easier if you store all of your trash in a plastic bag. When you get home, just toss the bag in the garbage. If you include a small plastic bag with your lunch, the bag makes for easy disposal of orange peels, pits, wrappers, etc.

Never vandalize prehistoric sites. Adding graffiti to petroglyphs (prehistoric rock art) or creating your own contemporary petroglyphs may seem artistic at the moment. To the rest of us who enjoy viewing petroglyphs, the new graffiti destroys a piece of history and culture. Trip leaders should suggest that potential graffiti addicts draw in the sand (not on the rock) and then smooth over the sand before leaving. Digging or removing artifacts is not permitted and is prosecutable by law. Even taking potsherds that are exposed on the surface is not allowed. Enjoy them, but leave them for the next person to admire. Sometimes we can damage a prehistoric site by just being there. Loss of vegetation from overuse of an area can increase erosion.

Horse travel in the Wilderness is common and still holds the romance and color of the Old West. The following suggestions will help minimize the effects of stock use and preserve the Wilderness for your next trip. Tie horses directly to trees only for short rest periods. For longer periods, use hobbles,

Natural Resources Conservation Service conducting the trend monitoring transect study in the Tule pasture of the Quarter Circle U Ranch. Left to right: Chuck Backus, Steve Barker, Shai Schendel, Missy Debnar, and Howard Horinek. November 2004 photo.

pickets, highlines, or hitch rails. Setting up a picket line between two trees will keep the horses from damaging tree roots and bark. When breaking camp, scatter manure piles to aid decomposition. Pack in your own feed, because natural forage is very limited, and grazing stock is not allowed. Avoid using whole grain feeds, which can grow if spilled and compete with the natural vegetation.

Human waste should be buried in a hole four to six inches deep (in soil, not sand) at least 300 feet away from water sources and dry washes. After use, fill the hole with soil. Do not burn or bury the toilet paper. Store the used toilet paper inside the cardboard tube or store the used paper in a plastic bag for disposal when you return home. Preserve the water sources by keeping human waste at least 300 feet from streams, springs, potholes, and dry washes. Do not contaminate the water with soap or any leftover food. Wash dishes and articles with soap away from the stream, not directly in it.

Personal items must not be stored in the Wilderness—it's illegal. Many former and some recent explorers and treasure hunters have stashed equipment and supplies in the Wilderness. Special Forest Order 12-59-R prohibits storing anything in the Wilderness for more than fourteen days. Outfitters and the Forest Service rangers take stashed equipment and supplies out to the trailheads for disposal outside the Wilderness.

SAFETY AND DANGERS

Everything you do is your responsibility. Your safety is determined solely by your judgment, skill, condition, and actions. Visiting the Superstition Wilderness carries the individual responsibility of knowing your own abilities. You will need to recognize the potential dangers of outdoor activities without the help of warning signs, handrails, or rangers pointing out the hazards. The hints and suggestions we provide should complement your outdoor skills and not be considered a substitute for proper training and outdoor experience. Be a safe visitor to the Wilderness by knowing your limits. See Useful Addresses in the back of the book for a list of emergency telephone numbers.

The desert mountain range in the Superstition Wilderness can get very hot. Extreme heat poses a very real threat in the summer when temperatures can reach more than 120 °F in the lower elevations. Always carry adequate water to avoid dehydration or heat exhaustion. See the section on Water, which describes the amount of water we carry.

At elevations above 4,800 feet, you will often encounter snow in the winter months. Nighttime temperatures can dip down to -10 °F with daytime temperatures ranging from 20 to 55 °F. To avoid frostbite and hypothermia, be prepared with warm and waterproof clothing.

All trips listed in this book are physically and mentally challenging—even the easy trips. Ascertain your own abilities from previous experience, and know when to abort a trip or modify the original plan.

Off-trail travel, *bouldering*, and climbing are inherently more dangerous than travel on a trail. Injuries due to falling are common. Loose or slippery rocks, on and off the trail, are the primary cause of falls. *Bouldering*, climbing, and travel near cliffs are hazardous and may result in injury or death.

As an individual in a larger group, you must be aware of the inherent danger in this activity and must use your own judgment, based on your own skill level, when confronted with a difficult situation. The responsibility always lies with you as an individual and not with the group. Do not let peer pressure force you into a situation that may be dangerous.

A special caution to horse riders is in order. For your safety, we do not recommend riding off the established trails unless you have considerable experience doing this. Although some riders successfully follow off-trail routes, we have heard that riders have been injured in an attempt to emulate their heroes. The government does not have restrictions on where you may ride, but the Forest Service classifies several steep or rocky trails as "Not Recommended for Horses." The list includes Peralta Trail (102), Boulder Canyon Trail (103), Red Tanks Trail (107), Rogers Canyon Trail (110), Frog Tanks Trail (112), Fire Line Trail (118), Haunted Canyon Trail (203), and Bluff Spring Trail (235). Before you go, consult the Forest Service or your favorite outfitter for current trail conditions. Don't injure yourself or your animal by attempting a ride that is above your ability.

Falling

Injuries due to falling can be a major problem whether it be from slipping on an algae-covered rock in a stream, stumbling on an obstacle in your path, or careening off a precipice. Falling has probably caused more injuries than rattlesnakes and scorpions. The chances of incurring an injury from a fall will increase as you get tired. Lack of attention and declining physical ability are sure signs of danger and increase the likelihood of injury from a fall.

Rattlesnakes

Letting rattlesnakes know you are in their territory will help you avoid an unwanted encounter. We found that a snake stick (any small wooden stick) is handy for beating the brush where you suspect snakes. When you hear that rattlesnake *buzz,* there will be no question whether it is really a rattlesnake.

Beating the brush is not a foolproof technique since rattlesnakes don't always buzz, so look around when you're walking, and check nearby vertical walls of stream banks and ravines. Never put your hands or feet where you can't see.

The snake stick is useful for probing overhead rock ledges before you climb up. Also, throwing a small stone in the bushes helps to announce your presence. Forget about trying to shoot a rattlesnake. If you have time to pull out a gun and have a steady enough hand to shoot, you are probably not in danger of a snakebite. Don't kill rattlesnakes; just learn to avoid them.

Venomous Critters

Along with rattlesnakes, hikers and riders need to be aware of scorpions, centipedes, black widow spiders, brown recluse spiders, tarantulas, Gila monsters, and more. Any venomous bite or sting can be serious.

Flash Floods

During the rainy season, flash floods are a real danger. Most people don't realize the danger of a flash flood until they see the power and force of the water in action. Camp on high ground. Crossing a flooded stream with water up to your knees is dangerous—water at waist level will result in an almost

Howard Horinek, former manager of the Quarter Circle U Ranch, on the Coffee Flat Trail coming into the Reeds Water area. Howard is riding Little Buddy and leading packhorse Clem. Cow dogs are Ruff, Spike, Gus, and Tuff. Buzzards Roost is on the right horizon. October 2007 photo.

certain swim and possible drowning in the current. Horses may buck you off when crossing a fast-moving stream.

Heat and Cold

Heat exhaustion and hypothermia (a drop in body temperature) are potential hazards in the Superstition Wilderness. Extreme changes in weather during a single day and the extremes during the seasons require hikers, riders, and campers to be prepared with the right equipment and provisions. The single most important provision is adequate water. Be sure to read the section in this book on Water. Because of the heat and lack of protection from the sun, heat exhaustion and dehydration are very real dangers. Extreme caution must be exercised between the months of June and September and anytime the temperature exceeds 100 °F.

Firearms

Shooting is not permitted in the Superstition Wilderness except for taking game with a valid hunting license. This means no target shooting. More people are hiking and riding in the mountains than you realize, so you could put the life of another hiker or horse rider in danger with a misdirected shot or the accidental discharge of your gun.

RANCHING AND TOURISM

Ranching began on federal land when people claimed possessory rights to the land—commonly known as squatter's rights. In the western Superstition Mountains, Matt and Alice Cavaness established their headquarters in 1876 by building the *board house* on the site of the present-day Quarter Circle U Ranch. Alfred Charlebois and George Marlow bought the business in 1882; then Marlow bought out Charlebois in 1883 and owned the ranch until his death. James Bark, Frank Criswell, and J. L. Powell bought the ranch from the Marlow estate in 1891. All of these transactions were purchases of the ranch improvements—buildings, windmill, fences, etc.—but not the land, since the land was still owned by the federal government.

In 1911, William "Tex" Barkley and Thomas Buchanan purchased the ranch from Criswell. Then, in 1913, C. S. Steward bought out Buchanan. Sometime after 1919, Barkley obtained full ownership of the ranch. Tex Barkley and his wife Gertrude managed the business as three ranches— Quarter Circle U, First Water, and 3R. The open range method of ranching where owners let their cattle roam free gave way to fences, rules, grazing leases, and limits on the number of cattle. In the mid-1940s, the Quarter Circle U and 3R Ranch headquarters—140 and 588 acres respectively—were purchased from the Arizona State Land Department, but the First Water Ranch headquarters was never patented.[1]

Soap Pot branding iron used at the present-day Quarter Circle U Ranch. The ranch uses the freeze branding method of branding, which is gentler on the calves. October 2007 photo.

After Tex died in 1955, Gertrude and their son Bill Barkley ran the operation. With Bill's failing health, his daughter Nancy and her husband, Ken McCollough, took over the ranch management in 1964. Bill died in 1967. That same year A. H. and Rachel Nichols bought the Quarter Circle U portion of the ranch. Thereafter, the 140 acres of patented land was divided between many owners. Chuck and Judy Backus bought the headquarters property and the Soap Pot brand in 1977 from Guy and Juanita Hill. In 2020, they sold the ranch to their daughter and son-in-law, Amy and Mike Doyle, who are the current owners. The Quarter Circle U brand was sold with the First Water Ranch.[2]

Charles F. "Fred" Weekes II established the Weekes Ranch headquarters on the west side of SR88 around 1900—across the road from the present site of the Superstition Mountain Museum. After he died in 1949, his son Charles F. Weekes III, realizing that the U.S. Land Department was promoting five-acre small-tract sales of federal land to veterans near his ranch, decided to apply for a patent to the Weekes Ranch headquarters, which had been established as a possessory right back in 1900. In 1943, Weekes purchased Joseph Miller's former homestead land and used it for his cattle operation. He traded part of the Miller homestead in 1953 with the federal government to obtain the patent for 160 acres at his Weekes Ranch headquarters in Section 11.[3] See the map on page 31 for some of the early patented properties in the Apache Junction area.

In 1931, George Curtis received his homestead patent for 320 acres in the center of present-day Apache Junction. He took advantage of the traffic at the "Y" highway intersection to establish his gas station and store. Other homesteaders—John Bailey, William Cavanagh, and Irene Rodriguez—filed for patents on the surrounding property.[4]

The property along the Tonto National Forest attracted homesteaders interested in obtaining stock-raising homestead rights to the land, which allowed for a full section (640 acres) to be patented. In 1933, Joseph Miller homesteaded Section 25, between Broadway and Southern Avenues. Within a year, Miller sold his homestead to William and Emma King. The next year, William Van Horn obtained the patent for Section 24 just north of Miller.[5]

In 1926, Wayne "Barney" Barnard filed mining claims on the Dutchman and Dutchman No. 1, 2, and 3, which were located on the western slopes of Superstition Mountain, just outside the Tonto National Forest. In

1936, he received the homestead patent for 320 acres in Section 34, which straddled present-day US60 and bordered Goldfield Road on its eastern boundary.[6]

Barnard became more interested in the land where his mining claims were located and, in 1950, he exchanged most of his homestead property for 240 acres in Section 13, just north of Van Horn. He saw the warm climate, open vistas, and lore of the Lost Dutchman Gold Mine as potential tourist attractions. Pioneer rancher Charles Weekes III, on the other hand, believed this was cattle country and opposed Barnard's land exchange. During a somewhat heated disagreement, Barnard, in a friendly gesture, modified his exchange plans, and the Bureau of Land Management dismissed Weekes's protest. Barnard went on to promote his property as a tourist destination calling his place Rancho del Superstitions. In 1954, Barnard started selling small parcels of his land to the public.[7]

On the southern slopes of Superstition Mountain in 1941, George Woodard homesteaded 160 acres on the north side of Baseline Avenue at the end of present-day Kings Ranch Road. In 1946, Woodard sold his 160-acre homestead to Julian and Lucille King where they established Kings Ranch

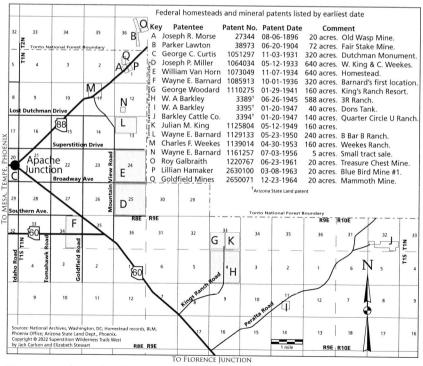

Federal homesteads and mineral patents listed by earliest date

Key	Patentee	Patent No.	Patent Date	Comment	
A	Joseph R. Morse	27344	08-06-1896	20 acres.	Old Wasp Mine.
B	Parker Lawton	38973	06-20-1904	72 acres.	Fair Stake Mine.
C	George C. Curtis	1051297	11-03-1931	320 acres.	Dutchman Monument.
D	Joseph P. Miller	1064034	05-12-1933	640 acres.	W. King & C. Weekes.
E	William Van Horn	1073049	11-07-1934	640 acres.	Homestead.
F	Wayne E. Barnard	1085913	10-01-1936	320 acres.	Barnard's first location.
G	George Woodard	1110275	01-29-1941	160 acres.	King's Ranch Resort.
H	W. A Barkley	3389[†]	06-26-1945	588 acres.	3R Ranch.
I	W. A Barkley	3395[†]	01-20-1947	40 acres.	Dons Tank.
J	Barkley Cattle Co.	3394[†]	01-20-1947	140 acres.	Quarter Circle U Ranch.
K	Julian M. King	1125804	05-12-1949	160 acres.	
L	Wayne E. Barnard	1129133	05-23-1950	240 acres.	B Bar B Ranch.
M	Charles F. Weekes	1139014	04-30-1953	160 acres.	Weekes Ranch.
N	Wayne E. Barnard	1161257	07-03-1956	5 acres.	Small tract sale.
O	Roy Galbraith	1220767	06-23-1961	20 acres.	Treasure Chest Mine.
P	Lillian Hamaker	2630100	03-08-1963	20 acres.	Blue Bird Mine #1.
Q	Goldfield Mines	2650071	12-23-1964	20 acres.	Mammoth Mine.

[†] Arizona State Land patent

Sources: National Archives, Washington, DC; Homestead records, BLM, Phoenix Office; Arizona State Land Dept., Phoenix. Copyright © 2022 Superstition Wilderness Trails West by Jack Carlson and Elizabeth Stewart

Homesteads and mineral patents in the Apache Junction area.

Resort. In 1949, King received title to the adjoining 160 acres to the east by purchasing the land from the federal government. King describes life in the Superstition foothills in his memoir, *Sand In Our Shoes*.[8]

William A. Barkley had the grazing rights to the western Superstition Mountains, but only held the possessory right to the 3R, First Water, and Quarter Circle U Ranch headquarters. In 1945 and 1947, probably in response to the other land transactions in the area, the Barkley Cattle Company obtained title to its headquarters' properties through a purchase from the Arizona State Land Department.[9]

Charles Hastings, one of the early pioneers along the headwaters of Queen Creek, obtained his mineral patent for the Surprisor No. 2 Mine and Windsor Mine in 1882. That same year, the Hastings Townsite (later named Superior) was surveyed—adjoining his mining claims on the east side of Hastings. Following Queen Creek downstream, the homesteaders were Espiridion Acosta, Jose Lopez, Rosa Nunez, Filomeno Ruiz, Clayton Brown, George Halvorsen, John McGrew, William Boyce Thompson, Robert Clevenger, James Herron, and William Murphey.[10] See the map on page 33 for early patented properties in Superior, Queen Valley, and Florence Junction.

In the Queen Valley area, Hart Mullins, Leon Baldwin, Juan Espinoza, and Richard Mattinson were the early homesteaders who received land patents. Cleo and Roberta Allen, Harold Willoughby, and Allan Lewis were later homesteaders. John Olson (Bill Martin's half brother) received the stock-raising homestead patent for Section 24 at Elephant Butte in 1938.[11]

J. R. Willoughby was the first to purchase land in Florence Junction and receive a patent from the Arizona State Land Department in 1930. Later patentees were C. E. Caldwell, Thomas Boskon, and Ouita Swaney.[12]

Some early pioneers did not take advantage of the homestead laws. Charles Whitlow had a ranch at the present-day site of the Whitlow Dam, but he did not homestead that property. Neither did Phil Nicholas at the 88 Ranch, just south of the present-day Herron Ranch headquarters. Hugh Hewitt staked a mining claim near the Silver Chief Mine, but never homesteaded his property along Queen Creek.

JACOB WALTZ AND DUTCHMAN GOLD

Researchers Greg Davis, Tom Kollenborn, Thomas Glover, Jack San Felice, and many others have been sorting through the stories of Jacob Waltz and the Dutchman Gold to separate fact from fiction. Books that will immerse you in the history are: *The Curse of the Dutchman's Gold* by Corbin; *The Lost Dutchman Mine of Jacob Waltz* and *Treasure Tales of the Superstitions* by Glover; *Superstition Mountain*, (Parts 1 and 2) by Swanson and Kollenborn; *Jacob's Trail* by Feldman; and *Lost El Dorado of Jacob Waltz* by San Felice.

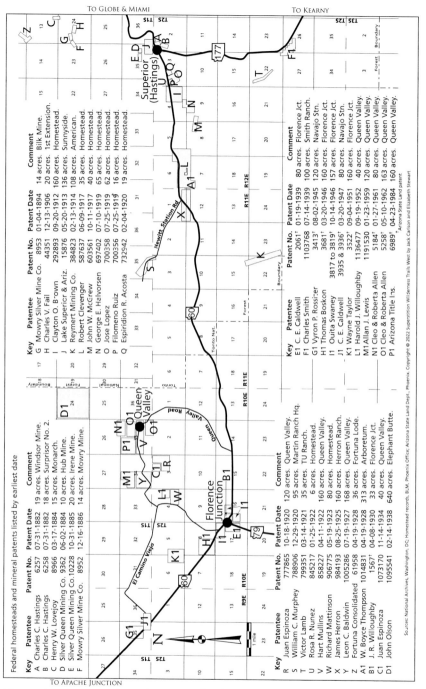

Federal homesteads and mineral patents listed by earliest date

Key	Patentee	Patent No.	Patent Date	Comment
A	Charles C. Hastings	6257	07-31-1882	19 acres. Windsor Mine.
B	Charles C. Hastings	6258	07-31-1882	18 acres. Surprisor No. 2.
C	Henry W. Lovejoy	8966	03-17-1884	15 acres. Monarch.
D	Silver Queen Mining Co.	9362	06-02-1884	10 acres. Hub Mine.
E	Silver Queen Mining Co.	10228	10-31-1885	20 acres. Irene Mine.
F	Mowry Silver Mine Co.	8952	12-16-1886	14 acres. Mowry Mine.

Key	Patentee	Patent No.	Patent Date	Comment
G	Mowry Silver Mine Co.	8953	01-04-1894	14 acres. Blk Mine.
H	Charles V. Fail	44351	12-13-1906	20 acres. 1st Extension.
I	Clayton O. Brown	292893	09-20-1912	160 acres. Homestead.
J	Lake Superior & Ariz.	15876	05-20-1913	136 acres. Sunnyside.
K	Reymert Mining Co.	384823	02-13-1914	108 acres. American.
L	Robert Clevenger	587637	06-09-1917	35 acres. Homestead.
M	John W. McCrew	603561	10-11-1917	40 acres. Homestead.
N	George E. Halvorsen	697402	07-10-1919	65 acres. Homestead.
O	Jose Lopez	700358	07-25-1919	62 acres. Homestead.
P	Filomeno Ruiz	700356	07-25-1919	16 acres. Homestead.
Q	Espiridion R. Acosta	732942	02-04-1920	19 acres. Homestead.

Key	Patentee	Patent No.	Patent Date	Comment
E1	C. E. Caldwell	2061†	01-19-1939	80 acres. Florence Jct.
F1	Charles Smith	1103768	07-14-1939	100 acres. Smith Ranch.
G1	Vyron P. Rossier	3413†	08-02-1945	120 acres. Navajo Stn.
H1	Thomas Boskon	3681†	03-20-1946	160 acres. Florence Jct.
I1	Ouita Swaney	3817 to 3819†	10-14-1946	157 acres. Navajo Stn.
J1	C. E. Caldwell	3935 & 3936†	03-20-1947	80 acres. Navajo Stn.
K1	Wayne Taylor	3522†	09-04-1951	160 acres. Florence Jct.
L1	Harold J. Willoughby	1136477	09-19-1952	40 acres. Queen Valley.
M1	Allan J. Lewis	1191530	01-23-1959	120 acres. Queen Valley.
N1	Cleo & Roberta Allen	5184†	01-27-1961	80 acres. Queen Valley.
O1	Cleo & Roberta Allen	5258†	05-10-1962	163 acres. Queen Valley.
P1	Arizona Title Ins.	6989†	04-23-1984	160 acres. Queen Valley.

† Arizona State Land patent

Key	Patentee	Patent No.	Patent Date	Comment
R	Juan Espinoza	777865	10-18-1920	120 acres. Queen Valley.
S	William C. Murphey	788906	12-29-1920	95 acres. Martin Ranch Hq.
T	Victor Lamb	799351	03-14-1921	35 acres. TU Ranch.
U	Rosa R. Nunez	845217	01-25-1922	6 acres. Homestead.
V	Hart Mullins	858227	04-11-1922	160 acres. Queen Valley.
W	Richard Mattinson	906775	05-19-1923	80 acres. Homestead.
X	James Herron	984193	08-25-1925	160 acres. Herron Ranch.
Y	Leon C. Baldwin	1005286	07-19-1927	168 acres. Queen Valley.
Z	Fortuna Consolidated	61958	04-19-1928	36 acres. Fortuna Lode.
A1	W. Boyce Thompson	1014831	04-19-1928	313 acres. Arboretum.
B1	J. R. Willoughby	1567†	04-08-1930	33 acres. Florence Jct.
C1	Juan Espinoza	1073170	11-14-1934	40 acres. Queen Valley.
D1	John Olson	1095541	02-14-1938	640 acres. Elephant Butte.

Sources: National Archives, Washington, DC; Homestead records, BLM, Phoenix Office; Arizona State Land Dept., Phoenix. Copyright © 2022 Superstition Wilderness Trails West by Jack Carlson and Elizabeth Stewart.

Homesteads and mineral patents in the Superior, Queen Valley, and Florence Junction areas.

One version of the story begins in the late 1870s or early 1880s with Jacob Waltz and his partner, Jacob Wiser, prospecting in the Superstition Mountains when they heard the sound of clanking metal. Approaching the sound cautiously, they spied two men mining gold. Thinking the miners were Indians, they shot them from behind. Later they discovered they had just killed two Mexican miners. The Mexicans may have been men who escaped the Apache massacre of the Peralta expedition in the 1850s. Waltz and Wiser mined the gold and packed it out to either Florence or Phoenix.

Another variation on the same theme recounts a Good Samaritan story involving Waltz and Wiser while they were in Mexico. After they rescued a wealthy Mexican from a card-game fight, the Mexican (named Peralta) gave Waltz and Wiser a map to his gold mine in the Superstition Mountains. In one variation of the story, the wealthy Mexican sends a guide with Waltz and Wiser to show them the location of the mine.

Some say that Jacob Waltz never had a mine, but he high-graded the ore from the Vulture Mine near Wickenburg. High-grading is a term used to describe the theft of ore when miners conceal it in their clothing. Thomas Glover, in his book, analyzed ore from the Vulture Mine, local mines, and other sources and did not find a match with the Dutchman's ore, so his findings discount the high-grading scenario.[13]

Others believe that Jacob Waltz stumbled on a buried cache or found a cache of gold ore in a cave. They claim Waltz made up the story about the mine to elude those who were following him. Indians, Jesuits, and Mexican miners were possible owners of the hidden cache of gold.

Dozens of prospectors have been searching the Superstition Mountains for the last century even though some geologists and authors continually state that the volcanic area is poorly mineralized and it would be unlikely for prospectors to find gold there. Others do not agree with the poor mineralization conclusion. Robert Sikorsky, author, geologist, and former Celeste Maria Jones employee, surveyed the Superstition Mountains and concluded that it was very possible that there could be metal deposits in the area.[14]

Clay Worst, author, prospector, and past president of the Superstition Mountain Historical Society, makes a case for mineralization in the Superstitions. He noted that many of the richest gold mines in the world are associated with volcanic geology—Goldfield, Nevada; the Capitol Mine in Cripple Creek, Colorado; the El Indio Mine in Chile; and the Hishikari Mine on Kyushu Island in Japan.[15]

Not everyone believes the Lost Dutchman Mine is located inside the Superstition Wilderness. John Wilburn, in his 1990 book *Dutchman's Lost Ledge of Gold*, places the Dutchman's mine west of the Superstition Wilderness at the site of the Bull Dog mine near Goldfield.[16] Jay Fraser

Bark and Criswell registered the Quarter Circle U cattle brand and earmark with the State of Arizona in April 1897. Diagram from Territorial Brand Book of Arizona, page 77. Courtesy of the Arizona State Archives.

establishes the Dutchman's mine northeast of Carefree, Arizona, in his 1988 book *Lost Dutchman Mine Discoveries*.[17] And Robert Blair, in his 1975 book *Tales of the Superstitions*, locates the one and only known Peralta Mine, originally owned by Miguel Peralta, at the Gloriana Mine (aka Valenciana Mine) west of Interstate Highway I-17 near the Bumble Bee exit.[18]

THE SEARCH FOR GOLD

The search for the Lost Dutchman Gold Mine began after Jacob Waltz died in Phoenix, Arizona, on October 25, 1891. Although labeled a Dutchman, Waltz was a German immigrant who started prospecting in Arizona about 1862.[19] Just before his death, Waltz told two close companions, Julia Thomas and Rhinehart Petrasch, the location of his gold mine.

Julia Thomas, Rhinehart Petrasch, and Rhinehart's brother Herman entered the Superstition Mountains in 1892 via the First Water Trailhead and searched for the gold mine without success. Julia Thomas died in 1917.[20] Rhinehart Petrasch died in 1943. Sims Ely, author of *The Lost Dutchman Mine*, credits cattle rancher Jim Bark with naming the Lost Dutchman Mine in 1893.[21]

The back cover of Helen Corbin's 1990 book *The Curse of the Dutchman's Gold* shows a picture of the matchbox reputed to have been made from the Dutchman's gold. Dick Holmes, Bob Corbin, and Tom Kollenborn are reported to have seen the actual gold that Waltz had in his possession.[22] The gold was taken from Waltz the day he died—from a box under his bed. Richard J. "Dick" Holmes Jr. said the Dutchman gave him the gold. The gold is now the property of an unnamed individual who received it from George "Brownie" Holmes (son of Dick Holmes).[23]

Apache Indians told stories of Mexican mining in the Superstition Mountains around the 1850s. The most famous story described the massacre of a large group of Mexican miners by Apache Indians in a running fight that lasted several days. In 1912, two prospectors, Carl A. Silverlock and Carl Malm, found gold ore on the north slopes of the Superstition Mountains at the present-day Massacre Grounds. Apache Indians supposedly had cut loose the ore from the Mexicans' pack animals after the massacre.[24] Thomas Glover's book *Treasure Tales of the Superstitions* describes the massacre and an alleged connection with the Dutchman's gold and Peters Mesa. See History and Legends on pages 235 and 240 for more of the story.

Jim Bark and later Tex Barkley, cattle ranchers in the Superstitions, played host to the many gold and treasure seekers since their grazing allotment covered the two main gateways to the Superstition Mountains—Peralta Trailhead and First Water Trailhead. Jim Bark and partner Frank Criswell bought the Superstition Cattle Ranch in 1891. Tex Barkley bought the ranch with partner Thomas Buchanan in 1911.[25]

In his 1953 book, *The Lost Dutchman Mine*, Sims Ely, general manager of the Salt River User's Association, with rancher Jim Bark, covers the early stories and interviews with Julia Thomas and Rhinehart Petrasch.[26] Early treasure seekers such as Dick Holmes, Brownie Holmes, and Herman Petrasch spent most of their lives searching for the Dutchman's Mine without success.

Travis Tumlinson and his uncle, Robert Tumlinson, claimed they found the famous Peralta stone maps northwest of Florence Junction—on the south side of Queen Creek in about 1949. There are many questions regarding the authenticity of the stones. Replicas of the stone carvings are on display at the Superstition Mountain Museum—with a temporary display of the original stones provided by the Flag Foundation.[27]

We have only described a few of the many famous Lost Dutchman men and women. More stories and famous personalities are included in the History and Legends section of each trip. The Lost Dutchman Gold Mine story continues; every year brings a new event of discovery or recollection of former episodes.

The Miners and Prospectors

The earliest recorded prospecting in the western Superstition Mountains and Goldfield Mountains took place in 1864. Since the Apaches still controlled that country, not much prospecting was done until the U.S. Army took control in 1873.[28]

James Rogers and partners Charles Ceslinger and Charles Fleming filed mining claims west of Superstition Mountain in 1876 on the Wild Cat Mine, two miles southwest of Rowe's Camp. In 1877, they filed on the Big Chief Mine, one mile west of Superstition Mountain.[29] After 1876, they had more success in Rogers Canyon and concentrated their efforts on the World Beater and Silver Chief Mines on the west ridge of Rogers Canyon.

On the western edge of the Superstition Wilderness in the Superstition Mining District, the Mammoth Mine, discovered in 1893, and the other nearby Goldfield mines were very successful. In 1893, Joseph Riley Morse located the Old Wasp Mine, which he patented in 1896—the earliest claim to be patented. Many claims were not patented during the boom years, but a few were patented in later years. Lillian and Reuben Hamaker patented the Blue Bird No. 1 in 1963, and Goldfield Mines patented the Mammoth Mine in 1964.[30] John Wilburn recalls the history of each of the Goldfield area mines in his book *Dutchman's Lost Ledge of Gold*.[31] Bob Schoose documents the Goldfield history in his book *Goldfield Boom to Bust*. We include more stories about the Goldfield area on page 214, Historic Mining District.

The Silver King Mine—located in 1875 in the Pioneer Mining District, north of present-day Superior—was a big producer. Ore from the Silver King and surrounding mines fed the smelter at Pinal City. Jack San Felice documents the history of the Silver King Mine and surrounding area in his book *When Silver Was King*.[32]

The Volcano Mining District, just upstream from the present-day Horse Mesa Dam on Apache Lake, was the site of several mining claims. In 1895, well-known men such as John Chuning and James E. Bark located the Defender Gold Mine, and in 1896, Frank, Harry, and William Criswell located the Shooting Star Mine in the Volcano District.[33] Other large mining operations in the western half of the Wilderness, such as the Carney Mines near Carney Trailhead and the Miller Mines near Tortilla Trailhead, were not very productive. As a result, the land was never patented.

MINING AND TREASURE HUNTING

The 1964 Wilderness Act closed all wilderness lands to new mineral claims effective January 1, 1984. In the Superstition Wilderness, the Forest Service requires existing valid mining claims to show valuable and locatable minerals. These mineral claims must operate with an approved Notice of Intent and Plan of Operations. The Forest Service has defined several categories of mineral-related activities to help clarify the regulations. Ask the Forest Service, or check their website for a copy of the regulations.

Mining is the extraction of minerals and is subject to the Forest Service rules described above.

Prospecting is only allowed with an approved Plan of Operations. Extraction of a small grab sample is permitted. Anything more than what you can carry in your hands is considered mining.

Gold Panning is considered a type of mining if a mineral is extracted. If a mineral is not extracted, gold panning is allowed and is considered prospecting.

Treasure Trove Hunting is only allowed with a permit from the Forest Service. A treasure trove is defined as money, gems, or precious worked metal of unknown ownership. You must prove that treasure, gems, coins, etc., exist at a particular location before a permit will be issued. If a permit is approved, it is issued for a specific number of days, and the search site is subject to inspection. The only treasure trove permit issued in the Superstition Wilderness was to Ron Feldman's group, Historical Exploration and Treasures, L.L.C. (HEAT), for excavation at Rogers Spring in 2004. Even though a permit was issued, all equipment and supplies had to be carried into the site by foot or horseback. The mining operation had to be conducted without power tools or power machinery.[34]

Artifacts that are more than one hundred years old may not be removed under the Archaeological Resources Protection Act. Archaeological sites may not be disturbed. Historic sites and artifacts are government property, and your permit may exclude collection of these items.

Metal Detecting is allowed, but may be considered mining, prospecting, or treasure trove hunting depending on what you find.

WATER

It is more convenient on day trips to carry all the water you need rather than purify water found in the creeks and springs. In hot weather, carry some empty containers that can be filled with untreated water—from potholes, creeks, and springs. You can use this untreated water for keeping a bandanna or shirt wet, which will act as your personal evaporative cooler and reduce the amount of water you need to drink. On hot days and in the summer, we freeze plastic bottles of water in advance so we have something cool to drink. On day trips, we carry one to four liters of water per person depending on the season and weather. In the summer, four liters per person is a minimum requirement for a day-long trip. Summer heat can make the water so hot it is not very pleasant to drink.

If you are looking for water, check the map for springs and streams. Plan ahead by checking with other people and the Forest Service rangers for the current conditions of springs and water sources. Many springs are seasonal, which means they are dry for long periods of time (months or even years). In the field, observe the color and type of surrounding vegetation. Cottonwood and sycamore trees sometimes indicate water. Green areas may have water or just catch more runoff than nearby areas. Potholes in ravines and intermittent streams are often good sources of water.

Purify all water to be certain it is safe for drinking. Boil water for at least five minutes, or use a purifier designed to remove *Giardia, bacteria,* and *viruses.* Some equipment classified as a filter does not remove viruses. Be sure you use a purifier that removes viruses. Always take your water from sources that are impacted by the minimum amount of human and animal traffic.

Although many of the springs developed by the former ranchers and cattlemen are in disrepair, you can often obtain water by following the metal pipes back to the spring. Some of the more reliable water sources are Charlebois Spring, La Barge Spring, Bluff Spring, Hackberry Spring, Rogers Spring, Campaign Creek, and Reavis Creek. For the latest information on water conditions, check with the rangers at the Mesa Ranger District in Mesa, Arizona.

EASY TRIPS

Here are several easy hike ideas to get you going. If you turn around at our suggested destination or when you get tired, these trips will make ideal easy treks. The difficulty of each trip varies within the easy category. Some of the selections are portions of more difficult trips, so you must read the trip description carefully to identify our suggested turnaround point. The distance and time are given for the round-trip. Horse riders can use this as a guide, but they need to read the full description to avoid trips where hikers could scramble over obstacles that would block horses.

Trip	Miles	Hours	Elev.	Turnaround Point	Condition
8	1.8	1.0	±350	Barkley Basin [7-L, 0.9]	good trail
26	2.2	1.5	±200	Wilderness Gate [5-SS, 1.1]	good trail
30	1.2	1.0	±110	Wilderness Gate [12-SS, 0.6]	good trail
31	2.8	2.0	±600	Petroglyph Site [15-P, 1.4]	good trail
33	2.0	1.5	±220	Quicksilver Draw [12-K, 1.0]	good trail
34	5.4	3.5	±320	Shade Rock [17-T, 2.7]	good trail
35	3.6	2.5	±950	Broadway Cave [17-C, 1.8]	fair trail
36	2.2	1.5	±390	Green Gate [16-II, 1.1]	good trail
37	3.8	2.5	±1,190	Siphon Draw Basin [19-H, 1.9]	good trail
38	2.1	2.0	±240	Jacob's Crosscut Loop Trip	good trail
39	2.3	2.0	±550	Green Boulder Loop Trip	good trail
40	2.0	1.5	±90	Treasure Trail Junction [18-I, 1.0]	good trail
42	5.2	4.0	±1,040	Massacre Grounds [18-W, 2.6]	fair trail
43	1.0	1.0	±210	First Water Creek [20-O, 0.5]	good road
44	2.4	2.0	±290	Hackberry Spring [20-J, 1.2]	creek bed
45	3.6	2.5	±390	Garden Valley [20-GG, 1.8]	good trail
47	1.6	1.5	±170	West Fork First Water [20-EE, 0.8]	creek bed
48	5.0	3.5	±580	Parker Pass [20-Z, 2.5]	good trail
56	1.2	1.0	±330	Wilderness Sign [25-B, 0.6]	good trail
57	1.6	2.0	±440	La Barge Creek [25-N, 0.8]	creek bed
58	2.2	3.5	±270	Jct. with Peters Canyon [26-L, 1.1]	creek bed
62	1.2	2.5	±140	Fish Creek [29-N, 0.6]	creek bed
64	1.2	2.5	±50	Tortilla Creek [30-U, 0.6]	creek bed

Equipment and Clothing

Equipment and clothing needs will vary from trip to trip, but we can offer some general guidelines. In our day packs for hiking, we each carry a small homemade emergency first-aid kit, flashlight, compass, GPS, camera, toilet paper, knife, maps, pencil, extra bandanna, sunglasses, snacks, and water. On our key chain, we carry a small pliers tool and pointed tweezers. We usually wear quick dry long or convertible pants, long-sleeved cotton shirt, bandanna, and a wide-brimmed hat or baseball cap. Loose fitting long pants help protect our legs on cross-country treks and on the lesser-traveled trails.

We always add a breathable waterproof jacket with hood, a wool or fleece hat, and liner gloves in the winter and in periods of changing weather. If the weather is cool or really looks nasty, we take polypropylene long underwear tops and bottoms that can be worn under our shirt and pants. In very cold weather, we take a lightweight (about one-pound) down jacket. If we expect rain or snow, we take rain pants. We wear wool socks in the winter and summer. Short gaiters on our boots keep the stickers and foxtails out of our socks. Leather gloves protect our hands when bushwhacking.

When riding horseback, we wear denim jeans, long-sleeved shirt, bandanna, wide-brimmed western hat (straw in summer, felt in winter), western-style work boots, denim jacket, and leather gloves. If the weather looks like rain, we take a full-length rain slicker to cover our legs and saddle. In brushy country, we wear leather chaps.

Our first-aid items are stored in a small mesh bag. You can also use a small plastic bag. The SPOT electronic device is stored in a waterproof bag with spare batteries. Our emergency first-aid and rescue kit contain:

❐ first-aid antibiotic ointment	❐ sunscreen
❐ moleskin	❐ Arnica gel
❐ gauze pads	❐ aspirin and Advil
❐ adhesive tape	❐ lip balm
❐ adhesive bandages	❐ nail file
❐ alcohol swab pads	❐ thread and needles
❐ SPOT rescue satellite device	❐ lighter
❐ Swiss Army knife with scissors and tweezers	❐ money ($20 or more in small bills and four quarters)

Horse riders will also need to assemble an emergency kit for their horses. For overnight trips, hikers and riders should consult one of the many instructional books on packing and develop their own list of equipment.

TRAILHEADS

These brief descriptions will quickly get you on the road to the trailhead, but the maps and detailed Trailhead descriptions in the trip section of the book will give you a better idea of what to expect. Paved road mileage is rounded to the nearest mile. Roads are suitable for passenger cars except as noted. The GPS coordinates identify the start of the trail from the parking area. Starting with Woodbury Trailhead, the trailheads are listed clockwise around the perimeter of the Superstition Wilderness.

Woodbury Trailhead

From Florence Junction, go east 2 miles on US60. Between mileposts 214 and 215 turn north on Queen Valley Road, and go 1.8 miles to FR357 (Hewitt Station Road). Go right on FR357 for 3 miles to FR172, and go left 9 miles on FR172 to the junction with FR172A. Bear left and continue on FR172 for another 1.4 miles to the end of the road. High-clearance vehicle is required on FR172. (N33° 24′ 33.8″, W111° 12′ 19.5″)

JF Ranch Trailhead (Relocated to Woodbury Trailhead)

Peralta Trailhead

Go 8 miles east of Apache Junction on US60. Between mileposts 204 and 205, turn north onto Peralta Road, FR77, and go 7.2 miles to end of road. (N33° 23′ 51.4″, W111° 20′ 49.7″)

Dons Camp Trailhead

Go 8 miles east of Apache Junction on US60. Between mileposts 204 and 205, turn north onto Peralta Road, FR77. Go 7 miles on Peralta Road. Turn left at the Lost Goldmine Trail sign, and drive west across the large parking area to the Lost Goldmine Trail kiosk. (N33° 23′ 32.0″, W111° 21′ 11.9″)

Carney Springs Trailhead

Go 8 miles east of Apache Junction on US60. Between mileposts 204 and 205, turn north onto Peralta Road, FR77, go 6 miles, and park in a small area along Peralta Road that is bounded by metal posts and a steel cable. Carney Springs Road has been closed to vehicle traffic since June of 2006. (N33° 23′ 08.8″, W111° 21′ 45.0″)

Hieroglyphic Trailhead

Go 6 miles east of Apache Junction on US60. Between mileposts 202 and 203, turn north on Kings Ranch Road, and go 2.8 miles to Baseline Avenue. Turn right (east) on Baseline Avenue for 0.25 mile. Turn left (north) on Mohican

Road for 0.3 mile, then left (west) on Valleyview Road. Valleyview Road meanders into Whitetail Road, which intersects Cloudview Avenue. Go right (east) on Cloudview Avenue for about 0.5 mile to the large parking lot for Lost Goldmine Trail. (N33° 23' 23.2", W111° 25' 26.0")

Broadway Trailhead

Go 3 miles east of Apache Junction on US60. Between mileposts 199 and 200, turn north on Mountain View Road and go 1.6 miles to Broadway Avenue. Turn right (east) on Broadway for 1 mile until the road curves and turns into South Broadway Lane. Park on the left (north) in the small unsigned parking area. (N33° 24' 28.3", W111° 28' 34.0")

Tonto Trailhead

The complementary parking at the former Mining Camp Restaurant for the Tonto Trailhead was closed in December 2016. The restaurant burned to the ground in July 2017 and there are no plans to rebuild it. This Wilderness boundary gate and access point is only useful for local residents that can hike or ride their horses from home. Please do not park on the residential streets.

Lost Dutchman State Park Trailheads

Go 5 miles north of Apache Junction on SR88. Between mileposts 201 and 202, turn east into the Lost Dutchman State Park.
(N33° 27' 33.2", W111° 28' 45.4")

Crosscut Trailhead

Go 5 miles north of Apache Junction on SR88. Between mileposts 201 and 202, turn east on FR78 (First Water Road) and drive 0.6 mile. Park on the right (south) side of FR78 in the signed parking area.
(N33° 28' 15.7", W111° 28' 08.2")

Massacre Grounds Trailhead (Relocated to Crosscut Trailhead)

First Water Trailhead

Go 5 miles north of Apache Junction on SR88. Between mileposts 201 and 202, turn east on FR78 (First Water Road), and go 2.6 miles to the end of the road. (N33° 28' 47.7", W111° 26' 32.5")

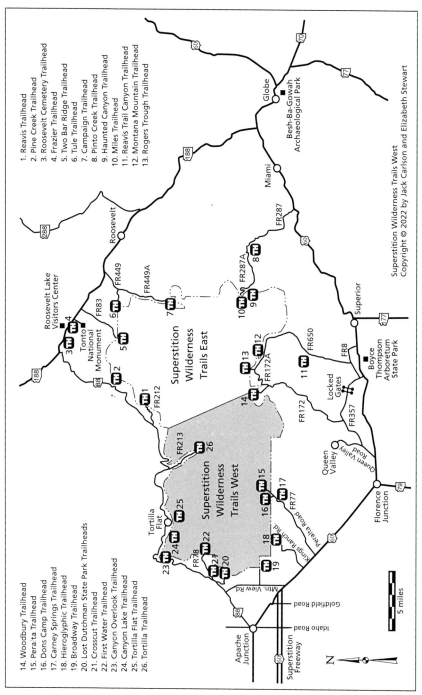

1. Reavis Trailhead
2. Pine Creek Trailhead
3. Roosevelt Cemetery Trailhead
4. Frazier Trailhead
5. Two Bar Ridge Trailhead
6. Tule Trailhead
7. Campaign Trailhead
8. Pinto Creek Trailhead
9. Haunted Canyon Trailhead
10. Miles Trailhead
11. Reavis Trail Canyon Trailhead
12. Montana Mountain Trailhead
13. Rogers Trough Trailhead

14. Woodbury Trailhead
15. Pera'ta Trailhead
16. Dons Camp Trailhead
17. Carney Springs Trailhead
18. Hieroglyphic Trailhead
19. Broadway Trailhead
20. Lost Dutchman State Park Trailheads
21. Crosscut Trailhead
22. First Water Trailhead
23. Canyon Overlook Trailhead
24. Canyon Lake Trailhead
25. Tortilla Flat Trailhead
26. Tortilla Trailhead

Superstition Wilderness Trails West
Copyright © 2022 by Jack Carlson and Elizabeth Stewart

Trailhead Locator Map

Canyon Overlook Trailhead

Go 12 miles north of Apache Junction on SR88. Between mileposts 207 and 208, park at two different pullouts; Tower 174 (N33° 31' 59.7", W111° 27' 13.7") and MP208 (N33° 32' 14.9", W111° 27' 11.1").

Canyon Lake Trailhead

Go 15 miles north of Apache Junction on SR88. Between mileposts 211 and 212, turn into the Canyon Lake Marina parking lot on the north side of fence adjacent to SR88. (N33° 32' 02.2", W111° 25' 19.7")

Tortilla Flat Trailhead

Go 17 miles north of Apache Junction on SR88. Between mileposts 213 and 214, park at Tortilla Flat or on vehicle pullouts down the road near milepost 214. Tortilla Flat is private property. Obtain permission from the store manager before parking at Tortilla Flat. We park near milepost 214. (N33° 31' 50.6", W111° 22' 51.5")

Tortilla Trailhead

Go 24 miles north of Apache Junction on SR88. Between mileposts 221 and 222, turn right and park in the parking area at the start of FR213, or take four-wheel-drive road FR213 to Tortilla Well. (N33° 29' 33.2", W111° 17' 41.2")

Reavis Trailhead

Go 28 miles north of Apache Junction on SR88. Between mileposts 227 and 228, turn east on FR212 and drive 2.8 miles to end of road. High-clearance vehicle is required. (N33° 33' 23.8", W111° 13' 38.6")

Pine Creek Trailhead

Go about 33 miles north of Apache Junction on SR88. Between mileposts 232 and 233, turn east on FR665, and drive 0.5 mile over the hill to the first water trough. Or, go south on SR88 for 9 miles from Roosevelt Dam to FR665. High-clearance vehicle is required and sometimes four-wheel drive is required. (N33° 35' 01.8", W111° 12' 18.5")

Roosevelt Cemetery Trailhead

Go about 27 miles north of Globe on SR188. Between mileposts 242 and 243, turn left (south) into Lakeview Park, then turn right into the paved trailhead parking area. (N33° 40' 02.0", W111° 08' 05.6")

Frazier Trailhead

Go about 26 miles north of Globe on SR188. Between mileposts 242 and 243, turn southwest on FR221, and drive around the power substation to the end of the gravel road. (N33° 39′ 43.6″, W111° 07′ 23.3″)

Two Bar Ridge Trailhead

Go about 23 miles north of Globe on SR188. Turn south onto FR83 between mileposts 239 and 240. Drive southwest on FR83 for 1.9 miles to junction with the Black Brush Ranch (aka Two Bar Ranch), which is private. Stay left on FR83 for 3.3 miles to end of four-wheel-drive road. (N33° 35′ 51.2″, W111° 07′ 40.2″)

Tule Trailhead

Go about 20 miles north of Globe on SR188. Turn south onto FR449 (J Bar B Ranch Road) between mileposts 235 and 236. Drive west on FR449 for 2 miles to junction with FR449A. Stay right on FR449 for 1.2 miles to end of road. (N33° 35′ 35.9″, W111° 04′ 32.5″)

Campaign Trailhead

Follow directions to Tule Trailhead, but after 2 miles on FR449, bear left on FR449A, and go 5.1 miles to Campaign Trailhead near Reevis Mountain School (former Upper Horrell Place). Reevis Mountain School is private property. Since 1994, the Campaign Trail has provided access to the Wilderness by going around the west side of Reevis Mountain School. Deep sand and seasonal water make FR449A a four-wheel-drive road although some high clearance vehicles can make it. (N33° 31′ 54.3″, W111° 04′ 42.8″)

Upper Horrell Trailhead (Renamed Campaign Trailhead)

Pinto Creek Trailhead

From Apache Junction, drive 29 miles on US60 to Superior. Continue on US60 for 12 miles to FR287 (Pinto Valley Mine Road) between mileposts 239 and 240. The FR287 junction is 1 mile east of the Pinto Creek highway bridge. Coming from Globe on US60, drive about 4 miles from Miami to the Pinto Valley Mine Road. Drive north on FR287, to the Iron Bridge on Pinto Creek. Before you cross the Iron Bridge, turn left (west) on a dirt road marked as *Trail 203*. Park near the locked gate, but do not block the road. A medium-clearance vehicle is required. (N33° 25′ 31.4″, W111° 00′ 09.7″)

Haunted Canyon Trailhead

Follow Pinto Creek Trailhead directions to the Iron Bridge. Cross the Iron Bridge over Pinto Creek, turn left on FR287A in 0.1 mile, go another 3.8 miles, and park in a small pullout on the right (east) side of FR287A. A medium-clearance vehicle is required. (N33° 25' 33.0", W111° 03' 17.3")

Miles Trailhead

Follow Pinto Creek Trailhead directions to the Iron Bridge. Cross the Iron Bridge over Pinto Creek, turn left on FR287A in 0.1 mile, and drive another 5.7 miles to end of FR287A. A medium-clearance vehicle is required. (N33° 26' 14.3", W111° 04' 01.9")

Reavis Trail Canyon Trailhead (Arizona Trail)

From US60 between mileposts 222 and 223, near the Arboretum, take FR357 (Hewitt Station Road) north for about 250 feet, turn right (east) on FR8 (Happy Camp Road) for 1.8 miles, go left (north) on FR650 for 4.3 miles to the metal *Arizona Trail* sign [37-K]. A high-clearance vehicle is required on this part of FR650—and in wet weather you might need four-wheel drive. (N33° 21' 09.9", W111° 07' 53.1")

Rogers Trough Trailhead

From Florence Junction, go east 2 miles on US60. Between mileposts 214 and 215 turn north on Queen Valley Road, and go 1.8 miles to FR357 (Hewitt Station Road). Go right on FR357 for 3 miles to FR172, and go left 9 miles on FR172 to the junction with FR172A. Continue right for 4 miles on FR172A to end of road—staying left at the junction with FR650. (N33° 25' 19.9", W111° 10' 21.7")

From Superior, go west on US60 to Queen Valley Road. Turn north on Queen Valley Road for 1.8 miles to FR357, go right 3 miles to FR172 and use the directions above. Locked gates across FR357 block access to FR172 from the east. A high-clearance vehicle is required on FR172. After seasonal rains, steep and rocky sections of FR172A make this a four-wheel-drive road.

Montana Mountain Trailhead

Follow directions for Rogers Trough Trailhead to the junction with FR172A and FR650. Go right (east) on FR650 for 2 miles to Montana Mountain Trailhead, which is marked by a wooden sign *Trail 509*. FR650 always requires four-wheel drive. (N33° 24' 19.6", W111° 09' 22.3")

WOODBURY TRAILHEAD

From Apache Junction, go east 15 miles on US60 to Florence Junction. Go 2 more miles east on US60. Between mileposts 214 and 215, turn north on Queen Valley Road and go 1.8 miles to FR357 (Hewitt Station Road). Go right 3 miles on FR357 to FR172. From Superior, go west to Queen Valley Road. Turn north on Queen Valley Road for 1.8 miles to FR357, go right 3 miles to FR172. Locked gates across FR357 block access to FR172 from the east.

FINDING THE TRAILHEAD

After reaching FR172, go north on FR172, using a high-clearance vehicle,

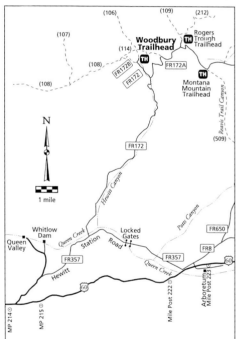

for 10.4 miles to the end of the road. Turn right at the locked gate to FR172B and the JF Ranch Headquarters. The trailhead parking lot is at (N33° 24′ 33.8″, W111° 12′ 19.5″).

FACILITIES

You'll find no facilities at this trailhead except for a hitching post. Bring your own water.

THE TRAILS

See Map 1 on page 53. The JF Trail (106), an abandoned dirt road, begins at a vehicle barricade at the parking lot [1-A] and heads north to the Woodbury cabin site [1-B]. A half mile north of the parking lot, the JF Trail reaches a signed trail junction [1-B] with Woodbury Trail. From here, the JF Trail goes straight ahead (north) toward a windmill [1-C]. The Woodbury Trail (114) goes east from the junction [1-B] 1.3 miles to FR172A [1-V] and west 1 mile to the JF Ranch Headquarters and the Coffee Flat Trail (108) [1-X]. The Coffee Flat Trail starts on the north side of the large corral [1-X]. This is still cattle country so you will likely find cows around the water holes.

HISTORY AND LEGENDS

JF Ranch, named for pioneer cattleman Jack Fraser, has existed since the 1880s when Fraser ran cattle here and in the Reavis area until 1910. George Martin, son of Bill and Teta Martin, and wife Lynn hold the grazing allotment. They use the JF Headquarters during roundups. The Martin Ranch main headquarters is located on Hewitt Station Road, at the Queen Creek crossing.

The JF Ranch buildings are located just outside the Wilderness boundary. George and Lynn Martin use these buildings in conjunction with their cattle operation under a permit with the Forest Service. The main building is a modern cinder-block structure with a large porch for sleeping outdoors. Just to the west stands a wood and metal barn with historic shoeing equipment behind it. In past years, the windmill pumped water into a cement cistern in front of the ranch house. In 2010, new storage tanks that are filled by a solar pump in the well were installed. On the north side of Fraser Canyon wash, you'll find a large corral area made of vertical logs. Huge cottonwood trees grow here, and some have fallen due to the eroding soil.

The old barn and windmill at JF Ranch headquarters in 1993. In past years, the windmill fed a concrete tank in front of the headquarters building, but now the water is pumped to larger storage tanks on the nearby hill.

The wooden corral at JF Ranch in 1993. The Coffee Flat Trail (108) skirts the right (north) side of the corral [2-X], which is off the right side of the photograph. The Coffee Flat Trail goes through an unsigned, barbed-wire gate, then the trail is marked with small rock cairns.

On March 4, 1873, the U.S. Army, under the command of Major William H. Brown, camped in the Rogers Trough area [1-U]. The army had been combing the mountains for Apache rancherias for more than two months and had come up from West Fork Pinto Creek via Spencer Spring Creek. According to the field notes of Second Lieutenant John Bourke, aide-de-camp to General Crook, the army followed an itinerary that started at Camp McDowell on January 6, 1873, and crisscrossed the mountains on the way to Camp Grant and Fort Bowie.[35]

On March 5, they broke camp and proceeded south through the "Gap" [1-I] and probably down the alignment of FR172A. We guess they went through the JF Ranch and Woodbury area [1-B], which they recalled as a former camp. The column continued up to Tortilla Pass [1-J] on the alignment of the JF Trail and then followed the JF Trail to the Tortilla Ranch area [30-A] where they made their March 5, 1873, camp.[36]

Archie McIntosh, who later homesteaded at present-day Roosevelt Lake, was one of the guides on this Fifth Cavalry expedition. See Trip 62 (Fish Creek Loop) on pages 349 and 350 for the military's activities on March 6, 1873.

ROGERS CANYON CLIFF DWELLINGS

This trip takes you to the prehistoric cliff dwellings in Rogers Canyon. Rogers Canyon at Angel Basin, just down canyon from the ruins, is an ideal place to camp. Tall Arizona black walnut, Arizona sycamore, and netleaf hackberry trees surround a large, flat grassy area here. Along the canyon floor are shaded camping places under the emory oaks, making this is a great destination for an overnight trip.

ITINERARY

From Woodbury Trailhead, follow JF Trail (106) to Tortilla Pass. Continue on Rogers Canyon Trail (110) to Rogers Canyon and the cliff dwellings. Return the same way.

DIFFICULTY

Difficult hike or moderate back-pack. Difficult horse ride. Elevation change is +1,500 and -1,280 feet.

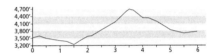

LENGTH and TIME

5.7 miles, 5 hours one way.

MAPS

Arizona USGS topo maps NAD27: Iron Mountain and Pinyon Mountain. Superstition Wilderness Beartooth map, grids L14 to L12. Map 1.

FINDING THE TRAIL

See the trailhead map on page 47. JF Trail (106) starts at the barricade on the north side of the Woodbury Trailhead parking lot [1-A] (N33° 24' 33.8", W111° 12' 19.5").

THE TRIP

Start on Map 1 on page 53. From the Woodbury Trailhead parking lot [1-A, 0], walk around the road barricade and proceed up the dirt road signed as the JF Trail to a small saddle. The old road descends to a signed trail junction with Woodbury Trail (114) [1-B, 0.5]. At this junction, continue straight ahead (north) on the JF Trail. The JF Trail curves around the right side of a dirt water tank, heading westerly, and is marked with a few small rock cairns. It is easy to lose the trail here, so be sure to keep the Woodbury windmill [1-C, 0.6] and the tall water storage tanks on your right as you curve around the dirt tank. Many flat places to camp lie along the trail near the windmill, but the cows have made claim to the area.

The trail becomes more defined as it passes the wooden Superstition Wilderness boundary sign [1-D, 0.8]. After crossing Randolph Canyon Wash twice, the JF Trail follows the west hillside of Randolph Canyon, which is dotted with honey mesquite, sugar sumac, single-leaf pinyon, redberry buckthorn, and mountain mahogany.

The JF Trail crosses the bed of Randolph Canyon [1-N, 1.5] for the last time where the trail begins the uphill climb to Tortilla Pass on the left (west) ridge of Woodbury Gulch.[37] Farther up the ridge, the trail is surrounded by a dense growth of mountain mahogany, sugar sumac, juniper, and shrub oak. At Tortilla Pass [1-J, 3.2], a wooden trail sign marks the junction of the JF and Rogers Canyon Trails. Leave the JF Trail, continue straight (north), and take the Rogers Canyon Trail (110). From Tortilla Pass, Rogers Canyon Trail (110) goes through an open gate, climbs up a grassy slope, heads north to a higher pass, descends on a long switchback to the bottom of the drainage, and finally meets the seasonal streambed of Rogers Canyon.

Rogers Canyon cliff dwellings [1-G]. May 1999 photo.

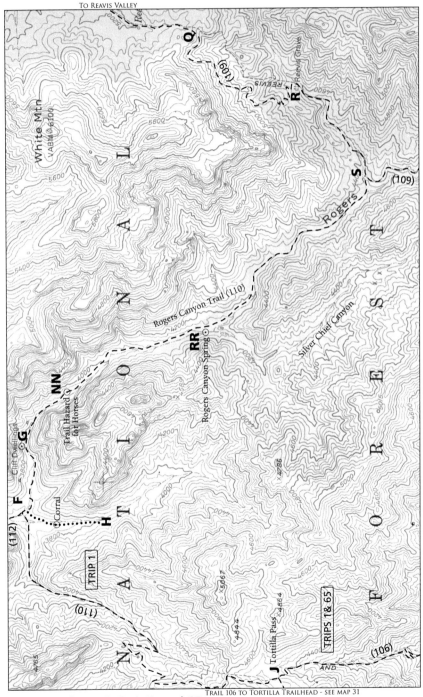

To Reavis Valley

Map 1 – Trips 1, 2, 3, 4, 5, and 65.

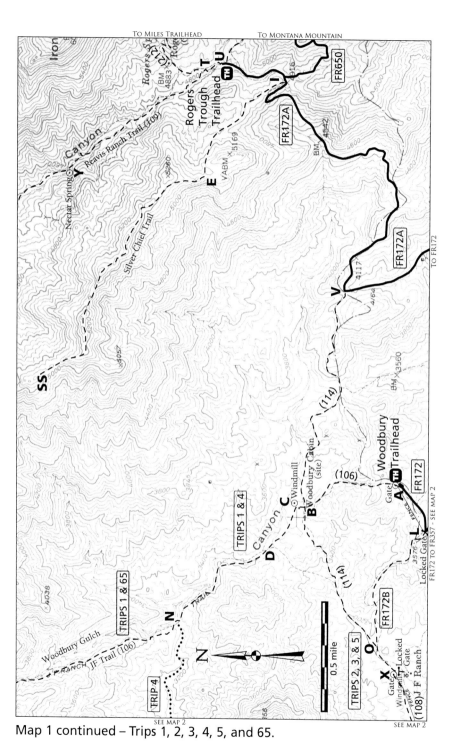

Map 1 continued – Trips 1, 2, 3, 4, 5, and 65.

Across the Rogers Canyon drainage, you can see a large inviting grassy area [1-F, 5.4] where a wooden sign marks the junction with Frog Tanks Trail (112). This is Angel Basin. Large Arizona black walnut, netleaf hackberry, and Arizona sycamore trees shade this ideal camping area.

From Angel Basin, follow the Rogers Canyon Trail right (east) as it crosses the drainage several times. You will find several more ideal camping places along here under the large emory oaks.

When the trail starts to go uphill, look across Rogers Canyon to the left (north) and you will see the Rogers Canyon cliff dwellings in a cave [1-G, 5.7] (N33° 27' 49.3", W111° 12' 19.9"). The cliff dwellings are located on the north side of the canyon about 100 feet up from the bottom of the wash. A rough trail goes steeply up the slope to a Forest Service sign that provides some useful information. The Salado occupied these dwellings around A.D. 1300. Don't take anything. Don't camp here. Don't do anything to degrade the ruins. Climbing on the walls can cause them to crumble, and building a fire may cause a hidden roof structure to burn.

Rogers Canyon wash may be dry near Angel Basin, but you may find water up canyon near the cliff dwellings in a waterhole that people call Angel Springs. We have only seen water at Rogers Canyon Spring [1-RR] when water was abundant in Rogers Canyon.

A trail leading southwest from the south side of Angel Basin ends at an abandoned corral and cement water trough. The troughs are dry, but we followed the pipes going south to a seep that had some water in shallow pools in the dirt [1-H], which may be the Angel Spring referenced on some older maps. Don't count on this spring for water. We saw a lot of bear scat around the area, so be sure to make some noise to let the bear know you are visiting.

The June 2019 Woodbury Fire spared the Angel Spring corral, but the nearby area and the land north to Angel Basin was burned to the ground. The fire burned the old wooden fence posts, so a lot of fence barbed wire is lying on the ground. A few old trees in Angel Basin were burned, but many of the tall trees survived the fire.

This is the end of the trip description. Return the same way to Woodbury Trailhead [1-A, 11.4].

A more popular approach to the Rogers Canyon Cliff Dwellings [1-G] starts from the Rogers Canyon Trailhead [1-U]. Our companion book, *Superstition Wilderness Trails East*, gives a full description of that trip including the history and legends. Horse riders should be aware that the trail from Rogers Trailhead [1-U] to the ruins [1-G] is hazardous for horse travel in one location [1-NN] on the Rogers Canyon Trail.

DRIPPING SPRING

Below JF Ranch, Fraser Canyon narrows, and rounded hilltops turn to jagged cliffs. Seasonal water in Fraser Canyon supports cottonwood, sycamore, and willow trees. The junction of Fraser and Randolph Canyons is very pretty with smooth, reddish bedrock and shallow pools of seasonal water. Dripping Spring seeps from the ledges above the canyon floor. A small cave is nearby.

ITINERARY

From the Woodbury Trailhead, go down FR172B to the JF corral, north of JF Headquarters. Follow the Coffee Flat Trail (108) down Fraser Canyon to Dripping Spring. Return the same way.

DIFFICULTY

Moderate hike. Difficult horse ride.
Elevation change is +110 and -990 feet.

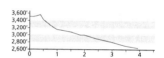

LENGTH and TIME

3.9 miles, 3.25 hours one way.

MAPS

Arizona USGS topo maps NAD27: Iron Mountain and Weavers Needle. Superstition Wilderness Beartooth map, grids L14 to J15. Map 2.

FINDING THE TRAIL

See the trailhead map on page 47. From the west side of Woodbury Trailhead parking lot [2-A, 0] (N33° 24′ 33.8″, W111° 12′ 19.5″), go west on FR172.

THE TRIP

Start on Map 2 on page 57. From the west side of Woodbury Trailhead parking lot [2-A, 0], follow FR172 to the locked gate [2-L, 0.2] for FR172B at the top of the hill. Climb over the metal gate and take FR172B to the JF Ranch Headquarters corral [2-X, 1.1].

    To avoid the locked gate on FR172B [2-L], horse riders need to take the longer route using the JF Trail to the junction of Woodbury Trail [2-B] and continue on the Woodbury Trail to the corral at JF Ranch Headquarters

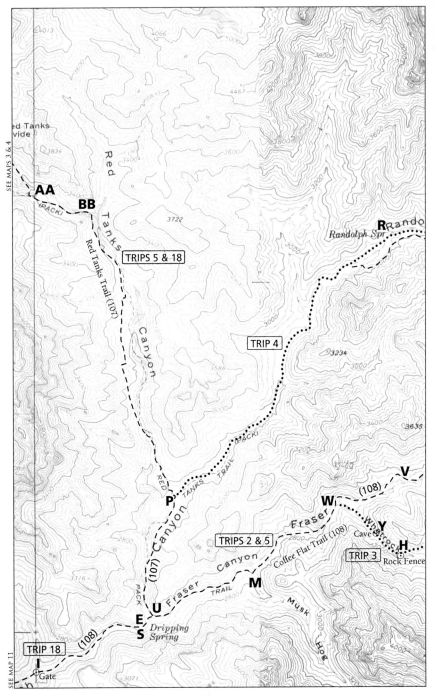

Map 2 – Trips 1, 2, 3, 4, 5, 18, and 65.

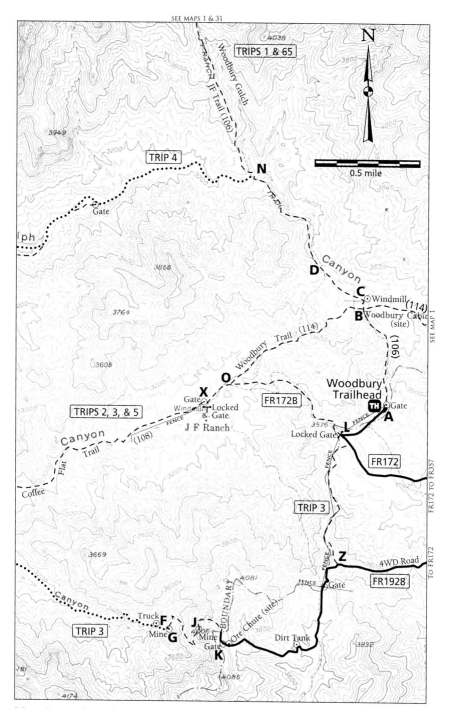

Map 2 continued – Trips 1, 2, 3, 4, 5, 18, and 65.

[2-X], which adds about 0.4 mile to the trip. For the return ride, horse riders should note the junction of Woodbury Trail and FR172B [2-O] (N33° 24' 39.5", W111° 13' 06.8"), which is marked only with a small rock cairn.

FR172B ends at the locked gate to the JF Ranch headquarters (private). The Coffee Flat Trail (108) goes through a barbed-wire gate [2-X, 1.1] (N33° 24' 35.5", W111° 13' 13.1") and heads around the right (north) side of the wooden corral. If the Coffee Flat Trail sign is missing from the barbed-wire gate, look west beyond the gate and you may see small rock cairns marking the Coffee Flat Trail, which follows the right (north) side of the corral fence for about 0.4 mile. At the corner of the fence line, the trail heads left toward Fraser Canyon where it enters the wash and goes down the sandy creek bed. Fraser Canyon usually has seasonal water after a rain.

Large rock cairns—sometimes hidden by tall grass—mark the trail as it crosses Fraser Canyon many times. Horse riders have kept the vegetation from invading the trail, and the walking is fairly easy. Hikers can elect to walk down the bed of the wash or follow the trail. Look for the freight road construction along the trail as it climbs the right (north) hillside [2-V, 2.3] (N33° 24' 12.5", W111° 14' 14.5").

If you follow the trail as it zigzags downstream, you might miss the mouth of Whetrock Canyon [2-W, 2.7] (N33° 24' 06.0", W111° 14' 37.2"), which is bypassed when the trail goes up on the right (west) bench of Fraser Canyon. See Trip 3 (Whetrock Canyon Loop) for the trek up Whetrock.

About 15 minutes west of Whetrock Canyon, the trail enters the creek bed where several willow trees populate the area. The 1991 Tonto National Forest map (but not the current map) shows a spring here—Whetstone Spring. Don't count on Whetstone Spring for water.

The trail is on the left (south) bank when it crosses Musk Hog Canyon [2-M, 3.3]. Small groves of sugar sumac, Arizona sycamore, and mesquite dot the canyon floor as the trail continues west. Overnight trekkers will find several flat places to camp between Musk Hog Canyon [2-M, 3.3] and Dripping Spring.

The wooden sign [2-U, 3.8] (N33° 23' 40.0", W111° 15' 32.1") for the Coffee Flat Trail (108) and the Red Tanks Trail (107) is on the left (south) side of the trail just before the Coffee Flat Trail goes into the creek bed of Randolph Canyon. Fraser Canyon ends here where it joins Randolph Canyon. The smooth, reddish bedrock, shallow pools of seasonal water, and openness of the canyon make this a special place.

Dripping Spring [2-S, 3.9] is on the south wall of the canyon—a short distance in Randolph Canyon from the wooden trail sign. Water drips from the ledges into the wash.[38] From the spring, look north across Randolph

Canyon to see a small cave [2-E] in the low cliff. The cave, with a low ceiling, extends back 40 to 50 feet. Seven grind holes in the boulders next to the creek, on the northwest side of Randolph Canyon between the cave and spring, remind us that prehistoric people were here centuries ago. The flat bench along the creek below the cave offers good camping or a shady place for lunch. Return the same way to Woodbury parking lot [2-A, 7.8] where the trip ends. See Trip 4 (Randolph Canyon Loop) for more return route ideas.

HISTORY AND LEGENDS

John Dahlmann, in his 1979 book *A Tiny Bit of God's Creation*, describes the old freight road through Fraser Canyon. Unless you see the road for yourself, it is hard to believe freight wagons traveled this canyon. You can see the retaining wall and roadbed along the north side of the canyon where it cuts through a cliff to bypass the smooth bedrock canyon [2-V]. Dahlmann said this was only a freight wagon road since it was too rough for stage coaches.[39]

Gertrude Barkley, Tex Barkley's wife, described the route of the old freight road to John Dahlmann. From Mesa, it ran along the southern slopes of Superstition Mountain, past Barkley's Quarter Circle U Ranch, up Whitlow

Allen Blackman on the old freight road (now part of the Coffee Flat Trail) in Fraser Canyon [2-V]. Photograph by Nyle Leatham, 1977. Courtesy Superstition Mountain Historical Society, Tom Kollenborn Collection.

Canyon, and into Fraser Canyon. It continued past the JF Ranch and Woodbury Mill before reaching Superior.[40]

Bob Ward, in a 1984 *Superstition Mountain Journal* article, describes the mines he located in the late 1950s using the Polka maps. J. J. Polka was an Apache who gave three maps to Bob Ward when they met in the Armed Services. Polka Map #2 makes reference to Fraser Canyon and Red Tanks Canyon. We haven't tried to find these mines, but it seems the area described is on the steep, rugged northern slope of Fraser Canyon near the junction with Randolph Canyon. Copies of the maps are reprinted in the 1984 *Superstition Mountain Journal.*[41]

On one occasion, when Elisha Reavis was packing his produce to market, he met Waltz in Fraser Canyon and had a conversation with him.[42] These chance encounters with the Dutchman never produced enough clues to reveal the location of his mine.

Fraser Canyon officially ends when it meets Randolph Canyon at Dripping Spring, but the ranchers downstream at the Quarter Circle U Ranch refer to Randolph Canyon as Fraser Canyon. Even when Randolph Canyon joins Whitlow Canyon farther downstream, the ranchers still use the Fraser name—probably because the grazing pasture for the Quarter Circle U Ranch in the upper Whitlow Canyon area is named Fraser.[43]

See Trip 23 (Whiskey Spring Trail) on page 156 for the Wagoner lost gold mine story and Barry Storm's map on page 157 showing the route through Whitlow, Randolph, and Red Tank Canyons.

The Coffee Flat Trail crosses the red bedrock of the creek near Dripping Spring at the junction of Randolph Canyon and Fraser Canyon [2-U]. December 1993 photo.

WHETROCK CANYON LOOP

This loop trip takes you up Whetrock Canyon to several abandoned mines.

ITINERARY

From the Woodbury Trailhead, go down FR172B to the corral north of JF Headquarters. Follow the Coffee Flat Trail (108) down Fraser Canyon to Whetrock Canyon. Go up Whetrock Canyon to the mines, then follow an abandoned road back to Woodbury Trailhead.

DIFFICULTY

Difficult hike. Not recommended for horses. Elevation
change is ±1,470 feet.

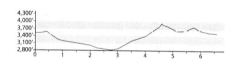

LENGTH and TIME

6.6 miles, 6.5 hours round-trip. Add 2.4 miles and 3 hours if you go to Dripping Spring.

MAPS

Arizona USGS topo map NAD27: Iron Mountain. Superstition Wilderness Beartooth map, grids L14 and K14. Map 2.

FINDING THE TRAIL

See the trailhead map on page 47. From the west side of Woodbury Trailhead parking lot [2-A, 0] (N33° 24′ 33.8″, W111° 12′ 19.5″), walk west on FR172.

THE TRIP

Start on Map 2 on page 57. Follow Trip 2 (Dripping Spring) on page 55 to Whetrock Canyon for the first part of the trip. Whetrock Canyon [2-W, 2.7] (N33° 24′ 06.0″, W111° 14′ 37.2″) is difficult to locate for two reasons: (1) it is only a narrow cut in the bedrock on the east side of Fraser Canyon, and (2) Coffee Flat Trail is on the opposite bench when it passes Whetrock Canyon.

Enter Whetrock Canyon [2-W, 2.7] and walk along the canyon floor until you see an easy place to go up on the east bench. Walking on the east bench is sometimes easier than walking in the bottom of the canyon, but the

Falling rocks collapsed the timbers to the incline shaft at this mine [2-J] on Fraser Mountain, 1993. These timbers and the nearby ore-loading chute were completely burned in the 2019 Woodbury Fire.

last time we checked the canyon, it had a trickle of water, and we decided to stay in the ravine for the complete trip. Thick grass and the foxtails that stick to your socks also influenced our decision to stay in the ravine.

Watch for the Teapot locator rock on the eastern horizon, which marks the general location of John Dahlmann's cave at the base of the cliffs. Leave Whetrock Canyon [2-Y, 2.9] (N33° 24' 00.0", W111° 14' 25.8") and hike up the steep bank to view the cave, which is only a small alcove.

At a sharp bend in Whetrock Canyon, a barbed-wire fence [2-H, 3.1] across the channel extends a stone wall from the western hillside. A few yards up the wash on the north bench, you can see an open barbed-wire gate in the stone wall.

The mine tailings on the mountain at the far end of the canyon come into view (N33° 23' 41.7", W111° 13' 46.2") as you continue up Whetrock Canyon. If you are hiking on the east bench, stay high until you are directly across from the mines. Below, in the ravine, you will see the remains of a rusty, white panel truck [2-F, 4.0] (N33° 23' 42.1", W111° 13' 27.7"). Walk down to the truck, then up to the lower mine with the gray-white tailings.

The entrance to the lower mine [2-G, 4.1] (N33° 23' 40.8", W111° 13' 23.9") has been covered with dirt, but you can see the smooth rock face where the adit entered the hill. Look for the abandoned mining road to the east. Following the road is easier than bushwhacking up the steep hill. The mine at the top of the hill [2-J, 4.4] (N33° 23′ 40.6″, W111° 13′ 14.7″) has an open incline shaft that could be dangerous. Don't enter the mine. The wide, timbered shaft went down at a steep incline toward the west. The entrance timbers were consumed in the 2019 Woodbury Fire. Another mine lies farther up on the west side of the same hill.

From the mine [2-J], follow the dirt road north as it curves around the peak of the hill heading southeast. The road crosses the Wilderness boundary and connects with FR1928.[44] From the Wilderness boundary, the walk back to the Woodbury Trailhead is easy. Go through the closed barbed-wire gate [2-K, 4.7]. A few hundred yards down the road is the site of the ore-loading chute that was burned in the 2019 Woodbury Fire. Continue down the road to the earth stock tank, and head north to another closed, barbed-wire gate. About 0.1 mile north of the gate, an abandoned road [2-Z, 5.6] (N33° 23′ 56.5″, W111° 12′ 34.1″) heads north, while FR1928 turns east. Take the abandoned road, which eventually follows the fence line and brings you to FR172 100 yards south of the locked gate on FR172B [2-L, 6.4]. From here, go east on FR172 to the Woodbury Trailhead parking lot where the trip ends [2-A, 6.6].

HISTORY AND LEGENDS

John Dahlmann, in his 1979 book *A Tiny Bit of God's Creation*, describes a horse ride he and others made from Millsite Canyon to the mines at the end of Whetrock Canyon. From the mines, he continued down Whetrock Canyon to Fraser Canyon. We hiked the same route and wondered how he negotiated that rough canyon on a horse. The canyon floor is mostly smooth bedrock. It seems that he followed the canyon floor beyond the stone wall [2-H] to a slick, rock passage where he dismounted and walked up the east slope about 100 feet. Here he found a cave [2-Y] that contained a skeleton, some prospector tools, and supplies. On previous trips, we had looked for the cave, but couldn't find it. Steve Bowser located the cave for us in 2008, and we inspected it on a trip in 2010. This trip is not recommended for horses.[45]

The rusty carcass of a panel truck [2-F] in the ravine below the Whetrock Canyon mines is only a shell. The engine and all mechanical parts are missing. The faded paint on the white rear doors reads, NEW MODERN DAIRY, GLOBE, ARIZONA.

Robert Garman, in his book *Mystery Gold of the Superstitions*, tells the story about James Whetlach and his silver mines. He wrote that Jesse Mullins met Whetlach in 1893 when Whetlach was loading silver ore into a wagon. Jesse was never able to locate Whetlach's mine although he was sure it was in Whetrock Canyon—Garman spells the name of the canyon as Whetlach. One of Garman's treasure maps shows a trail that goes north through Millsite Canyon and seems to end at the Whetrock Canyon mines. Jesse, who lived in

Superior, died on January 17, 1959, at age eighty-three, in the Pinal General Hospital, Florence. He is buried in the Mesa City Cemetery.[46]

The earliest mining claim we found for Whetrock Canyon was posted on June 16, 1937, for the Whit-Rock #1 and #11 by Hart Mullins, Jesse's brother. The description stated, "Beginning at a stone monument about 500 feet south of old workings done by Whit-Rock," which may be referring to a person named Whitrock. On June 21, 1947, Hart Mullins teamed up with George Morton and Charley Ellsworth to post claims on the Whet-Rock #2 through #10. On April 19, 1954, George Morton and Hart Mullins filed on the Whet Rock #21 and #22. New claimants show up in a filing on June 27, 1964, when Darlie Baker and Florence Olson posted claims on Whet Rock #4 through #24.[47]

Garman shows a picture in his book of the wooden ore chute [near 2-K], so we know significant mining was taking place before his book was written in 1975.[48] We do not know if Hart Mullins was taking silver out of his Whetrock Canyon claims or when the shafts and tunnels were dug in the mountain.

Garman named the mountain at the head of Whetrock Canyon "Frazier Mountain," which should be spelled "Fraser Mountain" after John "Jack" J. Fraser who established the JF Ranch. Fraser was born in Pictou County, Nova Scotia, Canada, in 1857 and died in Mesa, Arizona, in 1943. He was a U.S. citizen—due to his father Alexander's naturalization—as noted on voter and passport records. Thad Frazier, the owner of a store in the town of Roosevelt, Arizona, is often confused with Jack Fraser. We believe refer-

ences to J. J. Frazier in books and newspapers should read J. J. Fraser. Confusion with the spelling of Fraser's last name might have resulted from a different spelling for his father's last name of Frazer.[49]

Rancher John "Jack" James Fraser submitted this photo for his U.S. passport in 1918. He was traveling to Altar, Sonora, Mexico to investigate mining interests and the stock business. Photographer unknown. Courtesy National Archives, College Park, Maryland.[50.]

RANDOLPH CANYON LOOP

This loop trip takes you through a seldom-traveled section of Randolph Canyon. You'll find ample opportunity for viewing wildlife here.

ITINERARY

From the Woodbury Trailhead, walk down FR172B to the corral north of JF Headquarters. Follow the Coffee Flat Trail (108) down Fraser Canyon to Dripping Spring. Take Red Tanks Trail (107) to Randolph Canyon, hike up the bed of Randolph Canyon to JF Trail (109), and connect to the JF Trail going south to the Woodbury Trailhead.

DIFFICULTY

Moderate hike. Not recom-
mended for horses. Elevation
change is ±1,150 feet.

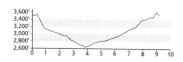

LENGTH and TIME

9.2 miles, 9 hours round-trip.

MAPS

Arizona USGS topo maps NAD27: Iron Mountain and Weavers Needle. Superstition Wilderness Beartooth map, grids L14 to J15. Map 2.

FINDING THE TRAIL

See the trailhead map on page 47. From the west side of Woodbury Trailhead parking lot [2-A, 0] (N33° 24′ 33.8″, W111° 12′ 19.5″), walk west on FR172.

THE TRIP

Start on Map 2 on page 57. Follow Trip 2 (Dripping Spring) on page 55 to Dripping Spring for the first part of the trip. From the wooden trail sign [2-U, 3.8] at the junction of Coffee Flat Trail and Red Tanks Trail, head right (north) on the Red Tanks Trail (107). The trail zigzags across the bed of Red Tanks Canyon where you often find seasonal pools of water. Then the trail leaves the wash and heads up a steep slope on the east side of the canyon where it climbs high above the canyon floor and bypasses the junction of Randolph and Red Tanks Canyons. Some hikers may enjoy staying in the canyon and walking along the smooth rock canyon floor rather than taking the trail over the hill.

When the trail drops down to creek level again, you are in Randolph Canyon. Several trails-of-use are here, so make your best guess, and cross to the north side of Randolph Canyon [2-P, 4.4]. The trail sign that was posted in the 1990s is gone. The unsigned Red Tanks Trail heads uphill (north) and goes over to Red Tanks Canyon, but Trip 4 leaves the trail and follows the bed of Randolph Canyon heading right (northeast). No continuous trails go up Randolph Canyon, so the best plan is to walk up the creek bed and make use of the cow trails on the benches.

Randolph Spring [2-R, 6.2], which has seasonal flow, is easy to find if you are following the creek bed. A cement dam, backfilled with rock, spans the wash at Randolph Spring. Several large willow trees grow here. When the wash went through a narrow, smooth rock section, we walked up the south slope where we found an old trail that took us a good distance up Randolph Canyon. This may have been the unimproved trail shown on the USFS Superstition Wilderness map. After crossing a ravine, we lost the trail, which may have turned south toward JF Ranch. Continuing on the south bank of Randolph Canyon, we soon passed through a normally closed gate in a barbed-wire fence before dropping into the creek bed again.

Black bear climbing out of a water trough on the Quarter Circle U Ranch in April 2010. This black bear could be the same bear that we encountered in Randolph Canyon on the Martin Ranch in the spring of 2008. Photo by Bobby Beeman.

JF Trail (106) crosses Randolph Canyon [2-N, 7.7] where a large wash enters from the north. No signs are posted, but you can see the eroded JF Trail heading up the red dirt bank to the south. From here [2-N], it is relatively smooth walking. The trail goes up the hill, crosses the wash twice, and then passes the wooden Tonto National Forest Superstition Wilderness sign [2-D, 8.4]. Continue on the JF Trail toward the Woodbury windmill [2-C, 8.6]. The Martin Ranch maintains the windmill and may disable it when the washes have plenty of water for the cattle. The trail near the windmill is very faint, so keep the windmill and tall water tanks on your left as you curve to the right around the dirt stock pond. The trail is more distinct as you proceed south to the signed junction [2-B, 8.7] with Woodbury Trail (114). The JF Trail follows the dirt road over a small hill to the parking lot at Woodbury Trailhead where the trip ends [2-A, 9.2].

HISTORY AND LEGENDS

On a December 1993 hike in Randolph Canyon, about a half mile west of Randolph Spring, we saw a full-grown javelina dart up the slope. The hooves striking the ground made a powerful sound. A few seconds later, two more large javelina ran up the slope after the first. These animals were a lot larger than the javelina we often had seen in La Barge Canyon.

After the trip, while driving down FR172 in the dark, we saw four more javelina cross the road—two adults and two of the smallest javelina we've ever seen. The two juveniles couldn't make it over the dirt embankment along the road, and one of the adults came back to give them directions. The family scurried into the darkness.

We encountered a black bear coming up Randolph Canyon in April 2008 as we were going down canyon. At first we thought it was one of the Martin Ranch black cows. Within seconds it saw us and ran into the bushes and up the hillside—not to be seen again that day.

In the spring of 2010, Bobby Beeman photographed a large bear taking a bath in a water trough and at other locations on the Quarter Circle U Ranch pastures. We think this could be the same bear that makes a yearly circuit through the canyons looking for food. Later in the spring of 2010, we saw more bear tracks in the wet sand—along with mountain lion tracks—where the JF Trail crosses Randolph Canyon [2-N] on the Martin Ranch.

RED TANKS DIVIDE LOOP

Because of its remote location, Red Tanks Divide cannot be reached from any trailhead on a leisurely day trip, but a loop trip can be made in a long day or on a multi-day trip. The open grassy hills in the high country will give you a sense of accomplishment as you reach Red Tanks Divide at 3,675 feet—the highest elevation on the trip. Some of these trails are used infrequently, so you will enjoy the solitude often missing on the more popular trails.

ITINERARY

From Woodbury Trailhead, follow Coffee Flat Trail (108) to Dripping Spring. Take Red Tanks Trail (107) over Red Tanks Divide and down Upper La Barge Box. Return on Whiskey Spring Trail (238), Dutchman's Trail (104), Coffee Flat Trail (108), FR172B, and FR172 to Woodbury Trailhead.

DIFFICULTY

Very difficult hike. Difficult backpack. Not recommended for horses.
Elevation change is ±3,300 feet.

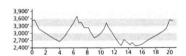

LENGTH and TIME

20.5 miles, 17 hours round-trip.

MAPS

Arizona USGS topo maps NAD27: Iron Mountain and Weavers Needle. Superstition Wilderness Beartooth map, grids L14-H14. Maps 2, 3, 4, and 11.

FINDING THE TRAIL

See the trailhead map on page 47. From the west side of Woodbury Trailhead parking lot [2-A, 0] (N33° 24' 33.8", W111° 12' 19.5"), walk west on FR172.

THE TRIP

Start on Map 2 on page 57. From the Woodbury Trailhead [2-A, 0], follow Trip 4 (Randolph Canyon Loop) on page 65 to the Red Tanks Trail [2-U, 3.8] near Dripping Spring and on to Randolph Canyon [2-P, 4.4]. Red Tanks Trail is marked only by scattered rock cairns when it crosses Randolph Canyon [2-P, 4.4] (N33° 24' 05.8", W111° 15' 26.0"), so look carefully for the trail as it heads uphill and goes over a small ridge before dropping down into Red Tanks Canyon.

Red Tanks Trail leaves Red Tanks Canyon [3-BB, 5.9] and makes a sharp left (west) turn.[51] From the large flat rock at that turn [3-BB], walk westerly about a minute or two on the trail and watch for the trail to cross the wash to the left (south) side. The crossing is often hidden by a thick growth of bushes, but the trail is well defined after you get through the bushes.

The Red Tanks Trail passes the metal pipe for the 1919 survey section-marker [3-AA, 6.2] and shortly drops into a ravine where water often collects in a pool below a large boulder (N33° 25' 21.4", W111° 16' 08.3"). Continue up the canyon to Red Tanks Divide [3-D, 6.6] (N33° 25' 35.4", W111° 16' 18.9"). The trail in the Red Tanks Divide area follows a different route than that shown on most maps. The Red Tanks Trail on Map 3 is shown correctly.

Brads Water [4-T] (N33° 26' 25.8", W111° 16' 53.2"), about 0.4 mile north of the trail, might be a possible water source if you are on a multi-day trip. The water is in a hard-rock tunnel a few yards up the slope from the abandoned concrete water troughs. The former corral [4-II] (N33° 26' 13.8", W111° 16' 58.4") is identified only by four wooden posts. The trails to the corral and Brads Water are overgrown and not usable, so traveling in the washes is the best approach.

Just before reaching the junction [4-B] with the Hoolie Bacon Trail, look for a group campsite (N33° 26' 10.1", W111° 17' 15.3") on the left (south) side of the Red Tanks Trail. The junction with the Hoolie Bacon Trail (111) [4-B, 8.1] is marked with a wooden trail sign. See the Alternate Return Routes for your trip options from this trail intersection.

Sign on the gate to the JF Ranch in 1993 [2-X].

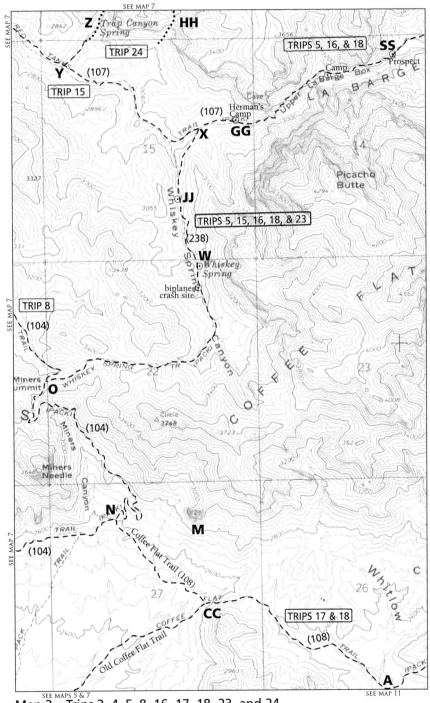

Map 3 – Trips 2, 4, 5, 8, 16, 17, 18, 23, and 24.

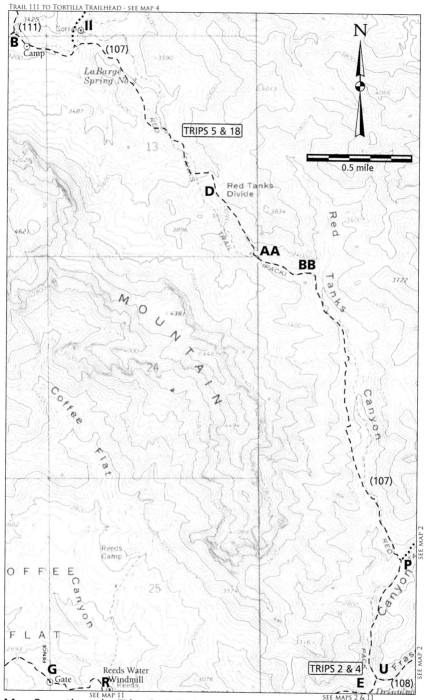

(111)

B

Camp

Corral

II

(107)

LaBarge Spring No 2

TRIPS 5 & 18

N

0.5 mile

Red Tanks Divide

D

TRAIL

AA

BB

Red

Tanks

M O U N T A I N

Canyon

Coffee

Flat

(107)

RED

C O F F E E

Canyon

Reeds Camp

SEE MAP 2

P

F L A T

FENCE

G

Gate

Reeds Water
Windmill
Reeds

R

TRIPS 2 & 4

U

E

(108)

Frasier

SEE MAP 2

Canyon

SEE MAP 11

SEE MAPS 2 & 11

Drinning

Map 3 continued – Trips 2, 4, 5, 8, 16, 17, 18, 23, and 24.

Continue on the Red Tanks Trail going down the Upper La Barge Box. Most horse riders will have trouble on this scary segment of trail—narrow and steep—with loose rock, slick rock, and sheer drop-offs. The Roy Bradford—and later Chuck Crawford—prospect [4-SS, 8.3] (N33° 26' 07.8", W111° 17' 30.8") is on the right (north) side of the trail.

About halfway down the Box, before you cross a large ravine coming in from the right (north), look for a fine campsite (N33° 26' 03.7", W111° 17' 49.7") on the left (south) side of the trail. The camp has great views of the rugged cliffs, and it is near seasonal water in the creek. Near the bottom of the Box, Herman Petrasch had a camp [4-GG, 9.2] (N33° 25' 53.2", W111° 18' 17.1") at a small cave on the north side of the creek and trail.

Watch for the wooden trail sign [3-X, 9.4] that marks the Whiskey Spring Trail (238). Go left (south) on the Whiskey Spring Trail, cross La Barge Creek, which is usually dry here, and follow the trail up and over the ridge. When the trail drops into Whiskey Spring Canyon, you will find some nice campsites [3-JJ, 9.8] along the trail under the laurel (sugar sumac) and cottonwood trees. Whiskey Spring is farther up the canyon [3-W, 10.1] on the left (east) side of the wash beneath the cottonwood trees.

At Miners Summit [3-O, 11.3], go left (south) on the Dutchman's Trail (104). Leave the Dutchman's Trail at the wooden trail sign [3-N, 12.8] and go left (southeast) on the Coffee Flat Trail (107). Bear left (east) at the wooden sign [3-CC, 13.4] and junction with the Old Coffee Flat Trail. Here the Coffee Flat Trail follows the 1880s alignment of a proposed Mesa-to-Globe Road.

The trip passes the unsigned trail [11-A, 14.4] going to Coffee Flat Spring [11-D] and Whitlow Corral—the wooden corral was destroyed in the June 2020 Sawtooth Fire. See Trip 17 (Reeds Water) on page 127 for information on the Coffee Flat and Reeds Water areas. At the gate [11-G, 14.9] in the barbed-wire fence, the trail crosses into the Martin Ranch grazing allotment and shortly arrives at the Reeds Water windmill [11-R, 15.2]. The water trough here is out of service. It is not a source of water anymore. There usually is water in the bottom of the rock well, although it is hard to get.

Go south through another gate to enter State Trust land and the Quarter Circle U Ranch leased pasture. At the out-of-service Cottonwood windmill [11-C, 15.3], cross the streambed of Randolph Canyon, immediately turn left (east), and head upstream—don't continue south on the better trail that will take you down to Whitlow Canyon. At the gate in the Wilderness boundary fence [11-I, 16.0], the trail leaves State Trust land and enters the Martin Ranch grazing allotment again, continuing up to Dripping Spring [2-S] to meet the signed junction with Red Tanks Trail (107) [2-U, 16.7].

See Trip 2 (Dripping Spring) on page 55 for the things to do in the Dripping Spring area and for the trip description back to Woodbury

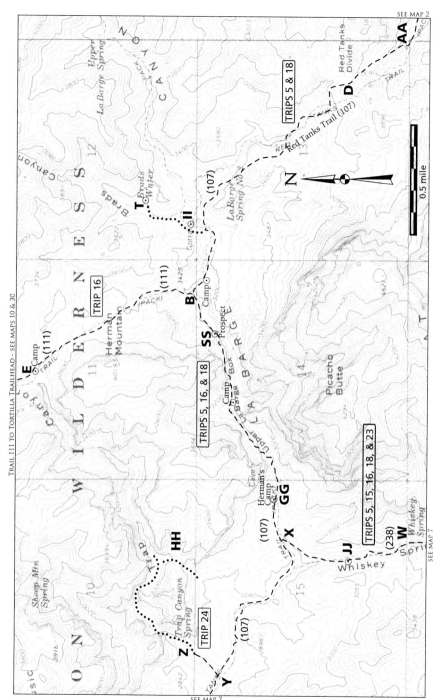

Map 4 – Trips 5, 15, 16, 18, 23, and 24.

Trailhead. A summary of the important mileages is: Whetrock Canyon [2-W, 17.8], road construction [2-V, 18.2], gate at corrals [2-X, 19.4], locked gate at FR172B [2-L, 20.3], and Woodbury Trailhead [2-A, 20.5].

Alternate Return Routes:

You have several opportunities for longer loops or shorter out-and-back treks.

(1) Backtracking from Red Tanks Divide [3-D, 6.6] to Woodbury Trailhead [2-A, 13.2] makes a fine out-and-back trip.

(2) Making a return loop on the Hoolie Bacon Trail (111) [4-B, 8.1], connecting with JF Trail (106) [30-D, 12.4] near Tortilla Trailhead, and returning over Tortilla Pass [31-J, 17.5] to Woodbury Trailhead [1-A, 20.7] is a nice loop that not many people consider.

(3) Exiting the trip described above in (2) at Tortilla Trailhead [29-A, 13.2] near Tortilla Well [29-B] or where four-wheel-drive FR213 meets the Apache Trail, SR88, [29-T, 16.4] is a possibility for a vehicle shuttle trip. It is a long shuttle—52 miles via Apache Junction or 89 miles via Miami.

(4) Hikers can also make a loop across Red Tanks Divide from Peralta Trailhead [7-A, 0] using the Dutchman's Trail (104), Whiskey Spring Trail (238), Red Tanks Trail (107), and Coffee Flat Trail (108). The return retraces the Dutchman's Trail to Peralta Trailhead [7-A, 18.1]. See Trip 18 (Upper La Barge Box Loop) on page 131 for the trip details.

Roy Bradford's Camp in La Barge Canyon above the Upper La Barge Box. Left to right: Walt Upton, Chuck Aylor, Peggy Aylor, Roy Bradford holding his pet cat Pinkey. Circa 1940s-1950s. Photograph by Al Reser. Courtesy Superstition Mountain Historical Society, Al Reser Collection.

Peralta Trailhead

From Apache Junction at Idaho Road, go 8 miles east on US60. Turn left (north) between mileposts 204 and 205 onto Peralta Road (also named FR77 and Peralta Trail). Peralta Trailhead is 7.2 miles, at the end of Peralta Road.

FINDING THE TRAILHEAD

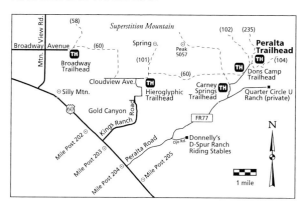

Trailhead parking is at the end of FR77 (N33° 23' 51.4", W111° 20' 49.7").

FACILITIES

Accessible pit toilets are located at the main parking lot. No drinking water is available. Be sure to bring your own water. Seasonal water in Peralta Canyon creek, just north of the parking lot, is good for soaking your aching feet, but don't drink it.

In the prime hiking season, February and March, Forest Service rangers are here conducting visitor-survey information, and they are available for any questions you have. Theft and vandalism are common at this trailhead, so don't leave valuables in your vehicle. Thieves steal clothes, books, maps, camping gear, gasoline, tools, GPS equipment, etc. Be sure everything is locked in the trunk, or better yet, don't bring it to the trailhead.

THE TRAILS

See Map 5 on page 77. Three trails start from the northeast side of the Peralta Trailhead [5-A] (N33° 23' 51.4", W111° 20' 49.7") parking lot. Peralta Trail (102) goes left (north) up Peralta Canyon to Fremont Saddle in 2.1 miles where you have a spectacular view of Weavers Needle. Peralta Trail ends in East Boulder Canyon (5.9 miles) not far from Aylor's former Caballo Camp. This is the most popular and heavily traveled route in the area.

The Dutchman's Trail (104) goes right (east) and immediately crosses Peralta Canyon creek bed. Fifty yards up the path, Bluff Spring Trail (235)

Peralta Trailhead. From the trail sign, the Peralta Trail goes left and then up the canyon shown at the top of the photograph. The Dutchman's Trail goes right (behind the Wilderness sign), crosses Peralta Canyon wash, and heads east. February 2010 photo.

branches to the left (north). It goes to Bluff Spring in 3.4 miles and connects with the Dutchman's Trail again. The Dutchman's Trail takes you to La Barge Canyon in another 2.1 miles. The Bluff Spring Trail is the second most traveled trail in the area and is very useful for connecting many of the loop trips.

At the Bluff Spring Trail junction, the Dutchman's Trail heads right (east) and contours around some small hills before dropping down into Barkley Basin. It continues over Miners Summit to the junction with Bluff Spring Trail in 5.4 miles, Charlebois Spring in 8.9 miles, and ends at First Water Trailhead 17.4 miles later. The Dutchman's Trail winds its way through the legendary areas of the Superstition Wilderness. The Dutchman's Trail, from the Peralta Trailhead, seems to have less traffic than other trails and offers some solitude once you pass over the first saddle on the trail.

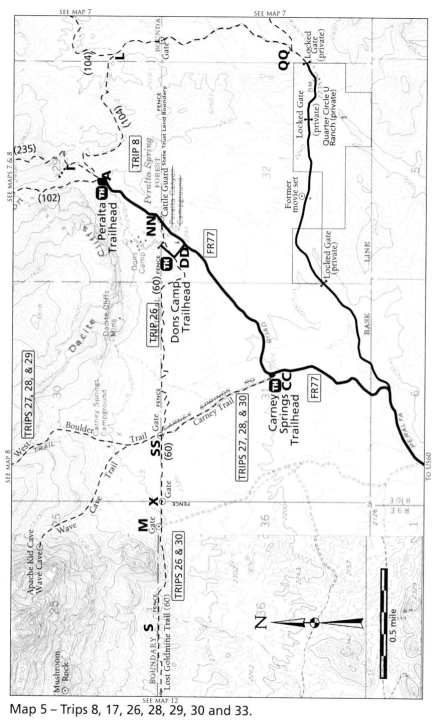

Map 5 – Trips 8, 17, 26, 28, 29, 30 and 33.

FREMONT SADDLE

For those who haven't seen Weavers Needle, this is a required trip. Peralta Trail is wide and easy to follow. It takes you directly to Weavers Needle. Look for the "Eye on the Trail" window rock on the eastern horizon and the hoodoo rock formations as you travel uphill to Fremont Saddle.

ITINERARY

From Peralta Trailhead parking lot, take the Peralta Trail (102), north, up Peralta Canyon to Fremont Saddle for a spectacular view of Weavers Needle. Return by the same route or by the Cave Trail and the Bluff Spring Trail.

DIFFICULTY

Moderate hike. Not recommended for horses. Elevation change is +1,360 feet.

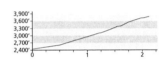

LENGTH and TIME

2.1 miles, 2 hours one way.

MAPS

Arizona USGS topo map NAD27: Weavers Needle. Superstition Wilderness Beartooth map, grids G15 to G14. Map 6.

FINDING THE TRAIL

See the trailhead map on page 75. Leave the northeast end of the Peralta Trailhead parking lot (N33° 23' 51.4", W111° 20' 49.7"), go left, and follow the Peralta Trail up Peralta Canyon.

THE TRIP

Start on Map 6 on page 81. Although Peralta Canyon is popular, it is a good choice for new visitors to the Superstitions. The view of Weavers Needle is spectacular, and the optional Cave Trail provides some experience in following rock cairns along a less-defined trail. The trip is rated moderate for hikers, which means experienced trekkers should be able to complete the trip without much difficulty. The 1,360-foot elevation change is large, so you may spend a few moments enjoying the view while you catch your second breath.

Peralta Trail is not recommended for horses due to heavy hiker traffic, slick rock, slanted tread, and many step-up sections of trail. Some outfitters walk their horses over the slanted, slick rock sections of trail.

The trip starts at the north end of the Peralta Trailhead parking lot [6-A, 0]. Follow the arrow on the Peralta Trail sign going left, which starts you up the west side of Peralta Canyon. The trail is wide and easy to follow. Rock hop across the seasonal water at each crossing—don't drink the water.

As you walk along the trail, let your imagination bring the spectacular rock formations on the ridgeline to life in the form of animals, faces, and figures. Look for a window-rock [6-B, 1.3] on the east ridge near the top of the cliffs—the Eye on the Trail.[52] Another window rock [6-C, 2.0], located next to the path just before the trail reaches Fremont Saddle, has also been referred to as the Eye on the Trail, but it doesn't have the distinctive eye features of the formation seen earlier.

At Fremont Saddle [6-D, 2.1], you won't need directions to find Weavers Needle, as it rises in the north, more than 1,200 feet from the bottom of East Boulder Canyon. Fremont Saddle is the turnaround point for Trip 6, but Peralta Trail (102) continues north, down the slope into East Boulder

Bob Corbin, Celeste Maria Jones, and Louis Roussette at the Jones Camp in East Boulder Canyon near Weavers Needle. From Superstition Mountain, A Ride Through Time *by James Swanson and Tom Kollenborn. Photograph by Jack Karie, circa 1950s.*

Canyon. For a closer view of Weavers Needle, follow the ridgeline from Fremont Saddle north along a faint path for about a quarter mile to a lookout point where a lone pinyon pine grows [6-L].

The easiest return route is to retrace your trip on Peralta Trail to the parking lot [6-A, 4.2]. The optional return for experienced hikers (not doable for horses) is via the Cave Trail starting at Fremont Saddle following the Trip 7 (Cave Trail) description on page 82 to the parking lot [6-A, 4.6].

HISTORY AND LEGENDS

Peralta Canyon was named by the Dons Club in 1934. It was formerly known as Willow Canyon[53] and has also been called South Needle Canyon.[54] At one time, Fremont Saddle [8-D] was called Fremont Pass. Fremont Saddle is named after General John C. Fremont who led a military campaign in the mid 1800s for American control of California.

Weavers Needle was named for Pauline Weaver in 1853.[55] Pauline Weaver was born in Tennessee in 1797. His parents, an Anglo-American father and Cherokee mother, named him Powell Weaver. He called himself Paulin and Paulino in Spanish, but became known as Pauline to the Anglos. He first ventured into Arizona in 1831 and became well known as a scout, trapper, mountain man, and miner. Both Indian and pioneer considered Weaver a friend for his fair judgment. He was a scout for Lieutenant Colonel Cooke when the Mormon Battalion made the trek from Santa Fe to southern California in 1846. In the late 1850s, he prospected for gold and for a short time prospected with Henry Wickenburg. Pauline Weaver died in 1867 while serving as a scout for the military at Camp Lincoln (near Camp Verde) and is buried in Prescott, Arizona, at the Sharlot Hall Museum.[56]

Experienced rock climbers ascend Weavers Needle starting from a gully on the west side—rated a 5.0 technical climb by Jim Waugh.[57] Tyler Williams rated the route a 5.3 technical climb in a more recent book.[58] Flat camping places on top of Weavers Needle, elevation 4553 feet, provide plenty of room for roaming around to view the surrounding Wilderness area. Some climbers make a day trip to the summit, but others haul their camping gear up the cliffs and spend the night on top of the Needle.

Piñon Camp [8-M] is just north of Fremont Saddle. The pinyon pine trees at the site of the 1949 Celeste Maria Jones camp—shown as Piñon Camp on the USGS topo map—died during the late 1990s. Jones was the leader of a party of treasure hunters in the search for gold here in the late 1950s and early 1960s.[59] Deteriorating ladders and steel spikes on the face of the Needle are evidence of her early explorations. Her adversary, Ed Piper, had a camp [8-O] farther down East Boulder Canyon.

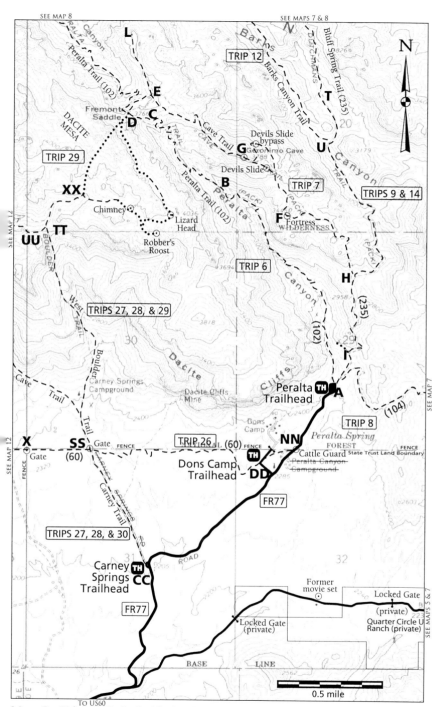

Map 6 – Trips 6, 7, 8, 9, 12, 14, 27, 28, 29, and 30.

CAVE TRAIL

The Cave Trail is a fine choice for ridgeline hikers who particularly enjoy walking on weatherworn rock—no dusty trail here. The route winds its way along cliffs and boulders, passing Geronimo Cave (alcove), with panoramic views into Peralta Canyon to the west and Barks Canyon to the east.

ITINERARY

Start on the Peralta Trail (102) at Fremont Saddle. The Cave Trail descends to the south along the east ridgeline of Peralta Canyon, connecting with the Bluff Spring Trail (235), which leads to the Peralta Trailhead parking lot.

DIFFICULTY

Moderate hike. Not doable by horses. Elevation change is -1,360 feet.

LENGTH and TIME

2.5 miles, 2.0 hours one way.

MAPS

Arizona USGS topo map NAD27: Weavers Needle. Superstition Wilderness Beartooth map, grids G15 to G14. Map 6.

FINDING THE TRAIL

See the trailhead map on page 75. The unsigned Cave Trail starts on the Peralta Trail (102) at Fremont Saddle [6-D, 0] (N33° 24′ 56.4″, W111° 21′ 50.9″) heading northeast along the top of the ridge.

THE TRIP

Start on Map 6 on page 81. The Cave Trail is much more challenging than the Peralta Trail. Even experienced hikers may have a difficult time staying on the trail as it crosses smooth rock surfaces—sometimes marked by rock cairns—and makes seemingly unnecessary twists and sharp turns around the cliffs.

      Many hikers use a mobile phone gps app to stay on the trail. Be sure to download your maps in advance since there is no internet service here. Avoid the Cave Trail if it is raining or if the trail is wet. Sheer cliffs and the always present loose pebbles on the smooth bedrock make the trail dangerous for a fall off the cliffs. Even in good weather the trail along the cliffs can be scary.

Start the trip by heading east from Fremont Saddle [6-D, 0] along the trail that leads to the overlook for Weavers Needle. After walking 5 minutes, you will come to a junction in the trail marked by a rock cairn [6-E, 0.2] (N33° 25′ 00.2″, W111° 21′ 43.3″). The left branch heads north to a pinyon pine tree [6-L] at the overlook for Weavers Needle. The right branch is the Cave Trail, which goes southeast and follows the east ridgeline of Peralta Canyon. After another 10 minutes, the Cave Trail makes a switchback and heads north for 100 yards to avoid a cliff, then doubles back and continues southeast.

Farther down, the trail goes in front of Geronimo Cave [6-G, 0.8] on a wide cliff face. You must scramble up about 80 feet to inspect the alcove. There is no actual cave here, only a large alcove. Continuing south, in a few minutes, the trail turns east at the top of Devils Slide. This is a very steep slickrock area that is steepest at the bottom where it is named Devils Slide.

Many people avoid Devils Slide, a dangerous section of the trail, by taking the bypass route on the east side of Geronimo Cave Butte. At the top of Devils Slide, look east and up about 20 feet to pick up a trail-of-use on the north side of a large boulder. That trail-of-use takes you on a cairned route to a less steep descent on the east side of Geronimo Cave Butte.

Geronimo Trail sign—now named the Cave Trail–in Peralta Canyon near Fremont Saddle, circa 1975. Photo by Richard Dillon.

About 25 minutes south of Geronimo Cave is a rock buttress that is named the Fortress [6-F, 1.3] (N33° 24' 32.5", W111° 21' 04.5"). The four technical climbs on this face are rated between 5.5 and 5.7.[60]

The Cave Trail continues to descend, and at times it might seem as if you will never get to the intersection with the Bluff Spring Trail. If you persevere for another 30 minutes following the cairns and most used trails, you will arrive in a relatively flat area at the unsigned Bluff Spring Trail intersection [6-H, 1.9] (N33° 24' 17.2", W111° 20' 43.6"). Take the well-traveled Bluff Spring Trail right (southwest), and follow it down the hill for 30 minutes to the Peralta Trailhead parking lot [6-A, 2.5]. The parking lot is visible along several sections of the Bluff Spring Trail.

HISTORY AND LEGENDS

The Dons Club established the Cave Trail in the late 1930s and guided people up the Cave Trail during their Dons Trek event until the Trek was terminated in 2006. They called the guided hike along the Cave Trail the "Long Hike." The *Superstition Mountain Journal* shows photographs (in the 1930s or 1940s) of women in long dresses and men in ties making this hike on the Cave Trail. In one photograph of the Dons Trek at Devils Slide [near 6-G], we counted twenty-six hikers.[61]

The Dons Club gave colorful names such as Cardiac Hill, Devils Slide, Geronimo Cave, and the Chimney to sections of the "Long Hike." Of all these interesting names, Geronimo Cave is the only one printed on the USGS topo map. We haven't found any records indicating Apache leader Geronimo was actually here. The present-day Cave Trail avoids the more difficult sections of the "Long Hike" by bypassing the Devils Slide and the Chimney.[62] See Dons Camp Trailhead on page 164 for more stories about the Dons Club.

A 1970 U.S. Forest Service survey of the Cave Trail (233) contained a note "90 percent no trail." We are not sure of the exact year that the Forest Service abandoned the trail, but the last Tonto National Forest Superstition Wilderness Maps that showed the trail and trail number were made in the mid-1980s. It is interesting that the Cave Trail was not shown on the official maps before 1970. We hiked the Cave Trail in 2021 and observed that the unofficial trail is now in better shape and easier to follow than it was in the 1970s. Now, it is sometimes marked with rock cairns with an improved alignment.

BLUFF SPRING LOOP

This traditional loop trip takes you by Miners Needle and on to Bluff Spring. The wide, flat valley, the large stand of sugar sumac, netleaf hackberry, oak shade trees, and the reliable source of water at Bluff Spring make this ideal for camping. You are rewarded with a superb view of Weavers Needle as you return past the site of Williams Camp.

ITINERARY

From Peralta Trailhead, the Dutchman's Trail (104) goes into Barkley Basin, climbs toward Miners Needle, and descends Miners Summit to Bluff Spring Trail. The return trip follows Bluff Spring Trail (235) to Peralta Trailhead.

DIFFICULTY

Moderate hike. Difficult ride.
Elevation change is ±1,460 feet.

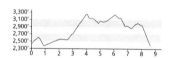

LENGTH and TIME

8.6 miles, 5 hours round-trip.

MAPS

Arizona USGS topo map NAD27: Weavers Needle. Superstition Wilderness Beartooth map, grids G15 to H14. Maps 7 and 8.

FINDING THE TRAIL

See the trailhead map on page 75. Leave the northeast corner of the Peralta Trailhead parking lot (N33° 23' 51.4", W111° 20' 49.7"), go right, and cross the creek bed coming down from Peralta Canyon. Walk north about 50 yards to a trail intersection, and take the Dutchman's Trail to the right (east).

THE TRIP

Start on Map 7 on page 89. This is a very popular loop trip. The hikers and riders are spread out over a long length of trail, and you will often be able to experience the quiet and solitude of the Wilderness. We prefer to travel counterclockwise starting on the Dutchman's Trail (104) and returning on the Bluff Springs Trail (235), but you can make the trip in either direction. The Dutchman's Trail starts out more gradually and goes over a rise, quickly leaving the parking lot [7-A, 0] behind, whereas the Bluff Spring Trail starts out very steeply on the appropriately named Cardiac Hill.

Follow the Dutchman's Trail (104) east, up and around the small hills. Keep a close lookout for mule deer on the left (north) side of the trail. We often see deer here. The trail continues down into Barkley Basin and meets an unmarked trail [7-L, 0.9] that leads south to the Quarter Circle U Ranch (private), which is an alternate return for Trip 17 (Reeds Water). This is the turnaround point for an easy trip.

Continue on the Dutchman's Trail across Barkley Basin toward some rock pinnacles in the distance—Cathedral Rock [7-M]. Go straight at the Coffee Flat Trail wooden sign [7-N, 2.6], where the Dutchman's Trail starts its climb up the switchbacks to Miners Summit.

The wooden sign at Miners Summit [7-O, 4.1] marks the Whiskey Spring Trail coming in from the right (east). Continue on the Dutchman's Trail as it leaves the summit in a northeast direction, making a long switchback down the hill. You'll find nice camp spots along the trail as it descends to Bluff Spring Canyon. The intersection with the Bluff Spring Trail [7-P, 5.4] is on the north side of the wash—identified by a wooden trail sign. The large stand of sugar sumac trees provides shade in Bluff Spring Canyon, where large groups often camp. It is a comfortable place to have a snack and get ready for the return trip.

View of Weavers Needle looking west from the Bluff Spring Trail in Bluff Spring Canyon.

To check out Bluff Spring [7-Q] (N33° 25′ 34.4″, W111° 20′ 04.4″) from the trail junction [7-P], go 0.2 mile northeast on the Dutchman's Trail, and take an unsigned spur trail to the left (northwest) for 0.1 mile toward the cliffs of Bluff Spring Mountain. The concrete water trough at Bluff Spring has been removed, but you can follow a well-worn path through the thicket to the pipe that normally has running water.

A horse trail [7-R] to the top of Bluff Spring Mountain [7-LL]—thought to be the trail used by Mexican miners in the mid 1800s—is located one minute (walking time) west of the wooden trail sign [7-P]. If time allows, check the start of the trail for a possible future trip. See the Trip 19 (Ely-Anderson Trail) for the exact trail location.

Bluff Spring Trail starts at the wooden trail sign [7-P], goes west up Bluff Spring Canyon, and crosses the wash numerous times. Weavers Needle soon rises on the western horizon, presenting an unforgettable image of the Needle in the background of Bluff Spring Canyon pass. This view of the Needle is another reason why we enjoy hiking the loop in this direction.

Williams Camp is to the right (north) of the trail just as it tops out of Bluff Spring Canyon. Walk up the small knoll to check out the remnants of the mining camp—broken china, tin cans, pieces of lumber, and other items. The remains of the mine diggings are to the north by the cliff.

After climbing out of Bluff Spring Canyon, the Bluff Spring Trail turns south and shortly intersects the Terrapin Trail [7-S, 6.4], which comes in from the right (west). At this point, you can continue with the traditional trip and follow the Bluff Spring Trail back to the trailhead or take the alternate return. The longer alternate return is described at the end of this section.

The easiest return follows the Bluff Spring Trail south down the hill into Barks Canyon. As the trail enters the wash [7-T, 6.9], it sometimes seems to disappear, but be assured it does continue. Bluff Spring Trail (235) stays in the bottom of the wash in Barks Canyon a lot longer than most people expect.

The trail continues across Barks Canyon, leaves the canyon [7-U, 7.1], and climbs up the west hillside. The unsigned Cave Trail enters from the north [7-H, 8.0] (N33° 24′ 17.2″, W111° 20′ 43.6″). Peralta Trailhead parking lot [7-A, 8.6] is another 20 minutes down the hill, where the trip ends.

ALTERNATE RETURN TRIP

The alternate return trek provides a bit of off-trail adventure as it cuts across the base of Weavers Needle before connecting with the Peralta Trail. Add about 2.9 miles and 2 hours for the Weavers Needle alternate return.

This alternate return takes the Terrapin Trail [8-S, 6.4] south to Bluff Saddle [8-JJ, 7.0]. About 0.2 mile north of Bluff Saddle, you leave the trail

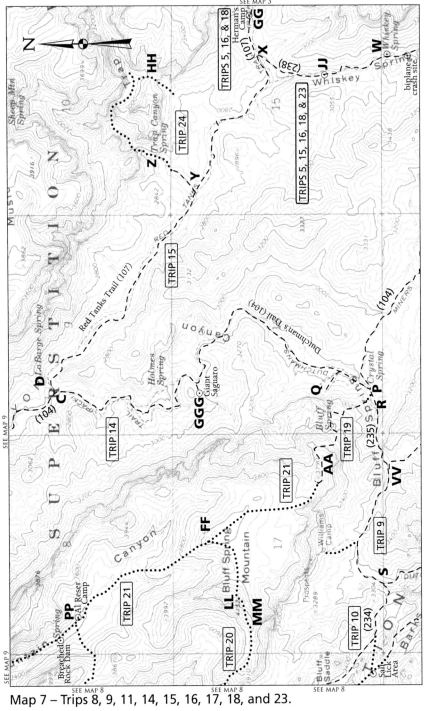

SEE MAP 3

N

Sheep Mtn Spring

LaBarge Spring

Whiskey Spring

biplane crash site

HH

TRIPS 5, 16, & 18

GG
X
JJ
W

Herman's Camp

Whiskey Spring

(101)

(238)

15

TRIPS 5, 15, 16, 18, & 23

Z
Trail Canyon Spring

TRIP 24

Y

Red Tanks Trail (107)

TRIP 15

Dutchman's Trail (104)

(104)

MINERS

Canyon

D

(104)

Holmes Spring

TRIP 14

GGG
Giant Saguaro

Q

Bluff Spring

R
P
Crystal Spring

Bluff (235) S.P.

TRIP 19

AA

TRIP 21

VV

S

TRIP 9

FF

Williams Camp

Mountain

17

Prospector (x3289)

Canyon

Bluff Spring

LL

MM

TRIP 21

TRIP 20

Bluff Saddle

TRIP 10
(234)

Barks

Al Reser Camp

PP
Breached Rock Dam

Salt Lick Area

SEE MAP 9

SEE MAP 9

SEE MAP 8

SEE MAP 8

SEE MAP 8

Map 7 – Trips 8, 9, 11, 14, 15, 16, 17, 18, and 23.

SUPERSTITION WILDERNESS TRAILS WEST

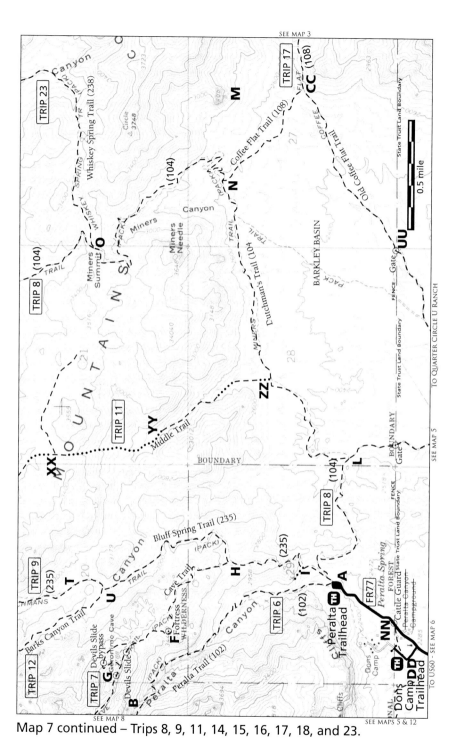

Map 7 continued – Trips 8, 9, 11, 14, 15, 16, 17, 18, and 23.

[8-II, 7.2] (N33° 25' 42.0", W111° 21' 32.8") and head left (west) on a trail-of-use going uphill. This trail-of-use is not suitable for horses beyond the pass at Weavers Needle. See Trip 13 (Weavers Needle Crosscut) on page 109 for a complete description. The route takes you to East Boulder Canyon [8-N, 8.1], where you pick up the Peralta Trail. Go up to Fremont Saddle [8-D, 9.4] and then down Peralta Canyon to the Peralta Trailhead [8-A, 11.5]. Refer to Trip 6 (Fremont Saddle) on page 78 and Trip 10 (East Boulder—Needle Canyon Loop) on page 95 for details.

HISTORY AND LEGENDS

In the early 1880s two soldiers, fresh out of the army, were traveling from Fort McDowell to the Silver King Mine to find work at the mine. They found some hand-sorted gold ore on their trip and showed it to mine owner Aaron Mason, who encouraged them to go back and set out claim notices and monuments at the mine. When Mason did not hear from the soldiers for a while, he sent out search parties to locate them. Jim Bark wrote that Mr. Whitlow found the body of a soldier who had been shot in the back and buried him where they found the body—northeast of the Quarter Circle U Ranch near the Wilderness boundary fence. Later the Whitlow boys showed Bark the grave, and he and ranch hand Huse Ward dug up the corpse for inspection and then reburied it. Another body was observed near Bluff Spring, and Bark surmised that it was the body of the second soldier.[63]

Speculation in Camp Pinal directed suspicion toward a saloon swamper as the murderer. When the citizens decided to run the suspected murderer out of camp, he took the stagecoach first to Florence, then Casa Grande, and out of Arizona.[64]

In 1884, Joe Deering allegedly found the same mine that the soldiers found, but he died in a mine accident before he could return to it. In 1915, Ernest Albert Panknin arrived in Phoenix from Alaska with a map to a lost gold mine in the Superstitions. Later in 1915, Sims Ely and Jim Bark tied the story together when they learned the man from Alaska who drew the map for Panknin was the Camp Pinal saloon swamper. Their key to the mystery was the fact that the man who drew the map had a twisted foot—the same as the saloon swamper. Panknin died in 1934 without finding the mine or revealing the memorized clues that accompanied the map.[65]

Abe Reid said the skull and bones of the soldier buried near the Quarter Circle U Ranch had been dug up when he and Tex Barkley rode by the grave in the 1950s. They were probably riding southwest down the former road between Miners Canyon and the Quarter Circle U Ranch. When they reached the ranch, Barkley asked ranch hand Roy Bradford to go back and bury the bones, which he did.[66] Researchers are still trying to identify the two soldiers' route and the location of their mine—the Two Soldiers' Lost Mine.

The ruins of Williams Camp, circa 1946–1948, with Weavers Needle in the background. The people in the photo were participants in the Dons Club Trek on an overnight backpack from First Water to Peralta Trailhead where the Dons Camp was then located. Photo by Arthur Weber (uncle of Gregory Davis). Courtesy of Gregory E. Davis and the Superstition Mountain Historical Society.

Miners Needle is the prominent rock formation on the west side of Miners Canyon. It is a Class 4 scramble to the eye of the needle, although some people prefer the security of a belayed climbing rope. The climbs to the top of the needle require technical equipment.

John Dahlmann describes what we believe was Williams Camp in his 1979 book *A Tiny Bit of God's Creation*. The camp was on a knoll just north of the trail near the head of Bluff Spring Canyon. The six cabins—three on each side of the trail—accommodated twelve miners. They were built of odd-shaped lumber remnants and roofed with galvanized sheet metal. Each cabin was about eight feet wide and twelve feet long.[67]

We prefer the older topographic maps since they contain the historical trails and landmarks, but the maps are always changing and can cause some confusion. The 1966 edition of the Weavers Needle USGS topo map shows the Dutchman's Trail as the Miners Trail, and on the same map, the Bluff Spring Trail is named the Dutchman's Trail. The 2004 edition removed all the trail names. The Forest Service and Beartooth maps show the correct names, and we overlaid the correct names on the topo maps shown in this book.

Most people probably don't have the older 1969 printing of the Weavers Needle USGS topo map (1966 edition) that interchanged the location of Bluff Spring and Crystal Spring. That was a topic of discussion for some of us map buffs until the 1978 printing of the map was issued with correct names.[68]

BLUFF SPRING TRAIL

The Bluff Spring Trail is the fastest way to reach Bluff Spring where you will find a pleasant cluster of shade trees and a fairly reliable spring. You can end your trek here, continue to the top of Bluff Spring Mountain, or go over to La Barge Spring and Charlebois Spring in La Barge Canyon.

ITINERARY

From the Peralta Trailhead, follow the Bluff Spring Trail (235) up Cardiac Hill, past the Cave Trail intersection, down into Barks Canyon, and up the hill to the Terrapin Trail intersection. Continue on Bluff Spring Trail down Bluff Spring Canyon to Bluff Spring. Return the same way or on an alternate route.

DIFFICULTY

Moderate hike. Not recom-
mended for horses. Elevation
change is +980 and -380 feet.

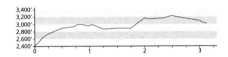

LENGTH and TIME

3.2 miles, 2 hours one way.

MAPS

Arizona USGS topo map NAD27: Weavers Needle. Superstition Wilderness Beartooth map, grids G15 to H14. Map 7.

FINDING THE TRAIL

See the trailhead map on page 75. Leave the northeast corner of the Peralta parking lot (N33° 23′ 51.4″, W111° 20′ 49.7″), go right (east), and cross the Peralta Canyon creek bed. Walk north about 50 yards up the path to a trail intersection, and take the Bluff Spring Trail to the left (north).

THE TRIP

Start on Map 7 on page 89. We included this trail description for those that want to get to Bluff Spring quickly on the most direct trail. Use the Trip 8 (Bluff Spring Loop) description on page 85 if you plan to make a loop trip. Horse riders may have difficulty on the first half mile of trail that goes up the steep, slick rock of Cardiac Hill and again on the climb out of Barks Canyon.

The trip begins at the Peralta Trailhead parking lot [7-A, 0] on the Dutchman's Trail. About three minutes up the trail, bear left (north) on the Bluff Spring Trail. Right away you begin to gain elevation on the section of trail dubbed Cardiac Hill. At several saddles on the way to the top, you have good views to the west into Peralta Canyon. The junction with the unsigned Cave Trail [7-H, 0.6] (N33° 24′ 17.2″, W111° 20′ 43.6″) to the north is not marked, but you can see the tread of the trail. Continue on the Bluff Spring Trail across a flat area, up to a saddle, and down into Barks Canyon.

At the trail intersection with the bed of Barks Canyon [7-U, 1.5], you can often find water. Those interested in a shorter trip can use this as a lunch and turnaround spot. Since this is a busy area, we do not recommend drinking the water. On a hot day, this is a good place for wetting a shirt or bandanna.

Almost everyone gets lost in the bed of Barks Canyon Wash [7-T, 1.7] as the trail weaves its way northerly. If you find yourself on one of the dead-end paths, backtrack and look for rock cairns marking the trail. When the trail goes up on the eastern hillside, the steep but well-defined trail may be a problem for some horse riders due to the slick rock. The spires, rock formations, saguaro cacti, and view of Weavers Needle on the western horizon make a good picture.

A little beyond the summit, the Terrapin Trail (234) [7-S, 2.2] comes in from the left (west). Continue on the Bluff Spring Trail northerly, then east as it crosses the saddle into Bluff Spring Canyon.

The rock inscribed with "A. P. Peralta" is located along the north side of the Bluff Spring Trail between [7-U] and [7-T]. November 11, 2010 photo.

You can walk up the small knoll to the site of Williams Camp on the north side of the trail. Not much is left of the mining camp except a few household remnants—broken china, tin cans, pieces of lumber, and other items. To the north by the cliff are the remains of the mine diggings. Back on the Bluff Spring Trail, continue east down to the wooden trail sign at the Bluff Spring Trail and Dutchman's Trail junction [7-P, 3.2].

It is another 0.3 mile to Bluff Spring if you need water or just want to check it out. Continue northeast from the wooden sign on the Dutchman's Trail for 0.2 mile. Take the well-worn spur trail 0.1 mile to Bluff Spring [7-Q] (N33° 25' 34.4", W111° 20' 04.4"), which is in a thicket of bushes up against the cliffs of Bluff Spring Mountain. Return the same way, or consider an alternate return. Be sure to read Trip 8 (Bluff Spring Loop) on page 85 for a narrative on the Bluff Spring area.

ALTERNATE RETURN ROUTE ON DUTCHMAN'S TRAIL

This return takes the Dutchman's Trail over Miners Summit and continues to Peralta Trailhead. See Trip 8 (Bluff Spring Loop) on page 85 for this alternate return—read the Trip 8 description in the clockwise (reverse) direction.

This return is 2.2 miles longer than retracing your trip on the Bluff Spring Trail. The summary of your important landmarks and mileages for the return is: wooden sign at end of Bluff Spring Trail [7-P, 3.2], Miners Summit [7-O, 4.5], Coffee Flat Trail sign [7-N, 6.0], and Peralta Trailhead [7-A, 8.6].

ALTERNATE RETURN ROUTE BY WEAVERS NEEDLE CROSSCUT

A second alternate return uses Weavers Needle Crosscut Route. It connects the Terrapin Trail (234) and Peralta Trail (102) and returns over Fremont Saddle via the Peralta Trail (102) or the Cave Trail. This return adds 2.8 miles and requires some off-trail hiking. It is not doable by horses.

From the wooden sign at the end of Bluff Spring Trail [7-P, 3.2], retrace your trip on the Bluff Spring Trail to the wooden sign at the junction with the Terrapin Trail [7-S, 4.2]. Turn right (west) on the Terrapin Trail, go over Bluff Saddle [8-JJ, 4.8], and meet the junction with the trail-of-use [8-II, 5.0] for Trip 13 (Weavers Needle Crosscut)—described on page 109.

The summary of your important mileages for the rest of the trip is: leave Terrapin Trail [8-II, 5.0], Peralta Trail [8-N, 5.9], Fremont Saddle [8-D, 7.2], and Peralta Trailhead [8-A, 9.3].

If you take the Cave Trail, your mileages are: Fremont Saddle [8-D, 7.2], trail junction [8-E, 7.4], trail junction [8-H, 9.1], and Peralta Trailhead [8-A, 9.7]. See Trip 7 (Cave Trail) on page 82.

EAST BOULDER—NEEDLE CANYON LOOP

This trip has more vistas of Weavers Needle than any other trip in the Wilderness. The trails are well defined, the views are great, and the trails are not crowded beyond Fremont Saddle. Weavers Needle attracted many prospectors, and the trail passes through their historic base camps. You may find seasonal water in East Boulder Canyon, Needle Canyon, and Barks Canyon. An optional side trip takes you to Aylor's Arch and Aylor's former camp.

ITINERARY

From the Peralta Trailhead, this loop trip takes Peralta Trail (102) north, up Peralta Canyon to Fremont Saddle for a spectacular view of Weavers Needle. The trip continues north on the Peralta Trail in East Boulder Canyon, east on the Dutchman's Trail (104), south on the Terrapin Trail (234), and returns to the Peralta Trailhead via the Bluff Spring Trail (235).

DIFFICULTY

Difficult hike. Not recommended for horses. Elevation change is ±2,880 feet.

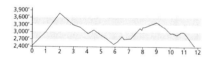

LENGTH and TIME

11.8 miles, 7.5 hours round-trip.

MAPS

Arizona USGS topo maps NAD27: Goldfield and Weavers Needle. Superstition Wilderness Beartooth map, grids G15 to F13. Map 8.

FINDING THE TRAIL

See the trailhead map on page 75. Leave the north end of the Peralta Trailhead parking lot (N33° 23' 51.4", W111° 20' 49.7"). Go left up Peralta Canyon.

THE TRIP

Start on Map 8 on page 99. This is a popular loop trip that circles Weavers Needle. The trip can be extended or shortened according to your particular plans as described later. From the Peralta Trailhead [8-A, 0], follow Trip 6 (Fremont Saddle), described on page 78, to Fremont Saddle [8-D, 2.1].

From Fremont Saddle [8-D, 2.1], descend into East Boulder Canyon on the well-defined Peralta Trail (102). The first landmark along the trail is Piñon Camp [8-M, 3.0], which was the 1949 camp of treasure hunter Celeste Maria Jones.[69] The four pinyon pine trees at Piñon Camp have died—only the trunks of two of them were left standing in 2010. The sugar sumac trees—locally called laurel trees—still provide a shady place to camp or rest.

The unsigned junction [8-N, 3.4] (N33° 25′ 40.3″, W111° 22′ 25.3″) with the Weavers Needle Crosscut Trail is sometimes marked with rock cairns. See Trip 13 (Weavers Needle Crosscut) on page 109 for the trail description that takes you over to the Terrapin Trail just north of Bluff Saddle.

Ed Piper established several camps in the area through the early 1950s. His last camp was located on a small flat along the Peralta Trail [8-O, 4.0] (N33° 26′ 04.9″, W111° 22′ 46.6″) near the bed of East Boulder Canyon. Piper Spring was located here in the bed of the wash, but it is no longer usable—look for the inscribed "Water" and arrow on the big boulder pointing to the spring. You can see the concrete frame of the spring box when it is not covered with sand and gravel.

North on the Peralta Trail, Hill 3113 is the prominent landmark on the horizon. The trail goes up over Granite Saddle [8-R, 4.5] and around the west side of Hill 3113, dropping through a pass that overlooks East Boulder

Al Morrow at his camp [8-EE] in Needle Canyon. Photograph by Al Reser, April 1968. Courtesy Superstition Mountain Historical Society, Al Reser Collection.

Canyon. Near here are flat areas along the trail that make good, but rather public, camping spots [8-W, 4.8]. Looking east, you can see the Dutchman's Trail going across Upper Black Top Mesa Pass [8-FF]. From this ridgeline, you have fine views of Weavers Needle to the south; spires on the horizon to the southwest; and Yellow Peak, Palomino Mountain, and Black Top Mesa to the north.

Heading down Peralta Trail into East Boulder Canyon, before the trail turns east into a switchback, a faint trail goes up to the ridge [8-X, 5.5] (N33° 27' 03.3", W111° 23' 10.5"). If you want to scout the route of the Quarter Circle U Trail[70] to West Boulder Canyon, follow this faint trail west about 150 feet to the ridge. Go north along the ridge to an eroded ravine, which was the former trail. This is as far as you should go now, since your objective today is to complete Trip 10. In earlier years, we found the tread of the trail going down the ravine, but by February 2010 it had disappeared. Map 23 shows Little Boulder Canyon, where we found parts of the cairned trail, which ends at the Dutchman's Trail [23-P] (N33° 27' 32.1", W111° 23' 54.4") in Boulder Basin.

Peralta Trail ends when it meets the Dutchman's Trail (104) at a wooden trail sign [8-AA, 5.8]. As an optional trip down East Boulder Canyon, take the Dutchman's Trail north to see Aylor's Arch [23-C] and the site of Aylor's Camp [23-A]. Allow an extra hour for the round-trip. See Trip 51 (Black Mesa Loop) on page 282 for a description of the attractions.

From the wooden trail sign [8-AA], Trip 10 continues on the Dutchman's Trail going right (south), crosses the bed of East Boulder Canyon to the east side, and begins the climb uphill. Just before the trail turns left, an unsigned trail [8-BB, 6.0] (N33° 26' 59.0", W111° 22' 56.1") enters the trees at Laurel Camp. Some outfitters make this the lunch stop for their horse rides out of First Water Trailhead.

From Laurel Camp, the trail heads up a long grade going across Upper Black Top Mesa Pass [8-FF, 6.5]. On the east side of the pass, the Dutchman's Trail intersects the Terrapin Trail (234) at a wooden trail sign [8-CC, 6.9]. At the trail junction, go right (south) on the Terrapin Trail. In 0.3 mile the Terrapin Trail crosses Needle Canyon, which only has seasonal water [8-DD, 7.2]. The old Needle Trail—now overgrown—went up the west bank following the Needle Canyon drainage. Al Morrow's main camp was located near here [8-EE] (N33° 26' 47.5", W111° 22' 07.1") and is hidden in the dense thicket of laurel trees. At the creek crossing [8-DD], Trip 10 leaves the Needle Canyon creek bed behind as it heads up on the right (west) bench.

Continue up the Terrapin Trail a few minutes. On the west side of the trail you will see a horseshoe-shaped stone wall surrounding the bed of the ravine [8-GG, 7.3]. It's about 1.5 feet thick, 3 feet high, 24 feet long, 36 feet

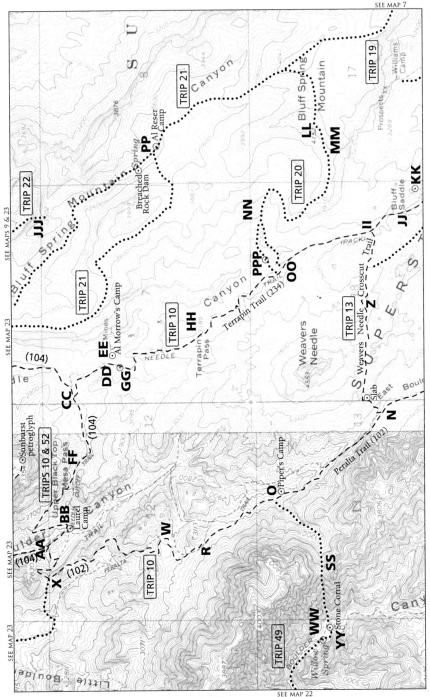

Map 8 – Trips 6, 7, 8, 10, 12, and 13.

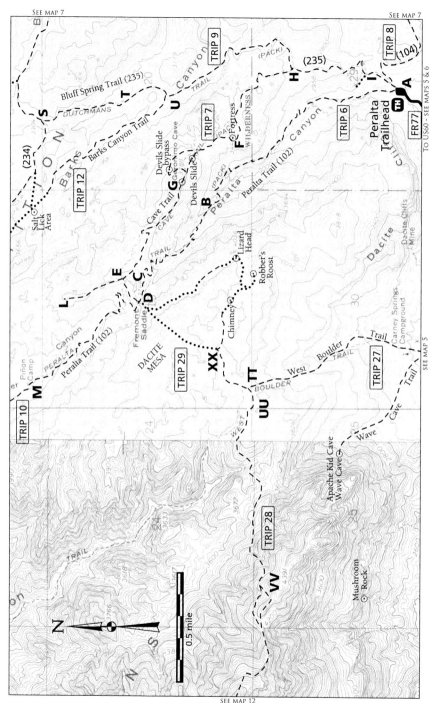

Map 8 continued – Trips 6, 7, 8, 10, 12, and 13.

wide, and made mostly of small stones. We don't know its·purpose, but we're guessing it could have been a wall to keep cattle out of the water basin.[71]

Terrapin Trail snakes up and down—with steep, slippery sections of trail—as it crosses several saddles and goes over Terrapin Pass [8-HH, 7.7]. On the east side of the trail you have limited views into narrow Needle Canyon, while the view to the west eventually opens up to a panoramic vista of Weavers Needle.

The ravine going down to Al Morrow's waterhole [8-PPP] (N33° 26′ 09.3″, W111° 21′ 40.3″) is not obvious because the trail crosses the ravine where it is shallow. The jumping off point [8-II, 8.8] (N33° 25′ 42.0″, W111° 21′ 32.8″) for Trip 13 (Weavers Needle Crosscut) is about 0.2 mile north of Bluff Saddle [8-JJ, 9.0]. On the south side of Bluff Saddle, the trail cuts through a scenic area of relatively flat basins circled by low rocky hills. Coming down the trail from Bluff Saddle [8-JJ], you pass an interesting rock formation—part of a rectangular window [8-KK, 9.1] about 90 yards east of the Terrapin Trail—that we named the Emperor's Dog.

At the wooden sign for the Bluff Spring Trail junction [8-S, 9.6], turn right (south) and follow the Bluff Spring Trail back to the Peralta Trailhead parking lot [8-A, 11.8]—about 1.5 hours more hiking time. See Trip 9 (Bluff Spring Trail) on page 92 for the trail description and possible side trips you might want to take from the Bluff Spring Trail junction.

HISTORY AND LEGENDS

The two canyons surrounding Weavers Needle, East Boulder Canyon and Needle Canyon, are rich in tales of the search for the Lost Dutchman Mine. Celeste Maria Jones, Ed Piper, Chuck Aylor, Al Morrow, Barry Storm, Glenn Magill, and Sims Ely were a few of the more famous searchers in this area. The names of these people are memorialized on government maps and in the journals of historians.

In upper East Boulder Canyon, treasure hunter Celeste Maria Jones established her 1949 base camp in the trees at Piñon Camp [8-M].[72] Jones was looking for a hidden treasure in Weavers Needle—the Lost Jesuit Gold.[73] Down the trail about one mile north of Piñon Camp, Ed Piper, in the early 1950s, located his mining camp [8-O] on a small flat area between the Peralta Trail and the bed of East Boulder Canyon. At his camp on the west side of the canyon, he used his skills as a rancher and farmer to grow vegetables, roses, and fruit trees.[74]

Bill Sewrey, veteran rock climber and former owner of Desert Mountain Sports, remembered two big army tents at Piper's camp and a trash can in the bed of the creek to catch water from the spring. In 1970 a Forest Service sign—Piper Spring—was posted here, and everyone considered it a

PRIVATE PROPERTY
$1000⁰⁰ FINE for TRESPASSING.
NO TRESPASSING on THESE GROUNDS
KEEP OUT of CAMP - NO LOITERING

Celeste Maria Jones posted this sign on the southeast side of Weavers Needle. Photograph by Bill Sewrey, December 1966. Courtesy Desert Mountain Sports, Phoenix, Arizona.

permanent spring.[75] On a trip in April 2000, we found the cement collar of the spring box in the bed of East Boulder Canyon, but the spring was not usable. We have not seen water here when the bed of East Boulder is dry.

John Dahlmann recounts his meetings with Ed Piper in the book *A Tiny Bit of God's Creation.* He describes an eight-by-sixteen-foot hut that Piper constructed with four-foot-high earthen walls (others recall a low wall) and a tarp roof. A drift tunnel at the rear of the hut ran a few feet into the mountain.[76] *Hunting Lost Mines by Helicopter*, by Erle Stanley Gardner, shows a picture of this drift, but we haven't seen it on our trips to Piper's Camp.[77]

Feuding between the Jones and Piper camps became violent between 1959 and 1962.[78] Robert Sikorsky, in *Quest for the Dutchman's Gold*, writes of his experiences during the early feuding. Employed as a geologist by Jones, Sikorsky would occasionally visit with Piper and get water from Piper's Spring. Ed Piper seemed to like him and offered him a job with his crew, but Sikorsky did not accept.[79] In the summer of 1959, after the Jones camp received rifle fire from the cliffs above, Sikorsky decided to leave the Jones crew.[80] It was getting dangerous.

Later that year, in November, Ed Piper shot and killed Robert St. Marie of the Jones Camp, in East Boulder Canyon. Ed Piper testified at the trial that Robert St. Marie pulled a gun from under a coat he was carrying and then he shot St. Marie. Jones testified in court that Piper and his men had them pinned down with rifle fire until dark while they shot up her camp from the boulders above. Inconsistencies in Jones's story led the jury to uphold Ed Piper's claim of self defense.

The feud continued in 1962 when Piper was accused of stealing rifles from the Jones camp, while Piper claimed Jones was stealing vegetables from his garden plot. On June 24, rock hunters found Piper incapacitated near his camp and had him helicoptered to the Pinal County Hospital in Florence. Symptoms of an ulcer turned out to be cancer. He was released from the hospital for a while and then readmitted. He died on August 10, 1962, at the age of sixty-eight.[81] Celeste Maria Jones left the Superstitions a few years later without finding the lost treasure.

Although many prospectors welcomed visitors to their camps and often offered coffee or a bite to eat, recollections of shootings and unexplained deaths created an atmosphere of uneasiness. With everyone carrying at least a sidearm, the Wild West was still alive. The secretive nature of prospecting led some miners to block public access to their claims. Since there was so much violence in the region, everyone took the warnings seriously.

For example, author Harry Black, in his book *The Lost Dutchman Mine*, tells of finding a barbed-wire fence in 1972, near the start of the Terrapin Trail, posted with Apex Mining Company, Danger, Keep Out. Harry Black contacted the Forest Service about this closure, and the rangers were successful in having these "improvements" removed.[82]

Lost Dutchman Mine researchers have tried to trace the early 1880s route of two soldiers who found gold ore on a cross-country trek through the Superstitions from Fort McDowell to the Silver King Mine near the town of Pinal. Barry Storm believed that the two soldiers crossed Upper Black Top Mesa Pass [8-FF] and found a partly exposed vein of ore halfway up a black-topped hill. That hill could be Black Top Mesa, although we do not know of any mineralization in that area. Barry Storm often referred to Black Top Mesa as the Peralta Mapped Mountain.[83] See Trip 8 (Bluff Spring Loop) on page 90 for a related soldier incident northeast of the Quarter Circle U Ranch.

Needle Canyon boasted at least six prospector camps established by well-known treasure hunters such as Al Morrow, Barry Storm, and Sims Ely.[84] The Glenn Magill camp [8-RR] was high above, to the east, on Bluff Spring Mountain. Albert Morrow had several camps in Needle Canyon while he prospected and lived in the Superstitions from 1950 until his death in a 1970 mine cave-in [8-EE]. Morrow was one prospector who never carried a gun.[85] Louis Ruiz, of the Bluebird Mine and Gift Shop, recalls Al Morrow cooking pancakes at his camp [8-EE] for the local Boy Scouts. Morrow would place some dynamite labels near the cooking area and tell the youngsters that a little dynamite added to the batter helped the flavor. Then, as the kids left camp with stomachs full of pancakes, he warned them not to be jumping off any rocks![86]

When Brian Lickman lived at Al Morrow's camp from 1965 to 1966, Brian said he obtained water in Needle Canyon about a mile upstream from camp [8-EE]. He carried two five-gallon glass jugs up to the waterhole [8-PPP], filled both, and carried one back to camp. Then he returned for the second one. Al stored the jugs in a tunnel to keep the water cool. He said it was easier to go up Needle Canyon than to use the Terrapin Trail to get to the year-round water source, which always had cool water in the summer months.[87] Water conditions changed yearly. In January 1968, Morrow commented that they had had the first rain in two years last December. He said, "Water was so scarce that I was forced to haul water from Charlebois Canyon [9-BB], which is three miles away."[88] In November 1968, Morrow commented again on the scarcity of water, but he said, "the big waterhole [8-PPP] up near the head of the canyon has lots of fresh water in it."[89]

Albert Morrow summarizes his feelings for the Superstition Mountains in his 1957 book *Famous Lost Gold Mines of Arizona's Superstition Mountains*, "I have found it a place of wonder and solitude where I could think clearly, enjoy the wonders of nature, and occupy myself in a pursuit that is interesting as well as healthful."[90]

Ed Piper at his camp in East Boulder Canyon near Weavers Needle. Hill 3113 appears in the background. Note the rock and dirt wall around the base of his tent. Courtesy Gregory Davis, Superstition Mountain Historical Society. Apache Sentinel, 1961. Doris J. Mathews, Editor.

MIDDLE TRAIL

The Middle Trail was used by the Quarter Circle U Ranch in the late 1800s and early 1900s as a direct route to Bluff Spring from the ranch headquarters. Although now abandoned, the route of the old trail can still be followed from the Dutchman's Trail over the ridge to Bluff Spring Canyon.

ITINERARY

From Peralta Trailhead, follow the Dutchman's Trail, turn north in the first canyon east of Barks Canyon, go over the ridge, and continue down to Bluff Spring Canyon. Return on the Bluff Spring Trail or on the Dutchman's Trail.

DIFFICULTY

Moderate hike. Not recommended for horses. Elevation change is ±1,390 feet.

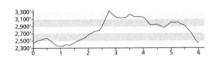

LENGTH and TIME

6.0 miles, 6 hours round-trip, with return on Bluff Spring Trail.
9.0 miles, 8 hours round-trip, with return on Dutchman's Trail.

MAPS

Arizona USGS topo map NAD27: Weavers Needle. Superstition Wilderness Beartooth map, grids G15 to H14. Map 7.

FINDING THE TRAIL

Trailhead map is on page 75. Leave the northeast side of the Peralta Trailhead parking lot (N33° 23' 51.4", W111° 20' 49.7") on the Dutchman Trail (104).

THE TRIP

Start on Map 7 on page 89. This trip is a good choice for those wanting to travel on historic routes. It is not all cross-country travel, since it connects with the Dutchman's Trail (104) and the Bluff Spring Trail (235).

Begin at the Peralta Trailhead [7-A, 0.0], and take the Dutchman's Trail to the northeast. You will pass the junction with the Bluff Spring Trail in a few minutes, which is one of the possible return trails. This trip continues on the Dutchman's Trail, goes around some small hills, and drops into Barks Canyon wash, which sometimes has a pool of water. This crossing is a major landmark for the trip, so take note of it.

Stay on the Dutchman's Trail until you see Middle Canyon wash coming in on your left (north) [7-ZZ, 1.6] (N33° 24' 07.2", W111° 19' 49.2"). Middle Canyon wash is the next big wash east of Barks Canyon wash. Leave the Dutchman's Trail and go left (north). Go cross-country on the left (west) bank of Middle Canyon. Middle Trail appears on the ground after the canyon narrows and the hill forces you close to the normally dry wash.

The Middle Trail is overgrown and washed out in many places, but it is possible to connect the existing sections of trail. Horse riders will need to turn around when the trail disappears into the wash at mile 1.8. One large and pointed rock cairn at mile 2.1 confirms you are on the route and marks the start of a rough section of missing trail across the slope of the hillside.

When the canyon opens up, the route crosses the bedrock [7-YY, 2.3] of Middle Canyon. This is a good rest spot before you tackle the uphill climb, cross-country trek, loose dirt, and unstable rocks on the next leg of this trip.

Verify north with your compass, take the Middle Trail route going north, and head for the ridge [7-XX] using your choice of the easiest route possible—mostly a bushwhack and scramble over loose rocks. At the ridge [7-XX, 2.8], you can travel east on the mesa for an optional side trip toward Miners Needle, but Trip 11 continues north, downhill, cross-country, and toward the ravine in the basin.

A trail in the bottom of the basin follows the ravine. It takes you northwest to intersect with Bluff Spring Trail [7-VV, 3.2] near a clump of trees and a camp area. Return on Bluff Spring Trail to Peralta Trailhead [7-A, 6.0] using Trip 9 (Bluff Spring Trail) on page 92 or return to Peralta Trailhead [7-A, 9.0] on Dutchman's Trail via Miners Needle using Trip 8 (Bluff Spring Loop) on page 85. The elevation change and elevation profile on page 104 is shown for the return on the Bluff Spring Trail.

OPTIONAL CROSS-COUNTRY ROUTES

From the bedrock section [7-YY, 2.3] of Middle Canyon, go northwest across a pass and connect with the Bluff Spring Trail [south of 7-T, 3.0] in Barks Canyon. Return on Bluff Spring Trail to Peralta Trailhead [7-A, 4.6].

Or, from the bedrock section [7-YY, 2.3], go west across a pass and drop into Barks Canyon within 0.2 mile. Go left (south) in Barks Canyon where you might find seasonal pools of water in the smooth bedrock. Connect with the Dutchman's Trail, turn right (west), and return to Peralta Trailhead [7-A, 4.5].

HISTORY AND LEGENDS

In 1866, before Jacob Weiser died in the care of Dr. John D. Walker, he gave the doctor a leather map that led to a gold mine—later to be known as the Lost Dutchman Mine. Thomas Weedin, editor of the *Arizona Blade Tribune* newspaper in Florence, made a tracing of the leather map in 1881.[91]

In two 1912 letters to Sims Ely, Weedin said the map tracing was lost, but he sketched, from memory, a map similar to Dr. Walker's leather map. The map below is similar to Weedin's sketch. Weedin said Dr. Walker described the trail to the mine "as leading up this long draw, on over the mesa, and down past the picacho on the left side into a big canyon."[92]

Weedin thought the "long draw" was Barks Wash, but considered other canyons. Middle Canyon is more suitable for a horse trail, so Middle Canyon could be a possibility for the "long draw." He thought the "picacho" was Miners Needle and the "big canyon" was La Barge Canyon.[93]

James Bark wrote that Waltz thought he could show Julia Thomas the route over the mountains from the board house, which was the Matt Cavaness Ranch house in the 1870s—now the present-day Quarter Circle U Ranch headquarters.[94] Waltz's route could have been the Middle Trail. The Middle Trail was still in use in the 1950s when Tom Kollenborn used it while working for Bill Barkley at the Quarter Circle U Ranch.[95]

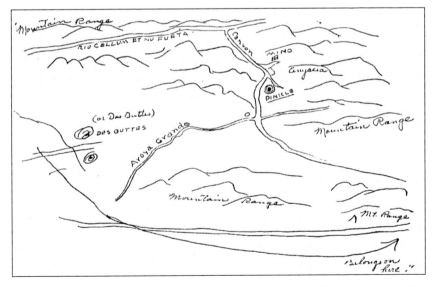

This Weiser-Walker Map is similar to the map that Thomas Weedin sketched from memory. Notice that the Des Buttes (North and South Buttes on the Gila River) are on the left of the map with an arrow pointing to the lower right corner where they belong. Weedin thought "Mino" was the Lost Dutchman Gold Mine. Courtesy Superstition Mountain Historical Society, Richard Peck Collection.[96]

SUPERSTITION WILDERNESS TRAILS WEST

BARKS CANYON TRAIL

Towering rock formations resembling images of animals and people surround this little-used cowboy trail. Good views into Barks Canyon and toward the Bluff Spring Trail give you a sense of depth as you look down into the valley.

ITINERARY

Start at Peralta Trailhead. Take Bluff Spring Trail (235). Leave the trail on the west side of Barks Canyon, follow a faint trail, and go north on the west side of Barks Canyon toward Weavers Needle. Cut over to Bluff Saddle, and return on Terrapin Trail (234) and Bluff Spring Trail (235) to Peralta Trailhead.

DIFFICULTY

Moderate hike. Not recom-
mended for horses. Elevation
change ±1,290 feet.

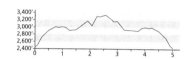

LENGTH and TIME

5.0 miles, 4.5 hours round-trip.

MAPS

Arizona USGS topo map NAD27: Weavers Needle. Superstition Wilderness Beartooth map, grids G15 to G13. Map 8.

FINDING THE TRAIL

See the trailhead map on page 75. Leave the northeast corner of the Peralta Trailhead parking lot (N33° 23′ 51.4″, W111° 20′ 49.7″) on the Dutchman's Trail (104). Bear left on the Bluff Spring Trail (235).

THE TRIP

Start on Map 8 on page 99. This trip covers new territory just off the popular Bluff Spring Trail. You can combine it with other trips to make longer loops—such as connecting with Trip 13 (Weavers Needle Crosscut).

From Peralta Trailhead [8-A, 0], follow Trip 9 (Bluff Spring Trail) on page 92 for the first part of the trip. At Barks Canyon [8-U, 1.5] (N33° 24′ 48.9″, W111° 20′ 52.2″), look for a trail on your left (west). We named this trail Barks Canyon Trail. The trail skirts the west side of a small hill where you will find some prospect holes in the red dirt up at the top.

Take the Barks Canyon Trail northwest to the north end of the low ridge at mile 1.9. Sections of the trail are washed out beyond this ridge and may be impassable for horse riders due to low-hanging vegetation. Missing trail sections are sporadically marked with rock cairns.

The Barks Canyon Trail descends as it approaches a fork in the wash at mile 2.0. Look for the trail on the opposite (north) side of the wash in the drainage of the right fork, and head for it. A well-defined trail follows the right bank near the bottom of the wash.

The next section of trail gets lost in the smooth rock of the wash, but it is marked by rock cairns higher up on the right bank. The Barks Canyon Trail ends in an open area (N33° 25' 19", W111° 21' 23") at mile 2.4, where Tom Kollenborn said the Barkley Cattle Company had a salt lick in the 1950s.[97] This trip turns southeast at the salt lick area and goes cross-country along the north side of a hill until it meets the Terrapin Trail (N33° 25' 22", W111° 21' 15") at mile 2.5. Take the Terrapin Trail, connect with the Bluff Spring Trail [8-S, 2.8], and return to Peralta Trailhead [8-A, 5.0].

OPTIONAL RETURN

To connect with Trip 13 (Weavers Needle Crosscut) on page 109, continue

north from the salt lick area to the next pass by following a game trail on the right (east) slope. From a high spot, identify the Weavers Needle Crosscut Trail in the basin below, and try to intersect the trail on the flat [between 8-II and Z]. It is somewhat of a bushwhack to get over the ridge and down to the basin. The summary of important mileages on this return is:
Basin [8-Z, 3.0],
Peralta Trail [8-N, 3.5],
Fremont Saddle [8-D, 4.8],
Peralta Trailhead [8-A, 6.9].

Bill Sewrey on the first ascent of The Glory Road route, Barks Canyon Wall, April 1966. Photograph by Dave Olson. Courtesy of Bill Sewrey, Desert Mountain Sports.

WEAVERS NEEDLE CROSSCUT

This seldom-used trek takes you around the south side of Weavers Needle where Celeste Maria Jones, Ed Piper, and their men searched for the Lost Dutchman Mine. A game trail over a low pass gets you up close to the Needle.

ITINERARY

From Peralta Trailhead, take Bluff Spring Trail and Terrapin Trail to Bluff Saddle. North of Bluff Saddle, take a trail-of-use along the south side of Weavers Needle. Connect to Peralta Trail, and return to Peralta Trailhead.

DIFFICULTY

Moderate hike. Not doable by horses. Elevation change is ±2,124 feet.

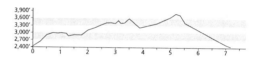

LENGTH and TIME

7.2 miles, 6 hours round-trip.

MAPS

Arizona USGS topo map NAD27: Weavers Needle. Superstition Wilderness Beartooth map, grid G13. Map 8.

FINDING THE TRAIL

See the trailhead map on page 75. Leave the northeast corner of the Peralta Trailhead parking lot (N33° 23' 51.4", W111° 20' 49.7") on the Dutchman's Trail (104). Bear left on the Bluff Spring Trail (235).

THE TRIP

Start on Map 8 on page 99. From Peralta Trailhead [8-A, 0.0], follow Trip 9 (Bluff Spring Trail) on page 92 to the Terrapin Trail [8-S, 2.2]. Take the Terrapin Trail over Bluff Saddle [8-JJ, 2.8] to the unsigned Weavers Needle Crosscut Trail [8-II, 3.0] (N33° 25' 42.0", W111° 21' 32.8"). Head in a westerly direction up the hill to the left (south) of a large rectangular butte on the horizon. Follow the trail across the basin [8-Z, 3.4] southeast of Weavers Needle, where horse riders should turn around. Go up the pass on the south side of Weavers Needle—the trail is on the right (north) side of the ravine.

The ravine reaches a saddle and then descends into the East Boulder Canyon drainage. As you are going down, look to the left (south) and walk through the passageway under the vertical slab of rock leaning against the cliff, or follow the rock cairns a few hundred feet down the ravine to another passageway. In either case, you come out on the slopes above East Boulder Canyon. A steep trail leads you down to the bed of East Boulder Canyon. Be careful and take your time. Follow the rock cairns a few yards up to the Peralta Trail [8-N, 3.9] (N33° 25' 40.3", W111° 22' 25.3"). Take Peralta Trail to Fremont Saddle [8-D, 5.2] and end at Peralta Trailhead [8-A, 7.3].

HISTORY AND LEGENDS

Bill Sewrey was a well-known outdoorsman in the Arizona rock-climbing and hiking community. He owned the Desert Mountain Sports store in Phoenix from 1970 until shortly before his death in 1998 and was known for his friendly advice and fair opinions. Between 1964 and 1969, Sewrey is credited with at least seven first ascents on the crags near Lost Dutchman State Park, Barks Canyon, and Miners Needle. He gained his technical rock-climbing expertise in the days before all the present-day high-tech hardware was available.[98]

Sewrey was exploring the Superstitions when well-known prospectors such as Piper and Magill were searching the earth for the elusive Lost Dutchman Mine in the 1960s. He recalled many encounters with these colorful characters. During her quest for the Lost Jesuit Gold, treasure hunter Celeste Maria Jones concentrated her searches on the well-known spire, Weavers Needle. Bill Sewrey had occasion to meet Jones and her men near Weavers Needle in the early 1960s.

Sewrey and friends were interested in technical rock climbing on the Needle and one day asked Jones if she would let them climb the spire. She said okay, but she wanted them to call her Phoenix residence before their attempt. Sewrey called several times, and Jones always refused permission. Finally they decided to go anyway—permission or not. Wasn't this public land?[99]

From the base of Weavers Needle in East Boulder Canyon, they hiked up the west slope into the gully of the Needle. A Jones henchman approached the climbers as they prepared to ascend the Needle. He was armed with a knife and revolver—a grubby sort of fellow and not pleasant. He told them to leave the area, but after much disagreeable discussion, the climbers proceeded, ignoring the threats. A little while later, rocks came raining down on them. Apparently the Jones men climbed the Needle by the east face route and, from above the climbers, tumbled rocks off the cliff. After the rocks stopped, the climbers continued up the west gully, around the chockstone, and up to the top of Weavers Needle, where they met the Jones men again and eventually found something in common to talk about. The Jones men wanted to know more about their rock-climbing techniques. Sewrey and the other climbers were happy to show them everything they knew. From that point on, there were no more confrontations with the Jones camp.

Bill Sewrey remembered every time they walked by the Jones camp, Maria would give them a look that seemed to say, "There they go again, what can you do?" Sewrey recalled that Jones eventually found a use for them and asked him and others to come over to her house on Van Buren Street in Phoenix. He knocked on the door, and one of her armed men answered. With arms folded, wearing a revolver and knife, just like in the Superstitions, he nodded them inside with a gesture of his head. They were motioned into the kitchen where they sat down at a table with a human skull. A candle was mounted inside the skull to light the room. It seemed a bit melodramatic.

Jones sat on one side of the table and explained her plan. She wanted Sewrey and the others to climb Weavers Needle and rappel off the north face to check out a notch in the rock. The treasure was supposed to be located there. A mining engineer employed by Jones was also to rappel with them. Sewrey said they needed to give the mining engineer some lessons in rappelling or he would be useless out on the cliff and would probably kill himself. The expedition never came off, but rock climbers Doug Black and Bill Forrest later made an agreement to do the work for Jones. They never got paid. Jones seemed to have a reputation for not paying the climbers.

View looking to the east from the Terrapin Trail just south of Bluff Saddle [9-II]. We named the rock formation on the right side of the photograph the Emperor's Dog [9-KK]. February 2010 photo.

CHARLEBOIS SPRING—LOOP 1

This trip takes you through the heart of the Wilderness to Charlebois Spring, where many prospectors, ranchers, and explorers have established their camps. The "Master Map" petroglyphs are located nearby.

ITINERARY

From Peralta Trailhead, take Bluff Spring Trail (235) to the Bluff Spring area. Connect with the Dutchman's Trail (104), follow it to La Barge Canyon, and go down to Charlebois Spring. Return the same way or on an alternate return.

DIFFICULTY

Difficult hike. Moderate backpack. Difficult ride. Elevation change is +1,230 and -1,060 feet.

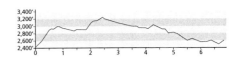

LENGTH and TIME

6.8 miles, 4 hours to Charlebois Spring one way.

MAPS

Arizona USGS topo maps NAD27: Weavers Needle and Goldfield. Superstition Wilderness Beartooth map, grids G15 to G12. Maps 7 and 9.

FINDING THE TRAIL

See trailhead map on page 75. Leave the northeast corner of Peralta Trailhead parking lot (N33° 23′ 51.4″, W111° 20′ 49.7″). Take the Dutchman's Trail about 50 yards to a wooden trail sign. Bear left on the Bluff Spring Trail.

THE TRIP

Start on Map 7 on page 89. This is the most direct way to get to Charlebois Spring from Peralta Trailhead [7-A, 0]. Start by following Trip 9 (Bluff Spring Trail) to Bluff Spring Canyon [7-P, 3.2]. Bluff Spring [7-Q] usually has water, but you have to push your way through the brush to get back to the pipe. The concrete water trough at the spring has been demolished and removed.

From the Bluff Spring area, follow the Dutchman's Trail (104) north through Bluff Spring Canyon. A spur trail to the left (west) leads to the site of a Giant Saguaro [9-GGG, 3.4] (N33° 26' 05.8", W111° 20' 04.2"). The saguaro was dying in 2015 and had fallen by 2019. At the wooden trail sign [9-C, 5.5] for Red Tanks Trail (107), the trip bears left in La Barge Canyon.

If you need water, take a detour going right (northeast) about 200 yards on the Red Tanks Trail to La Barge Spring [9-D] (N33° 26' 44.0", W111° 19' 59.5"), which is a reliable spring. The concrete water trough sits on the left (north) bench about 10 feet above the creek level—not in the creek bed—in a large grove of trees.

From the wooden trail sign [9-C, 5.5], the trip continues down La Barge Canyon. The trail is on the opposite (west) side of the creek when it passes Music Canyon [9-J, 6.0] and the seasonal Music Canyon Spring [9-K]. You should consult Trip 25 (Music Canyon) on page 160 if you want to determine the exact location of the canyon. A wooden trail sign [9-M, 6.5] marks the Peters Trail (105) coming in from the northeast. Charlebois Spring [9-BB, 6.8] is a short distance northeast of the Dutchman's Trail in Charlebois Canyon. A nice selection of flat, sandy campsites for large and small groups lies on the west bench of La Barge Canyon across from the mouth of Charlebois Canyon. Return the same way to Peralta Trailhead [7-A, 13.6].

While at Charlebois Spring, you should review Trip 52 (Marsh Valley Loop) on page 287, Trip 59 (Peters Canyon Loop) on page 323, Peters Mesa Area trips on page 331, and Bluff Spring Mountain Area on page 135 for things to do in these nearby locations.

Some believe these petroglyphs in La Barge Canyon near Charlebois Spring are the Spanish (Peralta) Master Map. December 1992 photo.

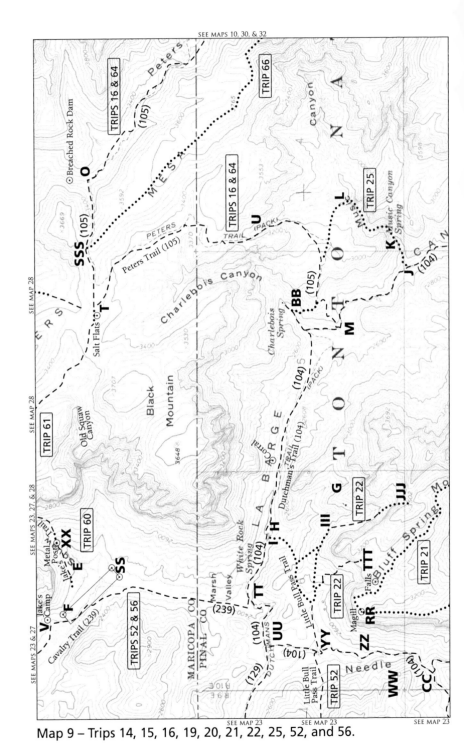

Map 9 – Trips 14, 15, 16, 19, 20, 21, 22, 25, 52, and 56.

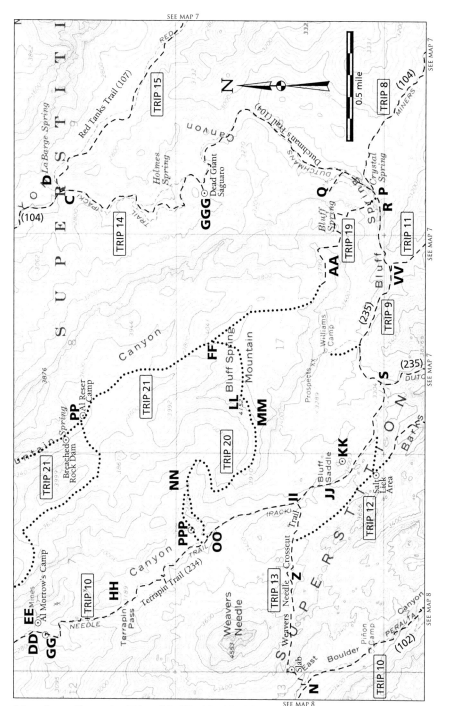

Map 9 continued – Trips 14, 15, 16, 19, 20, 21, 22, 25, 52, and 56.

OPTIONS FOR RETURN TRIP

The alternate return leaves Charlebois Spring [9-BB, 6.8] on the Dutchman's Trail (104) heading west, down La Barge Canyon. The trail passes the Cavalry Trail (239) intersection [9-TT, 8.3] and then turns south into Needle Canyon to the junction [9-UU, 8.6] with the Bull Pass Trail (129).

Continue west on the Dutchman's Trail to the junction [9-CC, 9.5] with the Terrapin Trail (234). Here you have a choice to return via the Terrapin and Bluff Spring Trails to Peralta Trailhead [8-A, 14.4] or to continue on the Dutchman's Trail over to East Boulder Canyon and then head south on the Peralta Trail (102) to Peralta Trailhead [8-A, 16.4]. In both cases you should read the descriptions for Trip 10 (East Boulder—Needle Canyon Loop) on page 95 and Trip 52 (Marsh Valley Loop) on page 287.

HISTORY AND LEGENDS

The French-named Charlebois Spring (locally pronounced "shar-le-boy") is often anglicized to Charlie Boy. Being a fairly reliable spring, it has been a natural destination and base camp for prospectors, ranchers, and outfitters.

Tom Kollenborn reported the history of the area in a 1992 *Superstition Mountain Journal* article titled "Superstition Mountain Place Names." The spring was originally named Black Mountain Spring—Black Mountain being the name of the mountain to the north. Later the spring was renamed for cattleman Martin Charlebois who lived in a cabin here. After his cabin burned in the early 1920s, rancher Tex Barkley rebuilt it, and then in 1948, it was moved to Bluff Spring where it remained until 1962.[100]

We found a death certificate for Martin N. Charlebois, who could be the Charlebois that Kollenborn wrote about. He was born in Alpino, Michigan, on September 4, 1879, to Joseph Charlebois and Mary Lyons. His wife was named Mattie. He died in Glendale, Arizona, on December 24, 1948. On his World War I draft registration card, he was listed as a sheepman for the Babbitt Sheep Company in Flagstaff, Arizona. On his death certificate, his occupation was noted as stockman in the cattle industry. His father may have been the Joseph Charlebois that registered the Diamond J brand in 1885 and also registered the Circle 5 brand for Martin in 1891, probably while they were living in Pinal, Arizona Territory.[101] See the History and Legends section of Upper La Barge Area on page 152 for more about the Charlebois and Lebarge families.

The petroglyphs that many believe to be the Spanish (Peralta) Master Map detailing the location of eighteen gold mines are south of Charlebois Spring.[102] They appear on a south-facing cliff at ground level on an inside bend of La Barge Creek. The petroglyphs are not difficult to find; a Forest Service sign marks the location. Don't touch them. Take pictures only.

The concrete water trough at La Barge Spring in La Barge Canyon has been a reliable water source for many years. The date inscribed on the rim of the water trough is 7-1-39. March 2010 photo.

CHARLEBOIS SPRING—LOOP 2

Like Charlebois Spring–Loop 1, this trip takes you through the heart of the Wilderness to Charlebois Spring on a wider trek than described in Trip 14 (Loop 1). We like this itinerary because it takes you past Miners Needle and down Whiskey Spring Canyon. A short side trip to Trap Canyon is worthwhile when there is seasonal water at the spring.

ITINERARY

From Peralta Trailhead, follow Dutchman's Trail (104) to Miners Summit. Take Whiskey Spring Trail (238) to La Barge Canyon. Follow the Red Tanks Trail (107) northwest to La Barge Spring. Take Dutchman's Trail (104) to Charlebois Spring. Return on the Bluff Spring Trail (235), or on the Terrapin Trail (234), or on the Peralta Trail (102).

DIFFICULTY

Difficult hike. Moderate back-pack. Difficult ride. Elevation change is +1,370 and -1,200 feet.

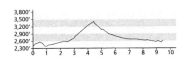

LENGTH and TIME

9.4 miles, 5.5 hours to Charlebois Spring one way.

MAPS

Arizona USGS topo maps NAD27: Weavers Needle and Goldfield. Superstition Wilderness Beartooth map, grids G15 to G12. Maps 7 and 9.

FINDING THE TRAIL

See the trailhead map on page 75. Leave the northeast corner of the Peralta Trailhead parking lot (N33° 23' 51.4", W111° 20' 49.7"). Take Dutchman's Trail about 50 yards to a wooden trail sign and bear right (east), staying on the Dutchman's Trail.

THE TRIP

Start on Map 7 on page 89. We think this is a more interesting route, compared to Trip 14 (Charlebois Spring–Loop 1), and it still allows you to return on the Bluff Spring Trail. Start the trip from Peralta Trailhead [7-A, 0] by following Trip 8 (Bluff Spring Loop) to Miners Summit [7-O, 4.1]. From Miners Summit follow the Whiskey Spring Trail (238) along the ridgeline east, over a pass, and then down into Whiskey Canyon. Trip 23 (Whiskey Spring Trail) on page 155 describes the features of this area. Whiskey Spring [7-W, 5.3] has had water most of the times we visited, but it can go dry. Check with the Forest Service or other hikers about the water conditions.

Not far down canyon from the spring, Whiskey Spring Trail drops into the bed of the wash where more tall cottonwood trees grow. You'll find several nice campsites [7-JJ, 5.6] along the trail and under the trees. The trail leaves the wash, climbs over a ridge, and heads up La Barge Canyon for a short distance before it crosses La Barge Creek to meet the Red Tanks Trail [7-X, 6.0] on the north bench at a wooden trail sign. La Barge Creek is often dry here, but you may find pothole water in the bedrock farther up or farther down canyon.

Cecil Stewart (aka Superstition Joe) with his wagon in Barkley Basin. Castle Rock [7-M] appears in the upper left corner of the photograph. Photo by Carl Broderick, circa 1950s. Courtesy of Superstition Mountain Historical Society, Carl Broderick Collection.

Trip 16 (Charlebois Spring–Loop 3) on page 121 goes right (easterly) on the Red Tanks Trail (107), where you might find water in the bedrock potholes of Upper La Barge Box. Trip 15 travels left (west) following La Barge Canyon downstream on the Red Tanks Trail.

Trap Canyon Wash [7-Y, 6.9] comes in on the right (north). See Trip 24 (Trap Canyon) for a description of the short trek and bushwhack up to the seasonal spring.

Farther down La Barge Canyon is La Barge Spring [9-D 8.0] (N33° 26' 44.0", W111° 19' 59.5"), which is a reliable water source. Look for the spring and concrete water trough up on the right (north) bank in a thick grove of trees—the spring is not in the creek bed. After continuing another 200 yards, the Red

In 1974, this USFS trail sign and another were posted at the junction [9-C] of Red Tanks Trail and Dutchman's Trail in La Barge Canyon near La Barge Spring [9-D]. They provided mileages for each trail and the popular destinations. Contemporary signage only gives the trail name and number.

Tanks Trail (107) ends at a wooden trail sign [9-C, 8.1], where that trail meets the Dutchman's Trail (104).

The trip now follows the Dutchman's Trail north, down La Barge Canyon, passing Music Canyon [9-J, 8.6] and the seasonal Music Canyon Spring [9-K]. The Dutchman's Trail meets the Peters Trail (105) intersection at a wooden trail sign [9-M, 9.1]. Charlebois Spring [9-BB, 9.4] is a short distance north of the Dutchman's Trail in Charlebois Canyon.

A nice selection of campsites rest on the sandy bench on the west side of La Barge Canyon across from the mouth of Charlebois Canyon. See Trip 14 (Charlebois Spring–Loop 1) on page 112 for a description and history of the Charlebois Spring area as well as the options for the return trek.

CHARLEBOIS SPRING—LOOP 3

This trip takes you on a wide loop to Charlebois Spring over trails that are lightly traveled. Seasonal water in La Barge and Peters Canyons provides ideal camping along the trail, where you can enjoy a good degree of solitude.

ITINERARY

Follow the Dutchman's Trail (104) from Peralta Trailhead to Miners Summit. Take Whiskey Spring Trail (238) to Red Tanks Trail (107), which leads you east through Upper La Barge Box. Continue north on Hoolie Bacon Trail (111) and trek cross-country to Peters Trail (105). Go west on Peters Trail, climb up to Peters Mesa, and descend to Dutchman's Trail (104). Charlebois Spring is a short distance to the north on the Dutchman's Trail. Return on Bluff Springs Trail (235), or through Needle Canyon on Terrapin Trail (234), or through East Boulder Canyon on Peralta Trail (102).

DIFFICULTY

Moderate backpack. Not recommended for horses. Elevation change is +2,930 and -2,760 feet.

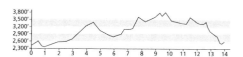

LENGTH and TIME

14.0 miles, 9 hours to Charlebois Spring one way.

MAPS

Arizona USGS topo maps NAD27: Weavers Needle and Goldfield. Superstition Wilderness Beartooth map, grids G15 to G12. Maps 4, 7, 9, and 10.

FINDING THE TRAIL

Trailhead map is on page 75. Leave the northeast corner of Peralta Trailhead parking lot (N33° 23′ 51.4″, W111° 20′ 49.7″). Take Dutchman's Trail about 50 yards to a wooden trail sign, bear right, and stay on the Dutchman's Trail.

THE TRIP

Start on Map 7 on page 89. This trip is too long for a day trip, but makes an enjoyable two- or three-day overnight trek that takes you through some lesser-traveled regions of the Wilderness. The trip is not recommended for horses. Riders will have problems on the rough and scary trail through the Upper La Barge Box, which is narrow and steep, with loose rock, slick rock, and sheer drop-offs.

From the Peralta Trailhead [7-A, 0], begin by following Trip 15 (Charlebois Spring—Loop 2) to Miners Summit [7-O, 4.1], to Whiskey Spring [7-W, 5.3], and to La Barge Canyon [4-X, 6.0]. Turn right (east) at the Red Tanks Trail wooden sign [4-X], and head up the narrow canyon named Upper La Barge Box. Potholes in the bedrock collect seasonal water. Herman Petrasch had a camp [4-GG, 6.2] (N33° 25' 53.2", W111° 18' 17.1") at a small cave on the north side of the trail.

About halfway up the Upper La Barge Box, after crossing a large ravine coming in from the left (north), look for a fine campsite (N33° 26' 03.7", W111° 17' 49.7") on the right (south) side of the trail. The camp has great views of the rugged cliffs, and it lies near seasonal water in La Barge Creek.

Roy Bradford's—and later Chuck Crawford's—prospect [4-SS, 7.1] (N33° 26' 07.8", W111° 17' 30.8") is on the left (north) side of the trail just as the trail exits the canyon. The Hoolie Bacon Trail (111) [4-B, 7.3] comes in from the north and meets the Red Tanks Trail at a wooden sign.

If you are looking for a large campsite, check the flat bench about 0.1 mile east on the Red Tanks Trail from the wooden sign [4-B]. The group campsite (N33° 26' 10.1", W111° 17' 15.3") is on the right (south) side of the trail. Back at the wooden trail sign for the Hoolie Bacon Trail [4-B], follow the Hoolie Bacon Trail north to the Trap Canyon area [10-E, 8.2], where you will find some smaller campsites under the juniper trees.

Farther north on the Hoolie Bacon Trail, a trail-of-use [10-N, 8.6] (N33° 27' 07.6", W111° 17' 53.6") branches off to the left. The faint trail is only marked by a small rock cairn. You will know you have passed the intersection if the Hoolie Bacon Trail heads up a steep slope in the northeast direction. See Trip 63 (Hoolie Bacon Trail—Peters Trail Loop) on page 351 for more information about the Horse Camp Basin area. Allow extra time along this route for getting lost and for exploring Horse Camp Basin.

Take the trail-of-use [10-N, 8.6] across the flat bench until it reaches the wash coming in on the left (west). Go right (northerly) in the wash for a short distance [10-H, 8.7]. Then you need to decide whether to stay in the wash or bushwhack in the catclaw on the left (west) bench. Wearing leather gloves makes it easy to push the catclaw aside and makes the going easier. For either route, follow the dotted lines on Map 10 to the ridge [10-OO, 9.3]. From the ridge, go cross-country to the Peters Trail, and intersect the trail [near 10-QQ] as it heads north just before it climbs up the hill—another catclaw trek.

Although Kane Spring [10-KK] (N33° 28′ 32.6″, W111° 18′ 23.8″) is not on the trip itinerary, it usually has water and may be worth checking if you need to fill up. Kane Spring is about a mile to the north on the other side of the hill—requiring significant uphill and downhill travel. Verify the water conditions with the Forest Service or other hikers.

Peters Trail continues over a low pass [10-PP, 9.9] named Peters Divide. The trail is on the north side of the knob on the horizon and goes down canyon, crossing the wash several times. The last crossing [10-O, 11.3] sometimes has water in the bedrock basins. If you plan to camp, check the campsite on the left (west) bench in the trees, or carry your water to the top of Peters Mesa for a dry camp with great views of the surrounding Wilderness. See Trip 59 (Peters Canyon Loop) on page 323 for a description of lower Peters Canyon.

The trail leaves Peters Canyon and climbs up to Peters Mesa where it makes a 90-degree turn [9-T, 11.8] in an area generally referred to as the Salt Flats. See History and Legends in the section titled Peters Mesa Area on page 331 for the history of this region. Tall grass often obscures the trail up here, so look for rock cairns to guide you toward La Barge Canyon. After losing the trail and then spotting some water in the Charlebois drainage, one of the authors decided to go straight down Charlebois Canyon. That was a big

Prospector Herman Petrasch at his camp on Hewitt Station Road. Herman Mountain is named for him. Photograph by Carl Boderick, Courtesy Superstition Mountain Historical Society.

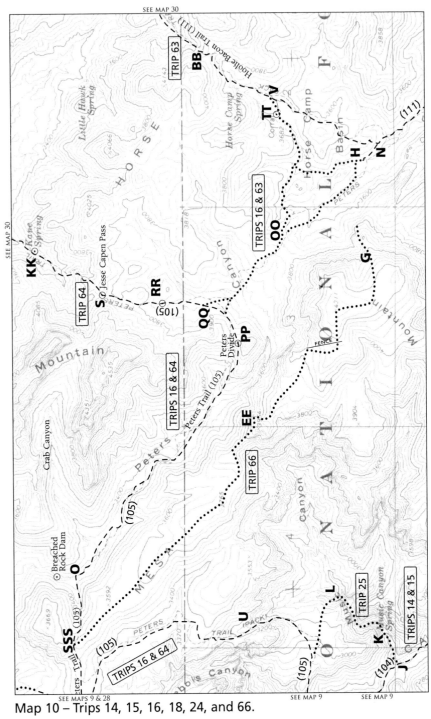

SEE MAP 30

Map 10 – Trips 14, 15, 16, 18, 24, and 66.

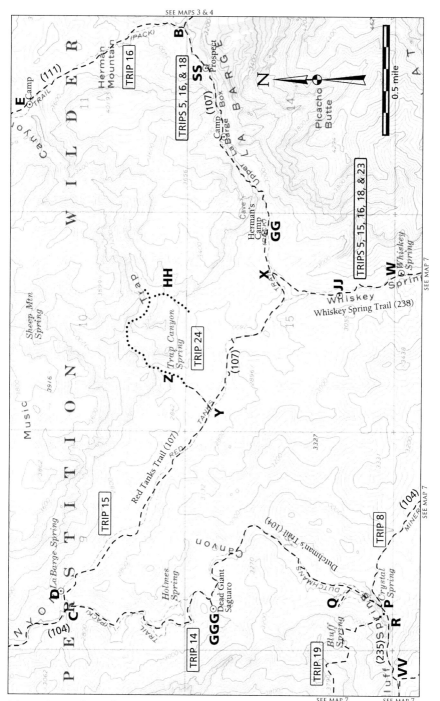

Map 10 continued – Trips 14, 15, 16, 18, 24, and 66.

mistake. Charlebois Canyon is filled with house-sized boulders and vegetation for about a quarter mile.

As the trail descends into La Barge drainage, you will see a rock wall [9-U, 12.8] built across the ravine. Tom Kollenborn suggested that the rock wall was a drift fence used to control cattle. Peters Trail ends [9-M, 13.7] in La Barge Canyon when it intersects the Dutchman's Trail (104). Go right (west) on the Dutchman's Trail as it turns into Charlebois Canyon. The spring is a short distance north of the Dutchman's Trail in Charlebois Canyon [9-BB, 14.0]. Check the west side of La Barge Canyon across from the mouth of Charlebois Canyon for a good selection of flat, sandy campsites.

See Trip 14 (Charlebois Spring–Loop 1) on page 116 for a description and history of the Charlebois Spring area. The return routes are also described in Trip 14.

HISTORY AND LEGENDS

Herman Petrasch established one of his camps [4-GG] on the north side of La Barge Canyon below the mountain named after him—Herman Mountain. He later lived along Hewitt Station Road, just west of the junction with FR172, on the Martin Ranch range. He died on November 23, 1953, at the age of eighty-eight and is buried with the Martin family in the Fairview Cemetery, Superior—not far from the grave of Abe Reid. Herman's brother, Rhinehart, died on February 3, 1943, at the age of seventy-five. He is buried in the Globe Cemetery. Their father, Gottfriet, died on May 23, 1914, at the age of eighty and is buried in the Arizona State Hospital Cemetery in Phoenix. All three were avid searchers for Jacob Waltz's mine.[103]

Roy Bradford had a cabin at Brads Water [4-T] and worked a prospect [4-SS] in Upper La Barge Box. The cabin is gone, but you can still see the ruins of the range improvements at Brads Water. He died at the age of seventy-two in Phoenix, Arizona, on September 4, 1951, and was buried in the Double Butte Cemetery, Tempe.[104]

Charles "Chuck" Crawford claimed Bradford's former prospect [4-SS] and named it Cheryl Anne after his daughter. He also had claims in Barks Canyon—named Casi 1 and Casi 2—and claims at Burns Ranch on Peralta Creek. Crawford ran for Pinal County Sheriff in 2000. He lost the race, but received a respectable 31 percent of the vote. He died on August 31, 2007, at the age of sixty-four, and his ashes were spread in the Superstition Mountains.[105]

For Sims Ely's stories about the Mexican camps, cut mine timber, and the Spanish Trails, see Trip 64 (Peters Trail to Charlebois Spring) on page 359.

REEDS WATER

Hikers and horse riders will enjoy this trip, which is relatively level compared to some of the trails in the Superstitions. Reeds Water windmill, in a grove of cottonwood and mesquite trees, pumped water for people, horses, and cattle, for many years, but the windmill and trough are now out of service. A short loop to Coffee Flat Spring on the return trek adds variety to the outing.

ITINERARY

Follow Dutchman's Trail (104) from Peralta Trailhead, and connect with Coffee Flat Trail (107), which takes you to Reeds Water. Return the same way or via Coffee Flat Spring in Whitlow Canyon.

DIFFICULTY

Easy hike. Moderate ride.
Elevation change is ±1,180 feet.

LENGTH and TIME

10.9 miles, 7.5 hours round-trip.

MAPS

Arizona USGS topo map NAD27: Weavers Needle. Superstition Wilderness Beartooth map, grids G15 to I15. Maps 5, 7, and 11.

FINDING THE TRAIL

Trailhead map is on page 75. Leave the northeast corner of Peralta Trailhead parking lot (N33° 23' 51.4", W111° 20' 49.7"). Head north about 50 yards to a trail intersection and bear right, continuing on the Dutchman's Trail.

THE TRIP

Start on Map 7 on page 89. From the Peralta Trailhead [7-A, 0], start on the Dutchman's Trail, and follow the trip directions for Trip 8 (Bluff Spring Loop) on page 85 to the intersection with the Coffee Flat Trail [7-N, 2.6].

Take the Coffee Flat Trail (108) going right (southeast) to the wooden sign at the junction with the Old Coffee Flat Trail [7-CC, 3.2]. The Old Coffee Flat Trail is described in the Optional Return at the end of this section.

Bear left (east) as the Coffee Flat Trail continues up to a low divide. East of the low divide, you enter the headwaters of Whitlow Canyon.

An unnamed trail [11-A, 4.2] goes right and continues down Whitlow Canyon. You can use this trail as the optional return route from Reeds Water. The wooden Whitlow Corral [11-W] (locally called Coffee Flat Corral) was destroyed in the June 2020 Sawtooth Fire and only the modern wire fence of the corral remains. But, if you want to see the corral site, take the unnamed trail 0.1 mile to the barbed-wire fence and gate.

Back on the Coffee Flat Trail [11-A, 4.2], continuing east, you pass through a gate [11-G, 4.7] and enter the Martin Ranch grazing allotment in the Superstition Wilderness. After crossing a small wash, you come to an unsigned trail junction where the Coffee Flat Trail goes right (south). Head left (north) 100 feet to see the Reeds Water windmill [11-R, 5.0]. The Reeds Water windmill over the rock-lined well and nearby trough are out of service. The bottom of the well often has water, but it is difficult to get since it is a deep well. The Martin Ranch maintains the windmill, well, and trough when they have cattle in this pasture. Please respect their range improvements.

For a shorter trip, you can return the way you came to Peralta Trailhead [7-A, 10.0], but Trip 17 continues south from the Reeds Water windmill [11-R, 5.0] on the Coffee Flat Trail. The land south of the Wilderness gate is managed by the Arizona State Land Department and requires a recreation permit to use the trails.

Follow the trail south to the bed of Randolph Canyon. The well, which is dry, at Cottonwood windmill [11-C, 5.1] will be on your right (west). Coffee Flat Trail goes left (east) up the right (south) bench of Randolph Canyon and meets the Red Tanks Trail (107) in 1.4 miles.

This trip continues straight (south) and follows Randolph Canyon on the course of a former road going downstream on the left bank. When the route changes to the right (west) side of the normally dry canyon, it becomes more difficult to follow. You will probably miss the vague horse trail that the cowboys use, so continue down to the junction with Whitlow Canyon [11-B, 5.9], and turn right (north) on the well-defined former road. If you miss this junction and bear left, you may end up on the Elephant Butte Road, which heads south to Queen Valley—not the way you want to go.

The north end of the former road in Whitlow Canyon ends near the Coffee Flat Spring metal water trough [11-D, 6.2], which is maintained by the Quarter Circle U Ranch. It often has water except during drought years. From the water trough, the trip follows an unnamed trail up the right bench of Whitlow Canyon. The trail crosses the normally dry wash two times and lies on the right (east) bench when it reaches Whitlow Corral (locally named Coffee Flat Corral) at the Wilderness gate [11-W, 6.6]. If you are riding, be sure to duck under the wire above the gate. Meet the Coffee Flat Trail [11-A, 6.7] a short distance to the north, turn left (west), and retrace your trip to Peralta Trailhead [7-A, 10.9].

OPTIONAL RETURN

You can make an additional loop on the return trip by bearing left on the Old Coffee Flat Trail at the trail signpost [7-CC, 7.7]. The Old Coffee Flat Trail takes you to the Upper Corral [7-UU, 8.6] on Arizona State Trust land where the Quarter Circle U Ranch maintains a water trough for cattle and wildlife. The Old Coffee Flat Trail, a dirt road, continues west to an unnamed road [5-QQ, 9.7] near the Quarter Circle U Ranch headquarters (private). Take the unnamed road north, go through the Wilderness gate, meet the Dutchman's Trail [5-L, 10.6], and turn left to Peralta Trailhead [5-A, 11.5].

HISTORY AND LEGENDS

Reeds Water is named for Abe Reid, who had a mine on the hill north of the Reeds Water windmill [11-R]. You can follow the outline of the former road up to his silver mine operation.[106]

After Abe Reid dug a six-foot well in the bed of the wash, he asked rancher Bill Martin Sr. to install a windmill on it. Martin told Reid that if he

Abe Reid's Camp at Reeds Water windmill [11-R] near Randolph Canyon. The vehicle belonged to Al Reser. Photograph by Al Reser, circa mid-1950s. Courtesy Superstition Mountain Historical Society, Al Reser Collection.

dug another well on the bench, away from the wash, he would install a windmill over the new well. Reid made his tent camp at the windmill. He died of natural causes in his tent in 1958 at the age of seventy-eight and is buried in the Fairview Cemetery, Superior, with members of the Martin family.[107]

Billy Martin Jr. said the Cottonwood windmill [11-C] on State Trust land just south of the Wilderness boundary has not produced any water for as long as he can remember. In 2003, Quarter Circle U Ranch owner Chuck Backus and ranch manager Howard Horinek cleaned out the well—13 feet down to bedrock. Only about one foot of water seeped into the well, so they did not consider it usable. Author Jack Carlson helped Horinek install a metal cover over the top of the well to keep it clean for possible future use.

Tom Kollenborn said that in the 1950s, Barkley used the names Upper Reids Water and Lower Reids Water for the windmills.[108] The Mesa-to-Globe road survey in 1891 used Little Cottonwood Gulch as the name for the wash at Reeds Water.[109]

The Quarter Circle U Ranch grazing lease on Arizona State Trust land covers both the Randolph and Whitlow Canyons, and the cowboys refer to this area as the Fraser Pasture. So, both Randolph and Whitlow Canyons are often referred to as Fraser Canyon by the ranch hands.

A cement structure near the Coffee Flat Spring is inscribed "7-14-1937 Tex Barkley," so we think Barkley may have been the rancher who developed the spring.[110] The spring improvements were in disrepair for many years, and the water dried up in the summer months. In 2003, author Jack Carlson helped ranch manager Howard Horinek build a new spring box [11-D] to capture the water. They piped the water down to a metal water trough, which Howard constructed out of metal panels and a concrete floor. All the material had to be packed into the site on horses. In 2006, ranch owner Chuck Backus hired a helicopter to deliver a 2,500-gallon storage tank, a coil of one-inch pipe, and a water trough to a site about 1,600 feet south of the spring. Drought conditions in 2020 and prior years have affected the reliability of the Coffee Flat Spring.

These range improvements provide water to cattle, wildlife, and people. Mountain lion, deer, javelina, fox, ringtail cats, coatimundi, and bobcats have been observed in the area after dark. In the daytime, the cowboys have seen a herd of bighorn sheep about a half mile south of the spring, so the wildlife seem to be using the water.[111]

UPPER LA BARGE BOX LOOP

Starting at Peralta Trailhead, this scenic trip takes you through the craggy cliffs of Upper La Barge Box and across Red Tanks Divide in a similar loop made from Woodbury Trailhead.

ITINERARY

From Peralta Trailhead, take the Dutchman's Trail, Whiskey Spring Trail, and Red Tanks Trail to Upper La Barge Box. Continue over Red Tanks Divide on the Red Tanks Trail, and meet the Coffee Flat Trail at Dripping Spring. Take Coffee Flat Trail past Reeds Water, and reconnect with Dutchman's Trail for a return to Peralta Trailhead.

DIFFICULTY

Very difficult hike. Not recommended for horses. Elevation change is ±2,760 feet.

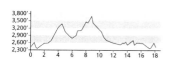

LENGTH and TIME

18.1 miles, 15 hours round-trip.

MAPS

Arizona USGS topo map NAD27: Weavers Needle. Superstition Wilderness Beartooth map, grids G15 to J13. Maps 3, 4, 7, and 11.

FINDING THE TRAIL

See the trailhead map on page 75. Leave the northeast corner of Peralta Trailhead parking lot (N33° 23' 51.4", W111° 20' 49.7"). Go about 50 yards to a wooden trail sign, and bear right on the Dutchman's Trail.

THE TRIP

Start on Map 7 on page 89. From the Peralta Trailhead [7-A, 0], start on the Dutchman's Trail. Follow the trip directions for Trip 16 (Charlebois Spring—Loop 3) on page 121, which takes you to Miners Summit [3-O, 4.1], down Whiskey Spring Canyon to the Red Tanks Trail [4-X, 6.0], and up the Red Tanks Trail in the Upper La Barge Box to meet the Hoolie Bacon Trail (111) at a wooden trail sign [4-B, 7.3]. Trip 16 describes the Hoolie Bacon Trail heading north, but Trip 18 continues east on the Red Tanks Trail. In about 0.1

mile from the wooden sign, a nice group campsite (N33° 26′ 10.1″, W111° 17′ 15.3″) lies on the right (south) side of the Red Tanks Trail.

Brads Water [4-T] (N33° 26′ 25.8″, W111° 16′ 53.2″), about 0.4 mile north of the Red Tanks Trail, might be a possible water source if you are on a multi-day trip. The water is in a hard rock tunnel a few yards up the slope from the abandoned concrete water troughs. The former corral [4-II] (N33° 26′ 13.8″, W111° 16′ 58.4″) is identified only by four wooden posts hidden in the brush. The trails to the corral and Brads Water are overgrown and not usable, so travel in the washes is the best approach.

Continue on the Red Tanks Trail up and over Red Tanks Divide [3-D, 8.8]. We have found water in a pool (N33° 25′ 21.4″, W111° 16′ 08.3″) in the ravine at the bottom of the hill a little before reaching the survey marker [3-AA, 9.2]. The 1919 survey marker identifies the section corner.

The Red Tanks Trail connects with Red Tanks Canyon [3-BB, 9.5] and immediately goes through an area thick with laurel trees, which might make a nice shady place to camp. In 1999, we photographed a wooden sign that was bolted to the large laurel tree, which showed the mileages—*Randolph Canyon 1½, La Barge Canyon 2.* The sign is gone, but the bolt is still in the tree.

At Randolph Canyon [11-P, 11.0], the Red Tanks Trail crosses the normally dry creek to the south side. You will have to watch carefully for rock cairns here to connect with the trail on the south bench. On the south bench, the trail goes up on the hillside and over a small ridge before coming down into Randolph Canyon again.

The 1919 survey marker on the Red Tanks Trail is near the water hole [3-AA]. January 1999 photo.

If you miss the trail [11-P] going up this hill, you can stay in Randolph Canyon and go downstream to the junction with Red Tanks Canyon where you bear left (south) and stay in the bed of Randolph Canyon. This is a pretty section of canyon. You can pick up the trail again when you see rock cairns marking the Red Tanks Trail as it zigzags across the creek bed. Seasonal water collects in the large red-colored potholes or tanks in the bedrock—possibly the origin of the Red Tanks name.

At the wooden sign for the Coffee Flat Trail [11-U,

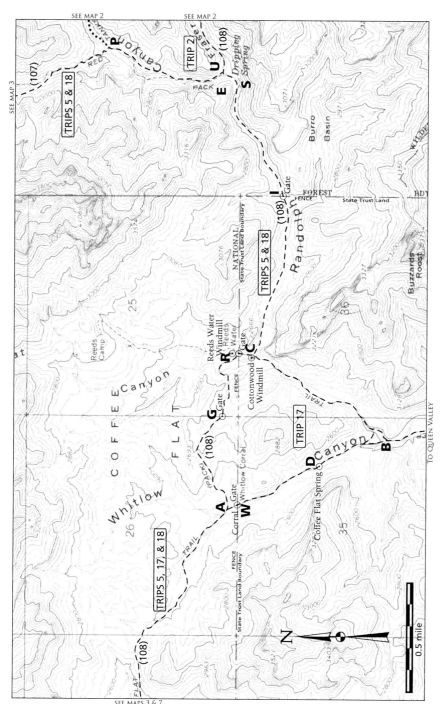

Map 11 – Trips 2, 5, 17, and 18.

11.6], this trip turns right (southwesterly). If you are camping, this might make a nice area to spend the night. Nearby Dripping Spring [11-S, 11.7] often has water, but we have seen it dry, so be sure to verify its condition before you go. See Trip 2 (Dripping Spring) on page 55 for a description of the Dripping Spring area.

Continue down Randolph Canyon on the Coffee Flat Trail, which meanders across the creek bed. At a gate in the fence [11-I, 12.3], the trail leaves the Superstition Wilderness and enters Arizona State Trust land. This is the boundary for the Martin Ranch (east side) and Quarter Circle U Ranch (west side) pastures.

At the out-of-service Cottonwood windmill [11-C, 13.0], bear right (north) and follow the trail as it re-enters the Wilderness through a gate in the fence just south of Reeds Water windmill [11-R, 13.1]. Reeds Water trough is dry, but you might find water at the bottom of the windmill well.

At Cottonwood windmill [11-C], you can also take a 0.7 mile longer alternate route, which goes down Randolph Canyon to the junction with Whitlow Canyon [11-B], up Whitlow Canyon, past Coffee Flat Spring [11-D], and through the gate at Whitlow Corral [11-W]. It connects with the Coffee Flat Trail [11-A] just north of the corral.

From Reeds Water [11-R, 13.1], the trip continues westerly on the Coffee Flat Trail. See Trip 17 (Reeds Water) on page 127 for the rest of the trip description—in reverse—returning to Peralta Trailhead. A summary of the important mileages is:
Gate [11-G, 13.4],
Trail junction [11-A, 13.9],
Trail junction [7-CC, 14.9],
Dutchman's Trail [7-N, 15.5],
Peralta Trailhead [7-A, 18.1].

For another perspective on this trip, see Trip 5 (Red Tanks Divide Loop) on page 68, which starts from Woodbury Trailhead and makes a similar loop through the Wilderness.

HISTORY AND LEGENDS

See Trip 17 (Reeds Water) on page 129 for the history of the Reeds Water area.

The trail sign was formerly bolted to a laurel tree by the Red Tanks Trail just south of [3-BB]. January 1999 photo.

SUPERSTITION WILDERNESS TRAILS WEST

BLUFF SPRING MOUNTAIN AREA

The top of Bluff Spring Mountain, Bluff Spring Mountain Canyon, and the trails to the top of the mountain make up the Bluff Spring Mountain Area, which is bounded by Bluff Spring on the south, Needle Canyon on the west and north, and La Barge Canyon on the east.

FINDING THE TRAILHEAD

Use Map 7 on page 88. From Peralta Trailhead [7-A] take the 3.2 mile Bluff Spring Trail (235) to Bluff Spring Canyon using Trip 9 (Bluff Spring Trail) on page 92. The trail description for the Bluff Spring Mountain Area starts near the intersection [7-P] of the Bluff Spring Trail (235) and the Dutchman's Trail (104) in Bluff Spring Canyon. The intersection is marked by a wooden sign in an area noted as Crystal Spring on some maps.

THE TRAILS

The Ely-Anderson horse trail, Trip 19 (Ely-Anderson Trail), is the best approach to the top of Bluff Spring Mountain (Peak 4152). Other hiking routes through the cliffs of the mountain are possible after you become familiar with the area—described in Trip 20 (Southwest Route) and Trip 22 (Northeast Route). Hiking on Bluff Spring Mountain is for experienced hikers only. Unmaintained trails, loose and moving rock, and exposed cliffs are true hazards here.

HISTORY AND LEGENDS

Bluff Spring Mountain became a topic of interest when Jimmy Anderson, brother of Gertrude Barkley,[112] discovered a trail [9-R to 9-AA] in 1911. He reported the discovery to Sims Ely, general manager of the Salt River Users' Association, who had collected information from other sources about a legend of an unnamed mountain where Mexicans grazed horses and mules while tending to their mining activities. Sims Ely connected the legend to the rediscovered trail and, along with rancher Jim Bark and cowhand Jimmy Anderson, explored the area. They concluded that Bluff Spring Mountain could have been the site of Mexican mining activity in the 1800s.[113]

Walter Gassler was exploring the Bluff Spring Mountain area in 1936, but he did not report any important discoveries.[114] It wasn't until May 5, 1966, when private investigator Glenn Magill and his partners filed The Dutchman claim on the northwest side of Bluff Spring Mountain that national

View of Weavers Needle from the top of the Ely-Anderson Trail on Bluff Spring Mountain [9-AA], just west of the rock wall. The tall plant in the right foreground is a century plant. December 2010 photo.

interest was aroused in another attempt at locating the Lost Dutchman Mine.[115] Glenn Magill's adventures are described in Curt Gentry's book *Killer Mountains.* Tucson KCUB radio announcer George Scott made an on-site broadcast from The Dutchman claim, and prominent Dutchman aficionados were interviewed about the discovery.[116] One photograph in Helen Corbin's book *The Curse of the Dutchman's Gold* shows Bob Corbin being interviewed by Scott at the mine.[117] Corbin, former Arizona Attorney General, has been a prominent figure in the search for the Lost Dutchman Mine since 1957. Corbin has written the foreword for many books published on the subject and is an active speaker and aficionado of the history of the region.

Glenn Magill used Adolph Ruth's famous maps to locate the Dutchman mine. Ruth's son, Erwin, supplied Magill with copies of the original Ruth-Gonzales maps. See Trip 49 (Willow Spring) History and Legends on page 272 for the story of Adolph Ruth. Magill's men set up a camp [9-RR] that looked into Needle Canyon from an overhanging ledge near a large flat area on the north end of Bluff Spring Mountain.[118] The pit that Magill's partners uncovered had walls of blackish stone, while the fill material was a reddish sandstone. The fill-material rocks were laid out in rows, and they found a cement-like seal farther down. Under a second seal, at a depth of 25 feet, the fill material changed to mine tailings and timbers in the pit, all of which led Magill to speculate that this was one of the mines covered over by the Apaches in the mid 1800s. After more work, they found the pit to be void of gold. The vein was played out. Shortly after the pit was uncovered, someone set off Magill's store of dynamite, which filled the pit with rubble.[119] The Forest Service has performed restoration work to fill in the diggings.

In his 1979 book *A Tiny Bit of God's Creation,* John Dahlmann describes his many trail rides across Bluff Spring Mountain starting up the Ely-Anderson Trail (Old Spanish Trail) on the south and descending a steep route to the north into Marsh Valley. Dahlmann's probable route [9-JJJ] off the north side is described in Trip 22 (Northeast Route) on page 149. It is not suitable for horses anymore. Dahlmann never located the site of Magill's diggings while searching on Bluff Spring Mountain between 1966 and 1977. Dahlmann accompanied artist Ted De Grazia on trail rides here on Bluff Spring Mountain as well as throughout the Superstition Wilderness. Dahlmann's book will be of special interest to horse riders for fascinating tales of his Superstition Wilderness trail rides.

Al Morrow helped Al Reser locate mining claims on Bluff Spring Mountain in 1966 and wrote about claims in that area by Richard Peck and Lloyd Sutton.[120] See Morrow's letter on page 143. Tom Kollenborn's map[121] shows the location of Al Reser's, February 18, 1984, camp [9-PP] just south of the breached dam in Bluff Spring Mountain Canyon. The Wilderness was closed to new mining claims just two months before—December 31, 1983.

ELY-ANDERSON TRAIL

This is a historic trip on a trail discovered in 1911 by cowhand Jimmy Anderson—often called the Mexican or Spanish Trail. The cliffs of Bluff Spring Mountain surround the long, open valley referred to as Hidden Valley. You have good views into Hidden Valley from the summit, and a feeling of openness surrounds you as you look across the landscape.

ITINERARY

From the south end of Bluff Spring Mountain, follow an old horse trail to the summit overlooking Bluff Spring Mountain Canyon (Hidden Valley). After exploring the top of Bluff Spring Mountain, return by the same trail, or take Trip 20 (Southwest Route) to Needle Canyon, or Trip 21 (Hidden Valley Loop) into the valley and Trip 22 (Northeast Route) to La Barge Canyon.

DIFFICULTY

Moderate hike. Not recommended for horses. Elevation change is +1,010 feet.

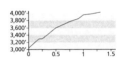

LENGTH and TIME

1.3 miles, 1.5 hours one way.

MAPS

Arizona USGS topo map NAD27: Weavers Needle. Superstition Wilderness Beartooth map, grid H13. Map 9.

FINDING THE TRAIL

Use Map 9 on page 115. The trip starts in Bluff Spring Canyon. From the wooden sign [9-P, 0] at the intersection of the Bluff Spring Trail (235) and Dutchman's Trail (104), walk west for 200 feet—about one minute—on the Bluff Spring Trail to an open area with a large fire ring [9-R] (N33° 25′ 23.0″, W111° 20′ 05.9″) on the right (north) side of the trail. Sometimes the fire ring is reconfigured as a large rock cairn. The fire ring is about 70 feet east of where the Bluff Spring Trail crosses the Bluff Spring Canyon wash.

From the fire ring, go toward the hill (north), and walk up the slope about 100 feet along the eroding bank (on your left) of the Bluff Spring Canyon wash where some rock cairns and evidence of a trail begin. Our

View to the northwest from the start of the Ely-Anderson Trail [9-R]. Two hikers can barely be seen going up the trail. November 2010 photo.

former trail marker on the Ely-Anderson Trail was a single-pole saguaro, but it has died. In the 2010 photo above, the saguaro with the small budding arm is about 120 feet up the trail. Its location (N33° 25' 23.9", W111° 20' 06.7") may still be useful for getting started on the route.

THE TRIP

Start on Map 9 on page 115. From the Bluff Spring Trail [9-R, 0], the trip goes up the slope of Bluff Spring Mountain heading directly north and then follows the natural contours of the terrain. The trail becomes easier to follow as it ascends. The buff-colored rock is worn through to the underlying white base where the trail crosses stretches of smooth rock. We do not think the rock cairns at the start of the trail mark the exact location of the old horse trail because of the steepness of the route, but several authors have written tales of experienced horse riders having problems on this trail due to the steepness and exposed cliffs.

When the trail turns southwest, you can see a small cave in the ravine to the north. At the top of the cliffs, the trail passes through a short section of stone wall [9-AA, 0.7] (N33° 25' 35.7", W111° 20' 29.1"). Some folks may have difficulty finding the top of the trail on the return trip, so you should take a look at the surrounding landmarks before you leave the rock wall.

Miners Needle rises on the south horizon with a good view of the window in the needle along several sections of this trail. Weavers Needle stands to the west.

From the stone wall [9-AA], the trail continues north and quickly becomes faint with overgrown grass. Within a quarter mile, the trail disappears, and the route continues across the grassy rolling hills. The horizon is broken only by the towering stalks of the century plant and sotol. If you continue northwest toward a high point on the mesa [9-FF, 1.3, 4041], you will be rewarded with a fine view of Bluff Spring Mountain Canyon, also known as Hidden Valley. The open views down into the valley and beyond the ramparts of Bluff Spring Mountain will please everyone. The trip description ends here, but you can continue to explore the area using Trip 21 (Hidden Valley Loop) before returning on the same trail, by Trip 20 (Southwest Route) on page 141, or by Trip 22 (Northeast Route) on page 149.

HISTORY AND LEGENDS

This trip follows a trail that is believed to be the one used by Mexican miners in the mid 1800s. They may have driven horses and mules to the top of Bluff Spring Mountain along this trail. Some have suggested that this ideal grazing area on top of the mountain could be protected from Apache raids with as few as six men with rifles. Jimmy Anderson, one of Jim Bark's cowhands, rediscovered the trail in 1911.[122] The worn rock along the trail is evidence of heavy use in the past, although not necessarily heavy use by Mexican miners, as Sims Ely suggests.

Sims Ely, in his 1953 book *The Lost Dutchman Mine,* tells the story of the rediscovered trail in detail.[123] Ely searched for the Lost Dutchman Mine in the early 1900s with rancher Jim Bark. Ely is pronounced "ee-lee."

Some authors refer to the Ely-Anderson Trail as the Mexican or Spanish Trail. Glenn Magill referred to it as the Ely-Anderson Trail on one of his maps, and we think that is a more appropriate name, since these were the men who rediscovered the trail and made it famous.[124]

At the top of the Ely-Anderson Trail, a stone wall [9-AA] is built on both sides of the trail. The wall, when viewed from the top of the mountain, is very low to the ground due to the steepness of the slope. So, instead of keeping Mexican mules on top of the mountain in the 1800s or acting as a fortification for defense, this wall might have been used as a drift fence in the 1900s to keep cattle from coming up the trail to the top of the mountain.

SOUTHWEST ROUTE

From the top of Bluff Spring Mountain, several hiking routes connect to the Forest Service trail system. This trip connects with the Terrapin Trail in Needle Canyon and provides spectacular views of Weavers Needle and the surrounding countryside. Off-trail hikers will enjoy this trek.

ITINERARY

Start on top of Bluff Spring Mountain at the summit of the Ely-Anderson former horse trail. A hiker route leads off the southwest side of the mountain into Needle Canyon connecting with the Terrapin Trail (234).

DIFFICULTY

Difficult hike. Not recommended for horses. Elevation change is +350 and -1,190 feet.

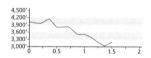

LENGTH and TIME

1.6 miles, 1.5 hours one way.

MAPS

Arizona USGS topo map NAD27: Weavers Needle. Superstition Wilderness Beartooth map, grid G13. Map 9.

FINDING THE TRAIL

Use Map 9 on page 115. This trip starts on top of Bluff Spring Mountain near the USGS 4041 elevation notation [9-FF, 4041].

THE TRIP

Start on Map 9 on page 115. Go cross-country from the end of Trip 19 (Ely-Anderson Trail) [9-FF, 0, 4041], heading south and then west, taking advantage of the flat ridge as you approach the summit of Bluff Spring Mountain [9-LL, 0.3, 4152]. From the top of Bluff Spring Mountain [9-LL], the view into the canyons below is spectacular—revealing colors and jagged rocks not evident from the trails below. Weavers Needle across to the west is impressive since this vantage point is almost 400 feet higher than Fremont Saddle and just 400 feet below the top of Weavers Needle.

View from Bluff Spring Mountain above Needle Canyon toward the northwest. November 1993 photo.

Before descending Bluff Spring Mountain, visually locate the Terrapin Trail (234) in Needle Canyon, and try to imagine where you will intersect the trail [9-OO]. From the high point [9-LL, 0.3, 4152], you have more than one way to descend into Needle Canyon, but the easiest is to walk south, then west through a break [9-MM, 0.4] in the ridge and rocks. Follow the contours of the terrain and select a route of your choice either along the ridgeline or directly into the bowl of the ravine. The ridgeline affords fine views into the valley, but dropping into the ravine here avoids some scrambling on steep slopes above the west facing cliffs. We didn't see any mine diggings along the ridgeline, but rock monuments along here look like prospector claim markers. We found loose rocks along the ridges and slopes, so be careful not to slide off the cliffs. Sims Ely, Glenn Magill, Walter Gassler, and others have had rock-sliding experiences on Bluff Spring Mountain, and all were lucky enough to be saved either by their companions or by a terrifying self-rescue.

The descent is slow due to the loose rocks and steepness of the terrain. Once you approach the bed of the ravine [9-NN, 1.1], it is best to stay on the north side. Avoid the brush and cliff areas by traversing on the slopes just above the bed of the ravine.

As the terrain begins to open up, cross the ravine to the south, head over the steep ridge, and pick a line-of-sight route down into Needle Canyon

SUPERSTITION WILDERNESS TRAILS WEST

and up to the Terrapin Trail [9-OO, 1.6] where the trip description ends. See Trip 10 (East Boulder—Needle Canyon Loop) on page 100 for directions for the 3.5-mile hike back to Peralta Trailhead.

If you want to check the waterhole [9-PPP, 1.5] (N33° 26' 09.3", W111° 21' 40.3") that Al Morrow used, take a more northerly route passing by the waterhole. Then climb out of Needle Canyon on the south side of the waterhole and meet the Terrapin Trail near mile 1.6 [9-OO, 1.6]. See History and Legends in Trip 10 (East Boulder—Needle Canyon Loop) on page 102 for more about Al Morrow and his camp in Needle Canyon.

Apache Junction, Arizona,
P.O. Box 327
August 16

Dear Al,
It was hard to do but I have laid out locations of some of the claims on Bluff Springs Mtn., at close approximate areas,
X marks Peck and Oklahoma groups of claims.
I have marked some of Sutton's claims as close as I can. He has so many claims that it is hard to tell if they are valid or not.
If there are others I don't know of them, although there are claims down canyon,
A search of records would be only accurate way to tell.
Glad to know that you found Pinta of Antrest. You didn't see me after you talked with pinta.
Weather still the same here. Nearly time for a late summer shower or two.
I visited Peggy yesterday. She is feeling the humidity and heat of recent days.
No news here.

Al M.

Letter from Al Morrow to Al Reser on August 16, 1966. Reser was living in California and Morrow was living at his camp in Needle Canyon [8-EE]. Three people mentioned in the letter, Peggy Aylor, Richard Peck, and Lloyd Sutton were prospectors. The Oklahoma group of claims refers to Glenn Magill's claims. We are not familiar with the name Pinta. Courtesy Superstition Mountain Historical Society, Al Reser Collection.

HIDDEN VALLEY LOOP

For experienced off-trail hikers, this long day-trip through Hidden Valley on Bluff Spring Mountain provides a challenging trek. From the sheer cliffs of Bluff Spring Mountain, you can look down into the surrounding canyons. The high cliffs provide an ideal vantage point for photographs. Hikers can still see the overhang at Magill's Camp on the north end of the mountain.

ITINERARY

Start on top of Bluff Spring Mountain at the summit of the Ely-Anderson former horse trail. Descend into Hidden Valley to Al Reser's Camp. Make a clockwise loop over a pass to the west, then contour along the cliffs to Magill's Camp. Return in the creek bed of Bluff Spring Mountain Canyon to Reser's Camp. Climb up to the end of the Ely-Anderson trip on the ridge.

DIFFICULTY

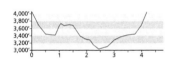

Very Difficult. Not recommended for horses. Elevation change is ±1,340 feet.

LENGTH and TIME

4.2 miles, 6.5 hours round-trip.

MAPS

Arizona USGS topo map NAD27: Weavers Needle. Superstition Wilderness Beartooth map, grids H13 to G12. Map 9.

FINDING THE TRAIL

Use map 9 on page 115. This trip starts on top of Bluff Spring Mountain near the USGS 4041 elevation notation [9-FF, 4041].

THE TRIP

Start on Map 9 on page 115. Scout this cross-country route from a high point before dropping down into Hidden Valley. From the end of Trip 19 (Ely-Anderson Trail) [9-FF, 0, 4041], walk north down into the bed of Bluff Spring Mountain Canyon to the site of Al Reser's 1984 camp [9-PP, 0.7] (N33° 26' 35.8", W111° 21' 08.3"), which is about 250 yards south of the breached dam. Only the built-up ground for a tent site remains at Reser's camp. We saw

Al Reser in Whitlow Canyon at the age of eighty-four. Photo by Al Reser. July 1992 photo. Courtesy Superstition Mountain Historical Society, Al Reser Collection.

the metal folding chair that was at Reser's Camp in the early 1990s about 75 yards to the north in another camp area. With water in the wash, this is a pleasant place to visit.

From Al Reser's Camp [9-PP, 0.7], this loop trip goes west, cross-country, up to the pass. From the pass, you have good views of Weavers Needle and the upper reaches of Needle Canyon. The route turns north and skirts the steep slopes of Hill 3999 where you may find some faint trails, one of which traverses a rocky area that has been blasted by prospectors. Some of the boulders along here contain thick bands of white quartz. Be careful on the steep slopes. Most of the rock is loose and the footing is not stable. The early prospectors often had problems with loose rocks. Large masses of rock and dirt have been reported to slide down the slopes carrying people with them. Beyond Hill 3999 and a small saddle, the terrain tends to be less steep. Head west and north, to the edge of the cliffs, for good views into Needle Canyon.

We looked for Magill's mine, The Dutchman, but could not find it. Greg Hansen, formerly of the Forest Service, said the mine diggings were restored to natural conditions. We don't advise you to climb around the cliffs looking for it. Most of the cliffs are a sheer drop into the canyon below. Continue to the north end of the mountain, and work your way down to the lowest, wide, flat terrace. No climbing is necessary, but you will have to look for breaks between the boulders. On the lower terrace, campers still use the overhang [9-RR, 2.3] (N33° 27' 16.0", W111° 21' 58.5") that Glenn Magill and his partners used as their camp. The large terrace in front of the overhang provides a fine view to the north into Needle Canyon and La Barge Canyon.

The return route follows the bed of Bluff Spring Mountain Canyon south, to the beginning of the loop. From Magill's overhang [9-RR, 2.3], walk south along the flat terrace until you see a ravine entering from the west. This is the best place to drop down into the bed of Bluff Spring Mountain Canyon. The canyon is narrow and full of boulders and vegetation. A few sections are easy walking, but most of the canyon entails some of the roughest cross-country trekking in the Wilderness. The only good aspect of the thrash-through-the-vegetation hiking is that it isn't that long. You will find a slightly overgrown trail to the left (east) of the water course—south of Hill 3502. Just as the canyon begins to open up, the breached rock dam (N33° 26' 40.3", W111° 21' 14.5") crosses the water course, which is marked as a spring on some maps. The rocks in the wall were set in cement.

From Al Reser's Camp [9-PP, 3.5], the route continues south to the ridge by retracing the route to the start of the trip on Hill 4041 [9-FF, 4.2 4041]. Follow Trip 19 (Ely-Anderson Trail) or Trip 20 (Southwest Route) to connect with a Forest Service Trail.

ALTERNATE RETURN

From Magill's overhang [9-RR], head south going cross-country. At the first ravine entering from the west, go south in the bed of Bluff Spring Canyon until you can head up the east side of Bluff Spring Canyon. Connect with Trip 22 (Northeast Route or Alternate North Route) on page 149 to descend through the cliffs at [9-JJJ] or [9-TTT]. That trip hooks you up with the Dutchman's Trail (104) in either La Barge Canyon or Needle Canyon.

HISTORY AND LEGENDS

Before you visit the top of Bluff Spring Mountain, it would be worthwhile to read Curt Gentry's book *Killer Mountains*, which describes Glenn Magill's adventures. Although their claims of discovery are a bit exaggerated, Curt Gentry tells a fascinating story of the Dutchman Mine on Bluff Spring Mountain. On the cliffs below the mine, they reported a tunnel that was rigged with "rock traps," which would send huge boulders tumbling down if any rocks were moved. In the cliff surrounding the tunnel were four two-man guardhouses built of stone. Also in the area were many tree stumps, assumed to have been cut for mine timbers.

To reach the mine above the tunnel, Magill's men used a helicopter on occasion, but often just scrambled up the steep cliffs. We haven't explored Magill's trails. One route was described as being straight down. Another

View looking north into Needle Canyon (left) and La Barge Canyon (right) from the overhang at Glenn Magill's camp [9-RR] on the north end of Bluff Spring Mountain. November 1993 photo.

route to the top of the cliffs piqued the interest of some Lost Dutchman Mine searchers since it involved climbing through a hole in two rocks without the use of footholds.[125] Jim Bark reported a similar story credited to Joe Deering in the late 1800s. In describing the area where he found gold, Deering said there was a trick to the trail where you had to go through a hole. As with many tellers of treasure stories, Deering died before revealing the location of his find.[126] Magill's Dutchman Mine on Bluff Spring Mountain did not produce any gold.

Al Reser filed several mining claims along Bluff Spring Mountain Canyon (Hidden Canyon) with his partner Monty Edwards. Three of his claims were located northeast of his camp [9-PP]—Tuffy 1, 2, and 3, named after his dog Tuffy. He also had two claims, Lena Bark 1 and 2, northwest of his camp on Hill 3999 with partner John Spangler.[127]

Close-up view of the North Route through the cliffs of Bluff Spring Mountain. The route goes through the break in the cliff [9-TTT] on the left side of the horizon. The waterfall from Bluff Spring Mountain Canyon is not shown in this photograph. March 2010 photo.

North Route through the cliffs of Bluff Spring Mountain is on the left side of the horizon. The close-up photo of the break in the cliffs [9-TTT] is shown in a separate photo above. The waterfall from Bluff Spring Mountain Canyon can barely be seen on the lowest part of the horizon. March 2010 photo.

Northeast Route

The little-known Northeast Route and the Alternate North Route provide access through the imposing cliffs at the northern end of Bluff Spring Mountain.

ITINERARY

Start on top of the northeast end of Bluff Spring Mountain in the saddle east of Hill 3502, go north down the ravine, and end in La Barge Canyon on the Dutchman's Trail (104) or in Needle Canyon on the Dutchman's Trail (104).

DIFFICULTY

Difficult hike. Not recommended for horses. Elevation change is -1,050 feet.

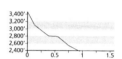

LENGTH and TIME

About 0.9 mile to La Barge Canyon or 1.1 miles to Needle Canyon, about 1 hour one way.

MAPS

Arizona USGS topo map NAD27: Weavers Needle. Superstition Wilderness Beartooth map, grid G12. Map 9.

FINDING THE TRAIL

Use Map 9 on page 114. Start at the saddle [9-JJJ] (N33° 27' 03.6", W111° 21' 28.3") just east of Hill 3502 on the top of the northeast end of Bluff Spring Mountain.

THE TRIP

Start on Map 9 on page 114. We have only taken this route downhill. Going uphill may require more intense route finding. To get on top of Bluff Spring Mountain, we either go up the Ely-Anderson Trail (Trip 19 on page 138) or go up the Alternate North Route described at the end of this section.

In 2003, Dave Cameron told us about the Northeast Route going through the saddle [9-JJJ] just east of Hill 3502 on Bluff Spring Mountain, where our trip description starts.[128] As you descend from the saddle [9-JJJ, 0],

View to the north of Hill 3502 on the left and the pass [9-JJJ] on the right where the Northeast Route begins. The gentle slope up to the pass shown in this photograph contrasts with the steep, rugged scramble down the north side of the pass. March 2010 photo.

stay high on the west side of the ravine, just below the cliff line. No trail is visible here, and the ravine is very steep. While staying close to the base of the cliffs on the left (west) side of the ravine, you have to anticipate when to descend toward the center of the ravine to avoid being cliffed-out on the ledges that form as you head downhill.

The former horse trail becomes visible on the ground about 0.2 mile downslope where the trail becomes less steep (N33° 27′ 11.7″, W111° 21′ 31.0″). The trail disappears [9-III, 0.4] (N33° 27′ 24.0″, W111° 21′ 35.8″) when you are able to cut to the left (westerly) around the point. Here the trail is more of a hiking route marked by rock cairns. That trail eventually becomes a bushwhack identified by sporadic rock cairns. We have not checked to see if the horse trail might continue directly north.

Scrambling and following the cairned route will take you north to the end of the mountain, where you can connect with the overgrown section of the Little Bull Pass Trail (N33° 27′ 32.5″, W111° 21′ 45.1″) at mile 0.7. This trail will take you north to La Barge Canyon [near 9-I, 0.9]. Alternatively, if you curve around the point of the mountain heading more westerly, you can go over the ridge and continue west to the unmaintained and overgrown Little Bull Pass Trail (N33° 27′ 29.2″, W111° 21′ 58.4″) at mile 0.8 near the Bluff Spring Mountain wash crossing. A short distance to the west, the Little Bull Pass Trail connects with the Dutchman's Trail [9-YY, 1.1].

ALTERNATE NORTH ROUTE

We have hiked the North Route several times to the top of the cliff on Bluff Spring Mountain, but we have always gone down the Northeast Route. The North Route should be hikeable in either direction. Greg Davis told us about this break in the cliff in March 2010.[129] We usually start on the east segment of the unmaintained Little Bull Pass Trail where it intersects the Dutchman's Trail [9-YY, 0] and follow the Little Bull Pass Trail a little bit beyond the Bluff Spring Mountain Wash crossing. When the trail turns northeast (N33° 27′ 29.7″, W111° 21′ 56.3″), we head cross-country on the east bench of Bluff Spring Mountain Wash and aim for a trail that begins on a narrow whitish ridge (N33° 27′ 25.5″, W111° 21′ 48.9″). Two waypoints along the faint trail, (N33° 27′ 22.2″, W111° 21′ 48.4″) and (N33° 27′ 20.1″, W111° 21′ 46.5″), will help you maintain the direction of the route up the slopes.

As you climb the steep hill, in the distance to the south you will be able to see the waterfall pouring off the north end of Bluff Spring Mountain—too far and too shadowed for a good photograph. When you get near the top of the route, the break that leads you through the cliff of Bluff Spring Mountain becomes more apparent. The last part of the route is steeper, requiring you to pull yourself over some boulders, but no technical rock climbing is required. The top of the cliff [9-TTT, 0.6] (N33° 27′ 16.3″, W111° 21′ 44.3″) is marked only by a small rock cairn near a fire ring. We don't believe this route was ever a horse trail.

Two useful waypoints for exploring Bluff Spring Mountain are:

Glenn Magill Overhang	[9-RR]	(N33° 27′ 16.0″, W111° 21′ 58.5″)
Breached Dam	[near 9-PP]	(N33° 26′ 40.3″, W111° 21′ 14.5″)

HISTORY AND LEGENDS

J. Alan Stirrat's 1948 map[130] shows a trail going from Bluff Spring to the top of Bluff Spring Mountain, then heading north down Bluff Spring Mountain Canyon. Stirrat's trail follows a canyon off the northeast end of Bluff Spring Mountain through a ravine that looks identical to the route Dave Cameron described to us. Stirrat does not name the trail, but only identifies it as "Old Trail." His map shows a corral [near 9-TT] at Marsh Flats (Marsh Valley).

Tom Kollenborn tells the story of riding his horse down the north end of Bluff Spring Mountain when he worked for Bill Barkley as a cowboy in the 1950s. This Northeast Route may have been the route he took.

Rancher George Martin told us that he rode his mule up the Ely-Anderson trail on the south end of Bluff Spring Mountain, across the valley, and then down the trail we call the Northeast Route. He said the Northeast Route was a steep trail going down, but he rode it several times when he worked for the Forest Service in the 1980s.[131]

UPPER LA BARGE AREA

The Upper La Barge Area begins south of Charlebois Spring and extends east, beyond La Barge Spring, to the Upper La Barge Box. All the trips in this area can be accessed from La Barge Canyon via the Dutchman's Trail (104) or the Red Tanks Trail (107).

FINDING THE TRAILHEAD

Use Maps 4, 7, 9, and 10. La Barge Canyon is one of the major drainages in the Superstition Wilderness. It runs northwest from La Barge Mountain through the heart of the Wilderness to Canyon Lake. The many small, scenic canyons entering La Barge Canyon offer the traveler enjoyable side trips. All trips are accessed from the Dutchman's Trail and/or Red Tanks Trail since we have not identified a specific trailhead for this area.

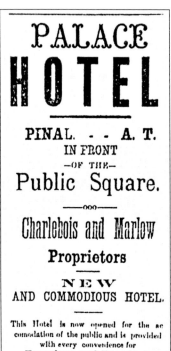

Alfred Charlebois and George Marlow were partners in several businesses including the Matt Cavaness Ranch and the Palace Hotel in Pinal.[132]

HISTORY AND LEGENDS

We do not have any evidence that John Lebarge was ever in La Barge Canyon, but it was probably named for him or one of his relatives. Lebarge spent his early years in Arizona Territory in the town of Pinal, had a stock ranch 3 miles south of the Matt Cavaness Ranch, and was living in Tempe when he died.

John Lebarge was born in Canada in 1856. He was naturalized as a U.S. citizen in Massachusetts in 1876.[133] We use the Lebarge spelling for John Lebarge although official records show variations of his name such as Le Barge, Lalarge, and Labarge. Place names will still be spelled La Barge.

In 1883, John Lebarge was living in Pinal, Arizona Territory. He was one of several witnesses—including Joseph Charlebois—in a civil case in District Court when Alfred Charlebois accused George Marlow of injuring his character with false statements made in the town of Pinal. Alfred Charlebois and Marlow were business partners in the former Matt Cavaness Ranch, the Palace Hotel, and the Pinal Meat Market. Lebarge spoke French as did Charlebois and Marlow; the complaint indicated that all of the witnesses understood the false statements that were spoken in both French and English. The lawsuit was discontinued by mutual consent.[134]

Jim Bark wrote that John Lebarge and Wiley Holman worked for George Marlow at his Marlow Ranch, which branded the ML. Lebarge and Holman found twelve head of Marlow cattle that had strayed to the top of Dacite Mesa. They were not able to coax the cattle down the steep trail, and all the cattle died of thirst up there. Bark credits Lebarge and Holman with finding a quartz outcrop containing metal on top of Dacite Mesa during their unsuccessful roundup. Later, Pete Carney ran a crosscut tunnel into the vein below the mesa at the present-day Dacite Mine.[135]

On May 21, 1891, John Lebarge filed a water location (water claim), named Cottonwood Spring, three miles southwest of the Marlow Ranch house. He knew Mary Charlebois, because he filed the Charlebois Spring location, 3.5 miles south of the Marlow Ranch house, for her, which she located on May 20, 1891—not far from his own location.[136] Note that this Charlebois Spring is not the one in La Barge Canyon. We think that Lebarge's

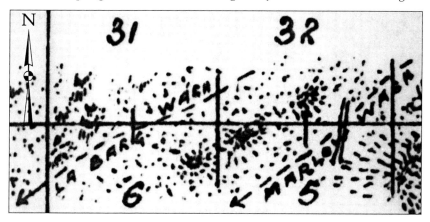

La Barg Wash (probably named for John Lebarge) is shown in the area of present-day Peralta Canyon Wash. Marlow Wash is present-day Barks Canyon Wash. Although not shown, the Quarter Circle U Ranch headquarters (former Matt Cavaness Ranch) is in Section 32 where Marlow Wash comes in from the right (east). The horizontal line is the baseline where Township 1 North (T1N) is above the line and Township 1 South (T1S) is below the line. The area shown with the Section numbers is in Range 10 East (R10E). We added the north arrow, and the sections are 1 mile square. The map is an excerpt from the Township Exteriors Plat Map of Gila and Salt River Base Line survey, April 18, 1899, by Albert T. Bolton. Courtesy of the Bureau of Land Management, Phoenix Office.

Cottonwood Spring was at West Tank as shown on the northwest side of the 1966 Florence Junction 7.5-minute USGS topographic map.

John Lebarge registered the JL brand on December 11, 1886, in Pinal County.[137] We speculate that he had his stock ranch at West Tank and that he was running cattle on the open range. An 1899 survey of the Salt and Gila River baseline (see map on previous page) shows that present-day Peralta Wash was named La Barg [sic] Wash, so he must have had some presence in the area. The wash through the Bark Ranch headquarters was named Marlow Wash.[138] Pinal County records show that Lebarge's house, canal, and personal property at the stock ranch were sold for back taxes of $45.43 on April 23, 1893. The assessed value of the property was $1,290.58, so it must have been a substantial operation.[139]

On June 10, 1893, John Lebarge sold his JL horse and cattle brand to Bark and Criswell who were then owners of the former George Marlow Ranch—previously the Matt Cavaness Ranch. Bark and Criswell registered Lebarge's JL brand in 1897 and listed the range as Superstition Mountains.[140]

Lebarge married Anna Gunson in Maricopa County on September 23, 1889. They had one child, named Joseph, who was two years old when his father died on July 27, 1893, while living in Tempe, Arizona Territory. His mother died soon after on October 21, 1893, which might have been related to her "successful" breast cancer operation in June.[141]

Barry Storm, in his book *Thunder Gods Gold*, writes that La Barge Canyon and Spring are probably named after Phil La Barge, who was the partner of cattleman Martin Charlebois.[142] We have not been able to find the name Phil La Barge in any official documents. You'll find information on Martin Charlebois in Trip 14 (Charlebois Spring—Loop 1) on page 116.

The 1984 book by Michael and Jan Sheridan *Recreational Guide to the Superstition Mountains and the Salt River Lakes*, suggests that "La Barge Canyon was named after John Le Barge [sic] a gold prospector who was born in Canada in 1856," which corresponds to our research.[143]

La Barge Spring [9-D] is one of the more reliable springs in the Superstition Wilderness, but you should always verify the water conditions with the Forest Service or other hikers before you go. La Barge Spring is located in a grove of tall trees on the east side of La Barge Canyon near the junction with Bluff Spring Canyon. The spring and concrete water trough—sometimes overflowing with water—are on the north end of a high bench—not in the creek bed as is often thought. The date inscribed in the concrete reads 7-1-39. We have not see any names in the concrete, but in 1957, Jerry Carr (Dan Hopper's stepfather) recorded the names inscribed in the concrete as "A. J. Vac hon and Harry McBride" with the Quarter Circle U Brand inserted between them. The date was the same, 7-1-39.[144]

WHISKEY SPRING TRAIL

Whiskey Spring, which may have water, makes a good destination for day trips from Peralta Trailhead. Many loop hikers and riders use the Whiskey Spring Trail to connect Miners Summit with La Barge Canyon. This is the site of a biplane wreck in the 1940s.

ITINERARY

From Miners Summit, follow Whiskey Spring Trail (238) to La Barge Canyon. The trail can be used as a side trip or as a connecting trail on longer loop trips.

DIFFICULTY

Easy hike. Moderate ride. Elevation change is +180 and -610 feet.

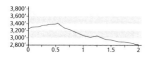

LENGTH and TIME

1.9 miles, 1.5 hours one way.

MAPS

Arizona USGS topo map NAD27: Weavers Needle. Superstition Wilderness Beartooth map, grid I14. Map 7.

FINDING THE TRAIL

The trail starts at Miners Summit or in La Barge Canyon. See Trip 8 (Bluff Spring Loop) on page 85 or Trip 15 (Charlebois Spring—Loop 2) on page 118 for the details.

THE TRIP

Start on Map 7 on page 89. From Miners Summit [7-O, 0], Whiskey Spring Trail (238) heads east along a ridge—going uphill more than you might expect—and tops out in about 0.5 mile. From the pass, the trail drops down into Whiskey Spring Canyon and turns north. Whiskey Spring [7-W, 1.2] is on the east side of the trail in a clump of cottonwood trees. The spring always has had water when we checked it in the cooler months, but it may go dry in drought years.

Glen Hamaker and O. E. Wagner found this whiskey still at Whiskey Spring in 1965. It is on display at the Bluebird Mine and Gift Shop. Courtesy of Louis Ruiz and Ray Ruiz, Bluebird Mine and Gift Shop. August 1993 photo.

About twenty minutes down canyon from the spring, many people camp in the shady area [7-JJ 1.5] under the cottonwood and laurel trees along the west bank of the ravine. The trail climbs out of Whiskey Spring Canyon, goes over a small ridge, and drops into La Barge Canyon, where it meets the Red Tanks Trail (107) [7-X, 1.9]. The Whiskey Spring Trail ends here.

HISTORY AND LEGENDS

In 1965, Glen Hamaker and O. E. Wagner found a metal whiskey still at Whiskey Spring and carried the whiskey still out of the Superstition Mountains via First Water Trailhead. Louis Ruiz has the whiskey still on display at the Blue Bird Mine and Gift Shop museum on North Apache Trail.[145]

In 1942 or '43, a Fleet Mark 7 PT-6 biplane crashed in Whiskey Spring Canyon directly south of Whiskey Spring. Bill Barkley reported that both pilots walked out to his Quarter Circle U Ranch after the crash. In 1946, Tom Kollenborn and his father hiked here and photographed the wreckage. The plane was removed in 1963 and later restored to flying condition.[146]

Fred Mullins,[147] a stagecoach driver out of Pinal, told a story about a man who discovered gold on the west side of Picacho Butte in 1894. Picacho Butte is the hill east of Whiskey Spring. The man, named Wagoner (also spelled Waggoner), would board the stage in Pinal and depart in the desert on the south side of the Superstition Mountains near the Whitlow Ranch. After taking out hand-picked rose-quartz gold ore, he would meet the stage again for a ride back to Pinal. Wagoner told Mullins his route from Whitlow Ranch was up Randolph Canyon, up Red Tank Canyon, down La Barge, and around Picacho Butte. Wagoner said he concealed the outcropping with brush and rocks and planted a circle of trees around the site so he could locate it in the future. In 1952, prospector and miner Ray Howland found gold in rose-quartz float on the west side of Picacho Butte. No one has reported the exact location of Wagoner's diggings.[148]

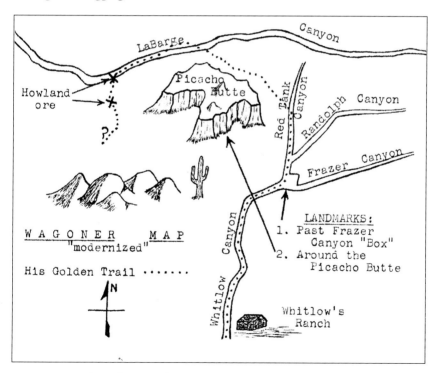

Barry Storm's "modernized" version of the Wagoner Map, with typewritten landmarks, from his 1945 book, Thunder Gods Gold. *Courtesy Robert Schoose, Schoose Publishing, Goldfield Ghost Town.*

Typical mining claim marker made of rocks. In 1993 when we took this photograph, we found Charles Crawford's March 1983 Certificate of Recording papers stuffed inside the beer can.

In 1974, a large tent camp occupied the north side of La Barge Canyon at the Whiskey Spring Trail and Red Tanks Trail junction. Author Jack Carlson recalls two large white-canvas-wall tents and some horses at the camp. One of the men from the camp was lying on an air mattress in a small pool in La Barge Creek. He was drinking beer and enjoying the sun. After a short conversation, our group walked back to Whiskey Spring. As we were returning, one of our fellow hikers asked us if we had noticed the other man, beside one of the tents, pointing a rifle at us. We were a bit naive about the dangers in those early years.

Trip 24

TRAP CANYON

Trap Canyon is a small canyon that has seasonal water. The easy walk up this intimate canyon is pleasant when there is running water.

ITINERARY

Starting from the Red Tanks Trail (107) in La Barge Canyon, this trip goes a short distance to Trap Canyon Spring and continues up canyon. Return the same way or over the pass [4-HH] to the south.

DIFFICULTY

Easy hike. Not recommended for horses. Elevation change is +320 feet.

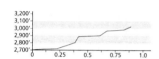

LENGTH and TIME

0.9 mile, 1 hour one way.

MAPS

Arizona USGS topo map NAD27: Weavers Needle. Superstition Wilderness Beartooth map, grid I13. Map 4.

FINDING THE TRAIL

Use Map 4 on page 73. Start on Red Tanks Trail (107) on the east bench of Trap Canyon [4-Y] (N33° 26' 06.6", W111° 19' 07.1"). Trip 15 (Charlebois Spring—Loop 2) on page 118 describes the directions from Peralta Trailhead.

THE TRIP

Start on Map 4 on page 73. From Red Tanks Trail [4-Y, 0], follow a faint trail on the east bench of Trap Canyon Wash. When the trail disappears, bushwhack up the wash through the trees to the Trap Canyon Spring area [4-Z, 0.3] (N33° 26' 18.4", W111° 18' 57.2"), which is marked by a brown metal post without a sign. A large willow tree towers over the seasonal spring. Farther upstream, you can loop over a low pass [4-HH, 0.9] for an optional return to the Red Tanks Trail. We haven't hiked the entire length of Trap Canyon, but others said it is a rough trip—best hiked in the downstream direction, east to west.[149] On one trip we found mining claim markers—white wooden stakes in a pile of rocks—that still contained the location papers.

MUSIC CANYON

Music Canyon has a seasonal spring. This is a seldom-traveled area that is ideal for one or two people.

ITINERARY

From the Dutchman's Trail (104) in La Barge Canyon, walk up the bed of Music Canyon. Return the same way or bushwhack over to Peters Trail.

DIFFICULTY

Moderate hike. Not recommended for horses. Elevation change is +450 and -450 feet.

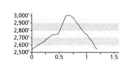

LENGTH and TIME

1.2 miles, 1.5 hours one way.

MAPS

Arizona USGS topo map NAD27: Weavers Needle. Superstition Wilderness Beartooth map, grid H12. Map 9.

FINDING THE TRAIL

Use map 9 on page 114. Start in La Barge Canyon on Dutchman's Trail (104) at Music Canyon. See Trip 14 (Charlebois Spring—Loop 1) on page 112.

THE TRIP

Start on Map 9 on page 114. Leave the Dutchman's Trail [9-J, 0] (N33° 27′ 04.4″, W111° 20′ 22.0″) and walk up the bed of Music Canyon. The trail-of-use though the bushes is completely overgrown, so traveling in the wash is easier. There is a fairly reliable water hole at the large cottonwood tree [9-K, 0.1] (N33° 27′ 05.9″, W111° 20′ 15.8″), but the actual Music Canyon Spring seeps from the bedrock farther up canyon at (N33° 27′ 07.8″, W111° 20′ 12.1″). The narrow canyon eventually widens with sloping hillsides. This is not a place for large groups, but lone hikers might find some very small, scenic places to camp below the low cliffs.

Return the same way [9-J, 0.2], or from [9-L, 0.5], bushwhack westerly 0.3 mile over the ridge to Peters Trail (105). Follow Peters Trail south, to the Dutchman's Trail [9-M, 1.2] in La Barge Canyon, where the trip ends.

DONS CAMP TRAILHEAD
(LOST GOLDMINE TRAIL, EAST TRAILHEAD)

From Apache Junction at Idaho Road, go 8 miles east on US60. Turn left (north) between mileposts 204 and 205 onto Peralta Road (also signed as Peralta Trail and FR77). Follow FR77 for 7 miles to the unmarked Dons Camp Road. Turn left (west) into the large parking area, and look for the Lost Goldmine Trail kiosk.

FINDING THE TRAILHEAD

Dons Camp Trailhead for the Lost Goldmine Trail is located at the kiosk

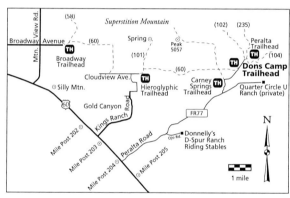

in the parking area south of the Dons Camp entrance gate. If you missed the turnoff for the Dons Camp, you can backtrack on Peralta Road about 0.2 mile, going south, from the cattle guard and Tonto National Forest boundary.

FACILITIES

No facilities are available except for a stone bench and hitching rail. Bring your own water. Peralta Trailhead has toilets.

THE TRAIL

From the kiosk at the Dons Camp Trailhead (N33° 23′ 32.0″, W111° 21′ 11.9″), Lost Goldmine Trail (60) goes east and west mostly following the southern boundary of the Superstition Wilderness. Going 0.2 mile northeast from the kiosk at the Dons Camp Trailhead, Lost Goldmine Trail ends at the cattle guard on Peralta Road (Peralta Road Access). Heading west from Dons Camp Trailhead at the kiosk, the Lost Goldmine Trail leads to West Boulder Trail gate in 1.1 miles, reaches Hieroglyphic Trailhead in 5.2 miles, and ends near Broadway Trailhead at Jacob's Crosscut Trail in 9.1 miles.

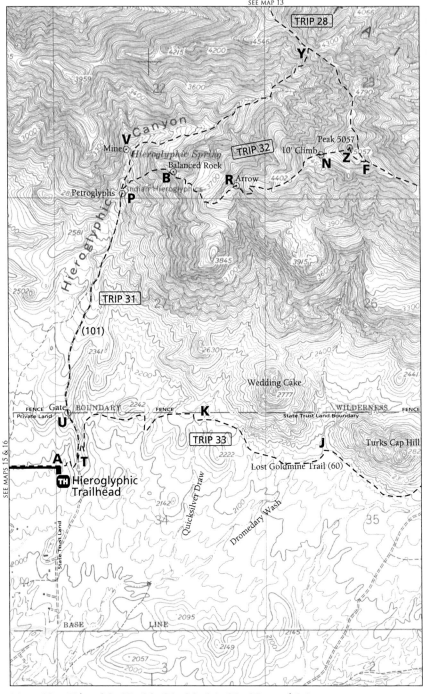

Map 12 – Trips 26, 27, 28, 29, 30, 31, 32, 33, and 36.

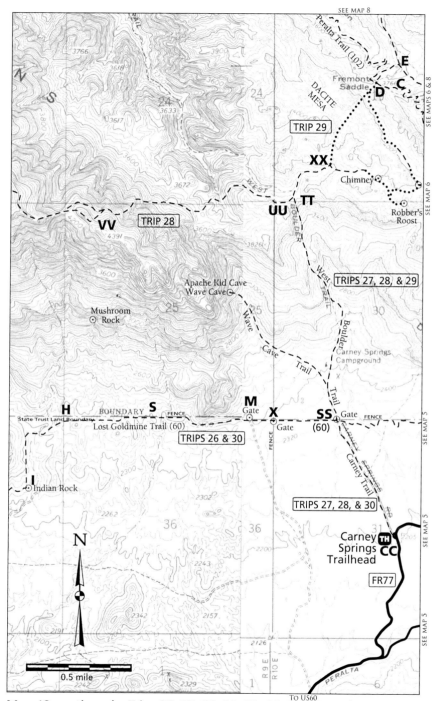

Map 12 continued – Trips 26, 27, 28, 29, 30, 31, 32, 33, and 36.

Pinal County manages the Lost Goldmine Trail, which is open for public use by hikers, horse riders, and bicycle riders. We refer to this trailhead as the Dons Camp Trailhead, but Pinal County has named it "Lost Goldmine Trail, East Trailhead." This updated name is much better than their previous name of "Peralta Road Trailhead." No permit is required to use the Lost Goldmine Trail, but leaving the trail requires a recreation permit for the use of the surrounding Arizona State Trust land.

HISTORY AND LEGENDS

In past years, the Dons Club held a big event in March, called the Dons Trek. It brought hundreds of people to the Dons Club Base Camp to enjoy the legends and lore of the Lost Dutchman Mine and the scenic beauty of the Superstition Wilderness.

The Dons led three guided hikes during the day-long Trek. The easy hike toured the north end of the base camp. The medium hike went up to the first saddle on Cardiac Hill, and the long hike climbed up the Cave Trail and returned on the Peralta Trail.[150] It was quite a scene to see a Dons Club leader, dressed in red and black in the old Spanish tradition, leading a group of twenty city folks along the trail. Standing in the Peralta Trailhead parking lot, we watched an unending stream of these groups come over the hill from the Dons Camp, walk across the parking lot, and then hike up the Bluff Spring Trail. The groups were spaced every 200 yards, which makes a spectacular show of humanity in the desert. Several hundred people must have stood on that small section of trail.

The Dons Trek was first held in 1934 and continued through 2005, except for the war years 1943, 1944, and 1945. In 2004, the Forest Service prohibited the future use of fireworks and the Fire Fall at the end of the evening program. In 2005, a laser light show ended the evening program, and that was the last Trek that was held. The lack of fireworks and Fire Fall may have led to the cancellation of future Treks. Since that time, the Dons have focused on daytime Discovery Camp events for school children.

Greg Davis, Director of Research for the Superstition Mountain Historical Society and member of the Dons Club, reported the history of the Dons Club in the 1982 *Superstition Mountain Journal*. The Dons Club began in 1930, when it was established as the Triangle Club within the Phoenix YMCA. The Triangle Club became an independent organization in 1931 and changed its name to the Dons Club. Oren Arnold, author of the 1954 book *Ghost Gold* and past president of the Dons Club, is credited with selecting the new name. The Dons Club Base Camp, north of the Dons Camp Trailhead parking area [5-DD], has operated since 1955 under a Forest Service permit on Tonto National Forest land. Between 1935 and 1954, the base camp was located at the present site of the Peralta Trailhead parking lot [5-A].[151]

LOST GOLDMINE TRAIL
FROM DONS CAMP TRAILHEAD

Everyone will enjoy this easy trail that provides access to the southern canyons and trails of Superstition Mountain. The trail travels just outside the Superstition Wilderness boundary, so hikers, horse riders, and bicyclists are allowed to use the trail.

ITINERARY

From the large parking area and kiosk at the Dons Camp Trailhead, follow the trail going westerly to the West Boulder Trail gate, Hieroglyphic Trailhead, or Broadway Trailhead. Return by the same way, or make a vehicle shuttle trip.

DIFFICULTY

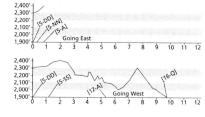

Easy hike. Moderate ride.
Elevation change to [16-Q]
is +620 and -1,040 feet.

LENGTH and TIME

Going east to Peralta Road Access [5-NN], 0.2 mile, 0.25 hour one way.

Going west to West Boulder Trail gate [5-SS], 1.1 miles, 0.75 hour one way.

Going west to Hieroglyphic Trailhead [12-A], 5.2 miles, 3.0 hours one way.

Going west to Broadway Trailhead [16-Q], 9.7 miles, 6.0 hours one way.

MAPS

Arizona USGS topo maps NAD27: Weavers Needle and Goldfield.
Superstition Wilderness Beartooth map, grid G15. Maps 5, 12, and 16.

FINDING THE TRAIL

See the trailhead map on page 161. Start at the Lost Goldmine Trail kiosk (N33° 23′ 32.0″, W111° 21′ 11.9″), south of the Dons Camp entrance.

THE TRIP

Start on Map 5 on page 77. This trail is a good choice if you only have a short bit of time and want to experience a trip in the Sonoran Desert. Follow the trail as it meanders through washes and crosses small ridges until you tire or run out of time. The scenery is good in both directions, so returning the same way makes a pleasant trip.

From the Dons Camp Trailhead [5-DD, 0], start the trip at the Lost Goldmine Trail rock and metal kiosk. The trail heads southwest, contours through a steep wash, turns to the north, and then follows the Superstition Wilderness boundary fence as it continues west.

At 0.8 mile, the Lost Goldmine Trail crosses an unsigned dirt road. Going left (south) on the abandoned road takes you to the Carney Trail (formerly the Carney Springs Road) in about 0.3 mile.

The Lost Goldmine Trail reaches the unsigned West Boulder Trail gate at [5-SS, 1.1]. Going right (north) through the gate puts you on the unsigned West Boulder Trail in the Superstition Wilderness. Going left (south) takes you 0.6 mile to the Carney Springs Trailhead [5-CC] on the Carney Trail.

The West Boulder Trail is a gentle uphill grade for the first 0.5 mile, so you could use it to get closer to the mountain. After 0.5 mile, the West Boulder Trail becomes very steep, with poor footing, so you do not want to take a horse past 0.5 mile. No bicycles are allowed on the north side of the boundary fence, which is inside the Superstition Wilderness. See the Carney Springs Trailhead on page 167 for more trip details.

Heading west from the West Boulder Trail gate [12-SS, 1.1] on the Lost Goldmine Trail, your major landmarks will be: green livestock gate [12-X, 1.5], large stand of saguaro cacti [12-S, 2.0], Mushroom Rock viewpoint [12-H, 2.4], Indian Rock grind holes [12-I, 2.8], Dromedary Wash west of Turks Cap Hill [12-J, 3.5], Quicksilver Draw [12-K, 4.2], Hieroglyphic Trailhead [12-A, 5.2], and Broadway Trailhead [16-Q, 9.7]. See Trip 30 (Lost Goldmine Trail from Carney Springs Trailhead) on page 184 for more trail information on the above landmarks. Return the same way, or make a shuttle trip from any of the trailheads.

HISTORY AND LEGENDS

See Carney Springs Trailhead on page 168 for the history and legends.

CARNEY SPRINGS TRAILHEAD

From Apache Junction at Idaho Road, go 8 miles east on US60. Turn left (north) between mileposts 204 and 205 onto Peralta Road (also named Peralta Trail and FR77). Continue 6.2 miles on Peralta Road to an unsigned parking area on the left (west) side of Peralta Road. Carney Springs Trailhead is at the cable barricade across the former Carney Springs Road.

FINDING THE TRAILHEAD

Carney Springs Trailhead (N33° 23' 08.8", W111° 21' 45.0") is about 1 mile south on FR77 from the cattle guard near Peralta Trailhead parking lot.

FACILITIES

No facilities are here. Bring your own water.

THE TRAILS

From the Carney Springs Trailhead [5-CC], the Carney Trail begins at the open gate in the cable barrier on the west side of the parking area. Carney Springs Road was permanently closed to vehicle traffic on June 17, 2006. Hikers and horse riders can still use the Carney Trail on the south side of the former roadbed. No trailhead signs are posted here.

From the Carney Springs Trailhead, go northwest on the Carney Trail for 0.6 mile, on the south side of the old roadbed, to the Superstition Wilderness boundary fence. The West Boulder Trail begins at the gate [5-SS] in the barbed-wire fence, heads northwest toward the mountain, and reaches West Boulder Saddle in 1.8 miles. Continuing on the Superstition Mountain Ridgeline Trail takes you to Lost Dutchman State Park for a total of 10.5 miles.

From West Boulder Trail gate, Lost Goldmine Trail (60) goes east and west following the south side of the Wilderness fence. Mileages from Carney

Springs Trailhead using Trail 60 are 1.7 miles going east to Dons Camp Trailhead [5-DD] and 4.7 miles going west to Hieroglyphic Trailhead [12-A].

HISTORY AND LEGENDS

The Carney Springs area was named for Peter G. Carney, who began development of the Carney Mine in the Lava Cliffs (now named the Dacite Cliffs) in 1907. Ogden H. Bowers, a wool manufacturer from New York City, financed the venture. Initially, the camp was named after him—Camp Bowers. Mr. Bowers must have withdrawn his support by 1911 because Pete Carney formed the Carney Mines Development Company and sold stock in the company. The name Camp Bowers was dropped, and the site became known as Camp Carney. Carney, who was the majority stockholder, promoted his company to many mining people in Mesa, Ray, and Miami.[152]

Because access to the Carney Mine was important for promotional purposes, Carney employed his workmen to build a new road from Tom Buchanan's Ranch in 1908. This new route cut off 7 miles. At times, Carney Camp had stage service, but mostly visitors and investors traveled to the mine by automobile.[153]

Reports of a free-gold vein in his copper mine helped sell stock, which provided funds to pay workmen and suppliers. In 1912, to speed up the tunnel work, Carney installed an Ingersoll compressor and power drills that increased the progress in the main tunnel to 8 or 10 feet per day. In November 1912, preparations were being made to ship ore to the Hayden smelter—the only mention over the years of ore shipments.[154]

By October 1913, work was at a low point with only watchman Murphy on duty. Then on February 3, 1914, at 8:10 p.m., two explosions set by "unknown miscreants" destroyed the compressor and magazine that had been placed in the mouth of the mine. Pete Carney's wife, Rebecca, and her two children and niece left Camp Carney and rushed over to the Barkley Ranch for their safety. Tex Barkley went into Mesa to report the incident. Pete Carney was in Ray on business, but he and Pinal County Sheriff McGee came up to the mine the next day.[155]

In 1915, some men were at work on the Carney Mine, but operations must have been in decline since no shipments were noted in the newspapers. A claim of $702.07 by Jack Lander against the Carney Mining Company signaled the end of the Carney Mine era, when the June 1917 Sheriff's sale disposed of the seventeen mining claims, materials, and equipment.[156]

Peter Carney died at the Veterans Hospital near Prescott, Arizona, on March 13, 1924, at age fifty-nine. He held the rank of second lieutenant in the army and is buried in the Prescott National Cemetery (Whipple Cemetery).[157]

SUPERSTITION WILDERNESS TRAILS WEST

Matt Cavaness wrote in his memoirs that a Maricopa Indian gave him directions to a spring near the Superstition Mountains that would be good for a cattle ranch. About 1876, he found the spring and hired men to run pipes 300 feet down the slope and to build a corral and water trough. We think his spring was the present-day Carney Spring. Cavaness had about one thousand head of cattle on the range.[158]

Interest in the water rights near the Marlow Ranch (present-day Quarter Circle U Ranch) at the beginning of the summer in 1891 seemed to be high. George Marlow had died the year before, and his estate was being sold. In 1891, when Jim Bark, Frank Criswell, and J. L. Powell purchased the Marlow Ranch, they filed water rights claims on several springs south and west of the Quarter Circle U Ranch, but we have not found their claim for the Carney Spring (Criswell Spring).[159] Maybe the Carney Spring was considered part of the Bark and Criswell range and they did not realize they needed to file a separate water claim.

On June 27, 1912, Thomas Buchanan and William A. Barkley filed their claim on the Criswell Spring (now named Carney Spring). They said that the spring had been used for more than fifteen years on the cattle ranch, which indicates that they were trying to establish prior rights to the water. The spring was described as being 2.5 miles northwest of the Quarter Circle U Ranch. As the crow flies, we measured the distance on the map as 2 miles.[160] See the History and Legends section of Upper La Barge Area on page 153 for other water rights that were filed—John Lebarge and Mary Charlebois filed 3 miles southwest of the Marlow ranch house in 1891.

Jimmie Jinks, U. S. Bureau of Mines, assayed the Upper Carney Mine vein in 1980 and found 0.01 ounces of gold per ton, 0.9 ounces of silver per ton, 1.3 percent copper, and 1.5 percent lead. Although not common, this example of a mineral-bearing vein in volcanic dacite fuels the hopes and dreams of many prospectors for finding the Lost Dutchman Gold Mine in the Superstitions.[161] Dacite (pronounced "day-site") is a fine-grained igneous rock formed when the molten rock material, from volcanic activity, crystallizes on the earth's surface.

The abandoned Carney Mine (aka Dacite Mine) has been home to five species of bats including the Townsend's big-eared and California leaf-nosed bats—both considered special status species by the Arizona Game and Fish Department. The Townsend's big-eared bat is also on the Regional Forester's sensitive species list. In 2010, the Tonto National Forest closed the lower Dacite Mine to the public to protect the bat roost site within the mine. A steel entrance barrier allows bat access, but prevents access by hikers and other visitors. The killing of 89 Mexican free-tail bats in 2009 at the mine prompted the closure. Those nectar-feeding bats pollinate cacti and agaves and eat mosquitoes so it is important to provide a safe roosting site for them.[162]

WEST BOULDER SADDLE

This is a pleasant but steep trail that is less traveled than the nearby Peralta Canyon Trail. The trail passes Carney Spring and leads to West Boulder Saddle where you have good views of the north side of Superstition Mountain and West Boulder Canyon.

ITINERARY

From the Carney Springs Trailhead, follow Carney Trail and West Boulder Trail to the saddle with West Boulder Canyon. Return by the same route, or continue with either Trip 28 (Superstition Mountain Ridgeline) or Trip 29 (Dacite Mesa Loop).

DIFFICULTY

Moderate hike. Not doable by horses after the first 1.1 miles. Elevation change is +1,480 feet.

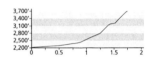

LENGTH and TIME

1.8 miles, 2+ hours one way.

MAPS

Arizona USGS topo map NAD27: Weavers Needle. Superstition Wilderness Beartooth map, grid G15. Map 12.

FINDING THE TRAIL

See the trailhead map on page 167. From the west side of the Carney Springs Trailhead, the trip starts on the Carney Trail at the opening in the parking lot barrier [12-CC, 0] (N33° 23' 08.8", W111° 22' 45.0") and connects with the West Boulder Trail at the Wilderness boundary gate [12-SS, 0.6] (N33° 23' 35.9", W111° 21' 01.4").

THE TRIP

Start on Map 12 on page 163. From Carney Springs Trailhead [12-CC, 0], take the Carney Trail (formerly the Carney Springs Road) 0.6 mile to the Wilderness boundary gate [12-SS, 0.6]. Just south of the gate the Lost Goldmine Trail, which is described in Trip 30 on page 184, goes east and west

View looking southeast down the West Boulder Trail toward Carney Springs Trailhead [12-CC].
Peralta Road is snaking across the flat desert in the upper part of the photograph. April 2010 photo.

on the south side of the Wilderness boundary fence. The West Boulder Trail starts at the Wilderness gate in the barbed wire fence and heads north.

Five minutes north of the boundary gate on the West Boulder Trail a rock cairn marks the trail junction (N33° 23' 43.6", W111° 22' 04.1") with the Wave Cave Trail, which heads northwest. From this junction, the Wave Cave (aka Apache Kid Cave) can be seen in the cliff to the northwest. The rock formation in the entrance of the cave resembles a giant wave. From the Carney Springs Trailhead, it is 1.4 miles with an elevation gain of 900 feet to the Wave Cave (N33° 24' 06.1", W111° 22' 34.3"). The last portion of the Wave Cave Trail is steep with slick rock so the trail is not suitable for horses.

Continuing on the West Boulder Saddle trip from the trail junction, the West Boulder Trail goes directly north. The trail can be difficult to follow through the trees, but it is always worth the extra effort to stay on the trail as it eventually turns northwest and works its way into Carney Springs Canyon. Fifteen minutes up the trail from the boundary gate, you'll see remnants of digging and cement footings along the trail. A fountain-like rock structure (no water) marks the former picnic area at the end of the iron pipe from Carney Spring. The concrete slabs once supported picnic tables.[163] Access to Carney Spring on the west hillside is difficult, so don't count on it for water.

The iron pipe from Carney Spring is sometimes visible along the left side of the trail. This pipe is a good guide for following the faint and sometimes overgrown trail. The trail turns northwest into Carney Springs Canyon at mile 1.1 and stays on the left (west) side of the canyon. This is the turn-around point for horse riders. Because some portions of the remaining trail have a 65 percent grade, we imagine that this was never used as a horse trail.

At mile 1.3, a large ravine comes in from the left. Here is where the trail leaves Carney Springs Canyon and follows the left side of this ravine to the northwest. The topography tends to make you head into the ravine on your right. If you lose the trail, look to your left, and you will usually see a rock cairn marking the trail. The general direction of the trail is up. Staying on the trail is fairly easy because the terrain is so rugged you can't go far without it. The trail becomes more obvious as it ascends to the first saddle.

You reach an intermediate saddle at mile 1.4 where you can catch your breath. After a short descent, the trail resumes its uphill trend. At West Boulder Saddle [12-TT, 1.8], you have a nice view down into West Boulder Canyon and the back slopes of the Superstition Mountain.

For a short optional trip from West Boulder Saddle, follow a well-worn trail to the left (west) for 0.1 mile to the 1919 brass survey marker [12-UU, 1.9]. Look for a short pipe in the ground on the right side of the trail. Return by the same route, or continue with Trip 28 (Superstition Mountain Ridgeline) on page 173, or Trip 29 (Dacite Mesa Loop) on page 180.

SUPERSTITION MOUNTAIN RIDGELINE

This is a very demanding trip that rewards energetic hikers with fine views from the crest of Superstition Mountain. A trail-of-use weaves its way across the rocky ridgeline where it is easy to find solitude among the hoodoos.

ITINERARY

From the Carney Springs Trailhead, follow Carney Trail and West Boulder Trail to the saddle with West Boulder Canyon. Follow the trail-of-use across the Superstition Mountain ridgeline all the way to Siphon Draw. Connect with the trail down Siphon Draw, and end at Lost Dutchman State Park.

DIFFICULTY

Very difficult hike. Not doable by horses. Elevation change is +4,000 and -4,140 feet.

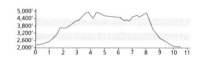

LENGTH and TIME

10.5 miles, 10 hours one way. Caution, some hikers require 17 hours or more to complete this hike. Vehicle shuttle is 20 miles one way.

MAPS

Arizona USGS topo maps NAD27: Weavers Needle and Goldfield. Superstition Wilderness Beartooth map, grids G15 to C13. Maps 12, 13, 14, 17, and 19.

FINDING THE TRAIL

See the trailhead map on page 167. From the Carney Springs Trailhead (N33° 23′ 08.8″, W111° 21′ 45.0″) on Peralta Road, the Carney Trail follows the former Carney Springs Road and connects with West Boulder Trail at the Wilderness boundary gate.

THE TRIP

Start on Map 12 on page 163. The route finding will be much easier if you use the detailed Goldfield, Arizona, USGS topographic map and follow the elevation benchmarks printed on that map. Since this is a one-way hike, park a shuttle vehicle at the Lost Dutchman State Park [19-K]. See Trip 37 (Siphon

Draw Trail) on page 215 and the Lost Dutchman State Park Trailheads on page 210 for more information. If you can't arrange a shuttle, you could do an up-and-back trip to Peak 5057.

This trip is quite different from most other hikes in the western Superstition Wilderness. The high altitude changes the local weather patterns. Rain, hail, sleet, and low clouds are always a possibility. Always be prepared for rain and wind. Make sure all the hikers in your party are capable of a sustained 10-hour strenuous hike. Carry your own water, and be sure to have some energy food in your lunch.

Begin at the Carney Springs Trailhead [12-CC, 0, 2220], and follow Carney Trail to the Wilderness boundary gate [12-SS, 0.6, 2330], where the West Boulder Trail leads you to West Boulder Saddle [12-TT, 1.8]. Follow the Trip 27 (West Boulder Saddle) description on page 170 for the first 1.8 miles.

At West Boulder Saddle [12-TT, 1.8, 3700], you have an exceptional view down into West Boulder Canyon and of the back slopes of Superstition Mountain. From the saddle, many of the high points on the Superstition Mountain ridgeline are in view. This is a good time to identify the peaks on your topo map.

Take the well-defined trail heading left (southwest) from the saddle to the corner-section marker at a big rock cairn [12-UU, 1.9]. The marker is a short iron post with a metal cap inscribed with General Land Office Survey 1919 (R9E/R10E S24-S19-S25-S30 T1N).

Continue in the same westerly direction along the left slope of West Boulder Canyon. The trail-of-use is marked with frequent rock cairns. After an easy stretch of trail, the trip makes an abrupt turn to the left and steeply climbs to the ridgeline [12-VV, 2.9, 4350] just northwest of Peak 4391. The highest point on the ridge is the peak [12-Z] of Superstition Mountain, 5,057 feet, which we go around on the right side (east). A well-defined trail [12-F, 3.6] on the southeast side of Peak 5057 [12-Z] leads to the peak for a 0.1 mile side trip.

See Trip 32 (Superstition Mountain Peak 5057) on page 192 for alternate routes from Hieroglyphic Trailhead to Peak 5057. The return for Trip 32 goes down Hieroglyphic Canyon on a steep trail-of-use starting from the ridgeline [12-Y, 4.3] (N33° 25' 03.1", W111° 24' 12.2"), which could be used as an alternate return using the Lost Goldmine Trail.

The trail goes around or over the peaks on the ridgeline. In a few places, the trail splits into two trails—one around the peak and the other over the top of the peak. Either trail will lead you in the correct direction.

A route down the north ridge of Old West Boulder Canyon starts near Peak 4562 and follows the dotted line on Map 14, marking the rough descent

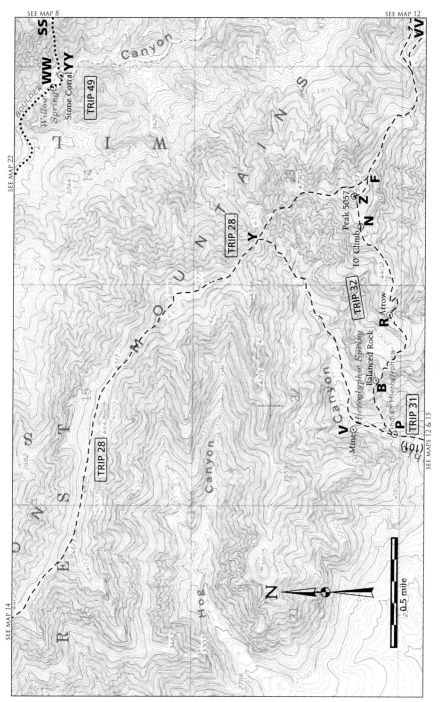

SS
WW
YY
Stone Corral
Willow Spring
BOULDER
Canyon

TRIP 49

T   I   M

3244

3426

4766

4766

4790

28

3800

3766

4700

TRIP 28

Y

4546

4660

4600

4600

511

4200

4215

3600

4200

4643

15

4400

TRIP 28

3882

3850

3862

3703

2786

2500

3805

3800

3959

Hog   Canyon

Canyon

V Canyon

Mine
Hieroglyphic Spring
Crater Hieroglyphics
Balanced Rock
B
TRIP 31
(101)
P
TRIP 32
R Arrow
S
4423
N
N
Z
Peak 5057
10' Climb
4527
F

M   O   U   N   T   A   I   N   S

R   E   S   T   S

N   0.5 mile

Map 13 – Trips 28, 31, and 32.

to Cross Butte near the head of O'Grady Canyon. See the History and Legends section of this trip for more about this route.

The only critical part of the hike is finding the descent into Siphon Draw [19-N, 8.0]. It starts down very steeply, just north of Peak 4861, but no technical climbing is necessary. We marked the correct location of the Flatiron formation on Maps 14, 17, and 19, but the location is incorrectly shown on the USGS topographical map. The Flatiron is west of Peak 4861, and it will be to the south as you descend the Siphon Draw Trail. At least one person in your party should have hiked to the top of Trip 37 (Siphon Draw Trail) to check out the landmarks at the edge of the cliff.

Take some time to stop on the ridgeline to enjoy the view to the south and north. In the north you can see the back slopes of the Superstition Mountain and the headwaters of West Boulder Canyon and First Water Creek. The Massacre Grounds are farther to the northwest. These are good places to explore where you rarely find many people.

Refer to Trip 37 (Siphon Draw Trail) on page 215 and the Lost Dutchman State Park Trailheads on page 210 for the scramble down Siphon Draw and the hike over to your shuttle vehicle [19-K, 10.5].

HISTORY AND LEGENDS

Hiking the Superstition Mountain ridgeline is fairly straightforward, but the weather can be unpredictable. On a hike across the ridgeline in 1985 with the Arizona Mountaineering Club, we were surrounded by clouds in a powerful September thunderstorm. We couldn't see more than 100 feet for about an hour. Several mule deer came up over a saddle and almost ran into us in the blinding rain storm. Both the deer and our group were surprised by the others' presence. Surrounded by thick clouds, our group had a tendency to drift off the ridgeline down into side canyons. A compass and map—before the days of the GPS—were essential in those low visibility conditions. We were lucky to have had a hike leader, Denis Duman, who knew the route from previous experience.

Tom Kollenborn, in his 1982 story "Al Senner's Lost Gold of Superstition Mountain," wrote an interesting account of a man accused of high-grading gold ore from the Mammoth Mine in Goldfield around 1894. The man, Al Senner, took revenge on the owners of the Mammoth Mine for cutting him out of the claim he helped develop. As a miner at the Mammoth, he stole gold ore each day, and then on Sunday, he would pack it up to the top of Superstition Mountain where it was cached. After he was run out of camp for his misdeeds, Senner made an attempt to remove his gold from Superstition Mountain. He died when his horse and pack animal fell off the steep cliffs. No one has ever located his cache, which is estimated to hold

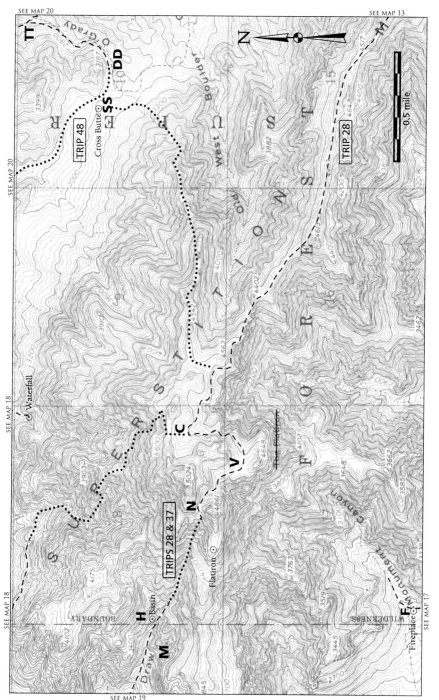

Map 14 – Trips 28, 37, and 48.

1,250 pounds of gold ore. It is worth reading the complete story, which tells of the doctor who found Senner's body. The doctor, many years later, fell in love with the woman Senner was planning to marry. Reprints are available at the Superstition Mountain Museum.[164]

Another account of Al Senner's story is given in Helen Corbin's *Senner's Gold*. Her 1993 book includes the story of Tom Kollenborn and Bob Corbin searching for Senner's cache of gold. The treasure map and Kollenborn's famous topo map will interest everyone. We hiked to the site of the three pinyon pine trees [14-V] shown on Bob Corbin's rendition of the treasure map. Two of the trees had a 12-inch trunk diameter and the third was 14 inches in diameter when we measured them in 2006. The diameters had each increased about 2 inches since our measurements in the mid 1990s.

Author Bruce Grubbs, in one of his interesting loop trips, described a route from Superstition Mountain ridge that leaves the Ridgeline Trail at Peak 4562 and goes north to the north ridge of Old West Boulder Canyon. See Map 14 on page 177. In 2008, Irv Kanode took GPS data to define that route.[165] Al Senner and modern day horse riders may have used this same route to reach the top of Superstition Mountain. Bruce Grubbs used the route that drops into Old West Boulder Canyon, but we think the horse route uses the trail in O'Grady Canyon. Irv came up O'Grady Canyon and returned via the waterfall on First Water Creek. We have seen horse tracks leading westerly out of O'Grady but lost them part way up the slopes, so we haven't traveled this route. Some people tell us that the route is a scary horse ride and that they do not recommend it for horse riders.

Another route—marked by a dotted line on Map 19—up to the Ridgeline Trail [19-C] meets the trail just east of Peak 5024. Joe Bartels made this trek by coming up from the Massacre Grounds Trail. Chris Coleman and Jesse Perlmutter used the trail behind The Hand [19-T] to approach the route up to [19-C]. All of the hikers agree that a loop in the clockwise direction with an exit down Siphon Draw is the safest way to complete the trip.[166]

Rancher Jim Bark held the grazing rights to much of the Superstition Mountains between 1891 and 1907 and always welcomed visitors to his ranch on the southeast side of the mountains. An 1899 *Arizona Daily Herald* newspaper article tells of a geological survey team that found arrowheads and other evidence of prehistoric Indians on the mountain. Later in 1899, a group of Mesa residents searched Superstition Mountain and recovered 106 arrowheads. Returning from the mountain, they stopped at Jim Bark's ranch, now the Quarter Circle U Ranch, and were surprised when Bark brought out a stash of 887 arrowheads he had recently found in an olla on Superstition Mountain. The rules have changed since those finds, and we must abide by the State and Federal laws that prohibit collecting artifacts.[167]

An account of a backpack trip across the Superstition Mountain ridgeline appeared in the Arizona Highways publication, *Outdoors in Arizona, A Guide to Hiking and Backpacking*, with photographs by John Annerino.[168]

View from the Superstition Mountain Ridgeline Trail at the spur trail [12-F] to the top of Superstition Mountain, Peak 5027 [12-Z]. The hoodoo rock formations up here are fantastic. February 2011 photo.

DACITE MESA LOOP

This rewarding loop trip takes you to the top of a 4,000-foot mesa with good views in all directions. You will enjoy the pinyon pine trees, hoodoo rock formations, and open space on top of this seldom-traveled mesa.

ITINERARY

From the Carney Springs Trailhead, follow Carney Trail and West Boulder Trail to West Boulder Saddle. Go right (northeast) on a cross-country route to Fremont Saddle. Return by the Cave Trail or Peralta Trail to Peralta Trailhead parking lot. Go south 1.3 miles on Peralta Road to your vehicle at Carney Springs Trailhead, or leave a shuttle vehicle at Peralta Trailhead.

DIFFICULTY

Difficult hike. Not doable by horses. Elevation change is ±1,950 feet.

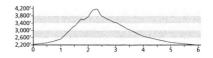

LENGTH and TIME

5.9 miles, 5 hours round-trip.

MAPS

Arizona USGS topo map NAD27: Weavers Needle. Superstition Wilderness Beartooth map, grids G15 to G14. Map 6.

FINDING THE TRAIL

See the trailhead map on page 167. The Carney Trail from the Carney Springs Trailhead [6-CC] (N33° 23′ 08.8″, W111° 21′ 45.0″) takes you 0.6 mile northwest to the Wilderness boundary fence and gate [6-SS], where you connect with the West Boulder Trail.

THE TRIP

Start on Map 6 on page 81. This is a loop hike. Depending on your hiking skills, finding a route from the top of Dacite Mesa down to Fremont Saddle could be difficult. Allow plenty of daylight for backtracking by the same route if you can't get through the maze of pinnacles and rock formations to Fremont Saddle.

Leave a shuttle vehicle at Peralta Trailhead [6-A] to shorten the trip by 1.3 miles. If you do not park a shuttle vehicle (bike or car) at Peralta Trailhead, starting at the Peralta Trailhead [6-A] or Dons Camp Trailhead [6-DD] will shorten your hike by 0.2 mile. Use the Lost Goldmine Trail from Dons Camp Trailhead to get over to the Wilderness gate [6-SS] at the start of the West Boulder Trail.

The hike begins at the Carney Springs Trailhead [6-CC, 0]. Follow the Trip 27 (West Boulder Saddle) description on page 170 for the first 1.8 miles. On the trek up to West Boulder Saddle, you will probably be thinking how distant the sculptured rock formations look on the horizon to your right (northeast). They are distant, but in about two hours, the hike will take you into this fairyland of rocks.

At West Boulder Saddle [6-TT, 1.8], the well-defined trail to the left is the Superstition Mountain Ridgeline Trail. Trip 29 goes right (northeast) following the Dacite Mesa Trail—a faint trail marked by small cairns. The Dacite Mesa Trail descends a little as it turns east into the ravine.

The trail crosses to the left (north) side of the ravine near the first pinyon pine trees. Bear right following the ravine on a trail marked by rock cairns on the left bench. Do not follow the rock cairns that head north and up the steep hillside.

Less than 10 minutes farther up the ravine, a large pinyon pine tree [6-XX, 2.0] (N33° 24′ 35.5″, W111° 22′ 05.8″) marks the location where the main ravine branches into three smaller ravines. Hike up the ravine on the left heading north. See the Alternate Robber's Roost Trail at the end of this section for a more difficult optional trip, which goes up the right ravine.

After starting up the left ravine, rock cairns mark the route, but be sure they lead you in the direction you intend to go—to Fremont Saddle. Pick your route carefully to avoid any major obstacles. Less than 10 minutes to the north, you can take a wide ravine to your right (east) and continue to the summit. Another option maintains a route north, bringing you to a ridge overlooking a drainage into West Boulder Canyon. In either case, you are pretty much on your own up here.

Your objective is to enjoy the rock pinnacles, views from the ridges, and maze of rock formations. Leave time for exploring and for working your way northeast toward Fremont Saddle. Spend some time exploring the ridge to the north since the interesting part of the hike is over once you drop down to Fremont Saddle [6-D, 2.5, 3766]. If you can see Weavers Needle, that is a good landmark—Fremont Saddle is south of Weavers Needle.

When you find a route through the ridgeline rocks to the Peralta or East Boulder side of the ridge, you will be able to see a direct scramble to Fremont Saddle. If you can't see a direct scramble to Fremont Saddle, you may "cliff-out," which requires you to climb back up to the top. Never descend anything that you can't easily climb back up. Try to descend the slope so you end up behind the rock formation at the west side of Fremont Saddle (on the USGS Weavers Needle topo map aim for the "e" in Saddle). The scramble from the ridge to Fremont Saddle might take about 25 minutes since it is steep and rocky (no technical climbing is necessary). Loose rocks on the scramble to the saddle make this route very hazardous. Be careful.

From Fremont Saddle [6-D, 2.5], the hike proceeds down the Peralta Trail to the Peralta Trailhead parking lot [6-A, 4.6]. If you did not park a shuttle car at Peralta Trailhead parking lot, hike southwest on Peralta Road for 1.3 miles to Carney Springs Trailhead, where the trip ends [6-CC, 5.9].

Or, from Fremont Saddle [6-D, 2.5], take the alternate Cave Trail to the parking lot [6-A, 5.0]. See Trip 6 (Fremont Saddle) on page 78 and Trip 7 (Cave Trail) on page 82 for a description of those trails.

ALTERNATE ROBBER'S ROOST TRAIL[169]

From the pinyon pine tree [6-XX, 2.0], which is near the location where the main ravine branches into three smaller ravines, take the right ravine and follow a cairned trail that we named the Robber's Roost Trail. It starts in the bed of the right ravine (N33° 24' 35.7", W111° 22' 04.2") and heads east going up the right (south) side of the ravine. The trail is easy to follow.

When you top out at mile 2.3, an impressive rock formation (N33° 24' 33.0", W111° 21' 50.7"), named the Chimney, rises on your left. This is a good place to take a rest and prepare yourself for the next segment of cross-country travel to Robber's Roost, which is poorly marked on the ground.

Sporadic rock cairns lead you east toward a green-lichen-covered boulder. From a rock cairn (N33° 24' 28.5", W111° 21' 47.1") on the west side of a flat that is overgrown with dense catclaw, skirt the catclaw to the right (south), and head east. Look to your right (south) for a pointer rock-cairn on top of a very tall boulder (N33° 24' 26.7", W111° 21' 44.4"). From the pointer rock, head east, follow traces of other hikers, and scramble about 100 or 200 feet down a congested area filled with boulders and vegetation to another rock cairn (N33° 24' 27.2", W111° 21' 43.1"). Continue east, bear right on well-trampled ground, and circle a large boulder until you descend to the basin of Robber's Roost at mile 2.5. You will know you are in Robber's Roost Basin when you see Boy Scout names and dates written on the walls— please do not add any more.

Retrace your steps out of Robber's Roost basin, and head north to connect with the Robber's Roost Trail (N33° 24' 30.5", W111° 21' 45.4") where it rounds the point below the hoodoo cliffs with yellow-green lichen. If you did not want to check out Robber's Roost, you could go directly from the Chimney to the above GPS location, which will keep you on the trail.

Rock cairns lead you easterly across the bedrock to a rock formation that looks like a Lizard Head (N33° 24′ 31.7″, W111° 21′ 38.1″) at mile 2.8. From the Lizard Head, go over the pass in a northerly direction, where you get your first view of Weavers Needle. Intermittent rock cairns and a few signs of a trail guide you northwesterly toward Fremont Saddle—with the hoodoo cliffs on the left (west) and Peralta Canyon on the right (east). Your course will take you to the large boulders (N33° 24′ 55.0″, W111° 21′ 52.9″) behind Fremont Saddle. Don't try to descend to the Peralta Trail before you get to Fremont Saddle. You will cliff-out and have to climb back up the slope.

From Fremont Saddle [6-D, 3.3], return to Peralta Trailhead using the Peralta Trail [6-A, 5.4] or the Cave Trail [6-A, 5.8]. If you did not place a shuttle vehicle at the trailhead, you need to hike southwest on Peralta Road for 1.3 miles to Carney Springs Trailhead [6-CC], where the trip ends.

Dick Walp is standing near the Chimney on the Robber's Roost Trail. Rock cairns mark the way across the slick rock between the hoodoos. April 2010 photo.

LOST GOLDMINE TRAIL
FROM CARNEY SPRINGS TRAILHEAD

This scenic trail, which is just outside the Superstition Wilderness boundary, provides access to the southern canyons of Superstition Mountain. Hikers, horse riders, and bicycle riders will be able to get close to the mountain through any of the four major trailheads.

ITINERARY

From the Carney Springs Trailhead, follow the Carney Trail northwest to the West Boulder Trail gate at the Wilderness boundary fence. Go east to Dons Camp Trailhead and Peralta Trailhead or west to Hieroglyphic Trailhead and Broadway Trailhead. Return by the same route, or make a vehicle shuttle trip.

DIFFICULTY

Easy hike. Moderate ride.
Elevation change is +610
and -950 feet to [16-Q].

LENGTH and TIME

Going east to Dons Camp Trailhead, 1.7 miles [5-DD], 1 hour one way.

Going east to Peralta Trailhead, 2.3 miles [5-A], 1.5 hours one way.

Going west to Hieroglyphic Trailhead [12-A], 4.7 miles, 2.5 hours one way.

Going west to Broadway Trailhead [16-Q], 9.2 miles, 5 hours one way.

MAPS

Arizona USGS topo maps NAD27: Weavers Needle and Goldfield. Superstition Wilderness Beartooth map, grids G15 to E15. Maps 5, 12, and 16.

FINDING THE TRAIL

See the trailhead map on page 167. Start at the unsigned Carney Springs Trailhead [5-CC] (N33° 23' 08.8", W111° 21' 45.0"), and follow Carney Trail 0.6 mile to the Wilderness fence [12-SS]. The Lost Goldmine Trail goes east and west along the south side of the Superstition Wilderness boundary fence.

THE TRIP GOING WEST

Start on Map 12 on page 163. We consider the Lost Goldmine Trail going west from West Boulder Trail gate [12-SS] to Hieroglyphic Trailhead [12-A] the most scenic length of the Lost Goldmine Trail. The Lost Goldmine Trail is always a good choice for a trip when you want to show visitors the beauty of the Sonoran Desert.

From the Carney Springs Trailhead [12-CC, 0], take the Carney Trail 0.6 mile to the West Boulder Trail gate [12-SS, 0.6] at the Wilderness boundary fence. The Lost Goldmine Trail follows the south side of the barbed-wire fence going east and west.

Go left (west) from the gate [12-SS, 0.6]. With the barbed-wire fence on your right, the first landmark on the Lost Goldmine Trail is a green livestock gate [12-X, 1.0]. The fence and gate divide two cattle-grazing allotments on Arizona State Trust land. The east side of the fence is leased by the Quarter Circle U Ranch, which brands the Soap Pot, and the allotment on the west side is leased to Donnelly's Stables, which brands the D-Spur. Be sure to close the livestock gate. The brass-cap section marker is located a few feet to the right (north) of the gate and is dated 1917, when the survey was made.

A gate [12-M, 1.1] in the barbed-wire Wilderness fence on the right (north) provides access to a small mine adit nearby. A faint trail leads to the adit, but bushwhacking is required to reach the mine dump that you can see from the gate. It is named the Green Door Mine because of some green-painted wood inside the mine—there is no door!

Farther up the canyon from the Green Door Mine adit is a large cave named the Wave Cave (aka Apache Kid Cave). Some game trails head toward the cave, but there is no continuous trail from this Wilderness gate [12-M].[170] If you want to visit the Wave Cave, the easiest approach is from the Carney Springs Trailhead [12-CC]. See page 172 for a short paragraph describing the Wave Cave Trail. This approach to the Wave Cave enters the Wilderness at the boundary gate [12-SS] on the West Boulder Trail.

After meandering away from the Wilderness fence to bypass a hill, the Lost Goldmine Trail passes through a large stand of saguaro cacti [12-S, 1.5], a good spot to photograph saguaros. The rocky cliffs form a picturesque background.

Mushroom Rock, to the right (north), can be seen from the Lost Goldmine Trail [12-H, 1.9] just below the cliffs. It is a 0.5 mile bushwhack (no trail) up the slopes to the base of Mushroom Rock. Following the low ridges makes the bushwhacking easier since some of the washes are clogged with vegetation.

The trail turns south as it detours around the butte that is locally called Turks Cap. Just before the trail resumes its westerly direction, you will see Indian Rock [12-I, 2.3] on your left (east). Within a hundred feet of the trail, look for bedrock grind holes in the rocks between the trail and the wash to the east. Prehistoric people made and used these holes in the rock to grind beans and corn by hand.[171]

The Lost Goldmine Trail continues to skirt the south side of Turks Cap, crosses Dromedary Wash [12-J, 3.0], and climbs the hill toward the Wilderness fence where the trail levels off again. Quicksilver Draw [12-K, 3.7] is the next landmark, and the trail soon follows the fence, except for some detours around small washes and hills.

The trail turns south as it approaches a ridge and a signed trail to Hieroglyphic Canyon [12-T, 4.6]. It is 1.3 miles going right (north) to the petroglyphs [12-P] in Hieroglyphic Canyon. You can see Hieroglyphic Trailhead from the trail junction, and it is only a short distance down the hill to the parking lot [12-A, 4.7] at the east end of Cloudview Avenue.

From the Hieroglyphic Trailhead parking lot [12-A, 4.7], the Lost Goldmine Trail follows Cloudview Avenue west and eventually takes you to Broadway Trailhead [16-Q, 9.2]. Return the same way, or make a vehicle shuttle to any of the trailheads.

THE TRIP GOING EAST

Start on Map 5 on page 77. The Lost Goldmine Trail going east is much shorter than the portion going west. The eastern part of the trail is useful for making loop trips connecting with Peralta Trailhead.

Starting from the Carney Springs Trailhead [5-CC, 0.0] on Peralta Road, take the Carney Trail 0.6 mile to the Wilderness boundary fence [5-SS, 0.6], where the Lost Goldmine trail parallels the south side of the barbed-wire fence. Heading right (east), the Lost Goldmine Trail crosses an unsigned road in 0.3 mile where you can go right (south) to the Carney Trail in 0.3 mile.

Most people end their trip at the kiosk for Dons Camp Trailhead [5-DD, 1.7] in the large parking area, but the official end of the Lost Goldmine Trail is on Peralta Road at the cattle guard on FR77 [5-NN, 1.9], which is the Tonto National Forest's southern boundary. We named the end of the trail here the Peralta Road Access.

From the cattle guard, you can continue north, up FR77, to the Peralta Trailhead [5-A, 2.3], connecting with the Peralta Trail (102), Dutchman's Trail (104), and nearby Bluff Spring Trail (235). Going south on Peralta Road from the cattle guard on FR77 [5-NN, 1.9] takes you 0.9 mile back to Carney Springs Trailhead [5-CC, 2.8] to complete the loop.

HIEROGLYPHIC TRAILHEAD

From Apache Junction at Idaho Road, go east on US60 about 6 miles to Gold Canyon. Between mileposts 202 and 203, turn left (northeast) onto Kings Ranch Road, go 2.8 miles to Broadway Avenue, and take local roads 1.2 miles to Cloudview Avenue and the parking area. Hieroglyphic Trailhead is also named Cloudview Trailhead and Kings Trailhead.

FINDING THE TRAILHEAD

The GPS for the trailhead is (N33° 23' 23.2", W111° 25' 26.0"). From Kings Ranch Road and Baseline Avenue, turn right on Baseline Avenue and drive 0.25 mile. Go left (north) on Mohican Road for 0.3 mile, then left (west) on Valleyview Road. Valleyview Road meanders north-northwest, connecting

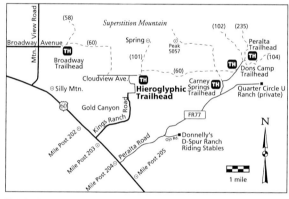

with Whitetail Road, which meets Cloudview Avenue. Go right (east) on Cloudview Avenue to the parking lot at the end of the road.

FACILITIES

No facilities are here. Bring your own water.

THE TRAILS

Only the Lost Goldmine Trail starts from the Hieroglyphic Trailhead [15-A] (N33° 23' 23.2", W111° 25' 26.0"). The Lost Goldmine Trail (60) runs east and west through Hieroglyphic Trailhead. Going east from the kiosk, the Lost Goldmine Trail connects with Hieroglyphic Trail (101) within 0.1 mile [15-T], which takes you to the petroglyphs [15-P] in 1.4 miles. Continuing east on the Lost Goldmine Trail brings you to the Dons Camp Trailhead [5-DD] in 5.2 miles. The trail ends at the cattle guard and Forest boundary on Peralta Road [5-NN] in 5.4 miles—near Peralta Trailhead [5-A, 5.8].

Heading west from the kiosk [16-A], Lost Goldmine Trail follows Cloudview Avenue, meanders on easements across private property and Arizona State Trust land, and ends at the Jacob's Crosscut Trail (58) [16-R] in 3.9 miles and connects with Broadway Trailhead [16-Q] in 4.5 miles.

HISTORY AND LEGENDS

The Lost Goldmine Trail, completed in 2001, is managed by Pinal County and is open for public use by hikers, horse riders, and bicycle riders. Pinal County, under the direction of Supervisor Sandie Smith, obtained the right-of-way easements across Arizona State Trust land, private property, and existing county roadways to provide a continuous trail. The Superstition Area Land Trust, under the direction of Rosemary Shearer, was the lead organization coordinating the volunteers and other groups that performed the trail design and construction.

Author and historian Tom Kollenborn reports that Hieroglyphic Canyon was called Apache Springs Canyon before 1930. Kings Mountain was named after early land owners William and Emma King and later changed to Silly Mountain by Bud Elrod. Kings Ranch Resort, formerly known as the Shadows at Kings Ranch, is named for Julian and Lucy King, who established the ranch in 1947. Julian King, in his memoirs, wrote a very interesting account of life on the slopes of Superstition Mountain in the 1940s. His story is told in the book *Sand in Our Shoes*. See the Ranching and Tourism section on page 29 for more about the early landowners.[172]

Hieroglyphic Canyon is a misnomer. The carvings and line drawings on the rock are actually petroglyphs, dated by most archeologists from A.D. 700 to A.D. 1100 during Hohokam habitation. Hieroglyphic Canyon was listed on the National Register of Historic Places in April of 1994.

Petroglyphs in Hieroglyphic Canyon [15-P]. This prehistoric rock art was carved on the cliffs more than eight hundred years ago.

HIEROGLYPHIC TRAIL

Everyone will enjoy the easy trip up to this special area with many Indian petroglyphs and pools of seasonal water. The trail follows a ridgeline, which offers good views in all directions.

ITINERARY

From the parking area, follow the Lost Goldmine Trail to the ridge and a wide track leading to the Wilderness boundary gate. Trail 101 begins at the gate and ends at the petroglyphs. Return by the same route.

DIFFICULTY

Easy hike. Moderate ride.
Elevation change is +600 feet.

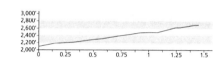

LENGTH and TIME

1.4 miles, 1.0 hour one way.

MAPS

Arizona USGS topo map NAD27: Goldfield. Superstition Wilderness Beartooth map, grid E15. Maps 12 and 15.

FINDING THE TRAIL

See the trailhead map on page 187. Start on the Lost Goldmine Trail at the kiosk on the north side of the parking lot (N33° 23′ 23.2″, W111° 25′ 26.0″).

THE TRIP

Start on Map 15 on page 191. This is a nice trip for visitors who are new to the area—much variety and something interesting to see at the trip's destination. The surrounding desert abounds with different kinds of healthy vegetation: jumping cholla, saguaro, palo verde, jojoba, brittlebush, bursage—visitors will see a lot of green here. The views are good, both going up and back.

The trip starts on the Lost Goldmine Trail at the kiosk on the north end of the parking lot [15-A, 0] and heads up a slope to intersect with a wide trail on the ridge [15-T, 0.1]. At the signed trail intersection [15-T], bear left (north), and continue to the Wilderness gate [15-U, 0.4].

Be sure to close the Wilderness boundary gate [15-U] at the start of the Hieroglyphic Canyon Trail (101). The trail follows an old road across the top of the ridge where large patches of wildflowers bloom. Near the end of the trail, take note of the large bedrock mortars (grinding holes) in a boulder right on the trail. Prehistoric people made these holes and used them to grind plants for food preparation.

A short distance beyond the bedrock mortars, look for the petroglyphs on the cliff face across the wash on an east-facing wall [15-P, 1.4]. The smooth bedrock in the wash catches seasonal rains. The small pools often have water, but they can go dry. Down the wash (south) about 200 yards on the west side, another cliff face displays more petroglyphs. The trip returns by the same route to the parking area [15-A, 2.8].

Continue up Hieroglyphic Canyon as far as you like before returning. Beyond the petroglyphs [12-P, 1.4], the trail stays on the right (east) bench of the canyon and does not go in the wash. A separate trail heads toward the wash and the filled-in mine shaft [12-V, 1.7] beside the wash.

To go up to the Superstition Ridgeline Trail [12-Y, 3.4, 4350] (N33° 25' 03.1", W111° 24' 12.2"), stay out of the wash and follow the trail-of-use on the right bench. See Trip 32 (Superstition Mountain Peak 5057) for a loop trip to the summit of the mountain and a return down Hieroglyphic Canyon.

Hieroglyphic Canyon petroglyph site [15-P]. The large panels of petroglyphs are on the left (west) side of the canyon off the left side of the photograph. February 2011 photo.

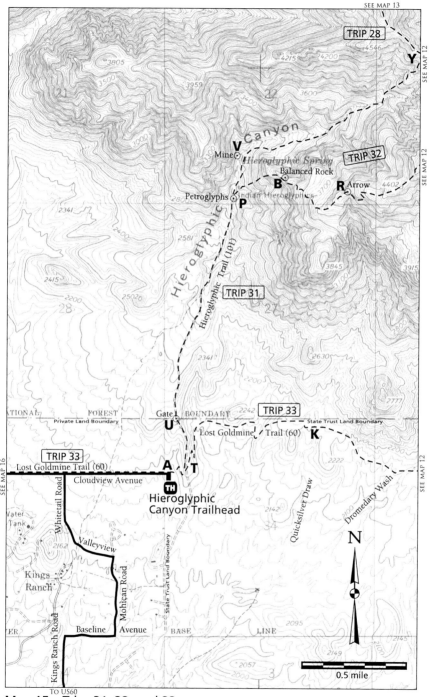

TRIP 28

Y

SEE MAP 12

SEE MAP 12

V
Mine

Hieroglyphic Spring

TRIP 32

Balanced Rock

B

R Arrow

Petroglyphs

Indian Hieroglyphics

P

Hieroglyphic Canyon

Hieroglyphic Trail (101)

TRIP 31

NATIONAL   FOREST
Private Land Boundary

Gate BOUNDARY

TRIP 33

State Trust Land Boundary

U

T

Lost Goldmine   Trail (60)

K

SEE MAP 16

TRIP 33
Lost Goldmine Trail (60)

A
T

Cloudview Avenue

TH

Hieroglyphic
Canyon Trailhead

Whitetail Road

Valleyview

Water
Tank

Kings
Ranch

Mohican Road

State Trust Land Boundary

Quicksilver Draw

Dromedary Wash

N

SEE MAP 12

Kings Ranch Road

Baseline   Avenue

BASE   LINE

TO US60

0.5 mile

Map 15 – Trips 31, 32, and 33.

SUPERSTITION MOUNTAIN PEAK 5057

The high point on Superstition Mountain, Peak 5057 provides scenic vistas of the mountains to the north and east as well as the city to the south and west. This challenging trek will test your endurance and navigation skills.

ITINERARY

From the Hieroglyphic Trailhead parking area, follow the trail to the petroglyphs in Hieroglyphic Canyon. Take the trail-of-use up the mountain to Peak 5057. Loop down Hieroglyphic Canyon or return the same way.

DIFFICULTY

Very difficult hike. Not doable by horses. Elevation change is ±3,040 feet.

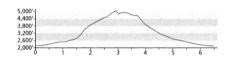

LENGTH and TIME

6.5 miles, 8 hours round-trip. Subtract 1 hour and 0.7 mile if you return the same way from Peak 5057.

MAPS

Arizona USGS topo map NAD27: Goldfield. Superstition Wilderness Beartooth map, grid E14. Map 12.

FINDING THE TRAIL

See the trailhead map on page 187. Start at the kiosk for the Lost Goldmine Trail on the north side of the Hieroglyphic Trailhead parking lot (N33° 23′ 23.2″, W111° 25′ 26.0″).

THE TRIP

This trip is for experienced hikers with some climbing ability. The trail-of-use contours along exposed cliffs, and a ten-foot-high technical climb (rated 5.1) [12-N] near the summit is required.

Start on Map 12 on page 162. From the Hieroglyphic Trailhead parking lot [12-A, 0], follow Trip 31 (Hieroglyphic Trail) to the petroglyphs [12-P, 1.4] in Hieroglyphic Canyon.

Start of route to Peak 5057 on Superstition Mountain. The landmarks on the horizon are (left to right); small hill to the north, saddle behind the hill, boulder speckled with holes sitting up high, and Balanced Rock [12-B]. The faint trail starts on the right side of the photo near the cholla cactus. Photo taken in February 2011 at the petroglyph site [12-P] in Hieroglyphic Canyon.

From the petroglyph site [12-P, 1.4], locate a large boulder, speckled with small holes. The boulder sits up high on the right (east) side of the canyon. From the south side of this boulder, a trail—not marked very well— heads northeast up to a saddle (N33° 24′ 31.4″, W111° 25′ 06.1″) behind the small hill to the north. At the saddle, a trail heading east is marked with rock cairns. Within 100 feet east of the saddle, you will see a petroglyph of a four-legged animal on a flat boulder, which will confirm that you are on the correct trail. Balanced Rock [12-B] will be on the horizon directly to the east.

Follow the rock cairns up the steep slope, go up a rock field, and contour to the right (south) along the cliff below the Balanced Rock [12-B, 1.8]. The cairned trail comes up onto a flat area (N33° 24′ 32.0″, W111° 24′ 51.1″) above and to the south of the Balanced Rock. You go near, but not next to, the Balanced Rock. Although not appropriate in a Wilderness area, white and red dots painted on the rocks guide you through the cliffy sections of the trail.

Below a high cliff, a painted white arrow [12-R, 2.2] (N33° 24′ 30.3″, W111° 24′ 33.7″) signals a right turn where the trail goes downhill, hugs the right side of the cliff, and contours east to a steep ravine. Heading up the steep ravine brings you to a field of hoodoo rocks and the open ridge.

An easy 10-foot technical rock climb (rated 5.1) up a narrow chute in the cliff [12-N, 2.8, 4780] (N33° 24′ 37.6″, W111° 24′ 08.9″) may deter some people due to the exposure on the cliff. From the top of the climb, the rock cairns become scarce, but you can see Peak 5057 straight uphill. As you near the peak, bear to the right (east), look for rock cairns, and approach the summit [12-Z, 2.9, 5057] (N33° 24′ 39.4″, W111° 24′ 00.3″) from the east. Look for the three metal survey markers and a sign-in register at the top. Return the same way from Peak 5057 to the parking lot [12-A, 5.8].

If you decide to return on the more rugged route down Hieroglyphic Canyon, descend from Peak 5057 to the southeast to meet the Superstition Ridgeline Trail [12-F, 3.0] (N33° 24′ 35.9″, W111° 23′ 54.5″). Go left (west) on the well-worn track of the Superstition Ridgeline Trail. The Superstition Ridgeline Trail descends to about the 4,350-foot elevation at a saddle [12-Y, 3.7] (N33° 25′ 03.1″, W111° 24′ 12.2″) where you turn left (south) and leave the Superstition Ridgeline Trail. Here you take a steep trail, marked by rock cairns, down the upper slopes of Hieroglyphic Canyon. Loose rocks make the hiking precarious, so take your time. The trail eventually leads to the left (east) bench of Hieroglyphic Canyon. You pass the petroglyph site [12-P, 5.1] and end the trip at the Hieroglyphic Trailhead parking lot [12-A, 6.5].

HISTORY AND LEGENDS

The benchmark on Peak 5057 was first established in 1899 with an aluminum tablet under a large rock cairn. The 1910 Station Recovery Report reads, "Peak is rugged, but with care, pack animals can be taken within 50 meters of top. Best approach is from Mesa via Criswell Ranch," which was probably up the West Boulder Trail from Carney Spring. Today, three metal disks are cemented into the bedrock and are marked with the dates that the bench-marks were inspected, installed, or reset. The date stamps are 1910, 1936, 1946, and 1965.[173]

Dave Hughes was the first person to bring the Peak 5057 route to our attention, after he made his February 1981 loop up Hieroglyphic Canyon and down the ridge from Peak 5057. No trails or paint dots marked the way in 1981. He said some backtracking was required to get through the cliffs on the 6.2-hour hike.[174] Local resident Larry Shearer makes the hike up and back to Peak 5057 by taking the northeast ridges—with a slightly different route through the cliffs each time. His trips take 4 hours to the summit, with a 3-hour return.[175]

In 2007, Chris Coleman field checked and took GPS data for us on both the trail in Hieroglyphic Canyon and on the ridge to Peak 5057. We used his route—the basis for Trip 32—through the cliffs and found the trail easy to follow, except at the start near the petroglyph site and near Balanced Rock.[176]

LOST GOLDMINE TRAIL
FROM HIEROGLYPHIC TRAILHEAD

The Lost Goldmine Trail extends east and west from Hieroglyphic Trailhead. It skirts the south side of Superstition Mountain providing scenic vistas of the mountain and access to trails and side canyons in the Wilderness. Since the trail is outside the Wilderness, it is open to bicyclists, hikers, and horse riders.

ITINERARY

From the Hieroglyphic Trailhead, going west takes you down Cloudview Avenue to Cloudview Access then northwest to Broadway Trailhead. Or, traveling east on the Lost Goldmine Trail takes you past the junction with the trail to Hieroglyphic Canyon and continues east to Peralta Road. Make an out-and-back or a one-way vehicle shuttle trip.

DIFFICULTY

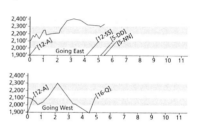

Easy hike. Moderate ride. Elevation change is +280 feet and -480 feet going west [16-Q], and +350 feet and -560 feet going east [5-DD].

LENGTH and TIME

Going east to West Boulder Trail gate [12-SS], 4.1 miles, 2.5 hours one way.

Going east to Dons Camp Trailhead [5-DD], 5.2 miles, 3.0 hours one way.

Going east to Peralta Road Access [5-NN], 5.4 miles, 3.1 hours one way.

Going west to Broadway Trailhead [16-Q], 4.5 miles, 2.5 hours one way.

MAPS

Arizona USGS topo map NAD27: Goldfield. Superstition Wilderness Beartooth map, grids E15 to C15 and E15 to G15. Maps 5, 12, and 16.

FINDING THE TRAIL

See the trailhead map on page 187. Start on the signed Lost Goldmine Trail at the north side of the Hieroglyphic Trailhead parking lot [16-A] (N33° 23′ 23.2″, W111° 25′ 26.0″).

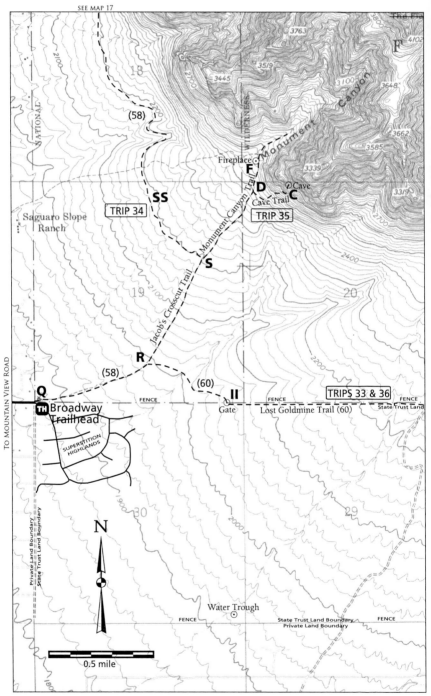

Map 16 – Trips 26, 28, 30, 31, 32, 33, 34, 35, and 36.

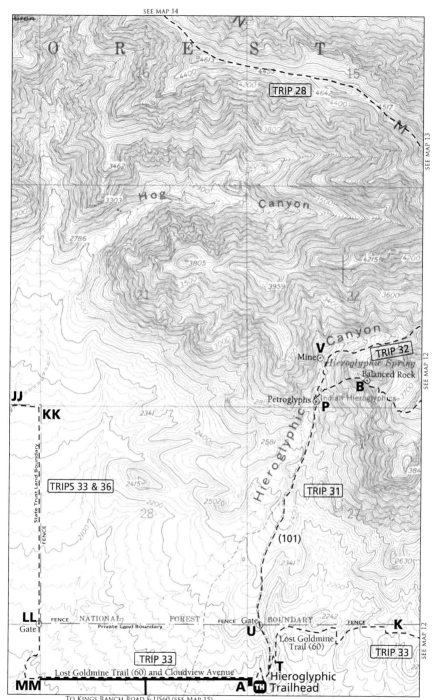

SEE MAP 14

O   R   E   S   T

N

15

TRIP 28

SEE MAP 13

Hog

Canyon

Canyon

V Mine

TRIP 32

Hieroglyphic Spring

Balanced Rock

B

Petroglyphs

Indian Hieroglyphics

P

SEE MAP 12

JJ

KK

TRIPS 33 & 36

TRIP 31

Hieroglyphic

(101)

LL
Gate

FENCE   NATIONAL   FOREST   FENCE Gate   BOUNDARY   FENCE   K

Private Land Boundary

State Trust Land Boundary
FENCE

Lost Goldmine
Trail (60)

U

TRIP 33

SEE MAP 12

TRIP 33

TRIP 33

Lost Goldmine Trail (60) and Cloudview Avenue

MM

T

Hieroglyphic
Trailhead

A TH

TO KINGS RANCH ROAD & US60 (SEE MAP 15)

Map 16 continued – Trips 26, 28, 30, 31, 32, 33, 34, 35, and 36.

Hieroglyphic Canyon Trailhead [16-A] and the Lost Goldmine Trail. February 2011 photo.

THE TRIP GOING WEST

Use Map 16 on page 197. Start on the Lost Goldmine Trail at the Hieroglyphic Trailhead parking lot [16-A, 0]. Follow the Lost Goldmine Trail going west on Cloudview Avenue, and go past Edgemore Road to the Cloudview Access [16-MM, 1.1]. The trail here is marked by a wooden sign and a large boulder. The carved map on the boulder face helps identify your location on the trail at the lower left edge of the "U."

No parking is available at Cloudview Access. The trail starts to cross private property on an easement donated by developer Harold Christ. Please stay on the trail and respect private property on either side of the trail.

At the green gate [16-LL, 1.4], the trail leaves the private property and enters Arizona State Trust land. Be sure to close the livestock gate. State Trust land is not public land, so if you wander off the trail and the 50-foot trail easement, you need to purchase a Recreational Permit from the Arizona State Land Department. The two square miles of Arizona State Trust land that the trail crosses here is part of the historic Quarter Circle U Ranch grazing lease.

The Lost Goldmine Trail follows the Wilderness boundary fence, turns west [16-KK, 2.4], and crosses the normally dry Hog Canyon Wash [16-JJ, 2.5]. Several man-made fires in recent years have burned the saguaros south of the trail, but along the Wilderness fence, large saguaros and palo verde trees make this a scenic part of the trail. At the green livestock gate

[16-II, 3.4], the Lost Goldmine Trail leaves Arizona State Trust land and enters the Tonto National Forest. Be sure to close the livestock gate.

The Lost Goldmine Trail ends at the signed junction [16-R, 3.9] with Jacob's Crosscut Trail (58). Go left (southwest) and end the trip at Broadway Trailhead [16-Q, 4.5]. Or, continue right (northeast) 5.8 miles on the Jacob's Crosscut Trail (58) to the Crosscut Trailhead [18-V]. See Broadway Trailhead on page 200 for more details. Return the same way, or make a vehicle shuttle.

THE TRIP GOING EAST

Use Map 12 on page 162. Start at the north side of Hieroglyphic Trailhead parking lot [12-A, 0]. Go right (east) to the top of the ridge [12-T, 0.1] and the signed trail for Hieroglyphic Canyon. A large boulder is inscribed with a map of the Lost Goldmine Trail. Your location is on the right side of the "U."

Bear right and continue on the Lost Goldmine Trail as it heads toward the Wilderness boundary fence. You immediately get a feeling of remoteness with the Superstition Mountain looming above and the desert trees closing in behind you. The trail winds through washes and around hills, mostly following the Wilderness boundary fence. After Quicksilver Draw [12-K, 1.0], the trail begins its descent to Dromedary Wash [12-J, 1.7] just west of Turks Cap Hill. Quicksilver Draw is a good turnaround point for a leisurely trip.

Shortly after crossing Dromedary Wash [12-J, 1.7], the Lost Goldmine Trail crosses an unnamed dirt road. Going left (north) on the east bank of Dromedary Wash, the road ends near the Wilderness fence. Going right (south), the road meanders for 4.4 miles and connects with Peralta Road.

The Lost Goldmine Trail continues east around the south side of locally named Turks Cap Hill on a relatively flat track. When the trail turns left (north), Indian Rock [12-I, 2.4] is on the right (east). Look for prehistoric bedrock grind holes in the rock between the trail and the large wash. Farther along the trail, look left (north) for a landmark named Mushroom Rock [12-H, 2.8] just below the lower cliffs on Superstition Mountain. It is a 0.5 mile bushwhack (no trail) up to Mushroom Rock. Stay out of the washes, and use the ridges to make the bushwhack easier.

The trail passes through a large stand of saguaro cacti [12-S, 3.2], and a little farther, it goes through a livestock gate [12-X, 3.7]. The gate separates two Arizona State Trust land grazing leases, so be sure to close the gate. Carney Trail goes right (south) at an unsigned junction [5-SS, 4.1] to Carney Springs Trailhead [5-CC, 4.7]. West Boulder Trail heads left (north) through the Wilderness fence gate [5-SS].

The Lost Goldmine Trail continues east to Dons Camp Trailhead [5-DD, 5.2] and ends at the cattle guard on FR77 (Peralta Road) [5-NN, 5.4].

Broadway Trailhead

From Idaho Road in Apache Junction, go 3 miles east on US60 toward Gold Canyon. At the end of the Superstition Freeway, between mileposts 199 and 200, turn left (north) onto paved Mountain View Road. Follow Mountain View Road north 1.6 miles, turn right (east) on Broadway Avenue, and go 1 mile until the road curves into South Broadway Lane. Park on the left (north) in a small parking area facing the fence.

FINDING THE TRAILHEAD

Spaces are marked by cement tire stops for six vehicles in the unsigned gravel parking area. The signed Jacob's Crosscut Trail (N33° 24' 28.3", W111° 28' 34.0") begins at the west end of the parking area. Please obey all *No Trespassing* and *No Parking* signs.

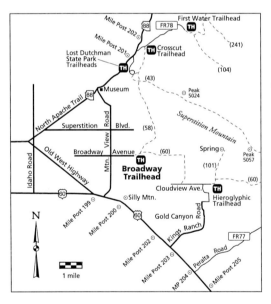

FACILITIES

No facilities are here. Bring your own water.

THE TRAILS

The signed Jacob's Crosscut Trail begins at the open gate [17-Q] in the Tonto National Forest boundary fence and connects with the Lost Goldmine Trail [17-R, 0.6] (N33° 24' 37.0", W111° 27' 59.5") and the Monument Canyon Trail [17-S, 1.1] (N33° 25' 2.0", W111° 27' 43.5") within a short distance.

    The Lost Goldmine and Jacob's Crosscut Trails are outside the Superstition Wilderness, so they are open to bicyclists, hikers, and horse riders. The Tonto National Forest land adjacent to these trails is regulated as a day use area, and no overnight camping is permitted. Lost Dutchman Park [18-K] does not provide horse access from the Jacob's Crosscut Trail, but riders can use the Crosscut Trailhead [18-V].

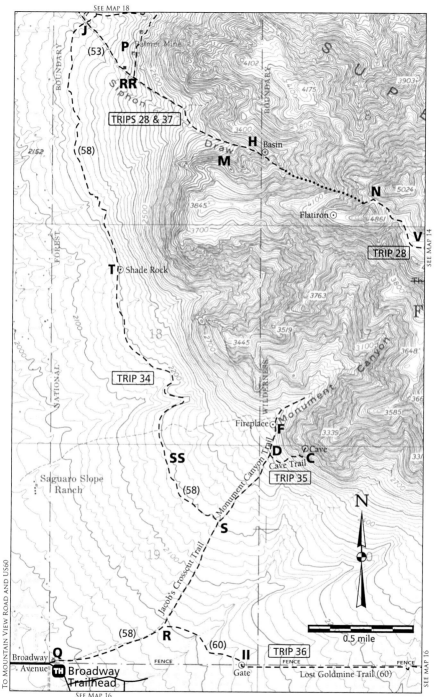

Map 17 – Trips 28, 34, 35, 36, and 40.

JACOB'S CROSSCUT TRAIL FROM BROADWAY TRAILHEAD

Jacob's Crosscut Trail is a relatively flat trail that follows the west face of Superstition Mountain all the way to the Crosscut Trailhead on First Water Road. You can expect spectacular sunsets to reflect red and orange hues off the majestic cliffs.

ITINERARY

From the Broadway Trailhead, go north and pass the trail intersections with Siphon Draw Trail (53), Prospector's View Trail (57), and Treasure Loop Trail (56). Meet the Crosscut Trailhead at First Water Road.

DIFFICULTY

Easy hike. Moderate ride. Elevation change is +410 and -180 feet.

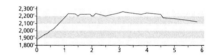

LENGTH and TIME

5.8 miles, 4 hours one way.

MAPS

Arizona USGS topo map NAD27: Goldfield. Superstition Wilderness Beartooth map, grids C14 to C12. Maps 17 and 18.

FINDING THE TRAIL

See the trailhead map on page 200. Start on the signed Jacob's Crosscut Trail at the open gate in the Tonto National Forest fence (N33° 24' 28.3", W111° 28' 34.0"). The open gate is a few feet west of the small parking area.

THE TRIP

Start on Map 17 on page 201. This is a good trail to take if you just want to walk a few hundred yards up the gentle slope to get a feel for the Sonoran Desert. Nice specimens of saguaro cactus along the trail will enhance your photos of Superstition Mountain and the Flatiron formation on top. The first part of the trail is covered with small, loose cobblestones, so the going is slower than normal.

From the Broadway Trailhead [17-Q, 0], the Jacob's Crosscut Trail (58) goes northeast and passes the signed Lost Goldmine Trail [17-R, 0.6]. The trail continues northeast and makes a sharp left turn (northwest) at a wooden signpost [17-S, 1.1]. Going straight (northeast) puts you on the Monument Canyon Trail, but our trip stays on the Jacob's Crosscut Trail heading left.

As the Jacob's Crosscut Trail heads north, it contours along the slopes of Superstition Mountain, and the bed of the trail becomes smoother. The trail passes through an unusually large stand of saguaro cacti [17-SS, 1.5] and continues on to Shade Rock [17-T, 2.7]. This large boulder offers the only reliable shade on the length of the trail. North of Shade Rock, the terrain becomes more open because the land has been burned by many wildfires.

Jacob's Crosscut Trail (58) crosses Siphon Draw Trail (53) at a signed intersection [18-J, 3.9]. Going left (west) on Siphon Draw Trail, hikers and bicyclists can reach the Lost Dutchman State Park boundary in 0.2 mile. The Siphon Draw Trailhead [18-K], inside the park, is another 0.6 mile. This is the first access to Lost Dutchman State Park (traveling north). The park has drinking water. See Lost Dutchman State Park Trailheads on page 210 for the description of park facilities and your trail options. Horses are not allowed in the park, but riders can end their trip at the Crosscut Trailhead [18-V].

Going right on the Siphon Draw Trail from the trail junction [19-J] takes hikers up Siphon Draw to the top of Superstition Mountain. See Trip 37 (Siphon Draw Trail) on page 215. Because of the steepness and congestion, horse riders and bicyclists are discouraged from using the trails branching east from Jacob's Crosscut Trail toward the cliffs of the mountain. But, all of Jacob's Crosscut Trail is open to horses, bicyclists, and hikers.

Although fires have removed the saguaros and palo verde trees here, the western slopes of Superstition Mountain are brilliant with wildflowers in the spring. The yellow brittlebush usually blooms each spring, but the orange poppies, blue lupine, and red chuparosa wait for the really wet years to bloom. Look in the washes for the red chuparosa.

Continuing north, the Jacob's Crosscut Trail passes Prospector's View Trail (57) [18-Z, 4.0], Treasure Loop Trail (56) [18-Q, 4.7], and Treasure Loop Trail (56) again [18-I, 4.8]. Horse riders and bicyclists are discouraged from using the Treasure Loop Trail going right (east), uphill, toward the mountain. Hikers and bicyclists can go left (west) on either of the Treasure Loop Trail branches and reach the State Park boundary within about 0.3 mile.

North of the Treasure Loop Trail intersection [18-I, 4.8], the view to the north opens up, and you can see Four Peaks Mountain in the far distance and the locally named Little Four Peaks in the near distance. Jacob's Crosscut Trail ends at Crosscut Trailhead [18-V, 5.8] on First Water Road. You will find plenty of room for parking vehicles and loading horses here.

Civilian Conservation Corps (CCC) camp in September 1935. CCC Company No. 2864 was under the command of Glenn J. Allen. Camp SCS-20-A was named Superstition Wash. The photograph is a partial view of a three-panel image. Photo by American Photo Service, San Antonio, Texas. Courtesy of Superstition Mountain Historical Society and National Archives, College Park, Maryland.

HISTORY AND LEGENDS

Before the land was developed for housing, a rectangular cement water tank stood near the informal parking area at Broadway Trailhead. We often climbed up on the open top rim to get above the desert vegetation for a photograph of Superstition Mountain.

In 1997, then Pinal County Supervisor Sandie Smith and others worked with Superstition Highlands developer John J. Jensen to establish trailhead parking for the Jacob's Crosscut Trail at Broadway Trailhead. Jensen donated the parking easement to Pinal County for six vehicles.

In 1935, a Civilian Conservation Corps (CCC) Camp was located about 2 miles west of the Broadway Trailhead. The Company No. 2864 camp was named Superstition Wash Camp, and the camp number was SCS-20-A. The SCS notation is the abbreviation for Soil Conservation Service. CCC projects performed by the men at the camp included soil conservation work such as the construction of rubble check dams, stock tanks, masonry dams, and telephone lines.[177]

The Jacob's Crosscut Trail is named for Jacob Waltz—he made the Superstition Mountains famous for his elusive Lost Dutchman Mine. See Lost Dutchman State Park Trailheads on page 214 for more area history.

BROADWAY CAVE TRAIL

The Broadway Cave Trail is an unmaintained trail that takes you to the cave in the lower cliffs of Superstition Mountain—a nice hike not far from town.

ITINERARY

From the Broadway Trailhead, follow the Jacob's Crosscut Trail (58) northeast for 1.1 miles to the start of the unmaintained Monument Canyon Trail. Take the Broadway Cave Trail to the cave. Return the same way.

DIFFICULTY

Easy hike. Not recommended for horses. Elevation change is +950 feet.

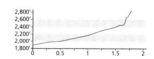

LENGTH and TIME

1.8 miles, 1.5 hours one way.

MAPS

Arizona USGS topo map NAD27: Goldfield. Superstition Wilderness Beartooth map, grid C14. Map 17.

FINDING THE TRAIL

See the trailhead map on page 200. Start on the signed Jacob's Crosscut Trail at the open gate in the Tonto National Forest fence (N33° 24′ 28.3″, W111° 28′ 34.0″). The open gate is a few feet west of the small parking area.

THE TRIP

Start on Map 17 on page 201. From the Broadway Trailhead, look northeast toward the lower cliff of Superstition Mountain for a dark spot with a larger tan-colored dot. That is the location of the cave and the trip destination.

Both the Jacob's Crosscut Trail, on this leg of the trail, and the Monument Canyon Trail have loose cobblestone-sized rocks. It is better to slow down, take it easy, and enjoy the trip rather than fight the loose rocks. The desert, with its lush vegetation, and the imposing view of Superstition Mountain compensate for the poor footing on the trail.

Starting at the Broadway Trailhead [17-Q, 0], take the Jacob's Crosscut Trail, go past the junction with the Lost Goldmine Trail [17-R, 0.6], and continue to the wooden signpost [17-S, 1.1] (N33° 25′ 2.0″, W111° 27′ 43.5″) where the Jacob's Crosscut Trail turns left (north).

Go straight, heading northeast, from the wooden signpost on the unmaintained Monument Canyon Trail until you come to a large rock cairn [17-D, 1.5]. If you miss the rock cairn and go too far, in about 0.2 mile, you will come to a fireplace chimney [17-F] in Monument Canyon. From the large rock cairn [17-D], go right (east) on the narrower Broadway Cave Trail. The last 100 yards is a scramble up the steep slope to the cave entrance.

The cave opening [17-C, 1.8] (N33° 25′ 18.6″, W111° 27′ 16.3″) is on a flat area, probably formed by the mine dump, with plenty of room for a large group. The cave does not go back into the cliff very far. It is more of a large alcove, but it will provide plenty of shade from the southern sun. Looking from the cave entrance toward Apache Junction and the west, you'll see the city roads radiate out in straight lines. The road to your right (west) that starts near the green water tanks is Superstition Boulevard. Return the same way.

HISTORY AND LEGENDS

The cave does not have a name, and no one seems to know much about its history. The mine drift inside of the cave is shallow.[178]

Jacob's Crosscut Trail at Broadway Trailhead. The small black dot in the top center of the photo is the location of the cave [17-C] described in Trip 35 (Broadway Cave Trail). July 2009 photo.

LOST GOLDMINE TRAIL FROM BROADWAY TRAILHEAD

The Lost Goldmine Trail follows the south side of Superstition Mountain providing good views of the mountain and access to many side canyons in the Wilderness. Since the trail lies outside the Wilderness, fewer restrictions apply, and it is open to bicyclists, hikers, and horse riders.

ITINERARY

From the Broadway Trailhead parking area, follow the Jacob's Crosscut Trail for about 0.6 mile to the junction of the Lost Goldmine Trail. The Lost Goldmine Trail goes east to Hieroglyphic Trailhead and continues east to Peralta Road. Make a one-way shuttle or an out-and-back trip.

DIFFICULTY

Easy hike. Moderate ride. Maximum elevation change is +280 and -480 feet.

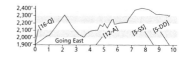

LENGTH and TIME

4.5 miles to Hieroglyphic Trailhead, 3 hours one way.

MAPS

Arizona USGS topo map NAD27: Goldfield. Superstition Wilderness Beartooth map, grids C15 to G15. Maps 16 and 12.

FINDING THE TRAIL

See the trailhead map on page 200. Start on the signed Jacob's Crosscut Trail at the open gate in the Tonto National Forest fence (N33° 24' 28.3", W111° 28' 34.0"). The open gate is a few feet west of the small parking area.

THE TRIP

Start on Map 16 on page 196. From the Broadway Trailhead, begin the trip on the Jacob's Crosscut Trail (58) [16-Q, 0.0], and go up the rocky trail to the signed junction with the Lost Goldmine Trail [16-R, 0.6] (N33° 24' 37.0", W111° 27' 59.5"). Bear right (easterly) and take the Lost Goldmine Trail. The trail becomes smoother as it contours along the gentle slopes of Superstition Mountain. The green gate [16-II, 1.1] marks the boundary where the trail leaves the Tonto National Forest and enters Arizona State Trust land. Be sure to close the livestock gate. Going east, the Lost Goldmine Trail follows the boundary fence with the fence on your left (north).

In 2000, Pinal County obtained a 50-foot easement across the State Trust land for the Lost Goldmine Trail. Trust lands are not considered public lands, so if you wander off the trail and the 50-foot easement, you need to purchase a Recreational Permit from the Arizona State Land Department. See Useful Addresses in the back of the book for the address.

The trail continues east, crossing several washes, until it meets the north-south Superstition Wilderness boundary fence [16-KK, 2.1]. Here the trail turns south, goes downhill on a gentle grade for about 1 mile, passes through another livestock gate [16-LL, 3.1], leaves Arizona State Trust land, and enters an easement across private land. Be sure to close the livestock gate.

South of the gate, the Lost Goldmine Trail closely follows Hieroglyphic Canyon Wash, heading southwest. Here the trail crosses private land on a Pinal County trail easement that was donated by developer Harold Christ. Respect private property on either side of the trail, and stay on the trail until it reaches Cloudview Avenue [16-MM, 3.4]. Cloudview Access is not a trailhead, because there is no parking and there are no other facilities here. Vehicles can drop off or pick up hikers, but there is no room for loading horses.

At Cloudview Avenue [16-MM, 3.4], turn left (east), and follow Cloudview Avenue for about 1.1 miles until Cloudview Avenue ends in the Hieroglyphic Trailhead parking lot [16-A, 4.5]. This trip description ends at the parking lot, but the Lost Goldmine Trail continues east 5.4 miles to Peralta Road [5-NN, 9.9]. See Trip 33 (Lost Goldmine Trail from Hieroglyphic Trailhead) on page 195 and Trip 30 (Lost Goldmine Trail from Carney Springs Trailhead) on page 184 for details on those parts of the Lost Goldmine Trail.

TONTO TRAILHEAD

Access at the Tonto Trailhead is only practical for local residents that can hike, bike, or ride horses from home. The Tonto Trailhead does not have parking facilities and parking along residential streets in not permitted.

Non-local hikers should use the Tonto National Forest access at the Lost Dutchman State Park where they have excellent facilities—picnic tables, water, rest rooms, camping, and great views of Superstition Mountain. Since horse access at the park is not available, horse riders can use two trailheads at each end of the Jacobs Crosscut Trail (58)—Broadway and Crosscut Trailheads—where there is parking and space for unloading horses. Hikers wanting to go to the Flat Iron at the top of Superstition Mountain should use the Siphon Draw Trail that starts inside the Lost Dutchman State Park.

HISTORY OF THE TONTO TRAILHEAD

The Tonto Trailhead was completed in December 2011 after a year or more of planning meetings with Pinal County Supervisor Bryan Martyn, Tonto Forest Service, Lost Dutchman State Park, horseman associations, and local residents. Mining Camp Restaurant owner, Vinton Fugate, agreed to allow parking at the northwest corner of the restaurant parking lot. In addition to parking, he provided a water trough and a hitching rail for horses.[180]

In 2016, non-restaurant visitors were filling the parking lot and hikers were taking advantage of the hospitality of the restaurant owners. The restaurant closed the parking lot to hikers in December 2016.

On July 25, 2017, the Mining Camp Restaurant, which was established in 1961, burned to the ground. The cause of the fire was an electrical short in the gift shop of the restaurant. Vinton Fugate bought the restaurant in 1984 and he had been working there before he purchased the business. After the fire, signs were erected later in 2017 that read "We Will Be Back," but in May 2018 Fugate made the decision not to rebuild.[181]

FACILITIES

There are no facilities. Do not park your vehicle on the residential streets.

THE TRAIL

The trail begins at the end of McKellips Road (dirt) at a green metal gate and continues to a step-over gate in the Tonto National Forest boundary fence. The trail is open to local hikers, horse riders, and bicycle riders.

Lost Dutchman State Park Trailheads

The Lost Dutchman State Park Trailheads are located about 5 miles north of Apache Junction on SR88 (between mileposts 201 and 202). From SR88 turn right (east) on the paved road, and drive into the State Park. SR88 is the famous Apache Trail, now designated as a National Forest Scenic Byway.

FINDING THE TRAILHEADS

After entering the park, three trailheads—Siphon Draw, Cholla Day Use, and Saguaro Day Use—offer several opportunities for making loop hikes. See the

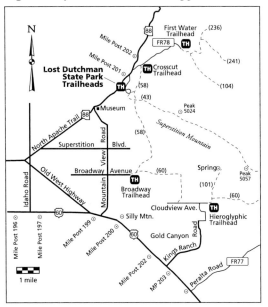

Map 18 inset detail on page 212 for the trailheads. For Siphon Draw Trailhead (N33° 27' 33.2", W111° 28' 45.4"), follow the road signs to the parking lot. Begin at the southwest corner of the Siphon Draw Trailhead parking lot on the signed Discovery Trail, which will take you to the Siphon Draw Trail (53) in about 0.5 mile.

The north segment of the signed Treasure Loop Trail (56) starts from the north side of the Cholla Day Use Area parking lot (N33° 27' 39.9", W111° 28' 36.5"), a few yards east of the restroom.

The south segment of the signed Treasure Loop Trail (56) starts from the southeast side of the Saguaro Day Use Area parking lot (N33° 27' 32.8", W111° 28' 38.0").

FACILITIES

The State Park has picnic tables, single and group ramadas, restrooms, showers, drinking water, telephone, developed campsites, RV hookups, and a dump station. See www.azstateparks.com for the overnight camping and daily

Lost Dutchman State Park entrance with Superstition Mountain in the background. July 1994 photo.

fees. Horses are not permitted in the park, but horse riders can access the Tonto National Forest Trails through the Crosscut Trailhead [18-V].

LOST DUTCHMAN STATE PARK

At the park entrance station, a quarter-mile native plant trail identifies the cacti, trees, and bushes seen throughout the Superstition Wilderness area. A short walk on the native plant trail is highly recommended. The park rangers have identified additional plants along the trails inside the 300-acre State Park. The park entrance station has a selection of free and for-sale literature. The rangers are happy to answer any questions you may have.

THE TRAILS

Starting from the Siphon Draw Trailhead parking lot [19-K], the Discovery Trail meets the Siphon Draw Trail (53) in 0.5 mile. The Siphon Draw Trail (53) intersects the Jacob's Crosscut Trail (58) [19-J] at 0.8 mile, reaches the Basin [19-H] at 1.9 miles, goes across the saddle on top of Superstition Mountain [19-N] at 2.4 miles, and crosses the Superstition Mountain Ridge to Carney Springs Trailhead [12-CC] for a total trip of 10.5 miles.

Two other parking areas—Saguaro Day Use Area and the Cholla Day Use Area inside the park—serve as the trailheads for both ends of the

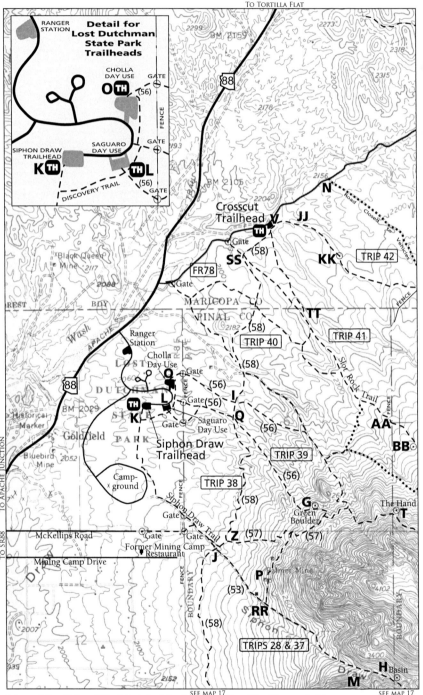

Map 18 – Trips 28, 34, 38, 39, 40, 41, 42, 45, 47, and 48.

SUPERSTITION WILDERNESS TRAILS WEST

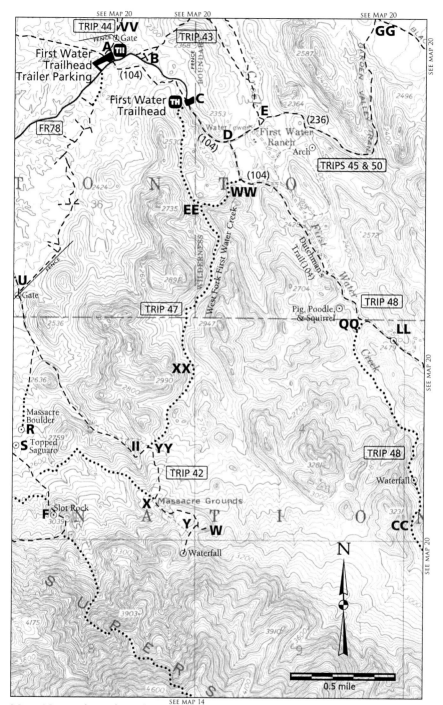

Map 18 continued – Trips 28, 34, 38, 39, 40, 41, 42, 45, 47, and 48.

Treasure Loop Trail (56). Treasure Loop Trail connects with Jacob's Crosscut Trail (58) and Prospector's View Trail (57), so you can make a variety of loop hikes. Rock climbers use the north segment of the Treasure Loop Trail to approach the rock climb on The Hand (Praying Hands) and the Siphon Draw Trail (53) to approach the rock climb on the Crying Dinosaur.

HISTORIC MINING DISTRICT

North Apache Trail (SR88) near the Lost Dutchman State Park was once a booming gold mining district. The center of gold mining activity was in the former town of Goldfield near the Mammoth Mine. John Wilburn, in his book *Dutchman's Lost Ledge of Gold*, documents the sites of fifteen gold mines, including the Mammoth, within a narrow corridor along SR88.[180] Twelve of the mines are on the west side of SR88, including the Bull Dog Mine, which John Wilburn suggests is the site of the Lost Dutchman Mine.

The Bull Dog Mine was the district's second largest gold producer, yielding an estimated 6,700 ounces of gold. The 1892 Bull Dog Mine received its name from the shape of a nearby rock formation that resembled the head of a bulldog. A portion of the face was blasted away in 1895, but if you look closely, you can still see the image of a bulldog.[181] The Bull Dog mine was located 1.7 miles west of the Lost Dutchman State Park just below the Pinal/Maricopa County line. The last of the Bull Dog Mine workings were bull-dozed over in 2007 during normal operations at the gravel pit.[182]

In his book, John Wilburn describes the operation and history of the mines and accounts for at least 58,620 ounces of gold removed from the mines in this region. Prospectors in Goldfield discovered the gold in veins of white quartz exposed on the surface. The Mammoth Mine accounted for about 43,300 ounces of gold and reached a depth of more than 1,000 feet.[183]

John Wilburn not only has written about the Lost Dutchman Mine, but also has searched for the gold. The Black Queen Mine was first staked in 1892 and was mined by several operators over the past century. In March of 1977, Wilburn obtained a lease from Goldfield Mines, Inc. on the old Black Queen, where he discovered new veins rich in gold. The new veins produced tons of high-grade ore. After the Mammoth and Bull Dog mines, the Black Queen was the third largest producer, yielding an estimated 6,000 ounces of gold in all its years of operation.[184]

You can see memorabilia and artifacts from the Goldfield Mining District at the Bluebird Mine and Gift Shop on the North Apache Trail, which was formerly owned by Ray Ruiz. Ray passed away on August 26, 2010. Ray's son, Louis, and others can often be found at the gift shop discussing all aspects of the Lost Dutchman legend with customers and friends.

SIPHON DRAW TRAIL

Siphon Draw is a scenic trip that takes you up a steep canyon under the towering cliffs of Superstition Mountain. Every spring the slopes are covered with wildflowers, dominated by the yellow brittlebush. You can walk by the site of the 1886 Palmer Mine, and you may see rock climbers on the Crying Dinosaur in Siphon Draw and on Praying Hands near Trail 56.

ITINERARY

This trip starts at Lost Dutchman State Park and heads east up the slopes into Siphon Draw. The trail ends after 1.9 miles, but a steeper and more difficult route continues another 0.5 mile to the Flatiron. Return by the same route.

DIFFICULTY

Easy hike. Not recommended for horses. Elevation change is +1,190 feet. The hike to the Flatiron is considered difficult, and it is not doable by horses. Elevation change to the Flatiron is +2,680 feet.

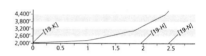

LENGTH and TIME

1.9 miles, 1.5 hours one way. Add 0.5 mile and 1 hour to the Flatiron.

MAPS

Arizona USGS topo map NAD27: Goldfield. Superstition Wilderness Beartooth map, grid C13. Map 19.

FINDING THE TRAIL

See the trailhead map on page 210. The Discovery Trail, which leads to the Siphon Draw Trail, starts inside the Lost Dutchman State Park at the Siphon Draw Trailhead parking lot (N33° 27′ 33.2″, W111° 28′ 45.4″).

THE TRIP

Start on Map 19 on page 217. This is a popular day trip and a nice hike for beginning hikers since it is difficult to get lost and turning around is possible at anytime. We rated the trip easy, but it is all uphill, and you will probably need to stop a few times to catch your breath. The view toward the Superstition Mountain cliffs is spectacular. We included this trip because some people prefer a less isolated trip. Additionally, this is the exit route for the dramatic and arduous Trip 28 (Superstition Mountain Ridgeline) from Carney Springs Trailhead [12-CC]. Although we rated the Siphon Draw Trail easy compared to other trips in our book, hikers should know the Lost Dutchman State Park rates this a difficult hike compared to other hikes in their information pamphlet.

From the Siphon Draw Trailhead [19-K, 0], follow the Discovery Trail and signs leading to Siphon Draw Trail, which takes you up to the junction with the Jacob's Crosscut Trail [19-J, 0.8] and continues southeast up the slope on the wide, well-traveled track of Siphon Draw Trail. Brittlebush is the dominate ground cover along the trail, and in the spring, the mountain slopes are a vibrant yellow color. The Palmer Mine Trail [19-RR, 1.2] branches off to the left (north) about 25 minutes into the trip just after passing an abandoned building foundation on your left (north).

Farther up the trail, Siphon Draw narrows. On the right (south) side of Siphon Draw is the Crying Dinosaur rock formation [19-M]. Continue up the trail through Siphon Draw as far as you like. After the trail goes into the

Hoodoos on top of Superstition Mountain. This rock formation, one of several in the area, is east of the saddle near the end of the hike to the Flatiron and north of the three pinyon pine trees [19-V]. February 1994 photo.

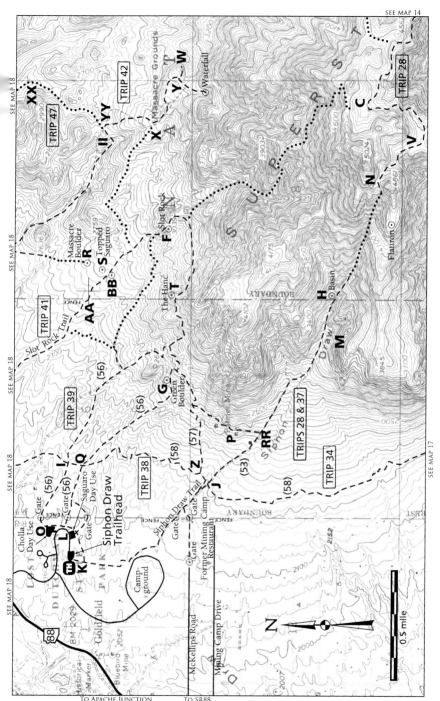

Map 19 – Trips 28, 34, 37, 38, 39, 40, 41, 42, and 47.

Goldfield area in the early 1900s with the Superstition Mountains in the background. Photograph by Walter Lubken. Courtesy Salt River Project History Services.

wash, the official trail ends at a smooth-rock alcove and seasonal waterfall in an area named the Basin [19-H, 1.9]. Return the same way to the Lost Dutchman State Park, Siphon Draw Trailhead [19-K, 3.8].

For those going to the top of the Flatiron, bypass the waterfall area on the right (south) side of the wash. Someone has painted white arrows and dots on the rocks, so it is easy to follow the route up Siphon Draw. No official trail exists here, but you can see where other hikers have established a path that takes you over a low ridge and back into Siphon Draw. The spray paint on the cliff, "Best Way, Stay in Canyon All the Way" has been partially covered. Although the advice is good, painting the rocks is not appropriate in the Wilderness; please don't paint the rocks. Most people hike up the bed of Siphon Draw. A trail lies on the south side of Siphon Draw, but we think the footing in the wash is better. Siphon Draw stays on the north side of the Flatiron, the prominent buttress, and becomes very steep before reaching the top of the cliffs. Loose rocks make the Siphon Draw route very hazardous. Don't roll rocks down onto hikers below you.

Several trails exist on top of the Flatiron. One goes south across the top of the Flatiron (west of Peak 4861), and another goes up to a saddle [19-N, 2.4] below some weathered rock formations. You can easily spend several hours up here photographing the rock formations and enjoying the views in all directions. Whenever you decide you have had enough exercise, return using the same trail to the Siphon Draw Trailhead [19-K, 4.8].

On the return trip, consider hiking over to the former mine site on the Palmer Mine Trail [19-RR]. The green steel-beam structures at the mine site were removed when the shaft [9-P] was covered and the area revegetated. Farther up an unmarked path, to the north, some smaller mine workings show a green chrysocolla mineral stain on the cliff. Continuing north on the Palmer Mine Trail connects you with the Prospector's View Trail (57).

HISTORY AND LEGENDS

The first mining claim in the Superstition District was the Buckhorn Claim, now known as the Palmer Mine. It was staked by W. A. Kimball in 1886. In 1900 and earlier, copper and gold ore were shipped from the mine. Dr. Ralph Palmer was a physician for the Roosevelt Dam construction site from 1903 to 1906 and mayor of Mesa in 1912. During this time, he became interested in gold mining. After Kimball's death, a group of businessmen and Dr. Palmer acquired the Buckhorn mine in 1917 and discovered small pockets of gold ore. In 1926, Dr. Palmer purchased the mine from his partners, but it wasn't until 1947 that the shaft was extended down from 215 feet to 265 feet. Unfortunately, only small traces of gold were found—nothing in commercial quantities. Dr. Palmer died in 1954. The Barkley Cattle Company used the

Weekes Ranch on the west side of Superstition Mountain circa 1930. Left to right, Dan Coverdale, Tex Barkley, Margaret Weekes holding Phil Peterson (child), Gene Peterson (child) at the front edge of her skirt, Fred Weekes, Merle Weekes Peterson, Charles Weekes III (kneeling), and Grant Peterson. Courtesy Gregory E. Davis, Superstition Mountain Historical Society, Weekes Ranch File; Ken and Nancy McCollough, and Betty Jean Schahrer.

shaft as a water well from 1950 to 1962.[185] The mine has been covered and revegetated, so you can't look into the shaft.

Rancher Bill Barkley's wife, Elizabeth Palmer Barkley, was the daughter of Dr. Palmer. While growing up, Nancy Barkley McCollough, granddaughter of Dr. Palmer, stayed with her grandfather in Phoenix so she could attend school. She spent the summers and weekends at the First Water Ranch with her parents. Nancy told us that she rode the haul bucket down into the Palmer Mine one time.[186] The cement and rock building foundation on the Siphon Draw Trail [near 19-RR] just west of the Palmer Mine Trail is said to have been the bunker where explosives were stored for the mine operation.

The cliffs of Superstition Mountain offer several technical rock climbs. Two of the more popular crags are the Crying Dinosaur and The Hand (Praying Hands). The Crying Dinosaur rock formation [9-M] is on the right (south) side of Siphon Draw. The vertical head and neck of the dinosaur and V-shaped mouth are visible from the trail. A long crack in the rock near the dinosaur eye looks like a tear. Rock climbers rate this a 5.5 climb.[187] Technical climbing equipment is required. The rappel off the top is a spectacular free rappel to the ground. See History and Legends in Trip 39 (Treasure Loop Trail to Green Boulder) on page 226 for the description of The Hand rock climb.

Cactus wrens, Arizona's state bird, have built many nests in the cacti and shrubs around the Lost Dutchman State Park. Watch for bird nests that look like bundles of hay woven between the branches of the cholla cacti and small trees. Some of the nests are built at eye level, which makes it easy to inspect the narrow, foot-long bundles of grass. Look for the birds' round entrance on one end of the nest.

Chain fruit cholla cactus on the northwest slope of Superstition Mountain. January 1993 photo.

Jacob's Crosscut Trail Loop

Jacob's Crosscut Trail lies just east of the Lost Dutchman State Park and is useful as a connecting trail on the Tonto National Forest. It is a fine trail for making loop trips on the western slope of Superstition Mountain and for viewing the wildflowers that bloom here in the spring following wet winters.

ITINERARY

This trip starts in Lost Dutchman State Park at the Siphon Draw Trailhead. When the Siphon Draw Trail (53) intersects the Jacob's Crosscut Trail (58), turn north and follow the Jacob's Crosscut Trail. Return to the Lost Dutchman State Park on either segment of the Treasure Loop Trail (56).

DIFFICULTY

Easy hike. Horses are not allowed in the State Park. Elevation change is ±240 feet.

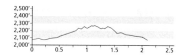

LENGTH and TIME

2.1 miles, 1.5 hours round-trip.

MAPS

Arizona USGS topo map NAD27: Goldfield. Superstition Wilderness Beartooth map, grid C12. Map 18.

FINDING THE TRAIL

See the trailhead map on page 210. The Discovery Trail, which leads to the Siphon Draw Trail in 0.5 mile, starts inside the Lost Dutchman State Park at the Siphon Draw Trailhead parking lot (N33° 27' 33.2", W111° 28' 45.4").

THE TRIP

Start on Map 18 on page 212. This is a pleasant trip that allows you to make a loop hike into the Tonto National Forest and to return to the Lost Dutchman State Park with little elevation gain. When the spring wildflowers are in bloom, the trip provides photographers with the ideal route for viewing the flowers against the backdrop of Superstition Mountain.

Photo at Weekes Ranch. Left to right: on burro, Melvin Ellsworth, Charles Weekes IV; in back row, Violet Weekes, Sam Elder, Ethel Brimhall, Betty Jean Schahrer, Florence Morse, Veda Elder, Felton Weekes, Jimmy Elder, Collins Riley Morse; kneeling in front row, Charles Weekes III, Stanley Elder. Photographer unknown. February 23, 1947 photo. Courtesy Gregory E. Davis, Superstition Mountain Historical Society, Weekes Ranch File; Ken and Nancy McCollough; and Betty Jean Schahrer.

From the Siphon Draw Trailhead [18-K, 0.0], go south on the wide, well-defined Discovery Trail. After about 0.2 mile, look for a small sign, near the Hiker-Biker Campsite, that directs you to the left (east) toward the Siphon Draw Trail (53). Shortly, the trail connects to a wider track that was once an old road and is now the Siphon Draw Trail. The Siphon Draw Trail leaves the Lost Dutchman State Park at the gate in the boundary fence and enters the Tonto National Forest. If the wildflowers are in bloom, they will cover both sides of the Siphon Draw Trail going southeast from the State Park boundary fence all the way up to the base of Superstition Mountain.

Leave the Siphon Draw Trail and go left (north) on the signed Jacob's Crosscut Trail [18-J, 0.8]. Several trail junctions here are a little confusing because they form a triangle to save you a few yards of travel, depending on the direction of your trip. The first landmark going north on the Jacob's Crosscut Trail is the intersection with the signed Prospector's View Trail (57) [18-Z, 0.9]. From here, you can make a longer loop up the hill and around the Green Boulder—returning on the Treasure Loop Trail (56).

The Jacob's Crosscut Trail contours across the slopes heading mostly north. Some shallow pits in the ground on either side of the trail are prospects that miners dug in earlier days in search of gold. The next landmark is the junction with the southern branch of the signed Treasure Loop Trail (56) [18-Q, 1.6]. You can turn left (west) to return to the Lost Dutchman State

Park through the Saguaro Day Use Area [18-L, 1.9] and end the trip at Siphon Draw Trailhead [18-K, 2.0].

For a slightly longer trip, continue north on the Jacob's Crosscut Trail to the northern branch of the signed Treasure Loop Trail (56) [18-I, 1.7]. From here it is 1.0 mile to First Water Road and the Crosscut Trailhead [18-V], but Trip 38 turns left (west) and returns to the Lost Dutchman State Park through the Cholla Day Use Area [18-O, 2.0]. The trip ends at Siphon Draw Trailhead [18-K, 2.2].

View looking southeast along the Siphon Draw Trail (53) at the junction [18-J] with the Jacob's Crosscut Trail (58). April 2008 photo.

TREASURE LOOP TRAIL TO GREEN BOULDER

This trip takes you up the western slope of Superstition Mountain. You can experience the closeness of the mountain cliffs as you look above to the towering hoodoos with the assurance that civilization is close by as you view the landscape below.

ITINERARY

This trip starts in Lost Dutchman State Park at the Cholla Day Use Area parking lot, follows Trail 56 in a loop around the Green Boulder, and returns to the Saguaro Day Use parking lot in the Lost Dutchman State Park.

DIFFICULTY

Easy hike. Horses are not allowed in the State Park. Elevation change is ±550 feet.

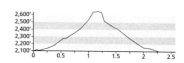

LENGTH and TIME

2.3 miles, 1.5 hours round-trip.

MAPS

Arizona USGS topo map NAD27: Goldfield. Superstition Wilderness Beartooth map, grid C12. Map 18.

FINDING THE TRAIL

See the trailhead map on page 210. The north branch of the Treasure Loop Trail starts inside the Lost Dutchman State Park at the north end of the Cholla Day Use Area parking lot [18-O] (N33° 27′ 39.9″, W111° 28′ 36.5″). The signed Treasure Loop Trail (56) starts a few yards east of the restroom.

THE TRIP

Use Map 18 on page 212. From the Lost Dutchman State Park, if you look closely, you can see the lichen-covered Green Boulder [18-G] on the western slope of Superstition Mountain. The Green Boulder is near the highest point on the Treasure Loop Trail that circles behind it.

Start at the north end of the Cholla Day Use Area parking lot at the trail sign [18-O, 0] just east of the restroom. The trail heads north to a gate in the park boundary fence, turns southeast, and intersects the Jacob's Crosscut Trail [18-I, 0.3]. Continuing on the Treasure Loop Trail (56) heading southeast, the trail gains elevation. Several benches along the trail give you a comfortable place to sit while you view the landscape and catch your breath.

The Treasure Loop Trail turns right (southwest) at an unmarked junction (N33° 27' 10.3", W111° 27' 45.3") with a steep trail-of-use that takes you to the rock formation and rock climb named The Hand [18-T, 1.1]. Trail 56 continues, contouring through some rough country. At mile 1.2, the trail meets the east end of the Prospector's View Trail (57) at a trail sign and bench. If you sit on the bench, the Green Boulder is the large butte in front of you. You cannot see the green-yellow lichen on the Green Boulder [18-G] until you proceed downhill and look back uphill toward the boulder.

As an optional route, you can return on the Prospector's View Trail (57) by connecting with the Siphon Draw Trail (53) and Discovery Trail for a total mileage of 2.7 miles to the Siphon Draw Trailhead [18-K, 2.7]. This trip

View from the Jacob's Crosscut Trail toward Superstition Mountain and the Green Boulder [18-G]. The Green Boulder is the stand-alone butte on the left side of the photo. The Jacob's Crosscut Trail appears in the lower right corner of the photo. March 2008 photo.

makes a sharp U-turn to the right at the trail sign and descends down a steep area with wooden water bars forming steps across the trail.

From the Green Boulder [18-G, 1.4], the Treasure Loop Trail continues downhill, intersects the Jacob's Crosscut Trail [18-Q, 1.9], and heads toward the State Park boundary. At an unsigned split in the trail, you can go either way. Going left takes you to the Saguaro Day Use Area parking lot and trailhead sign [18-L, 2.3]. Going straight takes you to the Discovery Trail. Here you can see the paved road as the Discovery Trail curves right (north) toward the Cholla Day Use Area parking lot [18-O, 2.3], where the trip ends.

HISTORY AND LEGENDS

To the northeast of the Lost Dutchman State Park, you can see interesting vertical rock formations that look like tall, thin fins. The farthest one to the north is named Praying Hands [18-T], but the rock climbers call it The Hand. The "hand" formation is actually easier to see as you drive from Apache Junction north on SR88. Bill Forrest, Key Punches, and Gary Garbert made the first ascent to the top of The Hand in 1965 on the Razor's Edge route. Later that same year, Bill Sewrey and Dave Olson made a first ascent using the Chockstone Chimney route. A 150-foot-free-fall rappel from the top is quite exciting. Technical climbing equipment is required for these climbs, which are both rated 5.6.[188] The approach to The Hand rock climb is usually made on the north segment of the Treasure Loop Trail (56) out of Cholla Day Use Area [18-O] in the Lost Dutchman State Park. The spur trail to The Hand begins at wooden sign (N33° 27' 10.3", W111° 27' 45.3") for the Treasure Loop Trail. Start on the uphill (east) side of the sign and follow any of the interconnecting trails for about 0.3 miles uphill to The Hand [18-T].

Most hikers use the Siphon Draw Trail (53) to ascend to the top of the western end of Superstition Mountain, but veteran hiker Joe Bartels made a "Reverse Flatiron" hike up the north side of Superstition Mountain from the Massacre Grounds [18-U] to the top [near 14-C]. We asked Chris Coleman to field check Joe's route. Chris and Jesse Perlmutter took the route that we added to Maps 14 and 18 as a dotted line, which is a continuation of the trail that goes by The Hand [18-T] rock climb. They followed washes and ridges most of the way. About a mile from the top and the Superstition Mountain Ridgeline Trail, Chris said the route got dangerous—"steep and rocky with scree fields and drop-offs." Once on the Superstition Mountain Ridgeline Trail, they said it was too dangerous to go back the way they came, so they descended on the Siphon Draw Trail. He said the lower part of the route in the canyon would make a fine up-and-back day hike, but he did not recommend going to the top. We have only field checked the route to the east end of the trail that goes by The Hand.[189]

CROSSCUT TRAILHEAD

Crosscut Trailhead is located on FR78. From Apache Junction, drive about 5 miles northeast on SR88 to the First Water Road (FR78), which is between mileposts 201 and 202. From SR88 turn right (east) onto dirt FR78 and continue 0.6 mile to the signed Crosscut Trailhead parking lot. The former Massacre Grounds Trailhead has been relocated to the Crosscut Trailhead.[190]

FINDING THE TRAILHEAD

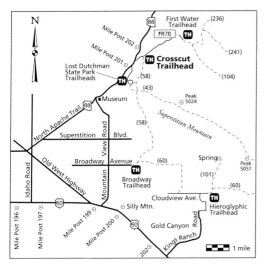

FR78 is about 0.2 mile north of Lost Dutchman State Park on SR88. The signed Crosscut Trailhead (N33° 28' 15.7", W111° 28' 08.2") is on the right (south) side of FR78. Look for the large trailhead sign to distinguish this parking area from several small pullouts along the road.

FACILITIES

No facilities are here. Bring your own water.

THE TRAILS

Two trails start from this trailhead—Jacob's Crosscut Trail and Massacre Grounds Trail. Jacob's Crosscut Trail is outside the Superstition Wilderness, so bicyclists, hikers, and horse riders are allowed to use the trail. Tonto National Forest land along the Jacob's Crosscut Trail is regulated as a day use area—no overnight camping or shooting is permitted. The Massacre Grounds Trail is outside of the Wilderness up to the boundary fence at [18-U].

The Jacob's Crosscut Trail (58) begins at the open gate [18-V] on the southwest corner of the Crosscut Trailhead parking lot at the information billboard. The trail sign is often missing, so bear right in front of the information billboard and follow the trail crossing the wash to the southwest. Don't take the unnamed trail heading southeast from here. On the southern side of the wash, the trail heads right (west) and goes up a small hill before leveling off.

From Crosscut Trailhead on the Jacob's Crosscut Trail (58), it is 1.0 mile to the Treasure Loop Trail (56) near Lost Dutchman State Park, 1.9 miles to the Siphon Draw Trail (53), and 5.8 miles to the Broadway Trailhead. The Lost Dutchman State Park has drinking water, restrooms, telephone, and many other facilities. Lost Dutchman Park does not provide access for horses, so riders on the Jacob's Crosscut Trail (58) must continue to the Broadway Trailhead [17-Q] or return to Crosscut Trailhead [18-V].

Abandoned roads and off-trail routes branch from the Jacob's Crosscut Trail not far from the Crosscut Trailhead. These routes give you the opportunity to venture up the foothills toward Superstition Mountain. See Trip 41 (Silverlock Prospect) on page 233.

The unsigned Massacre Grounds Trail starts from the east side of Crosscut Trailhead and goes to the Massacre Grounds. It is marked with rock cairns and is described in Trip 42 (Massacre Grounds Trail) on page 237.

HISTORY AND LEGENDS

The concrete on the east side of the Crosscut Trailhead parking area is the remains of the Salt Well and water tank.[191] See Trip 41 (Silverlock Prospect) on page 235 and Trip 42 (Massacre Grounds Trail) on page 240 for more of the area history.

Government Well in the early 1900s, about seven miles northeast of Apache Junction on the Apache Trail. Photograph by Walter Lubken. Courtesy Salt River Project History Services.

SUPERSTITION WILDERNESS TRAILS WEST

JACOB'S CROSSCUT TRAIL FROM CROSSCUT TRAILHEAD

Jacob's Crosscut Trail dips in and out of small ravines as it contours along the west face of Superstition Mountain, eventually ending at the Broadway Trailhead. This is pleasant trail traveling through the day use area of the Tonto National Forest on the boundary of the Superstition Wilderness. Wet winters cover the slopes of Superstition Mountain with spring wildflowers, and the evening sunsets on the mountain cliffs are often colorful.

ITINERARY

From the Crosscut Trailhead, the Jacob's Crosscut Trail (58) goes south; passes Treasure Loop Trail (56), Lost Dutchman Park, Prospector's View Trail (57), Siphon Draw Trail (53); and ends at the Broadway Trailhead. The Jacob's Crosscut Trail connects with the Lost Goldmine Trail near Broadway Trailhead. The trail is open to hikers, horse riders, and bike riders.

DIFFICULTY

Easy hike. Moderate ride. Elevation change is +180 and -410 feet.

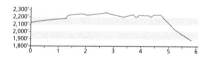

LENGTH and TIME

5.8 miles, 4 hours one way.

MAPS

Arizona USGS topo map NAD27: Goldfield. Superstition Wilderness Beartooth map, grids C12 to C14. Maps 17, 18, and 19.

FINDING THE TRAIL

See the trailhead map on page 227. Start at the southwest corner of the Crosscut Trailhead near the information billboard (N33° 28′ 15.7″, W111° 28′ 08.2″). From the open gate in the wire fence, the Jacob's Crosscut Trail (58) goes to the right (west) in front of the information billboard. Don't confuse Jacob's Crosscut Trail with an unnamed trail heading southeast from the billboard. The Jacob's Crosscut Trail crosses the dry wash and goes up on the south bank where it is marked with a wooden sign. The well-defined trail heads west up a small hill before leveling off.

THE TRIP

Start on Map 18 on page 212. This is an easy trail that lets you experience Superstition Mountain without a lot of effort. As with all trails, you can go a short distance and turn around, or you can make a day of it. The Jacob's Crosscut Trail is in the Tonto National Forest Day Use Area, so you can't camp along the trail except at Lost Dutchman State Park campground.

From the Crosscut Trailhead [18-V, 0], the Jacob's Crosscut Trail (58) goes southwest across the dry wash and heads up the small rise to the top of the hill [18-SS, 0.2]. Here the trail crosses an abandoned dirt road, which heads southeast on a ridge toward the Massacre Grounds area. The old road is a good choice for a moderate horse ride—see Trip 41 (Silverlock Prospect) on page 233. Continuing on the Jacob's Crosscut Trail, you will notice that the trail parallels the road for a short distance; then the trail heads in a more southerly direction. Ample opportunities exist along here to leave the trail to explore the washes or find a secluded spot for lunch.

Near the Maricopa and Pinal County boundary at mile 0.4, another abandoned road crosses the Jacob's Crosscut Trail in a southeast direction and follows a ravine for about 0.3 mile to an area that looks like it might have been prospected in the past. At the end of this road, you can go cross-country (no trail) a few hundred yards to the north to make a connection on the ridge with the previously mentioned road that started at the top of the hill [18-SS].

The next landmark along the trail is the signed Treasure Loop Trail (56) junction [18-I, 1.0]. Going right (west) 0.3 mile on the Treasure Loop Trail takes you to the Cholla Day Use Area [18-O] in Lost Dutchman State Park.

Going left (east) on the Treasure Loop Trail takes you uphill toward Superstition Mountain and the Green Boulder [18-G]. Looping downhill from the Green Boulder returns you farther south on Jacob's Crosscut Trail. Use either the Treasure Loop Trail to connect with Jacob's Crosscut Trail [18-Q] in 1.6 miles or the Prospector's View Trail to meet Jacob's Crosscut Trail [18-Z] in 1.5 miles. Tonto National Forest rules discourage bike and horse riders from using the narrow and steep trails east of Jacob's Crosscut Trail.

Staying on the Jacob's Crosscut Trail from the junction [18-I, 1.0] will bring you to the south segment of the Treasure Loop Trail (56), marked with a wooden sign [18-Q, 1.1]. Heading right (west) 0.4 mile on this branch of the Treasure Loop Trail takes you to the Saguaro Day Use Area [18-L] in the Lost Dutchman State Park. Heading left (east) on the Treasure Loop Trail takes you toward Superstition Mountain and the Green Boulder [18-G].

Continuing south, mining prospects in the wash on the south side of the trail are evidence of the search for minerals. We do not know who dug

Wedding photograph of William A. "Tex" Barkley and Gertrude "Gertie" Anderson in 1905. Courtesy of Nancy and Ken McCollough and the Superstition Mountain Historical Society, Barkley Collection.

those holes. The vegetation along the trail has been burned many times, so the saguaro cacti and palo verde trees are gone, but the open terrain is favorable to wildflowers, which bloom in abundance in the spring of wet years.

The signed Prospector's View Trail (57) branches to the left (east) from Jacob's Crosscut Trail [18-Z, 1.8] and takes you up the hill 0.6 miles, where it connects with Treasure Loop Trail (56) near the Green Boulder [18-G].

The wooden sign [18-J, 1.9] at the Siphon Draw Trail (53) marks a major intersection with the Jacob's Crosscut Trail. This intersection is one of our favorite locations for photographing the spring wildflowers. In fact, the cover photograph for this book was taken along the Siphon Draw Trail in March 1998.

Traveling right (northwest) 0.2 mile on the Siphon Draw Trail takes you to the Lost Dutchman State Park boundary, and another 0.6 mile on park trails brings you to the Siphon Draw Trailhead parking lot [18-K]. Traveling left (southeast) on the Siphon Draw Trail puts you on the trail to the Basin [18-H] and the route to the top of Superstition Mountain [18-N] and the Flatiron. See Trip 37 (Siphon Draw Trail) on page 215.

Continuing south on the Jacob's Crosscut Trail from the junction with Siphon Draw Trail, the trail is less busy. On sunny, hot days, the only reliable shade along the next section of trail is Shade Rock [17-T, 3.1], where a large boulder on the east side of the trail provides shade for a large group of people.

Farther south on the trail, the open landscape becomes dotted with saguaros and eventually passes through a large stand of saguaro cacti [17-SS, 4.3]. Wildfires have not burned this section of trail, so it is covered with dense Sonoran desert cacti and trees. The trail makes a 90-degree right turn to the southwest at the intersection [17-S, 4.7] with an unofficial trail named the Monument Canyon Trail. A wooden signpost [17-S] without a sign marks the intersection. The nearby Broadway Cave Trail takes you to a small cave in the low cliffs within 0.7 mile. Looking northeast from this trail intersection [17-S], you can see the black opening of the cave to the left of a light tan circle on the cliff face. See Trip 35 (Broadway Cave Trail) on page 205.

After the 90-degree right turn [17-S], the Jacob's Crosscut Trail heads down a slight grade on a rather rocky portion of the trail. Water has eroded the dirt from the small rocks, so they tend to roll under your feet. Take it easy, and enjoy the tall saguaros and the palo verde trees that offer a bit of shade.

The Lost Goldmine Trail branches to the east from the Jacob's Crosscut Trail at a signed junction [17-R, 5.2]. The Lost Goldmine Trail— open to hikers, bikers and horses riders—meanders east along the cliffs of Superstition Mountain to several trailheads including the Hieroglyphic Trailhead, which is 3.9 miles from this junction. You can travel all the way to Peralta Trailhead in 9.7 miles. For more trips on the Lost Goldmine Trail, see the Broadway, Hieroglyphic, Carney Springs, and Dons Camp Trailheads.

The last leg of the Jacob's Crosscut Trail continues down the gentle grade and rocky trail to the open gate [17-Q, 5.8] in the Tonto National Forest boundary fence. The Jacob's Crosscut Trail ends here at the Broadway Trailhead and a small parking area for six vehicles.

In 1905, Weekes Station was located across the Apache Trail from the Superstition Mountain Museum. Courtesy Gregory Davis, Superstition Mountain Historical Society, Weekes Ranch Family Collection.

SILVERLOCK PROSPECT

An abandoned dirt road takes you along a flat ridge to the site where Sergeant Edwards was alleged to have found the massacre bones in 1866. Later two men, Silverlock and Malm, found gold here. You can relive their stories while traveling up the gentle slope with terrific views of Superstition Mountain.

ITINERARY

From the Crosscut Trailhead, follow the Jacob's Crosscut Trail (58) south for 0.2 mile to the top of the hill, turn left (southeast) and follow the abandoned dirt road, pass through the Superstition Wilderness boundary fence, and stop at the massacre site or Silverlock prospect. Bikes are not permitted beyond the Superstition Wilderness boundary fence. Return the same way.

DIFFICULTY

Easy hike. Moderate ride.
Elevation change is +430 feet.

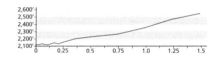

LENGTH and TIME

1.5 miles, 1 hour one way.

MAPS

Arizona USGS topo map NAD27: Goldfield. Superstition Wilderness Beartooth map, grid C12. Maps 18 and 19.

FINDING THE TRAIL

See the trailhead map on page 227. At the southwest corner of the Crosscut Trailhead near the information billboard, pass through the open gate [18-V] (N33° 28′ 15.7″, W111° 28′ 08.2″) in the wire fence. Go across the normally dry wash on a well-worn trail. On the south side of the wash, a wooden signpost without a sign marks the Jacob's Crosscut Trail as it goes up the hill.

THE TRIP

Start on Map 18 on page 212. This trip is ideal for a moderate horse ride on a wide dirt road. The abandoned road that we named the Slot Rock Trail follows the top of a flat ridge for great views in all directions. Experienced hikers and expert horse riders can make a rough cross-country loop trek

View to the north at the Silverlock cabin ruin on the north slope of Superstition Mountain. Gregory Davis (l) and Dick Walp (r). Dick is standing in the doorway of the stone building. April 2015 photo.

(no trail) through a boulder-strewn drainage to connect with the Massacre Grounds Trail, but most people will choose to return the same way they came.

Starting at the Crosscut Trailhead [18-V, 0], take the Jacob's Crosscut Trail across the dry wash and up the grade to the top of the hill. The Jacob's Crosscut Trail is wide and easy to follow. At the top of the hill [18-SS, 0.2], less than 10 minutes from the trailhead, look for an unmarked dirt road (N33° 28' 09.3", W111° 28' 16.2") heading left (southeast) toward Superstition Mountain. The road, which we named the Slot Rock Trail, has not been used for many years, but you can still see the track.

The abandoned road heads southeast with a slight uphill grade. The first landmark is an opening in the Superstition Wilderness Boundary fence [19-AA, 1.2] where the fence has been cut and pulled back. The cut fence looks as though it were cut years ago.

After passing through the fence, the road track turns into a trail. A topped (top cut off) saguaro cactus [19-S, 1.4] (N33° 27' 26.5", W111° 27' 23.9") marks the general area of the massacre site. The topped cactus is a few yards east of the trail. The site of the Massacre Boulder [19-R] (N33° 27' 30.6", W111° 27' 22.0") is 0.1 mile northeast of the topped saguaro [19-S].

Continuing up the trail, look for some large rock cairns to the south across the small wash. A red volcanic rock outcrop in the wash marks the spot where Silverlock had a prospect [19-BB, 1.5] (N33° 27′ 24.4″, W111° 27′ 24.8″)—a few feet south of the wash up on the bank. Farther up the hillside to the south, they had more diggings. Return the same way to Crosscut Trailhead [18-V, 3.0].

OPTIONAL ROUTES

From the end of the Silverlock Prospect trip [19-BB, 1.5], you can continue up the slope following the well-defined Slot Rock Trail to the slick rock and tall rock fins (aka Slot Rock) that are directly southeast [18-F, 1.8]. The rock formation named the Slot Rock can be viewed by looking westerly from the spine of the rock formation. Sitting beside the rock monoliths, you have the choice of shade or sun while taking in striking views in every direction.

A more traditional route to Slot Rock is a loop going by the Lost Dutchman State Park and up the hill to The Hand [18-H]. From Crosscut Trailhead [18-V, 0], go southerly on the Jacob's Crosscut Trail to the Treasure Loop Trail [18-I, 1.0], go left (southeast) and uphill to the top of the Treasure Loop Trail and take the unmarked trail going to The Hand. From The Hand [18-H, 2.0], continue easterly to Slot Rock [18-F, 2.6]. Return on the Slot Rock Trail, connect with the Jacob's Crosscut Trail [18-SS, 4.2], and end at the Crosscut Trailhead [18-V, 4.4]. A spur trail along the Slot Rock Trail [18-TT, 3.8] is another way to return north to the Crosscut Trailhead [18-V, 4.2].

Another return option for the Silverlock Prospect trip starts from the topped saguaro cactus [19-S, 1.4] and takes you cross-country (no trail) in a northeast direction to the Massacre Boulder [19-R, 1.5] (N33° 27′ 30.6″, W111° 27′ 22.0″), where Sergeant William Edwards was alleged to have found bones in 1866. Continue north, cross a large ravine, and connect with the Massacre Grounds Trail north of Hill 2336. It is a rough scramble going across the ravine, and it is not recommended for horses. Refer to Trip 42 (Massacre Grounds Trail) for the trail details going back to the Crosscut Trailhead. Your waypoints are: gate [18-U, 2.1], south end of ridge [18-KK, 2.6], north end of ridge [18-JJ, 2.8], and Crosscut Trailhead [18-V, 3.0].

HISTORY AND LEGENDS

Thomas Glover's book *The Lost Dutchman Mine of Jacob Waltz* describes the discovery of the massacre site and his *Treasure Tales of the Superstitions* book analyzes the evidence for the stories.[192] Although Glover and other reputable historians have not found documented evidence in the military or other historical records to support the Sergeant Edwards account, it still makes an intriguing tale.

The story begins in 1866 with William Edwards and Joe Green, possibly sergeants in the Arizona Volunteers, who allegedly found the bones of about 25 people on the northwest slope [19-R] of Superstition Mountain. Edwards thought the bones were those of Mexican miners killed by the Apaches. When he was able to return to the site, he found a clothed skeleton and a pouch of gold ore some distance from the fight. Eventually his back-tracking led to Marsh Valley and Peters Mesa. The story was allegedly passed down to his grandson Ben Edwards who confided the events and locations to his partner. The story was not made public until after Ben's death.

In the 1997 *Superstition Mountain Journal,* Gregory Davis compiled and analyzed the newspaper articles and documents of Carl A. Silverlock and Carl J. Malm—prospectors in the Superstition Mountains from 1901 through 1909.[193] Rumors circulated that they found $18,000 of gold ore on the northwest slope of Superstition Mountain, which they shipped from the Mesa express office.[194] It is generally accepted that this gold had been lost during the massacre in the 1860s.

Silverlock and Malm were immigrants from Sweden—entering the U.S. in 1868 and 1884 respectively. Both were educated men, and it is believed that Malm was Silverlock's nephew. Before coming to Arizona, Silverlock sold his ranch in Wyoming for about $15,000, which could account for some of their grubstake. In their final years, however, their luck may have run out, since they were receiving money from the county. Silverlock was committed to the State Mental Institution of Arizona in 1909, returned to the care of Maricopa County in 1917, and died on July 18, 1929, at age eighty-four. Malm died at Coffelt's Rest Home in Phoenix on April 25, 1947, at age seventy-eight.[195] See Trip 42 (Massacre Grounds Trail) for more history and legends.

View to the north along the Massacre Grounds Trail. The landmark conical butte (Hill 2636) is on the left horizon. November 2009 photo.

MASSACRE GROUNDS TRAIL

This very pretty and less-traveled area takes you up the north slope of Superstition Mountain into the foothills where a running battle took place at the historic Massacre Grounds. In the rainy season, you will find water in the washes and small waterfalls cascading from the lower cliffs of Superstition Mountain. The trail is surrounded by distant rock formations and the massive hulk of Superstition Mountain to the south.

ITINERARY

From the Crosscut Trailhead, follow a cairned trail southeast to the former Massacre Grounds Trailhead. Take the Massacre Grounds Trail to its end. Return the same way or go off-trail to First Water Trailhead.

DIFFICULTY

Easy hike. Moderate ride up to [18-II], then difficult. Elevation change is +1,040 feet.

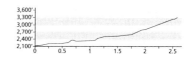

LENGTH and TIME

2.6 miles, 2 hours one way.

MAPS

Arizona USGS topo map NAD27: Goldfield. Superstition Wilderness Beartooth map, grids C12 to D12. Map 18.

FINDING THE TRAIL

See the trailhead map on page 227. The former Massacre Grounds Road, FR28, has been closed and abandoned for many years. The present-day route to the Massacre Grounds begins from the east side of the Crosscut Trailhead on a new trail, which is easy to follow.

The trip starts at the Crosscut Trailhead [18-V, 0.0] (N33° 28′ 15.7″, W111° 28′ 08.2″) at an unsigned open gate in the fence (N33° 28′ 17.3″, W111° 28′ 06.6″) on the east side of the parking lot. From the parking lot, the Massacre Grounds Trail follows the new cairned route to another open gate [18-U, 0.9] (N33° 28′ 02.2″, W111° 27′ 23.5″), where the former Massacre Grounds parking area was located.

To help you stay on track, the new trail heads in the general direction of the highest, craggy peaks to the southeast. When you get closer, follow the trail toward the rocky hill with yellow and green lichen, which is near the former Massacre Grounds Trailhead.

THE TRIP

Start on Map 18 on page 212. At the Crosscut Trailhead, look for the open gate (N33° 28' 17.3", W111° 28' 06.6") in the wire fence on the east side of the parking lot. Just east and straight ahead from the open gate is a large concrete slab, which is the floor of the former Salt Well Tank that stored water for the First Water Ranch. From the open gate, walk across the concrete slab and go 100 feet in a southeasterly direction to the sandy wash. Go left (easterly) in the sandy wash for 30 feet and look for the cairned trail, which resumes on the east (right) bench. Follow the rock cairns and the new Massacre Grounds Trail, which heads east to the north end of a flat ridge [18-JJ, 0.2] (N33° 28' 17.0", W111° 28' 59.4").

Most of the saguaros and palo verde trees on the flat ridge were burned in the August 2020 Superstition Fire. Although patches of jojoba and sugar sumac at the higher elevations up to the waterfall were burned, they should recover in a few years.

Continue east and southeast as the trail crosses the flat ridge to the south end of the ridge [18-KK, 0.4] (N33° 28' 09.1", W111° 27' 47.1"). From

View toward the southeast as the Massacre Grounds Trail approaches the craggy buttes. The rock-cairn arrow points the way across a big ravine beyond the south end of the ridge [18-KK]. The Massacre Grounds Trail goes left (east) of the conical butte (Hill 2636). November 2009 photo.

the south end of the ridge, the trail continues south and southeast across a series of gullies and into a large ravine. The top of the east side of the large ravine is marked by a rock cairn (N33° 28′ 02.7″, W111° 27′ 31.6″). Some horse riders may have trouble here on the smooth hard-packed dirt on the steep bank of the ravine, but most riders will be okay.

A short distance after you come up out of the wash, you will see the barbed-wire fence and the former Massacre Grounds Trailhead in the distance to the east. Continue to follow the rock cairns and faint trail, keeping your destination—the open gate in the barbed-wire fence—in sight [18-U, 0.9] (N33° 28′ 02.2″, W111° 27′ 23.5″).

Proceed through the open gate in the barbed-wire fence [18-U, 0.9] where the former trailhead was located. The trail follows an old road, heads southeast, and stays on the left (east) side of a prominent conical butte as the trail gains elevation. At the pass on the east side of the conical butte, the trail heads downhill. Stay on the most traveled trail through the brushy wash area. The trail makes a steep, slick-rock exit out of the brushy wash [18-II, 1.9] by going more easterly. Most riders will want to turn around here since the steep slick rock is difficult for many horses. Above the slick rock, the well-defined trail flattens out [18-YY, 2.0] and shortly continues to gain elevation.

Several trails-of-use lead uphill and to the south. Stay on the trail with the most rock cairns. After the trail crosses a large wash from the waterfall area, you arrive at the junction [18-Y, 2.5] (N33° 27′ 07.7″, W111° 26′ 29.7″) with the trail to the waterfall and the trail to the cliff. Bear left (east) to continue up to the edge of an impressive cliff that drops off to the east [18-W, 2.6] (N33° 27′ 06.7″, W111° 26′ 26.2″). This is the turnaround point for the trip and makes a good spot for a rest or snack.

From the turnaround point [18-W], the Massacre Grounds area stretches east and west along the base of Superstition Mountain. The final battle is said to have occurred about one mile northwest of here at Massacre Boulder [18-R]. That battle is described in Trip 41 (Silverlock Prospect).

To go up to the waterfall area, go back to the trail junction [18-Y, 2.5], and head southwest. The trail goes 0.2 mile through the bushes to the cliff below the waterfall. Here, water pours off the low, red cliffs after a rain. The cliff below the waterfall provides shade and makes a nice lunch spot, even when there is no water here. Return the same way to the Crosscut Trailhead parking lot [18-V], or try an optional return route.

OPTIONAL RETURN ROUTES

Several optional return routes are possible. They would be good for those desiring to experience off-trail travel and route finding. Refer to Map 18 for our route suggestions. Only the second route is doable by horses.

This century plant (agave) has not yet produced a tall showy stalk. It takes many years, but certainly not a century.

The first off-trail trek starts at a flat area on the trail [18-YY] and follows West Fork First Water Creek[196] heading north toward the Dutchman's Trail [18-WW]. See Trip 47 (West Fork First Water Creek) from First Water Trailhead on page 264 for the trip description in the reverse direction.

The second off-trail route[197] follows a series of abandoned dirt roads, starting from the north end of the Massacre Grounds Trail [18-U] and ending at the First Water Trailhead horse trailer parking lot [18-A]. The many intersecting dirt roads, which we marked on Map 18, will test your navigation skills as you try to stay on course.

The third route starts near a tall boulder [18-X] (N33° 27' 14.1", W111° 26' 41.8") and takes you northwest to what has become known as the Massacre Boulder and the final battle site [18-R] in about 1 mile. See Trip 41 (Silverlock Prospect) on page 233 for more information about the area.[198]

HISTORY AND LEGENDS

Sims Ely tells the story of the massacre in his 1953 book *The Lost Dutchman Mine*.[199] George Scholey was a friend of an Apache known as Apache Jack who related this episode to him. In 1848, when Apache Jack was about twelve years old, he and other reinforcements from the Apache village near the Picket Post military camp were summoned by the warriors to join the running fight against the Mexicans. Some authors believe the Mexican miners were part of the Peralta family expedition making the last trip to the mountains to recover gold, because the international boundary was being moved south to the Gila River at the end of the 1846–1848 Mexican-American War.

Apache Jack joined the fighting on the third day. The miners were being driven south and west against the cliffs of Superstition Mountain. The last of the Mexicans to die were killed at the Massacre Boulder [18-R] on the northwest slopes of Superstition Mountain. Several of the Mexicans escaped around the west side of the mountain, but their mules were either killed or scattered. Apache Jack said his group cut the packs and bags of rock (gold ore) off the mules and left them on the ground before taking the animals to their camp on a flat-topped mountain. Apache Jack said the place where Silverlock and Malm found their gold was the site of the massacre.

Scholey said that during a deer hunting trip in the Superstitions, Apache Jack took him near a gold mine on Black Mountain [west of 9-T], but then had second thoughts about showing him the exact location. Apache Jack was worried he would displease his tribal leaders by disclosing the location of a mine to a white man. Later, George Scholey learned that Apache Jack died from symptoms similar to arsenic or strychnine poisoning. Scholey attributed this poisoning to Apache Jack's medicine man, who may have upheld the legend that a horrid fate would overcome anyone who divulged the site of any mine to a white man. See History and Legends in the Peters Mesa Area description on page 332 for more on the poisoning incident, and History and Legends in Trip 41 (Silverlock Prospect) on page 235, which takes you to what has become known as the Massacre Boulder and the final site of the massacre [18-R].

Robert Garman, in his 1975 book *Mystery Gold of the Superstitions*, writes about several others that have found gold ore in circumstances similar to Silverlock. Legendary Lost Dutchman Mine hunter Herman Petrasch told Garman that a prospector came to his cabin with gold ore found in a pile next to a trail west of Weavers Needle. Another find was made about 1933 by two men, Mr. James and Mr. Ives. They found gold about 50 feet north of the trail in Needle Canyon on the pass going over to East Boulder Canyon. We believe this could have been the Upper Black Top Mesa Pass [8-FF].[200]

Garman includes a map in his book showing a possible trail that the fleeing Mexicans traveled during the Apache attack. The trail starts on the south side of the Wilderness, but it is unclear—due to misplaced landmarks on his map—how they arrived in East Boulder Canyon. From First Water, the Mexicans were fleeing west when the Apaches forced them south toward Superstition Mountain and the Massacre Grounds.

First Water Trailhead

First Water Road (FR78) is about 5 miles north of Apache Junction on SR88 between mileposts 201 and 202. The First Water Road turnoff is just 0.2 mile north of the Lost Dutchman State Park entrance. From SR88, turn right (east) on dirt FR78, and continue 2.6 miles to the First Water Trailhead parking lot at the end of FR78.

FINDING THE TRAILHEAD

While driving along FR78, you pass the Crosscut Trailhead parking lot at mile 0.6 on the right, the horse trailer parking lot on the left at mile 2.1, the entrance to the Dutchman's Trail (104) at mile 2.1 on the right, and the locked-gate dirt road at mile 2.2 on the left. FR78 ends at the main parking lot at mile 2.6 (N33° 28′ 47.7″, W111° 26′ 32.5″).

If the main parking lot is full, drive back on the dirt road about 0.5 mile, and park in the horse trailer area where the outfitters saddle up for their pack trips. An unmarked dirt road at the north side of the horse trailer parking lot is the start of a route to Hackberry Spring. The locked-gate dirt road between the horse trailer parking and the main parking lot goes down to a broken windmill and corral next to First Water Creek. The vehicle parking fee was eliminated in May 2006.

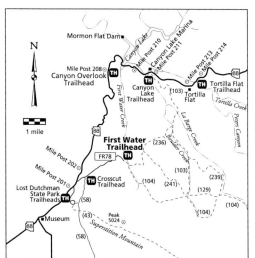

FACILITIES

Both parking areas have toilet facilities, but no drinking water. Theft is common at this trailhead, so don't leave valuables in your vehicle.

THE TRAILS

The main parking lot and the horse trailer parking lot are connected by the extension of the Dutchman's Trail (104). Starting from the horse trailer parking lot [20-A], hikers can walk on FR78 to get to the main parking lot [20-C], but horse riders should use the extension of the Dutchman's Trail

[20-A] (N33° 28′ 57.2″, W111° 26′ 54.6″), which starts on the right (south) side of FR78 at the horse trailer parking lot.

The Dutchman's Trail (104) leaves the east side of the main parking lot [20-C] (N33° 28′ 47.7″, W111° 26′ 32.5″) and heads east, down a rough dirt road. In about 0.3 mile, the Dutchman's Trail meets the Second Water Trail [20-D]; continues to Parker Pass in 2.5 miles, Aylor's Camp in 4.5 miles, Charlebois Spring in 8.5 miles, Bluff Spring in 12 miles; and ends at Peralta Trailhead in 17.4 miles. The Second Water Trail (236) goes east, crosses Garden Valley in 1.8 miles, passes Second Water Spring in 3.3 miles, and ends at Boulder Canyon Trail (103) in Boulder Canyon in 3.5 miles.

The August 2020 Superstition Fire burned most of the vegetation on the south side of FR78. The fire burned the area going southeast all the way to West Boulder Canyon and beyond.

Brian Lickman at First Water Trailhead in 1966. Unlike these interesting old signs, all mileages and place names have been removed from the contemporary Wilderness signage. Photo by Al Morrow. Courtesy of Brian Lickman.

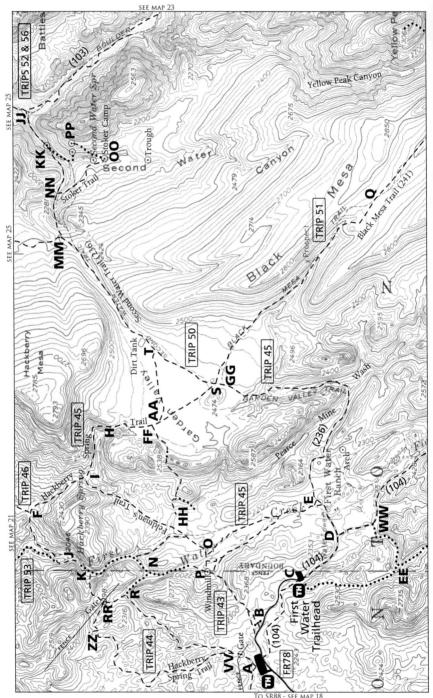

Map 20 – Trips 43, 44, 45, 46, 48, 49, 50, 51, 52, and 53.

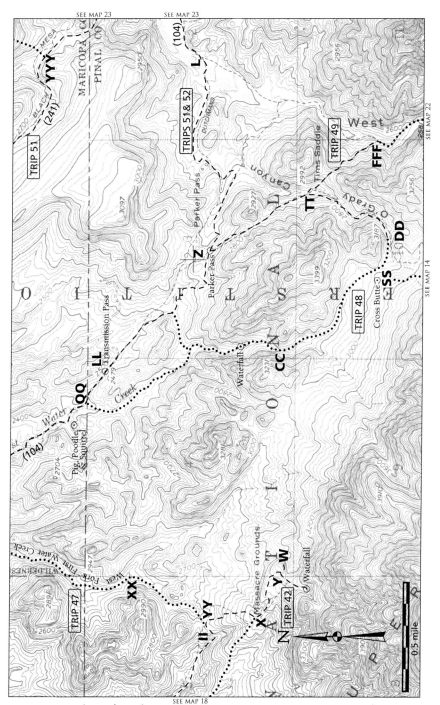

Map 20 continued – Trips 43, 44, 45, 46, 48, 49, 50, 51, 52, and 53.

WINDMILL

This easy trip is ideal for showing out-of-town guests the Ṣonoran desert. It follows a dirt road down to the former First Water Ranch corral just outside the Wilderness boundary. Across the Wilderness boundary fence, you may find small pools of seasonal water in the bedrock of First Water Creek.

ITINERARY

Start at First Water Trailhead horse trailer parking lot, go east on FR78 to the locked-gate road, and follow a dirt road down to a corral on First Water Creek. Choose one of three return routes. (1) Return the same way. (2) Go south, up First Water Creek to Second Water Trail (236), then proceed to the First Water Trailhead. (3) Go north, down First Water Creek to the first wash on the left, and follow a horse trail back to the horse trailer parking lot.

DIFFICULTY

Easy hike. Moderate ride. Elevation change is +60 and -150 feet.

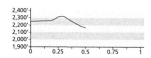

LENGTH and TIME

0.5 mile, 45 minutes one way.

MAPS

Arizona USGS topo map NAD27: Goldfield. Superstition Wilderness Beartooth map, grid D11. Map 20.

FINDING THE TRAIL

See the trailhead map on page 242. Start at the First Water Trailhead horse trailer parking lot [20-A, 0] (N33° 28' 57.3", W111° 26' 55.8"). Follow FR78 east to the locked-gate road [20-B, 0.2] (N33° 28' 58.4", W111° 26' 44.9"). The locked-gate road is about 0.1 mile east of the horse trailer parking lot [20-A] on the north side of FR78.

Or, from the First Water Trailhead main parking lot [20-C], walk west on FR78 about 0.4 mile to the locked-gate road—on your right (north). You can see the locked gate a few feet from FR78, beyond the sign that reads, "No parking, law enforcement vehicles only."

THE TRIP

Start on Map 20 on page 244. From the horse trailer parking lot [20-A, 0.0], go east on FR78 to the locked-gate road. Proceed through the opening in the fence next to the locked gate [20-B, 0.1], and continue northeast up the dirt road. Horse riders can bypass the gate by taking a horse trail from FR78 just north of the locked-gate road.

From the top of the ridge, the road drops down into the First Water Creek drainage. Visible from the road are a metal water tank, barbed-wire corrals, the windmill tower [20-P, 0.4], and a tin-roofed ramada. The blades and gear box of the windmill had toppled off the tower and were lying at the foot of the structure in December 1992, but in November 1993, we noticed they had been removed from the area. After looking at the former rancher's name in the concrete, "LAMB 79," continue east on one of the many paths to First Water Creek [20-O, 0.5].

The barbed-wire fence is the Superstition Wilderness Boundary. When First Water Creek is running with water or if the potholes have water, stop on one of the sculptured rocks—carved by the creek water—for lunch or a snack. Even without water, this is probably the best place to take a break.

Going down canyon (north) about 100 yards northeast of the windmill tower, just as the canyon walls become solid rock, be sure to look for the bedrock grind holes on the left (west) bench of the creek. The largest of the five grind holes is about 8 inches in diameter and 6 inches deep.

ALTERNATE RETURNS

You have three possible routes back to the start of the trip. The easiest is to return the same way (less than 30 minutes) [20-A, 1.0].

The second return route goes south and up First Water Creek bed or the unmarked trail on the east side of the creek to Second Water Trail [20-E, 1.2]. Turn right (west) on Second Water Trail, and go to the First Water Trailhead main parking lot [20-C, 1.7]. Continue west on the extension of Dutchman's Trail (104), or walk down FR78 to the horse trailer parking lot [20-A, 2.2]. This return adds about 1 hour and 1.2 miles to the trip.

The third return goes north and down the First Water Creek bed to the first wash on the left—before the creek narrows into a small canyon [20-N, 0.9] (N33° 29' 26.4", W111° 26' 31.8"). Proceed up the wash, which is initially blocked to stock animals, to a well-defined horse trail [20-R, 1.1], and continue in the bottom of the narrow ravine. The horse trail connects with the a dirt road (Hackberry Spring Trail) [20-VV, 1.7] leading south to the horse trailer parking lot [20-A, 1.8]. This return adds about 30 minutes and 0.8 mile to the trip description.

HACKBERRY SPRING

This trip takes you to Hackberry Spring, which often has water when every-thing else is dry. This well-shaded spring is a pleasant rest spot for lunch or for just sitting by First Water Creek below the sheer cliffs. Cottonwood and willow trees grow in the water course, and on the bench, you will find netleaf hackberry, honey mesquite, and oak trees.

ITINERARY

From First Water Trailhead, go to Hackberry Spring via: (1) Windmill Route, (2) Wash Route, (3) Ridge Route, or (4) Trip 45 (Garden Valley Loop).

DIFFICULTY

Easy hikes. Moderate rides, but Route (1) is not recommended for horses. Elevation change is +60, -230; +90, -250; +140, -300; and +310, -530 feet respectively.

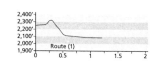

LENGTH and TIME

(1) Windmill, 1.2 miles, 1 hour one way.
(2) Wash, 1.1 miles, 1 hour one way.
(3) Ridge, 1.5 miles, 1 hour one way.
(4) Trip 45, 5.1 miles, 3.5 hours round-trip.

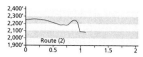

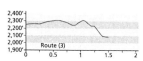

MAPS

Arizona USGS topo map NAD27: Goldfield. Superstition Wilderness Beartooth map, grid D11. Map 20.

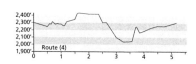

FINDING THE TRAIL

Trailhead map is on page 242. Route (1) starts at the entrance to First Water Trailhead horse trailer parking lot [20-A] (N33° 28' 57.3", W111° 26' 55.8").

Routes (2) and (3) start at the north side of First Water Trailhead horse trailer parking lot [20-A] (N33° 28' 58.9", W111° 26' 56.7").

Route (4), which is Trip 45 (Garden Valley Loop), starts at the First Water Trailhead main parking lot [20-C] (N33° 28' 47.7", W111° 26' 32.5").

THE TRIP

First time visitors, and those accompanying new hikers, should use Route (1) to go to Hackberry Spring. The walk down First Water Creek is very enjoyable. Horse riders will have difficulty in the narrows of First Water Creek because of the boulders and vegetation, so they should not use Route (1).

THE TRIP on WINDMILL ROUTE (1)

Use Map 20 on page 244. Refer to Trip 43 (Windmill) on page 246 for the first section of this trip [20-A, 0]. At the windmill tower [20-P, 0.4], continue north, down First Water Creek to Hackberry Spring. A few segments of a trail here make walking along the creek bed easy. Beyond a wash [20-N, 0.8] coming in from the left (northwest), the creek goes through a narrows with high cliffs on both sides—this narrow canyon is not recommended for horses.

Just on the other side of the narrows, you will see a well-traveled horse trail coming down a ravine from the left (west) [20-K, 1.1]. This is the trail that leads back to the First Water Trailhead horse trailer parking lot using Routes (2) and (3). Cross First Water Creek to the right (east) side, and when the trail crosses back to the left (west), look for Hackberry Spring [20-J, 1.2] and its water pipe on the right side of the creek. Return the same way, or use Routes (2), (3), or (4) for a return trip with new scenery.

THE TRIP on WASH ROUTE (2)

Use Map 20 on page 244. Starting on the north side of the First Water Trailhead horse trailer parking lot [20-A, 0] (N33° 28′ 58.9″, W111° 26′ 56.7″), follow Hackberry Spring Trail—a dirt road. About 75 yards beyond an open gate in a barbed-wire fence, a well-traveled horse trail [20-VV, 0.1] branches right (east) from the Hackberry Spring Trail. Your route parallels the dirt road for a short distance—the dirt road is left (west) of your route.

The Wash Route drops into a narrow wash and follows a winding trail in the wash. Watch for a well-used trail branching off to your left (north) [20-R, 0.7] (N33° 29′ 31.2″, W111° 26′ 37.0″), which takes you out of the wash and up the hill to the north.

If you missed the trail junction [20-R] leaving the wash, you will end up at First Water Creek [20-N, 0.9]. Horse riders will want to backtrack and take the branch trail [20-R] uphill to avoid the boulders in the narrows of First Water Creek. Hikers can just continue down First Water Creek and zigzag through the boulders to Hackberry Spring [20-J, 1.3].

Continuing on the branch trail [20-R], go uphill, and pass through an open gate [20-RR, 0.8] in the wire fence at the top of the hill near a flat spot. Proceed down the steep hill to First Water Creek [20-K, 1.0], cross First

Water Creek, turn left (north), and follow the creek on the right bank. When the trail crosses the creek to the left (west), look for a pipe coming out of Hackberry Spring on the right (east) side of First Water Creek [20-J, 1.1].

THE TRIP on RIDGE ROUTE (Hackberry Spring Trail) (3)

Use Map 20 on page 244. The Ridge Route is signed as the Hackberry Spring Trail. It follows a road and dips in and out of the ravines. Begin at the Hackberry Spring Trail sign on the north side of the horse trailer parking lot [20-A, 0] (N33° 28' 58.9", W111° 26' 56.7"), go through the open gate in the barbed-wire fence, continue up the dirt road, and follow the trail signs.

On an uphill segment of road (near the road's end), watch for a trail [20-ZZ, 1.1] (N33° 29' 38.7", W111° 26' 46.8") on your right (east), and take the trail. It will meet the branch trail from the Wash Route at an open gate [20-RR, 1.2] in a wire fence on a flat area. Turn left (east) through the gate, then continue down a steep hill to First Water Creek [20-K, 1.4]. The trail goes across First Water Creek and follows the creek on the right bank. When the trail crosses the creek to the left (west), look for the pipe coming out of Hackberry Spring on the right (east) side of First Water Creek [20-J, 1.5].

Return using Route (1), (2), (3), or (4). The return from Hackberry Spring, through Garden Valley, ending at First Water Trailhead horse trailer parking lot, is 4.0 miles from Hackberry Spring. Use Trip 45 (Garden Valley Loop) on page 252, and follow directions in reverse.

THE TRIP on GARDEN VALLEY ROUTE (4)

Use Map 20 on page 244. Follow the directions in Trip 45 (Garden Valley Loop) on page 252, starting from the main parking lot at [20-C].

HISTORY AND LEGENDS

Hackberry Spring [20-J] is on the east side of First Water Creek in a small hand-carved niche at the bottom of the cliff. From the streambed, you can see a metal pipe extending over the dirt bank. At one time, the pipe extended to the cement trough at the edge of First Water Creek. Louis Ruiz at the Blue Bird Mine and Gift Shop said he and John Cox installed a ¾-inch pipe, made regular repairs, and mucked the cement water trough at the spring when he worked for Cox on the First Water Ranch from 1969 through 1975. They branded the Quarter Circle U.

In January 1997, we observed the inscriptions on the rim of the Hackberry Spring cement trough. This is what we could read ("?" indicates illegible): "David" "1927" "FRO" "DOC" "W?E?LL?ABY" "?-22-82." On more recent trips, the trough was covered with sand, and the inscriptions were not visible.

Elizabeth Stewart at Hackberry Spring on First Water Creek. October 1993 photo.

Trip 45

GARDEN VALLEY LOOP

Garden Valley is the site of a prehistoric Indian ruin where potsherds litter the ground under a forest of chain fruit cholla cacti. Several trails traverse this level expanse, with Weavers Needle and Four Peaks rising above the surrounding low hills. Hackberry Spring often has water in the dry season, and First Water Creek has seasonal pools of water.

ITINERARY

From First Water Trailhead, follow the Dutchman's Trail (104) and Second Water Trail (236) east to Garden Valley. From Garden Valley, the signed Hackberry Spring Trail, a good horse trail, heads northwest to Hackberry Spring. Return on the Wash Route or one of four alternate routes.

DIFFICULTY

Easy hike. Moderate ride.
Elevation change is +310
and -530 feet.

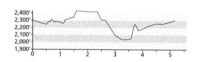

LENGTH and TIME

5.1 miles, 3.5 hours round-trip.

MAPS

Arizona USGS topo map NAD27: Goldfield. Superstition Wilderness Beartooth map, grid E11. Map 20.

FINDING THE TRAIL

See the trailhead map on page 242. From the sign-in register, the Dutchman's Trail [20-C] (N33° 28' 47.7", W111° 26' 32.5") leaves the First Water Trailhead main parking lot heading east.

THE TRIP

Start on Map 20 on page 244. From the main parking lot [20-C, 0], go east about 0.3 mile to the trail intersection where the Dutchman's and Second Water Trails diverge [20-D, 0.3]. Take the Second Water Trail, which goes left (east) and crosses First Water Creek—a rocky creek bed, usually dry or with little water.

252   SUPERSTITION WILDERNESS TRAILS WEST

Just after crossing the First Water Creek bed, look to the left (north) and remember the lay of the land. Possible return routes are through the creek bed or on a trail-of-use—marked by a railroad-tie fence post [20-E, 0.5] (N33° 28′ 42.7″, W111° 26′ 11.7″). Continue east following Second Water Trail over to Garden Valley [20-GG, 1.8].

Garden Valley is a very flat area that had been covered with mesquite trees and chain fruit cholla cactus in earlier years—but many were burned in the June 2020 Sawtooth Fire. The wooden sign at the trail intersection marks the Black Mesa Trail (241) branching off to the right (southeast). The Second Water Trail continues straight ahead (northeast) going over to Second Water Spring [20-KK, 3.3] and Boulder Canyon [20-JJ, 3.5].

For Trip 45, look for the signed Hackberry Spring Trail [20-S, 1.8+] (N33° 29′ 09.7″, W111° 25′ 36.9″) that branches left (northwest) about 100 feet north of the Black Mesa Trail sign. This horse trail has a well-defined track across the flat valley floor and begins just north of the small hill identified as 2474 on the USGS Goldfield topo map.

From the northwest corner of Garden Valley, the Hackberry Spring Trail, now a rough horse trail, drops into an unnamed ravine. A small hole in the hillside (below the trail) is evidence of old mine diggings [20-H, 2.5]. A few hundred yards down the trail, it is easy to look up canyon to see the small mine in the eroding bank, dug by Barry Storm in the late 1930s or early

Corral and buildings at First Water Ranch [near 20-E], circa 1975. Photograph by Richard Dillon.

1940s.[201] The landscape in this area is dominated by saguaro cacti, jojoba, and mesquite. Four Peaks can be seen through a break in the hills to the north.

At a trail junction [20-I, 2.7] on the saddle, the unsigned Feldman's Trail heads left (southwest) through an open gate down to First Water Creek, but Trip 45 continues straight ahead on the Hackberry Spring Trail. From the saddle [20-I, 2.7], the trail continues northwest, then west over another low saddle before dropping down into First Water Creek. Bear to your left, and head upstream along First Water Creek as the trail crosses the creek two times. Hackberry Spring [20-J, 3.5] is located in a small hand-carved niche at the bottom of the cliff on the left (east) side of First Water Creek. It often has water in the dry season. See Trip 44 (Hackberry Spring) on page 248.

ALTERNATE RETURN ROUTES

From Hackberry Spring, five return routes lead to First Water Trailhead. About 200 yards south of Hackberry Spring, two routes follow the horse trail [20-K, 3.6] up a steep hill to a ridge on the west side of First Water Creek. Horse riders should use this trail to avoid the narrows of First Water Creek. On the ridge, go through the gate [20-RR, 3.8] (N33° 29′ 37.6″, W111° 26′ 38.8″) in the wire fence where you have two choices—the Wash Route (left) or the Ridge Route (right) on the signed Hackberry Spring Trail. At the gate, the Wash Route takes the left (south) trail, goes down a ravine into a large

Elizabeth Stewart inspecting the bedrock grinding holes in Garden Valley. July 1993 photo.

wash [20-R, 3.9], and continues right (southwest) up the sandy wash. In 15 minutes, the trail goes west, out of the wash, up to a dirt road [20-VV, 4.5]. Follow the dirt road south to the horse trailer parking lot on FR78 [20-A, 4.6]. Continue to the First Water Trailhead main parking lot [20-C, 5.1] by taking the extension of the Dutchman's Trail (104)—look for the wooden (104) trail sign on the south side of FR78—or walk on dirt road FR78.

The Ridge Route, following the signed Hackberry Spring Trail, goes right (northwest) from the gate [20-RR, 3.8], turns left (south) on a dirt road [20-ZZ, 3.9] (N33° 29′ 38.7″, W111° 26′ 46.8″), passes the Wash Route intersection [20-VV, 4.9], reaches the horse trailer parking lot [20-A, 5.0], and ends at the First Water Trailhead main parking lot [20-C, 5.5].

The third, fourth, and fifth return routes from Hackberry Spring [20-J, 3.5] continue up First Water Creek (south) through the narrows, which are hazardous for horses. The third return route goes up the first wash on the right (northwest) [20-N, 3.9] (N33° 29′ 26.4″, W111° 26′ 31.8″), joins the horse trail [20-R, 4.1] (N33° 29′ 31.2″, W111° 26′ 37.0″), connects with the dirt road [20-VV, 4.7], and ends at the horse trailer parking lot [10-A, 4.8] or main parking lot [20-C, 5.3].

The fourth route leaves First Water Creek [20-O, 4.2] about 0.7 mile south of Hackberry Spring. Use the windmill tower [20-P] (N33° 29′ 10.8″, W111° 26′ 30.7″) as a landmark to mark the spot where you leave First Water Creek. From the corrals and windmill tower [10-P, 4.3], head west up the dirt road, which is visible on the hill on the western horizon. The dirt road takes you to the locked gate near FR78 [20-B, 4.6]. Turn left (southeast) on FR78, and end the trip at the main trailhead parking lot [20-C, 5.0]. See Trip 43 (Windmill) on page 246 for a description of the windmill and corral area.

The fifth route goes up on the east bank of First Water Creek—across the creek from the windmill tower—and follows a trail-of-use [starting near 20-O, 4.2] (N33° 29′ 11.1″, W111° 26′ 25.6″) that meanders south. The trail-of-use meets the Second Water Trail at the railroad-tie fence post [20-E, 4.9] (N33° 28′ 42.7″, W111° 26′ 11.7″). Turn right (west) on the Second Water Trail to return to the First Water Trailhead main parking lot [20-C, 5.4].

HISTORY AND LEGENDS

The *Arizona Daily Gazette*, in 1893, reported the ruins of a prehistoric stone house in Garden Valley. Estimated to be at least three stories high, the structure included a large stone-paved courtyard in the center. The outside dimensions were reported to be 300 by 500 feet. On the southeastern and upper side of Garden Valley, there was evidence of irrigation canals.[202] Today, the irrigation canals look like shallow washes coming down the hill from the south.

In a 1931 *Arizona Republic* story, Harvey Mott reported that the ruin was 97 feet wide, 192 feet long, and 20 feet high.[203] It is easy to miss the ruin today since it is covered with grass and palo verde trees. The ruin is 50 feet north of the wooden trail sign [20-GG] for the Second Water and Black Mesa Trails. You can still see the remains of a few walls, but it mostly looks like a big mound of rocks. The 1893 report seems to overestimate the size. The 1931 measurement is closer to our estimate of 75 feet wide, 150 feet long, and 10 feet high.

We found two large and two small metates in the bedrock on the southeast side of Hill 2474—about halfway to the top. The grinding holes are carved into flat rock and measure six to eight inches in diameter and two to ten inches deep. We found these in two locations. Parts of broken manos (grinding stones) can still be found on the valley floor. You can view another set of bedrock metates on the north end of Garden Valley. These metates are on the southeast side of Hill 2538 under a cliff overhang at ground level [west of 20-FF].

The pottery sherds in Garden Valley are usually about an inch to an inch and a half square with one side finished in a smooth, solid-red color and the other side an unfinished desert-sand color. A few sherds have designs painted in red (on buff). Specks of mica in the unfinished side sparkle in the sun. Some of the sherds have the smooth-edged feature of a vessel lip. This pottery was probably made by the Salado Indians between A.D. 1100 and 1400. Don't take any of the pottery sherds away from the site.

In 1866, Garden Valley was the site of a major skirmish involving the Apache and Yavapai Indians and the U.S. Infantry, led by army commander Lieutenant Dubois from Fort McDowell. Note that these were foot soldiers, not cavalry soldiers. Thirty Indians were killed and many taken prisoner. The trail coming up from Pearce Mine Wash [20-HH to FF] that the military used to approach Garden Valley is rough, but still usable.[204]

The Fifth Cavalry—outfitted with rations for twenty days—left Camp McDowell on January 6, 1873, in search of Apache rancherias. On the third day of the army's scout, the expedition, under the command of Major W. H. Brown, crossed the Salt River at present-day Canyon Lake. They made a 15-mile loop through the Superstition Mountains before making camp in Peters Canyon on the evening of January 8, 1873. We don't have a precise route for the day's march, but only one route fits this 15-mile excursion.

From the Salt River [24-V], we estimate that they marched south to Garden Valley [20-GG] and continued to West Boulder Canyon [23-R] where they "passed some tanks in rock, about 8 miles from last night's camp." Heading east over Bull Pass [23-M], they could have gone up Squaw Canyon [23-XX], but the mileage indicates they went farther—probably to Charlebois

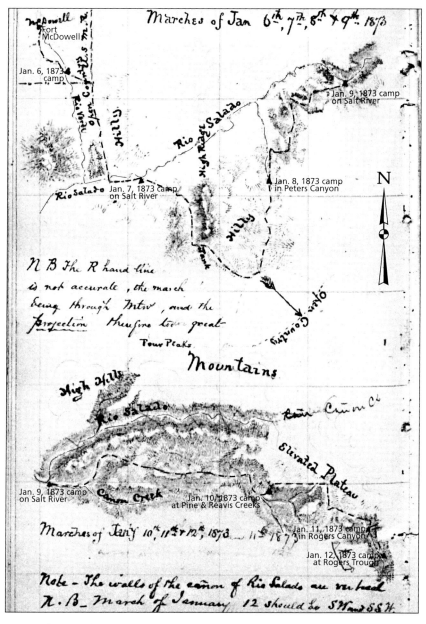

Page 101 from Second Lieutenant John G. Bourke's diary. The top map shows a loop march through Garden Valley and over Malapais Mountain with a Jan. 8, 1873, camp in Peters Canyon and a Jan. 9, 1873, camp on Salt River. The lower map shows the route to the Jan. 10, 1873, camp at the junction of Pine Creek and Reavis Creek; Jan. 11, 1873, camp in Rogers Canyon; and Jan. 12, 1873, camp at Rogers Trough Trailhead. We added the north arrow, dashed lines for trails and streams, and typeset dates for camps. Original color map from USMA Library, West Point, courtesy of Susan Lintelmann.

Spring [28-BB]. They continued up to Peters Mesa [28-T], followed the Spanish Trail across Malapais Mountain [27-Z to 27-J], and came down to their January 8, 1873, camp in Peters Canyon [27-M] where they noted a "feeble stream of water flowing north."[205] See Second Lieutenant Bourke's map on the top of page 257.

On January 9, the command camped on the Salt River near the confluence with Fish Creek, where Bourke wrote, "Our present camp within 600 or 800 yards of the scene of slaughter, Dec. 28th, 1872," which was the site of the Skeleton Cave Massacre. January 10 was another long march of 15 miles, which started in Cañon Creek (Fish Creek). Then, we surmise, they headed east to Pine Creek where they went left of "Weavers Needle" (Bourkes Butte) and came down into their camp at the junction of Pine and Reavis Creeks.[206] See Second Lieutenant Bourke's map on the bottom of page 257.

We speculate that on January 11 they headed up the Pine Creek Trail, went through Reavis Valley, and camped at the junction of Rogers and Grave Canyons for a march of 7 or 8 miles. This part of the route does not match Bourke's field notes or his map, but on January 12, they marched 1 to 1.5 miles and camped in the Rogers Trough area, which matches Bourke's notes for the following days when they traveled in the West Fork Pinto Creek area.[207] More of Bourke's commentary and maps on the Apache Wars in the eastern Superstition Mountains can be found in our companion volume, *Superstition Wilderness Trails East*.

In some areas of Garden Valley, you can see both Four Peaks and Weavers Needle. Some of the Lost Dutchman Mine maps show a reference line between these two peaks. Garden Valley lies to the west of that reference line. Another clue suggests that the Lost Dutchman Mine lies on a line drawn from Four Peaks when the four peaks are viewed as one peak. Four Peaks has that orientation when viewed from the Tortilla area.

Watch for the jumping cholla cacti. The literature inconsistently refers to both chain fruit cholla (*Opuntia fulgida*) and teddy bear cholla (*Opuntia bigelovii*) as jumping cholla. We use the jumping cholla name for the chain fruit cholla. Both plants drop spiny segments to the ground, but the teddy bear cholla has the reputation for being strongly barbed and more difficult to remove when embedded in your skin. It is easy to step on a cholla segment and transfer the spines from your shoe to your leg.

HACKBERRY VALLEY

The Hackberry Valley trip follows segments of former cowboy trails from Hackberry Spring to Canyon Lake. The trip goes through seldom-traveled country and a short slot canyon, making this an interesting trek. Horse riders can ride up to the slot canyon, but cannot get through to Canyon Lake.

ITINERARY

From First Water horse trailer parking lot, go to Hackberry Spring. Go down stream from Hackberry Spring, continue on the trail toward Garden Valley, leave the trail, go cross-country (northeast) into the Hackberry Valley, and follow Cholla Tank Wash to Canyon Lake Lagoon. Return the same way, or make a vehicle shuttle from Canyon Lake Trailhead.

DIFFICULTY

Moderate hike. Moderate ride, but beyond [21-X] not doable. Elevation change is +290 and -860 feet.

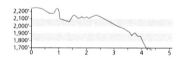

LENGTH and TIME

4.3 miles, 5 hours one way.

MAPS

Arizona USGS topo maps NAD27: Goldfield and Mormon Flat Dam. Superstition Wilderness Beartooth map, grid E10. Maps 20 and 21.

FINDING THE TRAIL

See the trailhead map on page 242. Start at the north side of the First Water Trailhead horse trailer parking lot [20-A] (N33° 28′ 58.9″, W111° 26′ 56.7″). Take Wash Route (2) to Hackberry Spring. See Trip 44 (Hackberry Spring) on page 249.

THE TRIP

Start on Map 20 on page 244. This route on abandoned trails provides an alternate way to get to Canyon Lake Trailhead rather than the popular Second Water (236) and Boulder Canyon Trails (103). The Hackberry Valley route is a little shorter than the maintained trails, but more rugged, and not passable for horses when it goes down a slot canyon in one spot [21-X]. It is a nice ride up to the slot canyon, but horse riders will have to backtrack the way they came or loop by Cholla Tank for a return to First Water Trailhead.

From the horse trailer parking lot at First Water Trailhead [20-A, 0], take Wash Route (2) to Hackberry Spring [21-J, 1.1] as described in Trip 44 (Hackberry Spring). From Hackberry Spring, the remaining part of the trip will be in open country and will not have much shade, so Hackberry Spring would be a good choice for a cool, shady rest stop. The spring is fairly reliable, but be sure to purify the water.

After zigzagging around the hills to get to Hackberry Spring, the Hackberry Valley route, in contrast, will provide open and scenic vistas. From Hackberry Spring [21-J, 1.1], continue down First Water Creek on the Garden Valley horse trail. About 0.3 mile north of the spring, the trail turns east, goes up a ravine, and tops out in a flat area. At the sharp right turn [21-F, 1.6], go left (north) on a cross-country route into Hackberry Valley.

From the trail [21-F, 1.6], head toward Gunsight Butte, and stay on the left (west) side of a small wash going northeast for about 0.2 mile where the faint trail crosses the wash to the right (east). Each time we travel this route, we look for the faint trail, but usually end up just going cross-country. Once in a while we find a well-worn section of trail and follow it for a short distance until it disappears. The trip crosses the low saddles of the seemingly endless ridges along the route. Gunsight Butte will serve as your major landmark for navigation. Head toward the butte, and keep it on your left as you pass it.

When the route connects with a sandy wash [21-D, 2.6], we found the walking to be easier in the wash than traveling on the hillside. This sandy wash intersects with Cholla Tank Wash [10-L, 2.9], where you may see a segment of trail and a former camp area on the west side of the intersection.

Continue down (north) Cholla Tank Wash using intermittent trails on either bench, or just head down the rocky bed of the wash. After a rain, the normally dry bedrock fills with water. Horse riders should follow the overgrown trails on the benches where there are flat places for camping.

The canyon narrows, and the benches disappear as the route heads into a narrow slot [21-X, 3.8] through the bedrock. Water flowing in the wash may make the route impassable. Even in dry weather, loose sand on the rock makes the footing hazardous. Negotiate three obstacles: (1) go through the hole in the rock—watch for slippery footing; (2) climb down the chute on the right using the right wall as in a chimney climb, and maybe have a buddy spot you from below; (3) bypass a pour-off and chockstone by going about 100 feet up on the right bench and then back down to creek level.

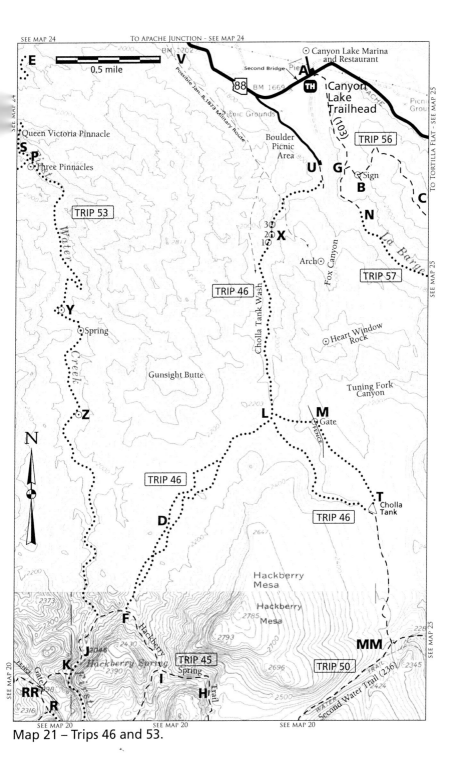

Map 21 – Trips 46 and 53.

From the narrows [21-X, 3.8], it is 0.5 mile down the bedrock of Cholla Tank Wash to the lagoon at Boulder Recreation site. When you reach the lagoon water, look for a trail heading out of the wash to the left (north). The trail goes up on the hill and then down to the lagoon waterline. Here, a well-used trail leads to the restrooms at the south end of the Boulder Recreation site parking lot [21-U, 4.3], which is a fee area. Free parking is available at the Canyon Lake Trailhead [21-A, 4.8] near the Canyon Lake Marina.

ALTERNATE RETURN ROUTE

Instead of going north down the narrow slot [21-X] in Cholla Tank Wash, hikers can start from the junction at the sandy wash [21-L, 2.7], go southeast, and follow Cholla Tank Wash up to Cholla Tank [21-T]—a dirt tank. This section of Cholla Tank Wash is rocky, brushy, and not suitable for horses.

Horse riders might try a steep cross-country route to the gate [21-M] in the fence on the ridge. We only found parts of the old trail from the wash [21-L] to the gate [21-M]—optimistically marked on Map·21 as a dotted line.

Cholla Tank [21-T, 3.4] is a rare sight in the desert when it is full of water and surrounded by a border of green grass. From Cholla Tank, take the track of the former road going south to the Second Water Trail (236) [21-MM, 4.1]. A side trip to Second Water Spring [20-KK] is 0.5 mile from here [21-MM]. On the Second Water and Dutchman's Trails, return to First Water Trailhead main parking [20-C, 6.9] or the horse trailer parking [20-A, 7.4] to complete the trip.

HISTORY AND LEGENDS

A 1966 Superstition Wilderness Forest Service map names the Hackberry Trail and shows it going from Garden Valley across Gunsight Butte, crossing the ridges, and ending at the Boulder Recreation site. A 1971 Superstition Wilderness map by Arizona Maps of Phoenix, Arizona, names the Hackberry Trail and identifies it as Trail 115. The 1971 map follows the same general route of the trail as the 1966 map, but the trail drops into the narrow slot canyon [21-X] that we named Cholla Tank Wash, which would disqualify it as a horse trail.

We originally thought Trip 46 (Hackberry Valley) would follow the former Hackberry Trail shown on the maps mentioned above until we came to the slot canyon and realized cowboys on horses could not use this route. So, the northern segment of the Hackberry Trail shown on the 1966 and 1971 maps is still a mystery.

Louis Ruiz rode the trails north of Hackberry Mesa when he was helping cattleman John Cox from 1969 to 1975 at the First Water Ranch.

John Cox branded the Quarter Circle U. Ruiz remembers a zigzag horse trail going off the north side of Hackberry Mesa and others that went over to Boulder Canyon and up to Cholla Tank [21-T]. Those trails are mostly overgrown now.

A January 8, 1873, account of a military expedition shows that the U.S. Army came south from the Salt River in the present-day Canyon Lake area—perhaps coming up through the wash that starts at Acacia Picnic area near milepost 210 on SR88 [24-V or 21-V]. We think the U.S. Army found a route through the cliffs west of the slot canyon [21-X] in Cholla Tank Wash or possibly on the mesa east of the slot canyon. We ruled out several other routes going south such as (1) First Water Creek, which is impassable to horses at a narrows [24-W]; (2) La Barge Canyon, which is impassable to horses at Box Spring [25-I]; (3) Boulder Canyon Trail, which did not exist in 1873; and (4) mountains east of First Water Creek, which are very cliffy. The route of the military is still a work in progress, so we continue to make field checks and research the literature.[208] See History and Legends on page 256 in Trip 45 (Garden Valley Loop) for more about the military marches through the Superstition Mountains.

Jack San Felice (left) and Bob Stambach (right) going through the narrow slot [21-X] in Cholla Tank Wash. March 2005 photo.

WEST FORK FIRST WATER CREEK

This trip is an alternate route to the Massacre Grounds Area. The route follows West Fork First Water Creek to its headwaters. The lower part of the canyon near the Dutchman's Trail makes a nice getaway for an easy hike.

ITINERARY

From First Water Trailhead, follow the Dutchman's Trail (104) southeast, go up West Fork First Water Creek, and connect with the Massacre Grounds Trail just below the Massacre Grounds.

DIFFICULTY

Moderate hike. Not recommended for horses. Elevation change is +910 and -50 feet.

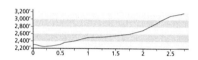

LENGTH and TIME

2.7 miles, 4 hours one way.

MAPS

Arizona USGS topo map NAD27: Goldfield. Superstition Wilderness Beartooth map, grid D12. Map 18.

FINDING THE TRAIL

See the trailhead map on page 242. The Dutchman's Trail leaves the southeast side (N33° 28' 47.7", W111° 26' 32.5") of the First Water Trailhead parking lot and heads east down a rough dirt road.

THE TRIP

Start on Map 18 on page 213. From the First Water Trailhead parking lot [18-C, 0.0], follow the Dutchman's Trail (104) beyond the junction with the Second Water Trail [18-D, 0.3] to the unmarked junction with West Fork First Water Creek [18-WW, 0.5] (N33° 28' 29.4", W111° 26' 17.2"). Boulder hop up the bed of the normally dry creek. The walking becomes easier once you get into the first curve of the creek. Seasonal water collects in the bedrock of the canyon, which makes hiking here enjoyable after a rain.

Elizabeth "Betty" Barkley at First Water Ranch headquarters [near 18-E]. Photo by Dewey Wildoner, 1963. Courtesy of Ken and Nancy McCollough—Betty's daughter.

For a short loop back to the First Water Trailhead, exit the canyon on the right (north) side [18-EE, 0.8] (N33° 28' 23.4", W111° 26' 28.7"). Follow a faint trail up the hill in a northerly direction toward a pass and a Hershey's-Kiss-shaped rock. From the left (west) side of the Hershey's Kiss rock, continue northerly to a second pass, but don't dip into the basin on your right (east). From the second pass, go down the ravine in a northerly direction, and then climb up to the trail on the ridge overlooking First Water Trailhead. You will need good off-trail hiking skills on this short cross-country trek to the First Water Trailhead [18-C, 1.3].

Resuming the trip description to the Massacre Grounds from the sharp bend [18-EE, 0.8], continue up the bed of the West Fork First Water Creek. Farther up canyon, bear right (southwesterly) at a fork in the canyon [18-XX, 1.6] (N33° 27' 45.9", W111° 26' 30.6"). Follow the drainage, and watch for rock cairns marking the route. Connect with the Massacre Grounds Trail near a flat camp area [18-YY, 2.1] (N33° 27' 27.7", W111° 26' 42.3"). Follow the Massacre Grounds Trail uphill to its end [18-W, 2.7]. Return the same way, or plan an alternate return using the information in Trip 42 (Massacre Grounds Trail) on page 237.

UPPER FIRST WATER CREEK

This enjoyable hike follows First Water Creek to its headwaters where you may find seasonal pools of water in the bedrock. You have a chance to find solitude here as you view the broad expanse of the Superstition Mountain northern slopes. Parker Pass provides a good view of Weavers Needle.

ITINERARY

From First Water Trailhead, follow the Dutchman's Trail (104) southeast. The route leaves the Dutchman's Trail, continues up First Water Creek bed, and climbs though a small canyon to the back slopes of Superstition Mountain. The return continues south to O'Grady Canyon, where a seldom-used trail circles north to Parker Pass, connects with the Dutchman's Trail, and retraces the Dutchman's Trail northwest back to the First Water Trailhead parking lot.

DIFFICULTY

Moderate hike. Not recommended for horses. Elevation change is ±1,050 feet.

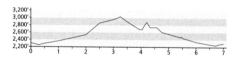

LENGTH and TIME

7.0 miles, 7 hours round-trip.

MAPS

Arizona USGS topo map NAD27: Goldfield. Superstition Wilderness Beartooth map, grid E12. Map 20.

FINDING THE TRAIL

See the trailhead map on page 242. The Dutchman's Trail leaves the southeast side (N33° 28′ 47.7″, W111° 26′ 32.5″) of the First Water Trailhead parking lot and heads east down the former dirt road.

THE TRIP

Start on Map 20 on page 244. Although not recommended for horses, riders can do the trip in reverse to reach the north slopes of Superstition Mountain near Cross Butte [20-SS]. From the First Water Trailhead parking lot [20-C, 0], take the Dutchman's Trail and bear right (south) at the wooden signpost

Prospector and treasure hunter Barry Storm, author of Thunder Gods Gold. *Photographer and date unknown. Courtesy Superstition Mountain Historical Society, John Burbridge Collection.*

for the Second Water Trail [20-D, 0.3]. Continue on the Dutchman's Trail over at least six stream or dry creek bed crossings. Be sure to look for the interesting rock formations resembling a pig, poodle, and squirrel on the right (west) side of the trail just before the trail crosses First Water Creek for the last time.

The trip leaves the Dutchman's Trail [20-QQ, 1.4] after about 20 or 30 minutes. At this point, the Dutchman's Trail heads southeast, away from the creek and up a small hill. If you continue up the hill for another 5 minutes on the Dutchman's Trail to Transmission Pass [20-LL, 1.6], you will see the top of Weavers Needle in the distance. This is the turnaround point for an easy trip. Another possible turnaround destination is at Parker Pass [20-Z, 2.5], where you have a better view of Weavers Needle before the trail drops down to West Boulder Creek.

From the bottom of the hill [20-QQ, 1.4], near a stone water-diversion bar on the trail, this hike continues south and up First Water Creek. You can walk up the creek bed if it is dry or on either side of First Water Creek, since there is no trail. The most interesting portion of the hike begins where First Water Creek makes a bend going due south—the creek climbs through a narrow canyon with a waterfall (N33° 27′ 18.5″, W111° 25′ 24.8″). We have seen water in the pools [20-CC, 2.5] above the waterfall even when the lower creek bed was dry. This would be a good place for lunch, or you could wait until you get to Cross Butte [20-SS].

If you are just coming up to the waterfall and returning the way you came, an easier return is to connect with the Dutchman's Trail south of

Transmission Pass. Going down canyon (north) from the waterfall, the terrain opens up and you can take a cross-country shortcut up and over a low pass to intersect the Dutchman's Trail (N33° 27' 34.6", W111° 25' 14.8").

Continuing on this trip to the top of waterfall canyon, the creek bed opens out into a large sloping plane on the back side of Superstition Mountain. A rectangular butte appears ahead as you continue up the wash. Then Cross Butte, which looks a little like a curved claw, comes into view on your left (southeasterly).[209] Stay in the wash that leads toward Cross Butte until you get to the saddle [20-SS, 3.2] at Cross Butte (N33° 26' 43.3", W111° 25' 05.4"). Don't let the trails-of-use on the right side of the wash lure you out of the wash—you will do a lot of unnecessary bushwhacking. From the saddle [20-SS], go 0.1 mile up and into the rock formation of Cross Butte. The smooth rocks make a nice place to rest. We named the butte after the small cross that is inscribed on the rocks. Please do not add more rock inscriptions.

From the saddle at Cross Butte [20-SS], head east until you see the narrow ravine of O'Grady Canyon. A few spotty cairns at the top of O'Grady Canyon [20-DD, 3.4] guide you down the ravine in a northeasterly direction. The O'Grady Trail is not well defined, so you must take your best guess for trail direction in some places. The O'Grady Trail ends at the intersection of the well-used Tims Saddle Trail [20-TT, 3.9] (N33° 27' 02.0", W111° 24' 41.1"). Turn left, take the Tims Saddle Trail over to the Dutchman's Trail at Parker Pass [20-Z, 4.5] (N33° 27' 26.0", W111° 24' 58.2"), and return to First Water Trailhead [20-C, 7.0].

EXTENSION OF TRIP TO THE RIDGELINE TRAIL

From Cross Butte [14-SS] near the top of O'Grady Canyon, you can follow a route up the north ridge of Old West Boulder Canyon to the Superstition Mountain Ridgeline Trail. The route meets the Ridgeline Trail near Peak 4562. See Trip 28 (Superstition Mountain Ridgeline) on page 178 for the route used by Bruce Grubbs and Irv Kanode. Use Map 14 on page 177.

HISTORY AND LEGENDS

In their 1978 *Hiker's Guide to the Superstition Mountains*, Dick and Sharon Nelson noted an abandoned vehicle along the north side of the Dutchman's Trail, just east of Transmission Pass [20-LL].[210] It has been rumored that the car may have belonged to Chuck Aylor or Obie Stoker.[211] Forest Service Ranger George Martin disassembled the car with a cutting torch and enlisted the help of the Sierra Club to pack it out of the Wilderness in March of 1980 or 1981.[212] While recognizing the need to restore and preserve the Wilderness, some Superstition Mountain aficionados felt a sense of loss when this rusty landmark was removed.

WILLOW SPRING

This trip takes you to the 1931 camp of Adolph Ruth in West Boulder Canyon. You can trace the route that the Barkley cowboys, Purnell and Keenan, used to pack Ruth into his camp. Gus Barkley told Ruth that it was a good spring. Even today, it has water in the dry season.

ITINERARY

From First Water Trailhead, follow the Dutchman's Trail (104) southeast. The route leaves the Dutchman's Trail at Parker Pass, goes across O'Grady Canyon and Tims Saddle, and drops into West Boulder Canyon. Return the same way or take an optional return on the Peralta and Dutchman's Trails.

DIFFICULTY

Moderate hike. Moderate ride, but difficult in West Boulder Canyon. Elevation change is +1,050 and -470 feet.

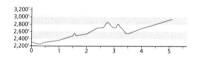

LENGTH and TIME

5.1 miles, 5.5 hours one way.

MAPS

Arizona USGS topo maps NAD27: Goldfield and Weavers Needle. Superstition Wilderness Beartooth map, grid F13. Maps 20 and 22.

FINDING THE TRAIL

See the trailhead map on page 242. The Dutchman's Trail leaves the southeast corner (N33° 28' 47.7", W111° 26' 32.5") of the First Water Trailhead parking lot.

THE TRIP

Start on Map 20 on page 244. From the First Water Trailhead parking lot [20-C, 0], take the Dutchman's Trail going east. Bear right at the wooden sign for the Second Water Trail [20-D, 0.3], and stay on the Dutchman's Trail. Proceed over Transmission Pass [20-LL, 1.6] to Parker Pass [20-Z, 2.5] (N33° 27' 26.0", W111° 24' 58.2"), which is the last pass before the trail goes downhill. At Parker Pass, look for the unsigned Tims Saddle Trail (aka O'Grady

Willow Spring [22-WW] emerges from the bed of the West Boulder Canyon in a clump of cattails and reeds—center right of the photo. The alternate return goes over the pass [22-SS] to the left of the peak on the horizon. October 2010 photo.

Trail), which goes uphill to the right (south) then curves southeast. Continue over the hill to O'Grady Canyon. Cross O'Grady Canyon wash [22-TT, 3.1] (N33° 27′ 02.0″, W111° 24′ 41.1″), go up on the bench following rock cairns, and look for the well-defined Tims Saddle Trail going up to Tims Saddle. At O'Grady Canyon, it is easy to lose the trail and incorrectly head south in the wash. Take a few moments here to make sure you are on Tims Saddle Trail.

The Tims Saddle Trail ends when it comes down the hill and meets West Boulder Canyon [22-FFF, 3.5] (N33° 26′ 44.6″, W111° 24′ 26.2″). From here, turn right (south), and follow the normally dry creek bed of West Boulder Canyon, or look for the old trail on the east bench. The August 2020 Superstition Fire burned this canyon and Old West Boulder Canyon.

The remains of a wire corral [22-W, 4.3] (N33° 26′ 10.0″, W111° 24′ 01.5″) still can be seen along portions of the former trail. Willow Spring [22-WW, 5.0] (N33° 25′ 55.8″, W111° 23′ 29.5″) normally has good water and originates from the middle of the creek bed. We have not determined the exact location of Aldolph Ruth's camp, but it was probably on the east bench across from the spring. The stone corral [22-YY, 5.1] (N33° 25′ 53.5″, W111° 23′ 25.2″) is upstream from the spring on the right (south) bench. Return the same way, or take the more difficult alternate return described below.

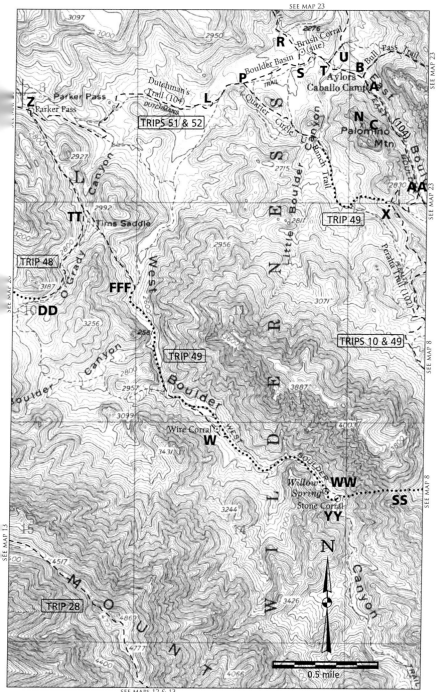

Map 22 – Trips 49, 51, and 52.

ALTERNATE RETURN ON PERALTA AND DUTCHMAN'S TRAILS

Start on Map 8 on page 98. From the stone corral [8-YY, 5.1], head east up a steep ravine to the pass [8-SS, 5.4] (N33° 25' 55.4", W111° 23' 09.7") for a spectacular view of Weavers Needle. Go cross-country following the left (north) slope of the ravine heading toward Weavers Needle and Peralta Trail (102). Staying on the slope and out of the ravine as long as you can will make the bushwhacking easier. At Peralta Trail (102)—just north of Piper's Camp [8-O]—turn left (north), and follow it around Hill 3113 [23-R, 6.3].

You have two choices for the remaining part of the return. First choice: Just before the Peralta Trail makes a switchback down to East Boulder Canyon [23-X, 7.3] (N33° 27' 03.3", W111° 23' 10.5"), you can go up and over the western ridge to connect with parts of the former Quarter Circle U Trail. It starts as a cross-county route—the old trail is washed out—and then turns into a cairned trail as shown on Map 23. The cairned trail takes you to the Dutchman's Trail [23-P, 8.3] (N33° 27' 32.1", W111° 23' 54.4") in Boulder Basin along West Boulder Creek. Turn left (west) and return on the Dutchman's Trail to First Water Trailhead [20-C, 12.1], where the trip ends.

Second choice: Remain on the Peralta Trail until it meets the Dutchman's Trail [23-AA, 7.6] in East Boulder Canyon at the wooden trail sign. Go left (north) on the Dutchman's Trail, pass Aylor's Camp [23-A, 8.2], cross West Boulder Creek [23-L, 9.1], go over Parker Pass [20-Z, 10.2], and end the trip at First Water Trailhead [20-C, 12.7].

HISTORY AND LEGENDS

On June 13, 1931, treasure hunter Adolph Ruth rode into the Superstition Mountains on the Dutchman's Trail from First Water Trailhead [20-C] to search for the Lost Dutchman Mine. At that time, First Water Creek was called Willow Creek as shown on the old maps. He was escorted by Leroy F. Purnell and Jack Keenan, two cowboys and prospectors from Tex Barkley's outfit. They took him up the trail in Willow Canyon (now First Water Creek), over Parker Pass, and down into West Boulder Canyon to a permanent pool of water at Willow Spring [22-WW].[213]

An extensive search was undertaken when Ruth was discovered missing from his camp on June 20. Ruth's skull was found near the Dutchman's Trail and Bull Pass Trail junction [23-UU] in Needle Canyon on December 11, 1931, by an expedition of the Arizona Archeological Commission, sponsored by *The Arizona Republic*. Staff writer Harvey Mott wrote a four-part series for the newspaper describing the expedition and their finds. *Phoenix Gazette* staff photographer E. D. Newcomer took the photographs.[214] Ruth's body was found a month later about one-half mile away on the lower east slope of Black Top Mesa [23-WW].

The last entry in Ruth's notebook was veni, vidi (I came, I saw). The notebook did not contain vici (I conquered), which has been reported in some literature.[215] Maps to the lost treasure, which Ruth had brought with him, were missing. Ruth's death was officially recorded as unknown, but many believe he was killed for his maps and information. An article by Greg Davis in the *Superstition Mountain Journal* shows a recently discovered photo of the right side of Ruth's skull.[216] The hole in the left side of the skull and the missing right side suggest that a gunshot to the head was probably the cause of death. Decades later, historians and treasure hunters continue to discuss and review the story of Adolph Ruth.

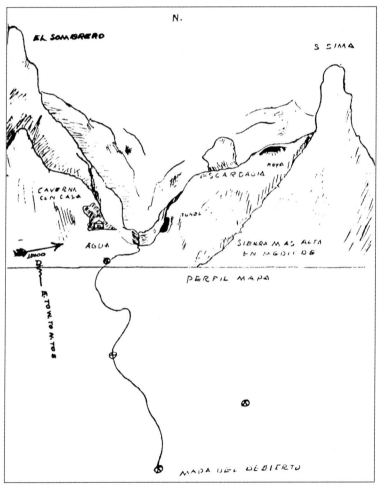

Ruth-Gonzales Map (Peralta-Ruth Map). Glenn Magill used this map to locate his mine on Bluff Spring Mountain. Courtesy Gregory Davis, Superstition Mountain Historical Society, Dons Club File.

SECOND WATER SPRING

This trip takes you beyond Garden Valley to a seasonal spring with cattails and reeds. Above the spring is the site of a former mining camp and caved-in mine shaft with good views of the canyons and surrounding mountains.

ITINERARY

From First Water Trailhead, follow the Second Water Trail (236) to Second Water Spring. Return the same way. An alternate approach takes an off-trail route to Obie Stoker's former camp and ends at Second Water Spring.

DIFFICULTY

Moderate hike and ride. Elevation change is +260 and -650 feet.

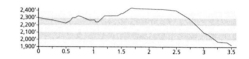

LENGTH and TIME

3.5 miles, 2.5 hours one way.

MAPS

Arizona USGS topo map NAD27: Goldfield. Superstition Wilderness Beartooth map, grid E11. Map 20.

FINDING THE TRAIL

See the trailhead map on page 242. This trip begins at the wooden trail sign in Garden Valley [20-GG, 1.8] (N33° 29′ 08.7″, W111° 25′ 36.7″).

THE TRIP

Start on Map 20 on page 244. From the First Water Trailhead parking lot [20-C, 0] (N33° 28′ 47.7″, W111° 26′ 32.5″), follow Trip 45 (Garden Valley Loop) on page 252 to the junction of the Black Mesa Trail in Garden Valley [20-GG, 1.8].

From the wooden sign for the Black Mesa Trail junction [20-GG, 1.8], continue on the Second Water Trail (236) northeast across the flat expanse of Garden Valley. At the northeast side of Garden Valley, the trail skirts a large earthen water tank [20-T, 2.2], and then the trail begins a rocky descent.

About 30 minutes from the Garden Valley trail-junction sign, you pass an old road [20-MM, 2.8] on the left (north) going over to Cholla Tank [25-T]. Note the rock cairn at the junction with the alternate Obie Stoker Trail [20-NN, 3.1], and continue down the trail to Second Water Spring [20-KK, 3.3]. The trail crosses the trickle of water just below the tangle of bushes and trees at the spring area.[217] Second Water Trail ends at Boulder Canyon [20-JJ, 3.5]. Return the same way.

ALTERNATE TRIP TO OBIE STOKER'S CAMP

Ten minutes down the trail from the Cholla Tank road intersection [20-MM, 2.8], a rock cairn [20-NN, 3.1] (N33° 29′ 48.0″, W111° 24′ 42.6″) on the right marks the faint trail that leads to Obie Stoker's former mining camp [20-OO]. Take the Obie Stoker Trail heading southeast, go across Second Water Canyon, and follow the faint trail to the camp on the flat bench.

A few remnants from mining work remain at Stoker's Camp [20-OO, 3.4] (N33° 29′ 36.6″, W111° 24′ 33.2″) on the east side of the ravine—rusty buckets, kitchen gear, a bed frame, etc. The trails going to the mine workings at the north end of the camp are overgrown—one heading steeply up the hill going east and another contouring around to the left (north). Unless you run across the tread of one of the trails, you will probably have to bushwhack through the overgrown area to reach the mines. At the upper mine, the trail

Sign at Obie Stoker's lower mine. Photo by Gregory Davis, circa 1985. Courtesy of Gregory Davis.

ends at a closed mine shaft [20-PP, 3.5] (N33° 29' 43.8", W111° 24' 28.0") filled in with rock and timber. Here, you are rewarded with a fine view of Second Water Canyon. The lower workings—in a short tunnel recently used as a black bear den—are on the slope a few hundred feet below the upper mine. It takes less than 10 minutes to reach either mine from the camp.

From the lower mine tunnel, drop down to the smooth bedrock of Second Water Canyon, and head down canyon to the area considered Second Water Spring [20-KK, 3.8]. If the larger bushes and trees block your progress in the ravine, scramble up the left (north) bank and connect with the Second Water Trail. The quantity and quality of water here will depend on the season. It is best to bring your own drinking water. Grasses, reeds, and cattails usually grow in small catch basins of water. Boulder Canyon [20-JJ, 4.0] is another 10 minutes down the trail (northeast). Return on Second Water Trail, or continue on the Boulder Canyon Trail.

ALTERNATE THROUGH TRIP TO CANYON LAKE TRAILHEAD

From the east end of Second Water Trail at the wooden trail sign [25-JJ, 3.5] in Boulder Canyon, continue the trip on the Boulder Canyon Trail (103), reach Indian Paint Mine [25-E, 3.9], cross La Barge Creek [25-D, 4.3], and end at Canyon Lake Trailhead [25-A, 7.4]. You will need to park your shuttle

Remnants of Obie Stoker's former mining camp [20-OO] above Second Water Spring [20-KK]. Tall grass has hidden most of the equipment in recent years. January 1993 photo.

vehicle at Canyon Lake Trailhead. See Canyon Lake Trailhead on page 304 and Trip 56 (Boulder Canyon Trail to Marsh Valley) on page 306 for more things to do in that area.

HISTORY AND LEGENDS

The 1956 Goldfield USGS map shows buildings at the First Water Ranch site along the Second Water Trail. Bill Barkley, son of Tex Barkley, and his wife Betty built a house, a barn, and some outbuildings here on the south side of the Second Water Trail near First Water Creek.[218] The Forest Service removed the structures, and all that remains today are some concrete footings. Greg Hansen and Russ Orr of the Forest Service recall that about 1972 the cattle operation—windmill tower and corrals—was moved 0.7 mile north along First Water Creek, just outside the Wilderness boundary fence [20-P].

In 1993 and the years following, we noticed new cow trails with fresh tracks, fresh-bed ground, and fresh manure in Second Water valley. We never saw any cattle, but others told us that they had seen them for several years. The Forest Service, in December 2003, authorized a roundup of the wild cattle in the Second Water and Garden Valley areas. About twelve animals were brought in one at a time, and the wranglers were allowed to keep them.[219]

Obie Stoker's lower mine was named Question Mark No. 1, and the upper mine [20-PP] was named Question Mark No. 2. An amended Question Mark No. 1 Notice of Mining Location in 1975 shows Obie Stoker's partners as Rollie Hubler, Floyd Hubler, Jerry Sherwood, and Bob Dierking. The paperwork mentions a 1969 tunnel and indicates that the first location was filed in 1924. Later partners were Warren Koneman and Bruce Gillette.[220] Apparently, the mining operation was not profitable. In 2010, we found that the lower workings were being used as a bear den. Fortunately, the bear was not home when we visited.[221]

Most people consider the water hole next to the Second Water Trail the location of the Second Water Spring [20-KK], but the Goldfield USGS map shows the spring just north of Stoker's Camp [20-OO]. In 2020, Greg Davis and author Jack Carlson finally verified the location (N33° 29′ 39.1″, W111° 24′ 33.5″) of that map designation for Second Water Spring. It is about 90 yards north of Stoker's Camp on the east side of the wash. A small seep of water comes out of the layered rocks, but there is no useable flow of water.

Water also surfaces in Second Water Canyon about a half mile directly south of Stoker's Camp—toward Black Mesa. That seasonal spring or catch basin probably fed the out-of-service concrete water trough (N33° 29′ 25.5″, W111° 24′ 33.6″) down canyon from the seasonal spring.

Black Mesa Loop

This popular loop trip goes from Garden Valley to the top of Black Mesa and then down to Boulder Basin, where you may find seasonal water in West Boulder Creek. A side trip to East Boulder Canyon takes you to the site of Aylor's Caballo Camp, Aylor's Arch, and wonderful views of Weavers Needle.

ITINERARY

This trip starts at First Water Trailhead, follows the Dutchman's and Second Water Trails to Garden Valley, and continues on the Black Mesa Trail over Black Mesa to West Boulder Canyon. Return on the Dutchman's Trail via Parker Pass to First Water Trailhead. An alternate return follows the Boulder Canyon and Second Water Trails back to First Water Trailhead.

DIFFICULTY

Moderate hike and ride. Elevation change is ±1,150 feet.

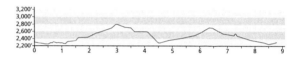

LENGTH and TIME

8.8 miles, 6 hours round-trip.

MAPS

Arizona USGS topo map NAD27: Goldfield. Superstition Wilderness Beartooth map, grids E11 to E12. Maps 20 and 23.

FINDING THE TRAIL

See the trailhead map on page 242. This trip begins at the wooden trail sign in Garden Valley [20-GG, 1.8] (N33° 29′ 08.7″, W111° 25′ 36.7″).

THE TRIP

Start on Map 20 on page 244. This is a favorite loop hike. It is a nice, moderate trip for people who enjoy the maintained trails. It is also a good introduction to many of the trails that connect to other parts of the Superstition Wilderness. We describe the trip in the clockwise direction. For those traveling in the counterclockwise direction, we provide the mileage waypoints at the end of this section.

From the First Water Trailhead parking lot [20-C, 0] (N33° 28' 47.7", W111° 26' 32.5"), follow Trip 45 (Garden Valley Loop) to the wooden trail sign for the Black Mesa Trail in Garden Valley [20-GG, 1.8]—next to the prehistoric ruin. Take the Black Mesa Trail.

The trail passes under towering saguaro cacti before leveling off at Black Mesa Pass [20-Q, 3.0] at the former forest of jumping cholla cacti, which was burned in the August 2020 Superstition Fire. The trail doesn't go to the ridgelines of Black Mesa, so for a better view of the valleys below, take a short cross-country walk to the ridges on the left or right, off the main trail.

The trail dips into the wash of Yellow Peak Canyon as it begins the descent to the south. You can take a cross-country side trip to the top of Yellow Peak by leaving the trail when the trail passes through a basin [23-YYY, 3.9].[222] And, for future trips, you might want to explore Yellow Peak Canyon all the way down to Boulder Canyon. The narrow canyon collects rainwater in the potholes that have been sculptured into the bedrock.

As you descend the Black Mesa Trail, look south into the flat valley of Boulder Basin for the West Boulder Creek crossing and the Dutchman's Trail intersection. Once in the valley, it will be difficult to get the big picture of the trail layout. Boulder Basin has endless flat places for tent camping

Riders out of the O.K. Corral Stables pause on the flat at Black Mesa. Left to right: packhorse Bill, Ken "Moose" Carter riding Shorty, packhorse Redman, and Rick Scheier riding Wyatt. January 2010 photo.

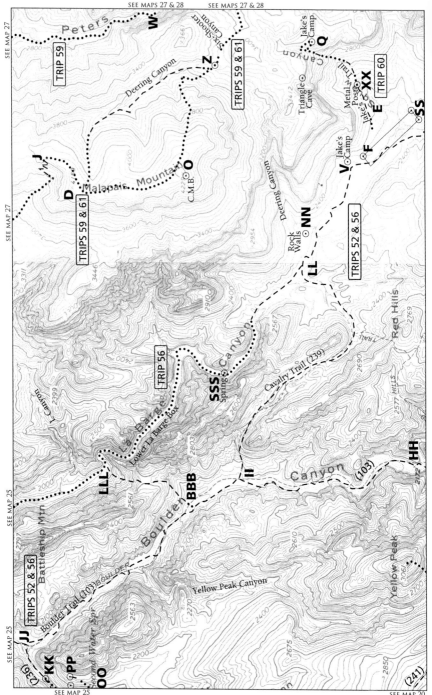

Map 23 – Trips 10, 21, 22, 49, 51, 52, 56, 59, 60, and 61.

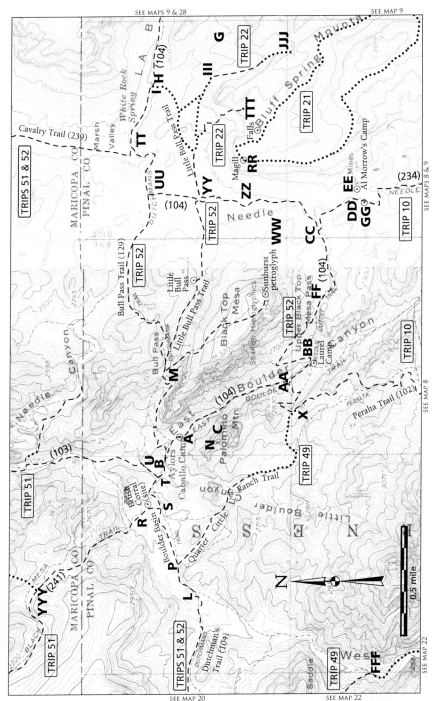

Map 23 continued – Trips 10, 21, 22, 49, 51, 52, 56, 59, 60, and 61.

and picnicking, but only a few small trees for shade. The trail crosses West Boulder Creek [23-R, 4.5] and quickly intersects the Dutchman's Trail at a wooden trail sign [23-S, 4.7]. From the wooden trail sign, the return trip goes right (west) and follows the Dutchman's Trail back to First Water Trailhead. The alternate return, described below, goes left (east) on the Dutchman's Trail for the longer trek via Boulder Canyon and Second Water Spring. The side trip to Aylor's Camp is also described below.

Go right (west) at the wooden sign [23-S, 4.7] on the Dutchman's Trail to take the easiest return to First Water Trailhead—about 4.1 miles and 2 hours. If you are planning a future camping trip, the flat areas south of Boulder Basin are ideal for tent camping—away from the trail and hidden by the low hills. The former Quarter Circle U Trail [23-P, 5.0] that comes in from the left (south) is marked only by a rock cairn.

Twenty minutes up the Dutchman's Trail, the trail crosses West Boulder Creek [23-L, 5.2] and heads up to Parker Pass [20-Z, 6.3]. From Parker Pass, it's mostly downhill to Transmission Pass [20-LL, 7.2] and on to First Water Creek. Looking left (south) [20-QQ, 7.4] up First Water Creek, you can see the route (no trail) of Trip 48 (Upper First Water Creek). The Dutchman's Trail follows the First Water Creek drainage back to the parking lot [20-C, 8.8]. The creek is narrow, and the several creek crossings are well defined by heavy use.

SIDE TRIP TO AYLOR'S CAMP FROM BOULDER BASIN

Whichever return route you select from Boulder Basin [23-S], you should take the short, quarter-mile side trip up the Dutchman's Trail, over the small hill, to the former site of Aylor's Caballo Camp in East Boulder Canyon. From the wooden sign at the Black Mesa and Dutchman's Trail intersection [23-S, 0.0], take the Dutchman's Trail east. After about 10 minutes, the Boulder Canyon Trail (103) branches to the left at a wooden trail sign [23-T, 0.2]. The Boulder Canyon Trail is the alternate return route.

Continue on the Dutchman's Trail going east for 5 minutes to the Bull Pass Trail wooden sign [23-B, 0.3] and another 5 minutes to Aylor's Caballo Camp [23-A, 0.4] (N33° 27′ 32.2″, W111° 23′ 18.1″). Only the flat camp area remains at Caballo Camp. If you look closely, you can still see "PEG Aylor" scratched in the black boulders to the west of the trail—please do not scratch your name on the rocks. For many years, Chuck Aylor and his wife Peggy had a tent camp here, but it was washed away in a flood around 1959.

From Aylor's Camp, the view of Weavers Needle looking up East Boulder Canyon is superb. You can see the image of a horse with a laid back ear on the horizon of Palomino Mountain on the left side of a square cut notch [23-N]. Clay Worst said it is best viewed in the afternoon from Aylor's

Chuck and Peggy Aylor's Caballo Camp [23-A] in East Boulder Canyon. Photograph by Al Reser, circa 1956. Courtesy Superstition Mountain Historical Society, Al Reser Collection.

Camp. The horse image is said to be a landmark for a lost mine, which is believed to be on the hill under the head.[223] A few minutes' walk south of Aylor's Camp—less than 300 yards—on the Dutchman's Trail brings Aylor's Arch [23-C] into view on the skyline of east-facing Palomino Mountain.

Another side trip in the area takes you to the site of an old and elusive arrastra that was used for grinding ore [23-U]. See History and Legends on page 286 for the story of the arrastra.

BLACK MESA LOOP—COUNTERCLOCKWISE

If you prefer to make the Black Mesa Loop in the counterclockwise direction, your mileage waypoints are: First Water Trailhead [20-C, 0], Parker Pass [20-Z, 2.5], Boulder Basin at the Black Mesa Trail sign [23-S, 4.1], Garden Valley [20-GG, 7.0], First Water Trailhead [20-C, 8.8].

ALTERNATE RETURN DIRECTIONS

The alternate return, from Boulder Basin [23-S, 4.7], using the Boulder Canyon and Second Water Trails is about 7 miles (4 hours) back to the First Water Trailhead. This return requires many crossings on boulders in the creek. The water is seasonal, so Boulder Canyon Creek might be just a dry creek bed, which makes the travel easier, though the scenery is not as pleasant.

Boulder Canyon Trail (103) starts at a wooden sign [23-T, 4.9] on the Dutchman's Trail. The trail junction is just 10 minutes away, over the low hill to the east, from the Black Mesa Trail intersection [23-S]. Boulder Canyon Trail goes north and follows East Boulder Canyon Creek. The trail soon passes West Boulder Canyon Creek as it enters from the left. This is the beginning of Boulder Canyon.

Boulder Canyon Trail continues down the Boulder Canyon water course on a trail marked by large rock cairns at each crossing. Needle Canyon enters on the right [23-HH, 5.7] and is marked by a naturally whitewashed, needle-shaped rock on the low cliff to the north. Here you'll find several flat, sandy camping places, which were formed by high water flowing through the canyon after heavy rains. Camp on high ground if it looks like it will rain.

Boulder Creek at flood stage. The view is looking downstream (north) from the wooden trail sign at the Cavalry Trail junction with Boulder Creek [23-II]. December 1992 photo.

If you have been following the rock cairns, the trail will pass by the wooden trail sign [23-II, 6.8] on the east bank, which marks the intersection with the Cavalry Trail (239). The Cavalry Trail is a convenient trail to use for trips over to La Barge Canyon [23-LL] and Marsh Valley [near 23-TT]. Across Boulder Canyon Creek from the Cavalry Trail sign, you will find some flat, sandy campsites.

A trail over the ridge to La Barge Box starts on the east side of Boulder Canyon [23-BBB, 7.1] (N33° 29′ 15.2″, W111° 23′ 38.4″). The unsigned trail is well defined, but too steep and rocky at the start for horses. It takes you to the sandy camp and pool of water at the bottom of Lower La Barge Box, which usually has water all year.

Continue downstream for about 30 minutes until you see Second Water Canyon [20-JJ, 8.2] break the horizon on the west side of Boulder Canyon. Second Water Trail (236) goes up this small drainage. The trail sign is on the west bank, and the large, smooth, flat white rocks in the middle of the creek will alert you to the upcoming trail intersection. The Boulder Canyon Trail continues downstream on the west bank, but for this trip, you want to take the Second Water Trail going west up the ravine for the final two hours of the trip. Follow the Second Water Trail to Second Water Spring [20-KK, 8.4], to Garden Valley [20-GG, 9.9], and to First Water Trailhead [20-C, 11.7], where the trip description ends. See Trip 45 (Garden Valley Loop) and Trip 50 (Second Water Spring) for more information about this last segment of the trail.

HISTORY AND LEGENDS

Boulder Basin was commonly referred to as Brush Corral Basin in the 1970s and earlier. Jesse Feldman showed us the site of Brush Corral, which is marked on Map 23 just north of the trail sign for Black Mesa and Dutchman's Trails [23-S]. It was a large wooden corral, which burned sometime around 1965. In their book *The History of Apache Junction, Arizona*, Swanson and Kollenborn show a 1948 picture of Brush Corral with rancher William T. "Bill" Barkley overlooking the branding operation.[224] Bill was William A. "Tex" Barkley's son.

A quarter mile southeast of Brush Corral, Charles "Chuck" and Martha "Peggy" Aylor located their camp in East Boulder Canyon [23-A]. From the late 1930s to 1959, they were actively prospecting for gold and enjoying the beauty of the Superstition Mountains. Their camp, located just south of the junction where East and West Boulder canyons meet, had a fine view up East Boulder Canyon toward Weavers Needle, with the sheer cliffs of Palomino Mountain on the west and Black Top Mesa on the east. They named their camp Caballo Camp, which is shown on the 1956 Goldfield USGS topographic map. Since the arch [23-C] on Palomino Mountain didn't have a name, we wanted to identify it for easy reference in our trip descriptions. Tom Kollenborn suggested Aylor's Arch, which we think is an appropriate name. He also said some storytellers call it the Eye of the Horse or Caballo Ojo.

Caballo Camp was destroyed in a flood about 1959 and was removed by the Forest Service, but you can still see the flat terrace beside the black basalt boulders where it was located. Sometime in the late 1950s, Chuck Aylor and Peggy Aylor were living separately. A 1959 auto accident put Chuck Aylor in the hospital, and it took some time for him to recover. About 1961 or 1962, Chuck Aylor established another camp [25-Z] in lower La Barge Canyon below the Lower Box. A letter from Peggy Aylor to Al and Martha Reser indicated that in 1967 she had partners in the mountains working with her. Chuck Aylor died in 1968, and Peggy Aylor died in 1970.[225] See Trip 56 (Boulder Canyon Trail to Marsh Valley) on page 311 for more about Chuck Aylor's La Barge Canyon camp.

Lost mine searchers speculate that an arrastra indicates that a hidden mine could be located nearby, so they are always on the lookout for such ruins. An arrastra is a fifteen-foot circular arrangement of flat rocks upon which large rocks are dragged to crush gold ore. A horse or mule was attached to a beam to supply the power that moved the rocks (similar to a children's pony ride). The Blue Bird Mine and Gift Shop, along the Apache Trail, has an arrastra on display behind the store. After a heavy rain in 1940, Brownie Holmes found an arrastra a few hundred yards south of the East and West Boulder Canyon junction [23-U]. After another heavy rain in 1944, he noted that it was covered with dirt again. A photo of the arrastra appears in T. E. Glover's book *The Lost Dutchman Mine of Jacob Waltz, Part 2, The Holmes Manuscript*. We have not seen the arrastra, but it may appear again, so we will keep looking.[226]

The Superstition Mountain Museum has an arrastra drag rock on display that was packed out of the mountains by Tex Barkley and his ranch hand "Boog" Barnett in the early 1930s. The drag rock was found at the junction of East and West Boulder Canyons. Nancy Barkley McCollough (granddaughter of Tex Barkley) and her husband Ken donated the drag rock to the Museum. The rock had been part of a wall at the 3R Ranch and later it was taken to Gertrude Barkley's home in Kings Ranch. The museum display notes that George Scholey packed the sweep pole, from the same arrastra, out of the mountains. The location of the sweep pole is unknown.[227]

Barry Storm claimed to have found gold ore in Boulder Canyon about a mile and a half north of the reported site of the arrastra. His February 27, 1940, assay report showed 28.64 ounces of gold valued at $1,002.40 when gold was $35 an ounce. From Barry Storm's topo map,[228] it appears that he found the ore in Boulder Canyon just south of Yellow Peak Canyon.

Trip 52

MARSH VALLEY LOOP

This classic trip loops through the interior of the Wilderness. While traveling on portions of four established trails, you discover seasonal water, cottonwood and sycamore trees, a large stone holding corral, former mining camps, unusual claim monuments and markings, stone walls, extraordinary views of Weavers Needle, the site of the Adolph Ruth stories, Aylor's Arch, and more.

ITINERARY

From First Water Trailhead, follow Second Water Trail to Boulder Canyon. Take Boulder Canyon Trail to Cavalry Trail, and follow the Cavalry Trail to La Barge Canyon. Explore La Barge Canyon south to the White Spring area. Return on the Dutchman's Trail going around Black Top Mesa, down East Boulder Canyon, over Parker Pass, and ending at First Water Trailhead. An alternate route uses the Bull Pass Trail over Bull Pass.

DIFFICULTY

Difficult hike. Moderate backpack. Difficult ride. Elevation change is ±1,880 feet.

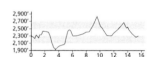

LENGTH and TIME

15.4 miles, 10 hours round-trip.

MAPS

Arizona USGS topo maps NAD27: Goldfield and Weavers Needle. Superstition Wilderness Beartooth map, grids E11 to G12. Maps 20 and 23.

FINDING THE TRAIL

See Map 23 on page 280. The trip starts in Boulder Canyon [23-JJ] (N33° 29' 56.1", W111° 24' 19.2") at the junction of the Second Water and Boulder Canyon Trails. See Map 20 on page 244 and Trip 50 (Second Water Spring) on page 274 for the trail description from First Water Trailhead.

THE TRIP

Start on Map 20 on page 244. This is one of our favorite trips. It takes you into the Boulder and La Barge drainages where you have spectacular views of the open valleys and mountain peaks. The trip provides majestic views of Weavers Needle at many points along the trail. Some folks can make the loop trip in one day, but plan ahead if you want to do much off-trail exploring. Many people camp for several days in La Barge Canyon and hike or ride to the surrounding mesas and canyons.

Start the trip from the First Water Trailhead [20-C, 0] (N33° 28′ 47.7″, W111° 26′ 32.5″) by following Trip 50 (Second Water Spring) beyond Second Water Spring to the junction with Boulder Canyon Trail [23-JJ, 3.5]. At the wooden trail sign [23-JJ, 3.5], take the Boulder Canyon Trail to the right (south) and follow the trail across the bed of the creek.

Boulder Canyon Creek is easy to follow if you spot the rock cairns at each creek crossing. The creek can be bone dry, or on rare occasions, it can be at flood stage and impassable. Flat camping is available on the low bench of the creek. If it looks like rain, though, use the higher benches to avoid the danger of flash flooding.

A trail-of-use [23-BBB, 4.6] (N33° 29′ 15.2″, W111° 23′ 38.4″) leaves the Boulder Canyon Trail, goes over the low ridge of Battleship Mountain, and drops into La Barge Canyon at the mouth of the Lower La Barge Box [23-LLL] (N33° 29′ 34.6″, W111° 23′ 29.6″), which normally has a bit of water at the sandy camp area. The trail starts out as a steep rocky climb—not doable by horses, but riders can find a gentler route to the left or right.

The Boulder Canyon Trail meets the Cavalry Trail (239) at a wooden trail sign [23-II, 4.9] on the left (east) side of Boulder Canyon Creek. Take the Cavalry Trail over the pass just north of the Red Hills, and drop down to the unsigned junction with La Barge Creek [23-LL, 6.3]. La Barge Canyon offers many places for camping and exploring. See the "Shorter Loop" description below if you want to make an alternate trip through Lower La Barge Box.

From the creek crossing [23-LL], the Trip 52 description continues south on the Cavalry Trail. Leave the trail, and go up on the left (north) bench to see the U-shaped rock walls [23-NN, 6.5] (N33° 28′ 45.5″, W111° 22′ 20.7″), which are located northeast of the junction of Deering Canyon wash and La Barge Creek. This was the first camp of Robert S. Jacob, or "Crazy Jake" as he liked to be called. About 100 feet northwest of the walls, trash buried in a large pit and a small stone enclosure against the south-facing rocks may be part of the former camp.

Farther south on the Cavalry Trail, you will find another of Crazy Jake's camps in a rock grotto [23-V. 6.8] (N33° 28′ 34.4″, W111° 22′ 01.0″) east of the trail. Yet another camp was at the head of Squaw Canyon [23-XX] (N33° 28′ 31.0″, W111° 21′ 38.8″), which was connected by a horse trail to his camp on Peters Mesa [23-Q] (N33° 28′ 43.5″, W111° 21′ 26.7″). The steep trail named the "Z" trail or "Jake's Trail" [23-XX to Q] is not doable by

John Burbridge leaning on an old-style descriptive trail sign at the junction of Second Water and Boulder Canyon Trails. Photographer unknown. March 1972 photo. Courtesy Burbridge Collection, Superstition Mountain Historical Society and Gregory E. Davis.

horses anymore, but hikers can bushwhack their way up the old trail.[229] See Trip 60 (Squaw Canyon) on page 335 for more about Jake's Trail.

A well-constructed, seven-foot rock monument [23-SS, 7.2] (N33° 28' 15.9", W111° 21' 48.6") stands at the mouth of Squaw Canyon on the high bench. A similar monument is about 320 feet to the north-east (N33° 28' 18.4", W111° 21' 45.9"). Looking southwest from the monuments provides a fine view of Weavers Needle. These two rock monuments, and another to the northwest [23-F, 6.9], could mark the boundaries of a mining claim, although the enclosed area is smaller than a typical 20-acre mining claim.

The Cavalry Trail, marked by a wooden trail sign [23-TT, 8.0], ends at the Dutchman's Trail (104) near Marsh Valley. Trip 52 takes the Dutchman's Trail going west. However, the east branch of the Dutchman's Trail offers several interesting attractions, which are described at the end of this section.

Continuing the trip from the signed Cavalry Trail junction [23-TT, 8.0], go west on the Dutchman's Trail to the wooden sign [23-UU, 8.3] at the Bull Pass Trail (129) intersection. The sparsely vegetated area at this trail junction is relatively flat, with Weavers Needle rising high on the southern horizon. The Spanish Race Track is presumed to be in this area, but we haven't found it. Also at this trail junction, Adolph Ruth's skull was found on December 11, 1931. A month later his body was found to the south on the lower, east slope of Black Top Mesa [23-WW].[230]

The alternate trail takes the Bull Pass Trail (129) west into Needle Canyon and then over Bull Pass [23-M] to Aylor's Caballo Camp [23-A].

Both the Bull Pass and Dutchman's Trails attain the same elevation, but the Dutchman's Trail is not as steep. As a consequence, it is 1.5 miles longer.

On Trip 52, with the spectacular view of Weavers Needle ahead, we continue on the Dutchman's Trail going south from the wooden sign [23-UU, 8.3] at the Bull Pass Trail intersection. After crossing the wash that comes from the top of Bluff Spring Mountain, the shortcut horse trail [23-YY, 8.5] (N33° 27' 26.8", W111° 22' 10.5") comes in on the left (east) bench. That horse trail—which we named Little Bull Pass Trail—crosses the Dutchman's Trail and Needle Canyon wash and heads right (west) up the hill toward Little Bull Pass.

Farther south on the Dutchman's Trail is a large stand of trees growing among house-sized boulders [23-ZZ, 8.9]. We believe this was Al Morrow's lower camp.[231] The signed Terrapin Trail (234) [23-CC, 9.2] comes in on the left (south) and leads to the southern part of Needle Canyon. Al Morrow's main camp [23-EE] (N33° 26' 47.5", W111° 22' 07.1") is 0.3 mile from the trail sign [23-CC]. The Dutchman's Trail continues over Upper Black Top Mesa Pass [23-FF, 9.6] and drops into East Boulder Canyon via a long switchback. A rock cairn [23-BB, 10.1] marks a trail-of-use going left (south) into the trees in an area named Laurel Camp by the horse outfitters. The Dutchman's Trail crosses East Boulder Canyon, meets the junction with Peralta Trail at a wooden sign [23-AA, 10.3], and heads northwest on the west side of the canyon to Aylor's Arch [23-C, 10.8] and Aylor's Caballo Camp [23-A, 10.9]. East Boulder Canyon has seasonal water that collects in the bedrock potholes. See Trip 51 (Black Mesa Loop) on page 282 for the attractions in this area.

Brian Lickman sitting on the fireplace in the kitchen area at Crazy Jake's Camp [23-NN] at the junction of La Barge and Deering Canyons. Photographer unknown. Circa 1967. Courtesy of Brian Lickman. Also, see a similar photograph on page 310.

Continuing from Aylor's Camp, you pass several trail junctions—Bull Pass Trail [23-B, 11.0] and

Boulder Canyon Trail [23-T, 11.1]—before arriving at the Black Mesa Trail junction [23-S, 11.3]. Here the final leg of the trip begins by following the Dutchman's Trail back to First Water Trailhead. Cross West Boulder Canyon [23-L, 11.8], continue over Parker Pass [20-Z, 12.9], enjoy the mostly down-hill trek to Transmission Pass [20-LL, 13.8] and First Water Creek [20-QQ], and end the trip at First Water Trailhead [20-C, 15.4]. See Trip 51 (Black Mesa Loop) on page 282 for the trail description from Aylor's Caballo Camp [23-A] to First Water Trailhead [20-C].

SHORTER LOOP THROUGH LOWER LA BARGE BOX

When the Cavalry Trail crosses La Barge Creek [23-LL, 6.3], you can explore downstream (north) in Lower La Barge Box for a short distance or continue on a shorter loop back to First Water Trailhead. Begin by heading left (north) on the east bank of La Barge Creek. When the sandy trail on the bench ends, drop into the creek bed for the scramble through Lower La Barge Box.

Your landmarks, going north, will be an unnamed spring [23-SSS, 7.0], the north end of box canyon [23-LLL, 8.0], Aylor's La Barge Camp [25-Z, 8.8] (N33° 30′ 11.1″, W111° 23′ 48.4″), Indian Paint Mine [25-E, 9.3], Second Water Trail [25-JJ, 9.7], Garden Valley [20-GG, 11.4], and First Water Trailhead [20-C, 13.2]. See Trip 56 (Boulder Canyon Trail to Marsh Valley) for more about this trip. Lower La Barge Box is not doable by horse riders.

SIDE TRIP ON EAST BRANCH OF DUTCHMAN'S TRAIL

If you opt for the side trip from the end of the Cavalry Trail [23-TT, 0.0], go left (east) on the Dutchman's Trail up La Barge Canyon about 0.3 mile to the first wash [23-I, 0.3] coming in from the right (south). A few yards west of the wash [23-I], the unmarked and overgrown Little Bull Pass Trail branches off to the right (south), which cuts southwest across the low ridge to Needle Canyon [23-YY]. Just past the wash is a rock wall [23-H, 0.3+] (N33° 27′ 39.6″, W111° 21′ 35.6″) that was built across the trail. The wall is most evident on the south side of the trail. It runs toward the cliff and is extended by a deteriorating barbed-wire fence bolted to the cliff face. If you bushwhack up the wash about 0.5 mile, you will see a 1967 prospector's claim marker painted on an east facing cliff [23-G] in three-foot-high white numbers, 6+5.

Back on the trail in La Barge Canyon, you will find nice shady cotton-wood trees growing in the creek bed near quiet pools of water. This is always a pleasant place to stop for a snack and rest. An abandoned corral (N33° 27′ 37.5″, W111° 21′ 15.2″), shown on Map 28, sits on the north side of La Barge Creek. If you have time, it is another easy 0.8 mile up to Charlebois Spring [28-BB, 1.5]. See Trip 14 (Charlebois Spring—Loop 1) on pages 112 to 116 for the description of the Charlebois Spring area. Return to the Cavalry Trail [23-TT] to continue with the Trip 52 itinerary.

HISTORY AND LEGENDS

Over the years, the Superstition Mountains have attracted many prospectors and treasure hunters. One of these men was Robert S. "Crazy Jake" Jacob, a colorful character who maintained a large camp of men in La Barge Canyon to search for the Lost Dutchman Mine. Local rancher Bill Barkley gave him the name Crazy Jake, because he was likely to be "the only one crazy enough to find the gold."[232]

In 1966 and 1967, Brian Lickman was working for Crazy Jake out of the camp that we often refer to as the stone corral [23-NN] at the junction of La Barge and Deering Canyons. Brian said they had a kitchen work counter and fireplace made of stone at that location. Today you can still see the rock walls, which are U-shaped, three to four feet thick, about four feet high, and about thirty feet square with the back wall missing. The fireplace was in the southwest corner. (See photo of Brian Lickman at the fireplace on page 290.) He said they did not use the walled area for a corral—they tied their horses to a picket line and never corralled the horses.[233]

Another large camp was based in a rock grotto [23-V] north of the Cavalry Trail—you can still see some camp materials, rocked-in terraces, and bolts in the rock.[234] Two other camps were in Squaw Canyon [23-XX] and on Peters Mesa above Squaw Canyon [23-Q].[235] A steep trail named the "Z" trail or "Jake's Trail" [23-XX to Q] went up Squaw Canyon to Peters Mesa connecting the camps.[236]

Unfortunately, Crazy Jake's keen ability to raise grubstakes led to his demise. Newspaper articles reported that Crazy Jake swindled prominent investors of $7 million over a period of twenty years, while leading them to believe he had found the Lost Dutchman Mine.[237] Crazy Jake's search for the Lost Dutchman Mine ended in 1986 when he was convicted of fraud and sentenced to ten years in prison for bilking investors out of $135,000 in his treasure hunting adventures.

In December 1992, at the site of one of his camps near the head of Squaw Canyon [23-XX], we found some recent stores of gasoline and camping equipment. The Forest Service said that this new prospector had been given orders to remove the equipment from the Wilderness. On a February 1994 trip, we found the camp restored to natural conditions, and during a 2010 hike, we observed that the camp area was completely over-grown with catclaw. Don Van Driel said the wire cable stretched out near that camp [23-XX] was used as a picket line for horses.[238]

Black Top Mesa, often called the Peralta Mapped Mountain, has inter-ested treasure seekers over the years because of the Spanish Hieroglyphics found on the south end and its proximity to Weavers Needle. In 1949, Clay Worst, with the help of Nyle Leatham, performed a survey on top of Black

Top Mesa to evaluate the clues of an 1854 Peralta survey. In 1924 Perfecto Salazar, acting as an interpreter for a Peralta family member, was shown some survey data of a mine in the Superstition Mountains. He memorized some of the survey figures, which are now commonly referred to as the Salazar Survey, and passed the information on to Frank Swento. Swento grubstaked local prospector Chuck Aylor; later Clay Worst was brought into the deal. Clay Worst set up a surveyor's transit on Black Top Mesa using the Spanish symbols (petroglyphs not hieroglyphics) on the northwest and southeast as the survey baseline and then triangulated a mine site. All of this excellent

Clay Worst evaluating the Salazar Survey clues on Black Top Mesa. Photo by Nyle Leatham in 1949. Courtesy of Clay Worst and the Superstition Mountain Historical Society.

work was to no avail, probably because the Salazar clues were incomplete. More recently in 2002, Steve Creager analyzed the Salazar data—Weavers Needle, Red Hills, and a cave (Triangle Cave)—and projected the mine to be near the north end of Peters Mesa. The lost Salazar Survey Mine remains undiscovered today.[239]

In 1989, Black Top Mesa was in the news when Patricia Kuhl (formerly Patricia Kuhl Murray) of Troy's Gallery in Scottsdale hid a bronze sculpture on the mesa. Artist Harland Young created the sculpture "In Search of the Dutchman" depicting Jacob Waltz and his two burros. Kuhl wanted to generate publicity so the public would buy the limited edition bronzes. The proceeds would benefit the town of Apache Junction in the effort to commission a life-size sculpture. Since the Wilderness rules prohibit certain commercial activities, Don Van Driel of the Forest Service advised Kuhl to move the bronze sculpture outside the Wilderness, which she did. Larry Hedrick, finder of the Hiram Walker Whiskey cache in 1978, said he discovered the place where the bronze had been hidden on Black Top Mesa a day after it was moved outside the Wilderness. The seventy-six-pound bronze sculpture was found on February 20, 1989, at a new, undisclosed hiding place outside the Wilderness by Andy Tafoya of Mesa, Arizona. Eddie Basha donated an identical bronze sculpture by Harland Young to the Superstition Mountain Museum, where it is now on display. From our observations, these men show that the competence of the treasure hunters is not in question. It's the obscurity of the clues to the Lost Dutchman Mine that seems to cause the problems.[240]

Trip 52 (Marsh Valley Loop) on page 287 and Trip 56 (Boulder Canyon Trail to Marsh Valley) on page 306, on the Cavalry Trail, take you by an area known as the Red Hills. The earth here is a reddish-brown color. One of the clues for the Lost Dutchman Mine refers to three red hills. The clue states that you have gone too far when you pass the three red hills.

Jim Bark tells a story about Mexican miners in the mid 1800s who were reputed to hold two-horse races along a dirt track in the Marsh Valley area. A bandit gang led by Joaquin Murietta would join the Peralta camp for mutual security and, during their stay in the mountains, would wager on the horse races. In the early 1900s, Jim Bark observed the race track to be 150 yards long. We have searched the elevated flat area north of Bluff Spring Mountain several times and have not been able to locate the impression of the race track, although, if you use your imagination, there are two eroded areas that might qualify as a two-horse race track. When Adolph Ruth's skull was found in 1931 at the junction of the Dutchman's and Bull Pass Trails [23-UU], this area was referred to as the Spanish Race Track.[241] One Lost Dutchman enthusiast said the race track is there, though overgrown with vegetation; however, others feel that this is just a myth.

LOWER FIRST WATER CREEK

This trip follows First Water Creek from Hackberry Spring to Canyon Lake. The seldom-traveled canyon offers wide open vistas as you leave Hackberry Spring with stretches of potholed bedrock that catch seasonal water. Near the end, tangled volcanic cliffs squeeze the canyon into a narrow gorge.

ITINERARY

This is an 8-mile vehicle shuttle trip. From First Water Trailhead, go to Hackberry Spring, and follow the bed of First Water Creek down canyon (no trail). Near Canyon Lake, take a trail up a side ravine to the Canyon Overlook Trailhead on SR88 where you parked your shuttle vehicle.

DIFFICULTY

Difficult hike. Not suitable for horses. Elevation change is +360 and -630 feet.

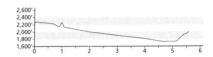

LENGTH and TIME

5.6 miles, 9 hours one way.

MAPS

Arizona USGS topo maps NAD27: Goldfield and Mormon Flat Dam. Superstition Wilderness Beartooth map, grids D11 to D9. Maps 20 and 24.

FINDING THE TRAIL

See the trailhead map on page 242. Start from the northeast corner [20-A, 0] (N33° 28' 58.9", W111° 26' 56.7") of the First Water Trailhead horse trailer parking lot, and follow the former dirt road heading north.

THE TRIP

This is a one-way trip, so you need to place a shuttle vehicle at the Canyon Overlook Trailhead near milepost 208 on SR88 [24-C]. See Map 24 on page 299 for the Canyon Overlook Trailhead.

Start on Map 20 on page 244. From the First Water Trailhead horse trailer parking lot [20-A, 0], follow the directions in Trip 44 (Hackberry

Spring) on page 249 using the Wash Route (2), which is the fastest way to get to Hackberry Spring [20-J, 1.1].

From Hackberry Spring [20-J, 1.1], the trip follows the trail going north for 0.3 mile until it makes a sharp turn to the east and heads uphill. At

Dick Walp at the water pool obstacle [24-W] in Lower First Water Creek. The spine, jutting out to the right, is in the top center of the photo above the pool of water. November 2010 photo.

the sharp turn, you drop into First Water Creek and go down the wide water course, which provides open vistas to the surrounding mountains. Stretches of bedrock collect seasonal water, and a few flat benches [24-Y and Z] offer camping above the creek level.

A narrow section of canyon with a deep pool of water [24-W, 4.4] (N33° 31' 50.4", W111° 26' 48.7") may deter some hikers from proceeding farther downstream. To get around the pool, proceed along the left (south) cliff face—about 15 to 20 feet above the water level. Near the west end of the cliff, a small spine juts out toward the right (north). Sparse handholds and footholds for about 5 linear feet make this a moderately difficult climbing move across the spine. Rock climbers will not have a problem here, but non-climbers should not try it. Beyond the spine, you need to do a lot of scrambling going upward or slide a few feet on a smooth rock to the creek bed.

For those who cannot proceed beyond the pool of water [24-W, 4.4], backtrack up canyon (south) to the Three Pinnacles area [24-P, 4.1] (N33° 31' 42.7", W111° 26' 42.4"). From the creek bed [24-P], go westerly up the ridge of the hillside, which is just downstream from the Three Pinnacles. Cross-country travel and a few game trails lead you steeply up to a saddle [24-K, 4.3] (N33° 31' 40.7", W111° 26' 52.8"). From the saddle [24-K], the route is fairly level as you head westerly over to SR88 at milepost 207 [24-L, 4.7] (N33° 31' 41.0", W111° 27' 10.9"). Walk down SR88 to your shuttle vehicle at milepost 208 [24-C, 5.4]. If you want to check out the lower part of the canyon that you missed by exiting the canyon near the Three Pinnacles [24-P], you can take Trip 55 (First Water Creek Canyon) on page 302, which leads you to the spot where Canyon Lake is backed up into First Water Creek Canyon.

Another route [24-S] that is used to avoid the water pool [24-W] is described in Trip 54 (First Water Creek Overlook Trail) on page 300. It is a steeper climb with poor footing, but it leads to a cairned trail and SR88.

It will be difficult to know exactly when you reach the exit ravine [24-D, 4.7] (N33° 32' 01.7", W111° 26' 49.7") that heads up to the Canyon Overlook Trailhead on SR88, so just walk down canyon until you reach the lagoon [24-E, 4.9] where Canyon Lake backs up into First Water Creek. This is as far as you can go, so from here, backtrack about 0.2 mile upstream and look for the exit ravine, which will be the first ravine on the right (west) [24-D, 5.1] after you go around the hairpin turn.

Hike up the bed of the exit ravine. At the cut barbed-wire fence, turn right (north), walk a few feet, and pick up a good trail on the right side of the ravine. Carefully follow the rock cairns to stay on a good trail that will take you up to SR88 and your shuttle vehicle near milepost 208 [24-C, 5.6], where the trip ends.

Canyon Overlook Trailhead

Canyon Overlook Trailhead consists of two different vehicle pullouts on SR88, about 12 miles northeast of Apache Junction between mileposts 207 and 208.

FINDING THE TRAILHEAD AND THE TRAILS

The first pullout (N33° 31′ 59.7″, W111° 27′ 13.7″) for this trailhead is for Trip 54 (First Water Creek Overlook Trail). The trailhead is about halfway between mileposts 207 and 208 at a metal electric tower on the east side of

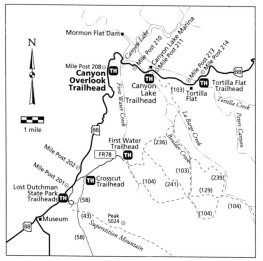

SR88. The metal electric tower can be identified by the painted number "#174" on the tower. From the vehicle pullout by the tower, follow the well-worn trail that heads south into the wash. The unsigned trail takes you to an overlook above First Water Creek within 0.4 mile.

The second vehicle pullout is for Trip 55 (First Water Creek Canyon), which is farther north on SR88 at the milepost

208 sign. Locate the nearby wooden power pole (N33° 32′ 14.9″, W111° 27′ 11.1″), and stand next to the pole with milepost 208 behind you. Look straight ahead for a steep trail that heads southeast into the wash. Go to the bottom of the wash, and follow the wash beyond a barbed-wire fence to the bed of First Water Creek within 0.5 mile. Turn left (north), and follow the normally dry creek to Canyon Lake or explore upstream as far as you like.

FACILITIES

The trailhead does not have any facilities. Bring your own water.

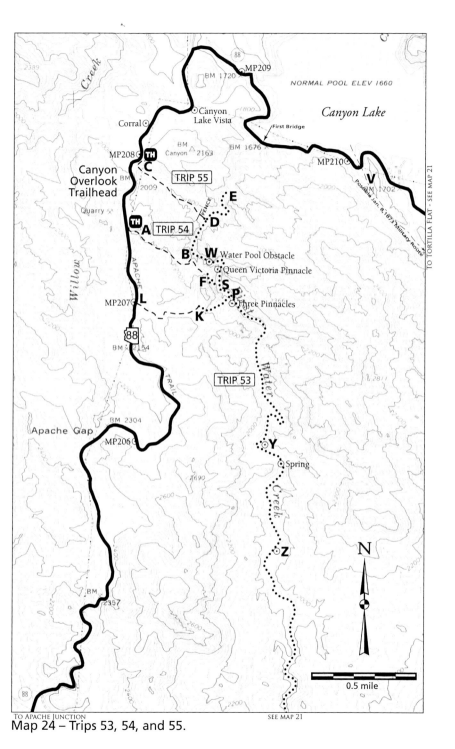

Map 24 – Trips 53, 54, and 55.

FIRST WATER CREEK OVERLOOK TRAIL

This is an easy hike close to the paved road. You can experience the rugged beauty of the canyons just minutes away from your car. This short walk leads you to a nice scenic overlook of First Water Creek Canyon. In the spring, wildflowers cover the slopes on both sides of the trail.

ITINERARY

From the vehicle pullout at electric tower #174 on SR88, follow a trail to an overlook into First Water Creek Canyon. Return the same way.

DIFFICULTY

Easy hike. Not recommended for horses.
Elevation change is +30 and -230 feet.

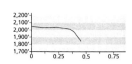

LENGTH and TIME

0.4 mile, 30 minutes one way.

MAPS

Arizona USGS topo map NAD27: Mormon Flat Dam. Superstition Wilderness Beartooth map, grid D9. Map 24.

FINDING THE TRAIL

See the trailhead map on page 298. From the metal electric tower #174 [24-A] (N33° 31′ 59.7″, W111° 27′ 13.7″) and vehicle pullout on SR88, the trail goes south.

THE TRIP

Start on Map 24 on page 299. From the vehicle pullout [24-A, 0], the well-defined trail goes south, descending into the wash. After a few minutes, the trail leaves the wash and stays high, going east as it crosses a small ridge and heads toward the rim of First Water Creek. In the spring, wildflowers are abundant. Views to the north and east look into the side canyons of First Water Creek and beyond to Canyon Lake.

You can turn around at any of the intermediate lookout points, or continue up the cairn-marked trail for about 25 minutes to a spur trail going

View to northeast from the First Water Creek Overlook Trail to Canyon Lake. November 2010 photo.

to the left. The spur trail goes down a small wash and within 200 feet reaches a cliff. During the wet season, water pours off the 150-foot cliff into First Water Creek. The view from the seasonal waterfall into the canyon is very scenic [24-B, 0.4] (N33° 31′ 51.7″, W111° 26′ 54.7″). Be careful not to fall off the cliff. The rocks are smooth here. Wet, smooth rocks and loose gravel can pose a footing hazard. Return via the same trail.

ALTERNATE ROUTE

Although some people continue beyond the spur trail to get into the narrow canyon of First Water Creek, we do not recommend this route because of the steepness of the trail. But if you want to check it out, go uphill a bit to a saddle [24-F, 0.6]. From the saddle, the trail careens down a steep, narrow ravine to the bed of First Water Creek. Loose dirt and small stones make this part of the trail a real challenge, but it is doable if you go slow and hang onto the rocks and vegetation. The trail enters First Water Creek [24-S, 0.6+] (N33° 31′ 45.8″, W111° 26′ 46.3″) in a pretty section of canyon with sculptured holes that hold seasonal water in the white bedrock. An exit route starting near the Three Pinnacles [24-P] leads back to SR88. This alternate route is described in Trip 53 (Lower First Water Creek) on page 297.

FIRST WATER CREEK CANYON

This short walk quickly takes you from the paved road, across the Wilderness boundary, into First Water Creek with its narrow canyon and pools of seasonal water. This is one of the fastest and shortest ways to get into a rugged canyon from the paved road.

ITINERARY

The hike starts at a vehicle pullout exactly at milepost 208 on SR88 and follows a trail into First Water Canyon. You can boulder hop down the canyon to Canyon Lake or up the canyon as far as you like.

DIFFICULTY

Moderate hike. Not recommended for horses. Elevation change is -280 feet.

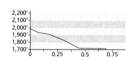

LENGTH and TIME

0.7 mile, 45 minutes one way.

MAPS

Arizona USGS topo map NAD27: Mormon Flat Dam. Superstition Wilderness Beartooth map, grids D11 to D9. Map 24.

FINDING THE TRAIL

See the trailhead map on page 298. Start a few feet east of the guy-wire anchor on the wooden electric power pole [24-C] (N33° 32′ 14.9″, W111° 27′ 11.1″). The wooden power pole is next to paved road SR88, and milepost 208 is right behind you.

THE TRIP

Start on Map 24 on page 299. From the vehicle pullout [24-C, 0], the hardest part of the hike is getting down into the wash that heads east toward First Water Creek. At first, the route is steep with many loose stones, but the cairned trail soon levels out in the bottom of the wash. Follow the well-worn trail, and look for rock cairns when the trail crosses rocky stretches of ground. The trail follows the bed of the wash when it passes through a cut barbed-wire fence—the Wilderness Boundary. First Water Creek is another

Canyon Lake backs up into First Water Creek at some large cottonwood trees [24-E]. This is as far as hikers can go downstream. Boaters often travel up the canyon to the cottonwood trees to explore the normally dry bed of First Water Creek. November 2010 photo.

minute or so down the wash [24-D, 0.5]. You will return using this same route, so look around at the landmarks, and put up a rock cairn to mark your exit route.

It is a short 15-minute hike down canyon, north, and around the hairpin turn to Canyon Lake. Several small cottonwood trees growing on the right bench of the canyon mark the end of the trip [24-E, 0.7]. When Canyon Lake is near full capacity, the water comes up the canyon to the cottonwood trees.

You can also hike up the canyon, but lots of boulder hopping is required if you go very far. When there is water in the canyon, you will need to wear shoes that are good for walking in water. Trip 53 (Lower First Water Creek) on page 295, starting from First Water Trailhead, describes the trek going downstream (north) in First Water Creek.

Return the same way to your vehicle [24-C, 1.4]. At the cut barbed-wire fence, look to your right (north) for the trail as it goes up on the low bench.

CANYON LAKE TRAILHEAD

Canyon Lake Trailhead is on SR88, about 14 miles northeast of Apache Junction between mileposts 210 and 211. The distance is 28 miles southwest on SR88 from Roosevelt Lake Dam.

FINDING THE TRAILHEAD

Coming from Apache Junction, you will cross two single-lane bridges along this stretch of road at Canyon Lake. After crossing the second bridge, the trailhead is on the right (south) side of SR88. Free trailhead parking is provided inside the fenced area at the Canyon Lake Marina complex on the left (north).

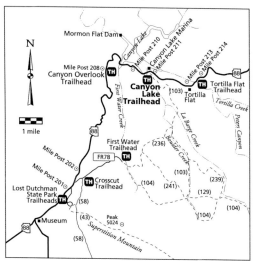

FACILITIES

Canyon Lake Marina has a restaurant, marina, beach area, Dolly Steamboat tour boat, and free fenced parking. You can also use the USFS Boulder Picnic Area (fee required) for parking. The USFS picnic area, located on the southwest side of the second bridge, has a fishing dock, ramadas, picnic tables, and toilets, but no water. Bring your own drinking water.

THE TRAIL

The Boulder Canyon Trail starts from paved road SR88 on the marina side of the bridge at a big sign reading *Boulder Canyon Trail 103* [25-A] (N33° 32′ 02.2″, W111° 25′ 19.7″). Heading south and uphill on Boulder Canyon Trail, the distance is 0.6 mile to the Spur Trail [25-G] leading to La Barge Creek, 0.6 mile to the viewpoint at the Wilderness sign [25-B], 3.1 miles to La Barge Creek [25-D], 3.5 miles to Indian Paint Mine [25-E], 3.9 miles to the junction with Second Water Trail (235) [25-JJ], and 7.4 miles to First Water Trailhead [20-C].

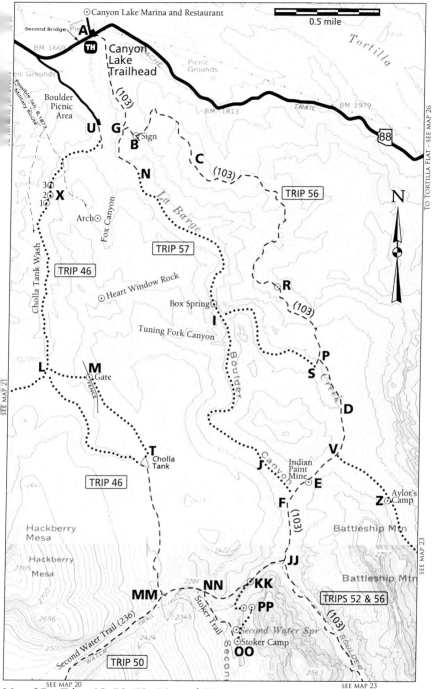

Map 25 – Trips 46, 50, 52, 56, and 57.

BOULDER CANYON TRAIL TO MARSH VALLEY

Boulder Canyon Trail offers a fine view of Weavers Needle and Battleship Mountain within the first half mile of the trip—a moderate uphill walk for almost everyone. The Indian Paint Mine, prospector camps, and the seasonal water and vegetation along La Barge and Boulder Canyons make this a good choice for an overnight trip.

ITINERARY

From the Canyon Lake Trailhead on SR88, Boulder Canyon Trail (103) goes over a high hill to La Barge Canyon and on to Paint Mine Pass. The trip meets Second Water Trail, takes Cavalry Trail over another ridge back to La Barge Canyon, and ends in Marsh Valley at the junction with the Dutchman's Trail. Return the same way, or make a loop back to the trailhead.

DIFFICULTY

Difficult hike. Moderate backpack. Difficult ride. Elevation change is +1,650 and -950 feet one way.

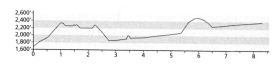

LENGTH and TIME

8.4 miles, 6 hours one way.

MAPS

Arizona USGS topo maps NAD27: Mormon Flat Dam, Goldfield, and Weavers Needle. Superstition Wilderness Beartooth map, grids D12 to G12. Maps 23 and 25. Make your own composite copy of the three USGS map corners.

FINDING THE TRAIL

See the trailhead map on page 304. The Boulder Canyon Trail [25-A] (N33° 32′ 02.2″, W111° 25′ 19.7″) starts from paved road SR88 on the east side of the single-lane bridge across from the Canyon Lake Marina complex.

THE TRIP

Start on Map 25 on page 305. From the paved road [25-A, 0], Boulder Canyon Trail heads south, up the hill. After traveling about 20 minutes, the Spur Trail [25-G, 0.5] bears right (west), while the main trail bends left (southeast). The Spur Trail continues south and goes 0.3 mile to the bed of La Barge Canyon [25-N], which has seasonal water. Another 3 minutes on the Boulder Canyon Trail brings you to the wooden Superstition Wilderness sign [25-B, 0.6] and a great view of Weavers Needle and Battleship Mountain to the south. If you only have a short time here, the Wilderness sign is a good turnaround place. Or, with more time and energy, you can go to the top of the ridge [25-C, 1.1].

At the Wilderness sign, Boulder Canyon Trail makes a sharp left turn as it heads up the ridge on the east side of La Barge Canyon. From the top of the ridge [25-C, 1.1], the trail continues south with lots of ups and downs.

A narrow section of trail [25-R, 2.3] (N33° 31' 01.8", W111° 24' 22.4") near the final descent into La Barge Canyon could be a problem for packhorses. The cliff juts out a bit, and a wide pack might catch on the cliff.

A shortcut trail into La Barge [25-P, 2.8] (N33° 30' 44.2", W111° 24' 09.5") goes off to the right (southwest) and, in a few hundred feet, reaches La Barge Creek [25-S] (N33° 30' 42.7", W111° 24' 10.3"). This shortcut trail is useful if you are making a loop down La Barge Canyon through the Box Spring area [25-I].

Boulder Creek (aka La Barge Creek) crossing on the Roosevelt Road (Apache Trail) in 1907 [near 25-A]. Photograph by Walter Lubken. Courtesy Salt River Project History Services.

Boulder Canyon Trail crosses the normally dry bed of La Barge Canyon [25-D, 3.1] (N33° 30' 33.4", W111° 24' 02.4") and picks up on the west bench. Rock cairns mark the trail on both sides of the creek, and the cut bank of reddish dirt makes the crossing easy to recognize.

An unsigned faint trail [25-V, 3.3] leaves the main trail in a flat area, turns into a bushwhack, and goes up the creek bed to Aylor's La Barge Camp [25-Z] (N33° 30' 11.1", W111° 23' 48.4"). If you take the 0.3 mile side trip to Aylor's former camp in the boulders along La Barge Creek, you have two choices for the next part of your trip—return to the Boulder Canyon Trail and head up to Indian Paint Mine [25-E], or continue up the bed of La Barge Canyon another 0.8 mile to Lower La Barge Box [23-LLL], which usually has some water. You can continue up the box or head over the ridge on a trail that goes to Boulder Canyon [23-BBB] and the Boulder Canyon Trail.

We pick up the trip description on the Boulder Canyon Trail as it goes up to Paint Mine Saddle and Indian Paint Mine [25-E].[242] Horses may have difficulty on the steep, eroded trail here. The rock walls and filled-in shaft at the Indian Paint Mine ruins [25-E, 3.5] are on the southeast side of the trail.

From Indian Paint Mine, the trail drops down into Boulder Canyon. The Boulder Canyon Trail goes directly across Boulder Creek (usually dry) [25-F, 3.6] and moves up on the west bench. You may find water down canyon (north) 0.3 mile beyond a small grove of Fremont cottonwood trees [25-J]. After crossing the ravine of Second Water Canyon, Boulder Canyon Trail meets the Second Water Trail (236) at a wooden trail sign [25-JJ, 3.9]. You can usually find water at Second Water Spring, about 0.2 mile up the Second Water Trail where the trail crosses the bed of the creek [25-KK].

If you ever lose the Boulder Canyon Trail in this area [25-JJ], the long section of smooth, white bedrock in the floor of Boulder Canyon is a good landmark for recognizing Second Water Canyon. Continuing south from the trail sign [25-JJ], Trail 103 crosses Boulder Canyon to the left (east) bench. The cairned trail is usually marked fairly well as it zigzags across the normally dry creek bed. It is always easier using the trails on the low benches rather than boulder hopping up the main channel.

In Boulder Canyon, look for a rock outcrop [23-BBB, 5.0] (N33° 29' 15.2", W111° 23' 38.4") on the left (east) side of the creek bed that marks the start of an optional shortcut trail over to the sandy camp at Lower La Barge Box [23-LLL] (N33° 29' 34.6", W111° 23' 29.6"), which always has water.

Trip 56 stays in Boulder Canyon until it reaches the wooden sign at the Cavalry Trail junction [23-II, 5.3], which enters on the left (east). The Cavalry Trail takes you over a pass just north of the Red Hills and drops down to La Barge Creek. Just before the Cavalry Trail (239) reaches La Barge Canyon [23-LL, 6.7], you will find a few flat camping places along the trail.

Cavalry Trail crosses to the left (east) side of La Barge Canyon, which has seasonal water and may have water after Boulder Canyon has gone dry.

About 0.2 mile from the junction of La Barge Canyon and the Cavalry Trail, look for rock walls [23-NN, 6.9] (N33° 28′ 45.5″, W111° 22′ 20.7″) on the northwest bench at the junction of La Barge and Deering Canyons. The U-shaped walls are three to four feet thick, about four feet high, and about thirty feet square with the back wall missing. See Trip 52 (Marsh Valley Loop) on page 288 for more information about the rock walls, Jake's Camp [23-V, 7.2], and other attractions in the area.

The Cavalry Trail ends at the Dutchman's Trail (104) in Marsh Valley [23-TT, 8.4]. The trip description ends here. Return the same way to the trailhead [25-A, 16.8], or plan a loop trip back to the Canyon Lake area.

HISTORY AND LEGENDS

The Indian Paint Mine ruin [25-E] is easy to inspect since most of the diggings are within 100 yards of the trail. Greg Davis, Director of Research and Acquisitions for the Superstition Mountain Historical Society, said early stories indicate that the Indians may have mined the red rock for paint, and the mine has been referred to as Indian Paint Mine as far back as 1911.[243] Stone walls, a filled-in shaft, building foundations, and a carved area in the cliff are all that is left of the former mining camp. Greg Davis suggests, "When seeing an old mine shaft, tunnel, tailing or mine dump, try not to look at it as

View from Boulder Trail (103) into La Barge Canyon. Battleship Mountain is in the center of the photograph, and Weavers Needle is in the distance. July 1993 photo.

The kitchen at Crazy Jake's Camp [23-NN] at the junction of La Barge and Deering Canyons. Ross Ackerly, in the photo, was one of the men working for Crazy Jake. Photo by Brian Lickman, 1967. Courtesy Brian Lickman and Ron Feldman. Also, see a similar photo on page 290.

a scar, but visualize an old miner searching for his golden dream. Think of the endless stories those old mines could tell if they could talk."

Carl Silverlock and Carl Malm had nine mining claims in the Indian Paint Mine area that were staked in 1904.[244] The men are more famous for their activities in the Massacre Grounds area [18-BB]—see Trip 41 (Silverlock Prospect) on page 233 and Trip 42 (Massacre Grounds Trail) on page 237.

Ralph Morris is reported to have erected buildings at the Indian Paint Mine site [25-E] in 1956.[245] Barry Storm[246] observed a deep shaft at the mine in 1937, and Dick and Sharon Nelson saw it about 1978.[247] Greg Hansen and Russ Orr said the Forest Service filled in the mine shafts sometime in 1991 or 1992. Rancher Jim Bark told of a tunnel, without timbering, that John Chuning blasted out near the Indian Paint Mine—150 feet long, along a boulder-filled 18-inch crack.[248] The Chuning Mine is across from the Indian

SUPERSTITION WILDERNESS TRAILS WEST

Paint Mine three-fourths of the way to the top of the hill, north of the old building foundation.[249] Several other holes and prospects are visible near the Indian Paint Mine ruins. The first is about 50 feet south of Paint Mine Saddle. Two more appear on the north side of Paint Mine Saddle; one is filled with mining camp trash—bed springs, cookware, and mining equipment. Find another set of holes across the ravine about 100 yards north-northwest of the main ruins. Some iron pipe fittings and iron bars are still there. All the mines that we saw have either collapsed or have been filled in.

Robert Schoose, in his 1986 reprint of Barry Storm's *Thunder Gods Gold*, describes several hand-picked Spanish mines not far from this area. Schoose located the mines using Hank D'Andrea's map—included in the book along with a photograph that shows one of the mines. He describes one mine that had fire pits and beds carved into the walls.[250]

In December 1992, during a rain storm, Jack Carlson was trapped on the Cavalry Trail when La Barge Creek and Boulder Canyon were flooding. The normally placid (often dry) creeks were raging with a force that recalled memories of white-water rafting rivers. Another hiker and Jack worked their way cross-country to the southern end of Weavers Needle, using Dutchman's Trail (104) to enter East Boulder Canyon, and then hiked to First Water Trailhead. At Aylor's Caballo Camp [23-A], two other campers were drying out after a soaking in a creek-crossing attempt. Their offer of hot chocolate and coffee made a pleasant pause in our adventure to escape the flood waters.

On August 20, 1959, Chuck Aylor was injured in an automobile accident on the Apache Trail.[251] After Aylor was released from the hospital, Dewy Wildoner let him recuperate at his house, because Aylor's Caballo Camp on East Boulder Canyon had been washed out in a flood. Then Aylor stayed with Dick Walp and later with Virgil Hammond. When he had worn out his welcome with them, Aylor's three friends decided they should build him a permanent camp in the Superstition Mountains.[252]

Two prospectors named Vic and Larry were vacating their camp [25-Z] in La Barge Canyon because they were leaving for Mexico, so they said Dick Walp and friends could have it. They tore out the old camp material and burned it in the creek. Over a period of weeks, they rebuilt a cabin inside the ideally spaced boulders. The three friends and their buddies backpacked concrete, lumber, roofing, and tools to the site. They enlisted Aylor's two burros to haul the stove, refrigerator, and electric generator. It was a nice camp with bunk beds, electric lights, and a large picture window looking out onto La Barge Creek. Dick commented that the food shelves looked like an A. J. Bayless grocery store, with all the canned items that visitors left behind.

Chuck Aylor lived alone at the La Barge Camp and hosted his friends and visitors on overnight stays. Ralph Morris was a good cook who baked pies and cooked vegetarian meals at his nearby Indian Paint Mine camp. Dick Walp said that Morris often brought food over to Aylor's Camp. Aylor enjoyed the pies, but complained about the meatless fare.

In 1964, Dewy Wildoner invited Mary Leonhard to Aylor's Camp, and she wrote a story in *The Arizona Republic* making the camp location widely known.[253] It is commonly thought that the newspaper story resulted in the demise of the camp, but Dick Walp said that it was Aylor's failing health that prompted him to move to Apache Junction. The Forest Service was not concerned about the camp.[254]

When Aylor's health deteriorated more, he was admitted to the Pinal County Hospital in Florence and died on January 3, 1968. His body was sent to the University of Arizona College of Medicine for medical research.[255] All of the appliances and building material have been removed from the camp, but you can still see the rock wall that supported the picture window and the interior walls where a cutout in the boulder made room for the refrigerator.

Chuck Aylor's Camp [25-Z] in La Barge Canyon. The view is through the missing front door to the white refrigerator. The torn canvas roof hangs from the rafters. Photo by Brian Lickman, circa 1967.

Trip 57

LOWER LA BARGE CREEK

La Barge Canyon offers a good opportunity for hikers to explore a canyon that has seasonal pools of water. Box Spring in the narrows always has water. A detour to Indian Paint Mine is a worthwhile side trip. An uphill trek on Boulder Canyon Trail provides an alternate return with scenic views.

ITINERARY

From the Canyon Lake Trailhead on SR88, take Boulder Canyon Trail (103) to the Spur Trail, which leads down to La Barge Canyon. Go up the creek bed (south) to the junction with Boulder Canyon Trail. Return the same way.

DIFFICULTY

Moderate hike. Not doable by horses at Box Spring. Elevation change is +330 and -200 feet.

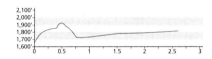

LENGTH and TIME

2.6 miles, 2.5 hours one way.

MAPS

Arizona USGS topo map NAD27: Mormon Flat Dam. Superstition Wilderness Beartooth map, grid E10. Map 25.

FINDING THE TRAIL

See the trailhead map on page 304. The Boulder Canyon Trail (N33° 32′ 02.2″, W111° 25′ 19.7″) starts from SR88 on the east side of the single-lane bridge—across from the Canyon Lake Marina complex. Don't try to access La Barge Canyon by taking the dirt road, at lake level, on the east side of the lagoon. The road connects, after some tough bushwhacking, with the Boulder Canyon Trail, so it is easier to start your trip at the trailhead on Trail 103.

THE TRIP

From the paved road [25-A, 0], Boulder Canyon Trail (103) heads south up the hill. In about 20 minutes, the Spur Trail, marked by a rock cairn, branches off to the right [25-G, 0.5] (N33° 31′ 39.5″, W111° 25′ 08.3″), while the main trail bends left. A recommended side trip of an additional 3 minutes on the main trail brings you to the wooden Superstition Wilderness sign [25-B] and a great view of Weavers Needle and Battleship Mountain.

Back at the Spur Trail [25-G], head down into La Barge Canyon [25-N, 0.8] (N33° 31' 29.3", W111° 25' 04.1"), which has seasonal water. Walking up the creek bed is just as easy as taking the trail-of-use on the east bench.

About 0.9 mile up canyon in the narrows, you come to Box Spring, which fills the creek bed wall-to-wall with water.[256] Even in the driest seasons, we have seen water here. Approach the clump of trees on the left (east) bench. Just before reaching a pool of water, cross through the cattails to the right (west) bank. When blocked by another pool of water, move diagonally to the left (east) and up canyon on stepping stones. Climb up a chute against the left (east) wall or scramble over the large boulder—whichever seems easier. A few hundred yards beyond Box Spring, La Barge Canyon makes a 90-degree left (east) turn [25-I, 1.7], while Boulder Canyon continues straight (south). Since GPS signals are weak in this stretch of canyon, you will have to rely on your ability to visually identify the narrow opening of La Barge Canyon through the trees and bushes at this stream junction.

Although you could continue up Boulder Canyon and loop over Indian Paint Mine Saddle [25-E], Trip 57 goes left, through the trees and bushes in La Barge Canyon. This short stretch of La Barge Canyon often has water and might be a good stop for a snack or lunch, because La Barge Canyon is often dry farther upstream. The trip description ends when you reach the shortcut trail to Boulder Canyon Trail (103) [25-S, 2.4] (N33° 30' 42.7", W111° 24' 10.3") or the Boulder Canyon Trail crossing of La Barge Canyon [25-D, 2.6] (N33° 30' 33.4", W111° 24' 02.4"). Both of the turn-around locations are marked with rock cairns and visually identified by the reddish-colored eroded bank on the left (northeast) side of the creek. Return the same way, or take one of the optional returns described below.

ALTERNATE RETURN ON BOULDER CANYON TRAIL (103)

Leave La Barge Canyon at a red-rock outcrop [25-S, 2.4] (N33° 30' 42.7", W111° 24' 10.3") on the left (east) side of the creek. The faint trail is marked with rock cairns and goes northeast a few hundred feet, where it connects with the Boulder Canyon Trail [25-P, 2.4+] (N33° 30' 42.2", W111° 24' 09.5"). Turn left (north), and take the Boulder Canyon Trail for about 2 hours over the big hill—with lots of up-and-down sections of trail—to Canyon Lake Trailhead [25-A, 5.2].

ALTERNATE TRIPS TO AYLOR'S CAMP AND INDIAN PAINT MINE

Continue up La Barge Canyon to the crossing of Boulder Canyon Trail (103) [25-D, 2.7] (N33° 30' 33.4", W111° 24' 02.4"). Boulder Canyon Trail crossing is marked by rock cairns, and the trail is well worn on both sides of the creek. An eroded bank of reddish dirt and boulders on the left (north) side of the creek is another good landmark.

Take the Boulder Canyon Trail to the right (south), and follow it along the west bench. A trail-of-use to Aylor's Camp branches off to the left (southeast) [25-V, 2.9] (N33° 30' 21.6", W111° 24' 03.5"). The faint trail is somewhat of a bushwhack and quickly goes into the bed of La Barge Creek. Aylor's Camp is on the right (west) bench a few feet above the creek bed [25-Z, 3.2] (N33° 30' 11.1", W111° 23' 48.4").

Back on the Boulder Canyon Trail [25-V, 3.5], continue southeasterly, and go up the eroded steep trail—horses may have some difficulty here—and continue over Indian Paint Mine Pass to the Indian Paint Mine ruins [25-E, 3.7]. You will find rock walls and a filled-in shaft on the left (south) side of the trail. Trip 56 (Boulder Canyon Trail to Marsh Valley) on page 309 describes the history of the Indian Paint Mine area and Aylor's Camp.

You have three choices for the return from Indian Paint Mine [25-E, 3.7] to Canyon Lake Trailhead [25-A]: (1) return the same way going down La Barge Canyon to Canyon Lake Trailhead [25-A, 6.8], (2) return on Boulder Canyon Trail (103) to Canyon Lake Trailhead [25-A, 7.2], or (3) head west

Ralph Morris building his cabin at Indian Paint Mine [25-E] in 1956. Photo by Jerry Carr. Courtesy Gregory Davis, Superstition Mountain Historical Society, Dan Hopper Collection.

Ralph Morris constructed the cabin at Indian Paint Mine [25-E] in 1956. Photo by Jerry Carr. Courtesy Gregory Davis, Superstition Mountain Historical Society, Dan Hopper Collection.

on the Boulder Canyon Trail, and go a short distance down to Boulder Canyon. Turn right (northwesterly) in the Boulder Canyon creek bed (no trail), pass some cottonwood trees [25-J, 4.1], and meet the junction with La Barge Canyon [25-I, 5.0] near Box Spring. Then retrace your trip down La Barge Canyon to Canyon Lake Trailhead [25-A, 6.7].

THE BIG FISH STORY

One early-spring day in 1984, we hiked the lower section of La Barge Canyon, encountering many large pools of water. Several pools contained fish that were trapped when Canyon Lake receded or the spring runoff ended. As we approached each pool, the fish darted into the shadows of the bank. John Stickney, a friend from Colorado, said we could easily catch one of these fish for closer inspection. He talked us through the exercise. The technique—lie spread eagle on the ground, with head almost in the water, move both hands in the water until you touch the fish, then hold the fish against the bank and slide it to the surface. And then, you have a fat, eighteen-inch trout looking you straight in the eye.

TORTILLA FLAT TRAILHEAD

Tortilla Flat Trailhead is on SR88, about 16 miles northeast of Apache Junction between mileposts 213 and 214.

FINDING THE TRAILHEAD

Tortilla Flat Trailhead is located at one of the vehicle pullouts about a half mile east of Tortilla Flat. We often park next to the power pole near milepost 214 (N33° 31' 50.6", W111° 22' 51.5") along the road east of Tortilla Flat.

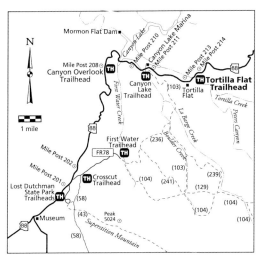

FACILITIES

The town of Tortilla Flat has a general store, restaurant, bar, ice cream shop, and gift shop. Restrooms are available when the stores are open. Bring your own water. The parking area at Tortilla Flat is posted, *No Overnight Parking*. For overnight and day-hike vehicle parking, talk to the friendly owners in the restaurant who are accommodating and may make special arrangements for you. Do not park here without permission. From October through May, you can reserve a campsite at the nearby Tortilla Campground. They have restrooms and running water.

THE ROUTE (NO TRAIL)

From milepost 214, walk down the slope to Tortilla Creek. Go upstream (south) in Tortilla Creek. At the junction with Peters Canyon in 1.1 miles, go right (south) into Peters Canyon to the bedrock potholes at 1.4 miles, or continue upstream to the cave at 2.3 miles.

HISTORY AND LEGENDS

L. L. Lombardi, in her 1994 book *Tortilla Flat, Then and Now*, describes the history of Tortilla Flat. In the late 1800s, Tortilla Flat was used as a camp along the Yavapai Trail (Tonto Trail), which was only a footpath then. The Yavapai Trail was renamed the Apache Trail in the early 1900s after the road to Roosevelt Dam was constructed. In 1942, Tortilla Creek flooded and washed away most of the structures north of the road. Few of the families living there decided to rebuild. In more recent times, owners have rebuilt the town after devastating fires. The town is now a popular day trip destination.

In 2010, when the Tortilla Flat Restaurant was expanded, the iron crucifix that sat on the bar inside the restaurant was moved to the museum at the east end of town. The iron crucifix was reported to have been found in the Superstitions in 1952, but it was actually purchased in Mexico. You can read all about the crucifix and other fascinating information in the Tortilla Flat Museum.[257]

Here at Tortilla Flat in the early 1940s, Barry Storm wrote his famous book *Thunder Gods Gold*, which includes the story of the Gonzales treasure map. In the 1870s, Charles Clark, who was the telegraph operator in Maricopa, Arizona Territory, grubstaked Gonzales, the son of Manuel Peralta. In exchange for his grubstake, Gonzales showed his map to Clark. A short time later, Gonzales returned with gold, bought a horse, and returned to Mexico. Clark and his son Carl unsuccessfully searched for the mine, and later Carl Clark told Barry Storm the story. Cañon Fresco appears on the Gonzales map and is thought to be an important clue in locating the lost Peralta mines. La Barge Creek and Fish Creek have been proposed as Cañon Fresco, but Barry Storm considered Tortilla Creek to be a more logical choice—and he speculated that the location of the mine was at the junction [26-L] with Peters Canyon.[258]

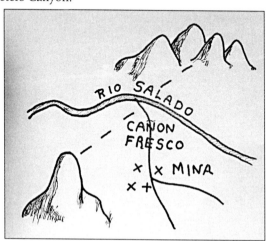

The Gonzales Mexican Mine Map shows Cañon Fresco. Barry Storm thought the mine could be located at the junction of Tortilla Creek and Peters Canyon [26-L].[259]

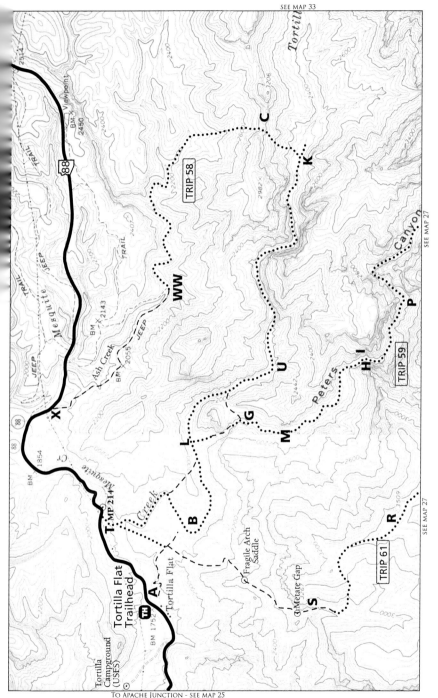

Map 26 – Trips 58, 59, and 61.

LOWER TORTILLA CREEK LOOP

After difficult hiking and bouldering in this narrow canyon, you will be rewarded by many refreshing seasonal pools of water shaded by giant cottonwood trees. It is possible to find water here in the summer, but the surrounding country can be unbearably hot.

ITINERARY

Park at milepost 214 on SR88 just northeast of Tortilla Flat. Follow the bed of Tortilla Creek east beyond the junction with Peters Canyon. The route leaves Tortilla Creek drainage at a break in the northern ridge. Descending from the ridge to the north, the route follows several washes westward and connects with a dirt road that intersects paved SR88 near Mesquite Flat. Return to milepost 214 on the paved road—SR88.

DIFFICULTY

Very difficult hike. Not doable by horses. Elevation change is ±1,130 feet.

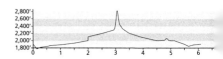

LENGTH and TIME

6.1 miles, 10 hours round-trip.

MAPS

Arizona USGS topo maps NAD27: Horse Mesa Dam and Mormon Flat Dam. Superstition Wilderness Beartooth map, grid F10. Map 26.

FINDING THE TRAIL

See the trailhead map on page 317. The trip starts northeast of Tortilla Flat at milepost 214 (N33° 31′ 50.6″, W111° 22′ 51.5″) on SR88.

THE TRIP

Start on Map 26 on page 319. This trip is mostly cross-country (no trails) except for the 2.4 miles of dirt road and paved highway at the end of the trip. The route takes you through Tortilla Creek, which may have water or pools of water, depending on the season. If you wear shoes that can get wet, the hiking will be much easier. You will need some experience in bouldering, since ome sections of the creek bed are blocked by large boulders that you must scramble over. No technical climbing equipment is required.

The hike starts at milepost 214 on SR88. Drop down to the bed of Tortilla Creek [26-T, 0.1]. After the creek turns south, it makes a big turn to the east [26-B, 0.7], signaling the approaching junction with Peters Canyon [26-L, 1.1]. Use this landmark to check your location on the map and to calculate an approximate hiking speed. In this area, 1.0 mph would be a typical pace for the authors. Hikers on an easy day hike should turn around along this stretch of creek.

As Tortilla Creek turns southeast, the walls of the canyon change to sloping hills, cut by many small ravines. At the bend to the east, the streambed is full of vegetation—grasses, reeds, Fremont cottonwood trees, and velvet ash trees. Hells Hole Spring [26-U, 1.8] is located in this area.

The canyon immediately narrows with steep walls on both sides. Large Arizona sycamore trees are wedged between massive boulders that choke the canyon. Pools of water make the hiking slow. A good estimate for hiking speed here would be less than 0.5 mph. This is another canyon that you would want to avoid if you expected a flash flood—very few places to camp exist and most of them would not be secure in a flash flood.

Depending on the season, the water may be intermittent. The canyon floor alternates between dry, white boulders and heavily overgrown areas of vegetation. About one mile upstream, beyond the creek's next bend to the east, the canyon opens with broad (but steep) sloping hills on either side. Farther up canyon [26-K, 2.9], in an area known as Hells Hole, two high points on the north ridge (elevations 2982 and 3206) silhouette a pass [26-C, 3.1] in the cliffs. It is possible to hike up and over the north side of the canyon in several places here. That is the route this hike takes. As a second alternate route, you can return the same way you came, although the hike through the pass [26-C] would be one to two hours shorter.

Before leaving the canyon [26-K], you could continue east to explore Tortilla Creek farther up canyon, but we have not field checked the canyon up to the waterfall [33-W]. You will have to return down canyon since the estimated 50-foot-high waterfall [33-W] blocks the canyon to hikers.

To approach the pass in the cliff, pick the easiest uphill slope, and head directly toward the pass [26-C, 3.1]. The authors crossed the ridge just west of the pass through a small notch, but the approach was steeper, and we had to climb higher than the pass. The best plan is to stay in the creek bed until you are parallel with the pass through the cliff, then head up the slopes. Even though this is remote and rough country, others have been here. We found two old sleeping bags stashed under a palo verde tree on a flat area about a quarter of the way to the top.

Tortilla Flat [26-A] in the early 1900s. Photograph by Walter Lubken. Courtesy Salt River Project.

At the top of the ridge [26-C], you can see Four Peaks to the north and a small slice of Canyon Lake to the west. Descend the slope on the north side, and drop into one of the washes. All the washes eventually lead west, connecting to Ash Creek, which intersects with the dirt road [26-WW, 4.4] at a cement and stone bridge abutment—from a former bridge on the old Apache Trail that spanned Ash Creek. Climb out of Ash Creek on the west side, and follow the dirt road to the intersection of the paved SR88 [26-X, 5.3]. At SR88 turn left (northwest), and walk 0.8 mile along the paved road toward Tortilla Flat to milepost 214, where the 6.1 mile trip description ends.

HISTORY AND LEGENDS

We think the area we labeled [26-K] in Tortilla Creek is Hells Hole. This could be the location where, in May of 1866, fifteen Yavapai and Apache Indians were killed in a battle with the U.S. Infantry from Fort McDowell.[260]

Along the dirt road [26-WW to X], just at dusk, we saw a coral snake, with the distinctive red and black bands separated by wide bands of white. The white on the coral snake is sometimes a cream or yellow color. In contrast, the non-poisonous king snake mimics a similar coloration, but without a separation between the red and black bands. Coral snakes are poisonous and should not be handled.

SUPERSTITION WILDERNESS TRAILS WEST

PETERS CANYON LOOP

Peters Canyon is a pleasant canyon with seasonal water and sheer cliffs. The loop trip goes up to historic Peters Mesa, where many Lost Dutchman Mine searchers uncovered evidence of nearby mines. The return trek across Malapais Mountain and Geronimo Head offers a spectacular view into the canyons below and then takes hikers down a steep, narrow break in the cliff above Tortilla Flat. Many day hikers enjoy a short walk up Peters Canyon and return the same way.

ITINERARY

Start northeast of Tortilla Flat at milepost 214 on SR88. Follow the bed of Tortilla Creek east to the junction with Peters Canyon. Follow the bed of Peters Canyon southeast to Peters Mesa. Return across the ridgeline, hiking southwest via Malapais Mountain and Geronimo Head. Descend the cliffs to the north, through a narrow break, 0.8 mile south of Tortilla Flat.

DIFFICULTY

Very difficult hike. Not doable by horses. Elevation change is ±3,410 feet.

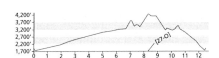

LENGTH and TIME

12.4 miles, 11 hours round-trip.

MAPS

Arizona USGS topo maps NAD27: Mormon Flat Dam, Horse Mesa Dam, Weavers Needle, and Goldfield. Superstition Wilderness Beartooth map, grids F9 to G11. Maps 27 and 28.

FINDING THE TRAIL

See the trailhead map on page 317. The hike starts at milepost 214 on SR88 just northeast of Tortilla Flat (N33° 31′ 50.6″, W111° 22′ 51.5″).

THE TRIP

Start on Map 27 on page 324. The route (no trails) takes you through Tortilla Creek and Peters Canyon, which may have water or pools of water—

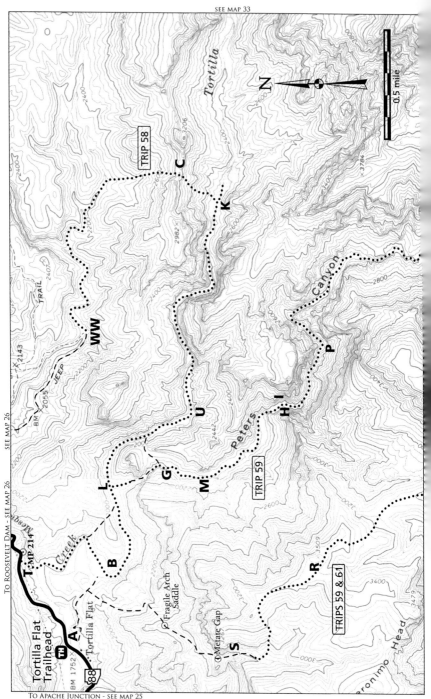

Map 27 – Trips 52, 56, 58, 59, 60, and 61.

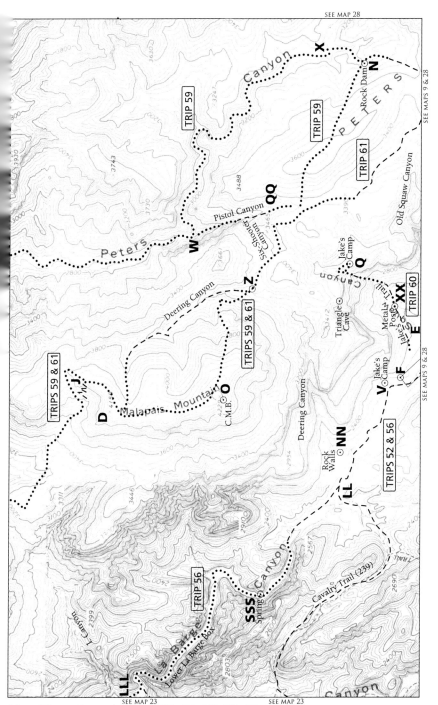

SEE MAP 28

SEE MAPS 9 & 28

SEE MAPS 9 & 28

Canyon

X

N Rock Dam

TRIP 59

TRIP 59

TRIP 61

Old Squaw Canyon

QQ

Pistol Canyon

SXShooter Canyon

Peters

W

PETERS

Deering Canyon

Z

TRIPS 59 & 61

Jake's Camp

Q

Canyon

Metal Trail Post

XX

TRIP 60

Jake's Cave

Triangle Cave

Jake's Grave

E

F

J

TRIPS 59 & 61

Malapais Mountain

O C.M.B.

Deering Canyon

Jake's Camp

V

D

Rock Walls

NN

TRIPS 52 & 56

LL

Spring Canyon

Cavalry Trail (239)

Trail

SSS

TRIP 56

La Barge

Lower La Barge box

LLL

L Canyon

Canyon

SEE MAP 23

SEE MAP 23

Map 27 continued – Trips 52, 56, 58, 59, 60, and 61.

depending on the season. If you wear shoes that can get wet, the hiking will be much easier. Map reading is awkward since the hike crosses the corners of four USGS topo maps. For a handy reference, make a composite copy of the corners of all four USGS maps. Drawing the water courses in blue will make the copied map more readable.

From paved SR88 at milepost 214, drop down to the creek level [27-T, 0.1]. After the creek turns south, it makes a big turn to the east [27-B, 0.7], signaling the approaching junction with Peters Canyon. We often avoid the big bend by taking a cross-country route over the low pass to the south. A steep game trail takes you over the pass to Tortilla Creek just downstream from the mouth of Peters Canyon. The entrance of Peters Canyon comes in from the right (south) [27-L, 1.1]. Across from the mouth of Peters Canyon, a six-foot hole that you can walk through penetrates the cliff at Tortilla Creek level.

From Tortilla Creek, turn right (southeast), and proceed up the bed of Peters Canyon. The beginning of Peters Canyon is blocked with house-sized boulders and large pools of seasonal water. Look for a trail on the left (east) bank below the cliffs that will take you on a rugged route around the boulders. A long stretch of smooth potholed bedrock is the turnaround place for leisurely day hikers [27-G, 1.4].

Hikers can proceed up canyon as far as they like and return the same way, or return on a cross-country route that goes over the low pass to Tortilla Creek. The pass is located south of the butte below the junction of Peters Canyon and Tortilla Creek.

The image of a face, with a large nose, is nestled among tall rock spires on the west side of the canyon [27-M, 1.6]. About 1 mile up (south) from the mouth of Peters Canyon [27-L], on the east side of the canyon, is another rock formation Estee Conatser describes as the Indian Head [27-I, 2.2]. The profile of the face is very flat. When you see the large cave [27-H, 2.3] on the west side of the canyon, the Indian Head profile will be visible on the opposite side of the canyon on a tall, freestanding rock. The large cave on the west bank contains stone walls and makes a good shelter high above the canyon floor.

Farther up canyon, another cave sits on the right (south) bank about ten feet above creek level. When we were first here in December 1993, we saw an old sleeping bag, pots and dishes, a five-gallon plastic bucket, and a lot of trash. Someone had been excavating the floor of the cave. On subsequent trips, the buckets were gone—removed by Forest Service volunteers—and then the buckets reappeared again.

A few hundred feet upstream, the water flows over a low, slick rock waterfall into a deep pool [27-P, 2.6]. In past years, it was possible to bypass he waterfall by climbing the broken cliff on the right (south) side of the canyon. But, flooding in 2019 scoured away several feet of sand and rock fill, so climbing the cliff is not doable without a long ladder. You can bypass the waterfall by starting down canyon from the waterfall and going up the right (south) hillside. After dropping back into the creekbed upstream of the waterfall, you will need to wade through the long, deep, and narrow pool. Be careful when climbing around these obstacles. A fall here could easily result in a serious injury or death. After the waterfall and pool, the canyon heads northeast for a short distance, then makes a sharp turn to the right. This is a pretty section of canyon with sheer walls on both sides.

In another 2 miles, when the canyon narrows, Pistol Canyon [27-W, 4.7] is due south, and Peters Canyon makes an abrupt turn to the left (east). Continue up Peters Canyon and turn right (south) at a small canyon [27-X, 6.2]. A short distance up the side canyon at the rock dam [27-N, 6.4] (N33° 28′ 39.1″, W111° 20′ 29.5″), take a cross-country route (northwest) up to Peters Mesa.

You won't have much time to look around on Peters Mesa if you are doing this trip as a loop day-hike, so continue northwest over the hill on Peters Mesa, and set a course toward the high point on the south end of Malapais Mountain [27-O, 4229]. Pistol Canyon [27-QQ] drains to the north, and Squaw Canyon drops off to the south. Metal pipes in the ground are the remains of Roy Bradford's former camp along Deering Canyon wash [27-Z, 7.7] (N33° 29′ 08.1″, W111° 21′ 33.7″), where you can sometimes find water.

View looking up canyon to the pothole area of Peters Canyon [26-G]. December 1993 photo.

To get to the top of Malapais Mountain, start from Roy Bradford's Camp [27-Z], cross Deering Wash to the west side, and look for several faint trails going northerly along the steep slope. The trails take you to a flat spot within 0.2 mile, on a little ridge (N33° 29' 15.9", W111° 21' 37.0"), where you can catch your breath.

Head westerly and sometimes southwesterly going cross-country up the open hillside—aiming toward a dark outcrop (N33° 29' 13.5", W111° 21' 46.6") around the 3,800-foot elevation. Go through the center of the dark outcrop of rocks, and bear right (northwesterly). We follow the terrain, which presents itself as somewhat of a natural course of travel up the rough slope. Another waypoint (N33° 29' 15.4", W111° 21' 53.6") at a small cliff line makes a fine resting spot on the flat rocks before tackling the last 400 feet to the summit.

A little bit southeast of the top of Malapais Mountain [27-O, 8.3, 4229], we found a white painted "C.M.B." inscription (N33° 29' 15.3", W111° 22' 05.2") on a boulder. Looking south from here, you get a fine view of La Barge Canyon with Weavers Needle in the background.

Follow the crest of Malapais Mountain going north, skirt Peak 4159 to the right (east), and drop down to the start of the switchback trail [27-J, 9.1]

View of C.M.B. inscription (lower left of photo), La Barge Canyon (center of photo), and Weavers Needle (on right horizon) from the northwest side of Malapais Mountain. March 2009 photo.

Route

View looking north to the break in the cliffs [27-S] north of Geronimo Head. The route hugs the cliff on the right side of the photo. April 2003 photo.

(N33° 29' 50.0", W111° 22' 00.6"). The switchback trail is eroded and recent reports in 2019 indicate that it may not be visible. You can try to go down the switchbacks to connect with the vegetation choked ravine, but a more reasonable route is to go farther north as shown on Map 27 near [27-J]. This route avoids much of the vegetation and steepness of the ravine. Follow sporadic rock cairns down the hill. On two trips we have taken the boulder field [27-D] to the west of the ravine, which avoids the vegetation in the ravine, but it does not follow the historic pack-trail route going down the ravine.

Follow our route shown on Map 27 as the trip turns northerly, goes across an open ridge, climbs up and skirts Peak 3509 [27-R, 10.5] to the left (west). Staying on the ridge north of Peak 3509 makes the hiking easier. At the north end of the ridge, drop down going westerly to the canyon that ultimately leads to the break in the cliffs [27-S, 11.3].

Once in the ravine leading to the break in the cliff [27-S, 11.2] and looking northwest, you will see a large butte to the west. Your hike takes you between the butte and the sheer cliffs on the east. Continue north toward the large butte and stay on the right (east) side of the ravine. When the ravine narrows between two rock outcrops, a trail-of-use takes you along the east side of the steep ravine. Eventually the trail heads up to the saddle that we named Metate Gap on the east side of the large butte.

From Metate Gap, follow a good trail-of-use down the slopes to Tortilla Creek [27-T, 12.3] and up to your vehicle at milepost 214, where the 12.4 mile trip description ends. Respect the private property at Tortilla Flat by taking an appropriately wide course around the developed land. If you receive permission from the owners of Tortilla Flat, you could start and end your trip at the upper parking area [27-A] for the restaurant.

HISTORY AND LEGENDS

Peters Canyon was named after Gottfried Petrasch, known as Peter or Old Pete, who searched here for the Lost Dutchman Mine. Gottfried Petrasch was the father of Herman and Reiney Petrasch. Reiney, also called Old Pete, and Julia Thomas were Jacob Waltz's friends. Jacob Waltz is reported to have told Reiney and Julia where his mine was located. Neither Gottfried nor his sons were ever successful in locating Waltz's mine. Gottfried died in 1914, Reiney in 1943, and Herman in 1953.[261]

Geronimo, a leader of the Chiricahua Apache, allegedly talked about a cave that held a large amount of gold. The cave, located somewhere in the Superstition Mountains, was supposedly marked by a large rock that resembled the head of an Indian. A similar rock formation in Peters Canyon, about a mile up canyon (south) from the junction with Tortilla Creek, piqued the interest of Estee Conatser. In her book *The Sterling Legend*, Conatser describes the rock and the cave under the nose. The profile of the face is very flat, and the nose points in a westerly direction. The rock stands almost one hundred feet high in the middle of Peters Canyon with nothing else around it [27-I]. After a thorough investigation and checking with a metal detector, Conatser found no gold.[262]

In his 1983 manuscript *The Lost Peralta-Dutchman Mine*, Walter Gassler describes the findings of his research at the Berkeley Library, Berkeley, California, between 1932 and 1935. The Peralta-Dutchman Mine was in a north-south running canyon with hundreds of potholes [27-G]. A large cave [27-H] with a house in it served as the Peralta headquarters. A water hole [27-P] lay a short distance up canyon from the cave. The mine was reported to be 1.5 miles up canyon, which places the mine near Pistol Canyon [27-Y].[263] All of these landmarks are still here today, but the most important landmark, the Lost Dutchman Mine, remains undiscovered.

Gassler wrote that an American Indian friend of rancher Tex Barkley took Tex up Peters Canyon to a large water hole at the waterfall [27-P]. At that point, the friend became nervous and decided to turn around. He pointed up canyon and indicated to Tex that the mine was in that direction. Tex should take the next right-hand canyon—Pistol Canyon.[264] Gassler also recalls Tex describing a cave in Peters Canyon that had posts and rafters. That might have been the remains of the two-room Peralta headquarters.[265]

PETERS MESA AREA

Trip descriptions for the Peters Mesa Area start on top of Peters Mesa [28-T]. Most people get up to Peters Mesa on the Peters Trail, but several off-trail routes developed by former treasure hunters provide rugged trails to the mesa and across this high country.

FINDING THE TRAILHEAD

Use Map 28 on page 333. Only one maintained trail crosses Peters Mesa— Peters Trail (105)—but information on the non-maintained routes is included in several trip descriptions in the Peters Mesa Area section of the book.

The shortest trail (4.7 miles) to Peters Mesa [28-T] is Peters Trail (105) starting from Tortilla Well [30-B]. This trail is described in Trip 64 (Peters Trail to Charlebois Spring) on page 357. Even if you have to walk the extra 3.3 miles on four-wheel-drive FR213, it is still the shortest approach at 8.0 miles. Some steep, rugged sections of trail make the Peters Trail a problem for some horse riders and pack animals.

The next shortest trail to Peters Mesa [28-T] starts from Peralta Trailhead [7-A] and uses the Bluff Spring Trail (235), Dutchman's Trail (104), and Peters Trail (105). Trip 14 (Charlebois Spring—Loop 1) on page 112 describes this route, which has a one-way mileage of 8.4 miles.

Another popular approach to Peters Mesa [28-T] is from First Water Trailhead [20-C] using the Dutchman's Trail (104), Bull Pass Trail (129), Little Bull Pass Trail shortcut, and Peters Trail (105). It is 9.8 miles one way.

Trip 60 (Squaw Canyon) on page 335 and Trip 59 (Peters Canyon Loop) on page 323 provide more options for off-trail approaches to Peters Mesa. Trip 61 (Spanish Trail and Malapais Mountain) on page 338 helps you get around in the Peters Mesa high country. Peters Mesa does not have permanent water, but you may find seasonal runoff in the ravines. The closest water is Charlebois Spring or seasonal pothole water in Peters Canyon and Deering Canyon.

HISTORY AND LEGENDS

Peters Mesa is a historic area that has been explored and prospected since the early 1900s. Some Lost Dutchman aficionados believe the area was mined in the mid 1800s. Many of the early books and manuscripts of the former prospectors describe the physical evidence and legends of Peters Mesa. A summary of the stories appears below, but additional reading on your own will greatly enhance your trip to this historic mesa.

About 1911, Sims Ely made a trip to Peters Mesa where he discovered evidence of about forty Mexican fires northeast of Black Mountain. These fire beds were six-by-four-foot areas in which coals were used to heat the ground and to surround a person sleeping there. Ely assumed they were used by Mexican miners. A year later, George Scholey and an Indian friend named Apache Jack hunted for game on Peters Mesa. Scholey was a miner and good friend of the local rancher Jim Bark. Apache Jack's intent (disguised as a hunting trip) was to indirectly show Scholey where the gold mine was located. When they approached the northeast corner of Black Mountain, overlooking the fire beds, Apache Jack became nervous and headed back to First Water Trailhead. Shortly after this hunting trip, Apache Jack died from what Scholey thought was arsenic or strychnine poisoning by his medicine man—punishment for talking too much.[266] It is not clear to us why Scholey could not identify the type of poison, since the symptoms of arsenic and strychnine poisoning are very different. Arsenic poisoning results in severe gastric pain. Strychnine poisoning attacks the central nervous system causing dramatic and exaggerated convulsions of the body. The poisoning account in the story, tends to cast suspicion on the validity of the episode.

Walter Gassler searched the Superstition Mountains from 1936 to 1984 for the lost mines and treasures. He documented his ideas and experiences in the 1983 manuscript *The Lost Peralta-Dutchman Mine*. From Gassler's writings, it is clear that he considered Peters Mesa an important link in the mystery of the lost mines. Gassler describes the physical evidence such as the Mexican fire beds, the Spanish saddle, the spurs, a pistol, a water hole in Peters Canyon, a cave on Malapais Mountain, and cut timber to support his theory that Mexican miners lived on the mesa. The Apache reportedly covered the mines and restored the landscape to prevent further mining there. Stories of the mine closures by several Indians included descriptions of three tepee-shaped boulders laid out in a semicircle, adding more evidence to the exact location on the mesa. Tex Barkley's observation of the mescal pit and numerous grinding stones on Peters Mesa provided support for the mine-closure theory. Although it is possible to develop other scenarios using this same physical evidence, most authors of the Lost Dutchman Mine legends have avoided discussions of other scenarios.[267]

When Gassler first investigated Peters Mesa in 1936, he described a herd of horses on top of the mesa led by a large white stallion. Later, Gassler realized Tex Barkley referred to Peters Mesa as Horse Mesa because of these horses.[268] This and his many other stories of the mesa revealed his fascination with the region. On his last trip to Peters Mesa in May 1984, Walter Gassler died of a heart attack while walking on the Peters Trail above Charlebois

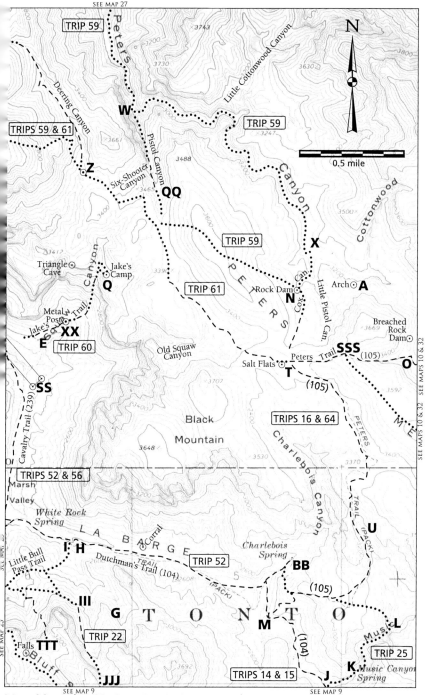

TRIP 59

Peters

Little Cottonwood Canyon

3743

3730

3200

3661

3800

3630

N

0.5 mile

W

Deering Canyon

TRIPS 59 & 61

Z

Six-Shooter Canyon

Pistol Canyon

3488

QQ

TRIP 59

3247

Canyon

Cottonwood

3500

X

TRIP 59

Triangle Cave

Jake's Camp

Q

3412

3397

TRIP 61

P E T E R S

Rock Dam

Arch A

Little Pistol Can.

N

Co. Can.

Metal Post

Jake's

E

XX

TRIP 60

3669

Breached Rock Dam

Old Squaw Canyon

Salt Flats

Peters Trail

SSS

(105)

O

SS

T

(105)

3592

SEE MAPS 10 & 32   SEE MAPS 10 & 32

Cavalry Trail (239)

Black Mountain

3707

3648

3530

TRIPS 16 & 64

Charlebois Canyon

3370

M I L E

PETERS

TRAIL (PACK)

1400

TRIPS 52 & 56

Marsh Valley

White Rock Spring

L A B A R G E

Little Bull Pass Trail

I H

Corral

Dutchman's Trail (104)

TRIP 52

(PACK)

Charlebois Spring

U

BB

(105)

III

G

T O N T O

3803

M

Music

L

TRIP 22

TTT

Falls

Bluff

3692

TRIPS 14 & 15

J

K

TRIP 25

Music Canyon Spring

(104)

JJJ

Map 28 – Trips 22, 25, 52, 59, 60, 61, and 64.

Spring. He never found the mine, but like many others, received great satisfaction in the search.[269]

Pistol Canyon is not shown on the Weavers Needle USGS topographic map, but Lost Dutchman Mine searchers and authors commonly refer to the north-draining canyon from Peters Mesa as Pistol Canyon. Clay Worst of the Superstition Mountain Historical Society told us that Pistol Canyon received its name in the early 1930s. Roy Bradford lost his six-shooter in the area, and Chet Dickerson later found and returned it. Since then, everyone calls the small drainage Pistol Canyon.[270]

On one trip to Peters Mesa, Walter Gassler was accompanied by a friend, Tom Reis. After looking around Peters Mesa, Reis, who was an experienced mining engineer, commented that if there was a mine here, it would be on the north slope, possibly facing down Pistol Canyon.[271]

On our trips to Peters Mesa, we have observed circular areas of black dirt, which we believe are the remains of agave roasting pits. These roasting pits could have been misidentified as Mexican fire beds.

Al Reser's Camp [27-Z] at the southeast end of Malapais Mountain in Deering Canyon. This was the site of Roy Bradford's former camp. Reser's first camp at this location in the late 1960s was burned by vandals. It looks like his dog Tuffy is sleeping by the left end of the tent. Photograph by Al Reser in 1972. Courtesy Superstition Mountain Historical Society, Al Reser Collection.

SQUAW CANYON

For expert hikers, who enjoy rugged hiking, the Squaw Canyon route offers a challenge and the chance to retrace the steps of former prospectors. This shortcut, cross-country trek provides another route to Peters Mesa.

ITINERARY

From La Barge Canyon, the Squaw Canyon route takes you up a steep ravine of Squaw Canyon to the top of Peters Mesa.

DIFFICULTY

Very difficult hike. Not recommended for horses. Elevation change is +860 and -20 feet.

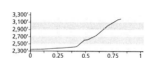

LENGTH and TIME

0.8 mile, 1.5 hours one way.

MAPS

Arizona USGS topo map NAD27: Weavers Needle. Superstition Wilderness Beartooth map, grid G11. Maps 23 and 28.

FINDING THE TRAIL

Use map 23. The route starts from the Cavalry Trail (239) in La Barge Canyon north of the mouth of Squaw Canyon. Look for Jake's Trail near the large boulders [23-E] (N33° 28′ 29.1″, W111° 21′ 45.8″).

THE TRIP

Start on Map 23 on page 280. Leave the Cavalry Trail (239) near the large rock cairn [23-F, 0]—a little south of Jake's Camp [23-V]. Walk easterly across the slopes on the north side of Squaw Canyon toward some large house-sized boulders [23-E, 0.2] (N33° 28′ 29.1″, W111° 21′ 45.8″). Look carefully on the uphill side of the boulders until you find a faint trail marked by rock cairns heading northeast into Squaw Canyon. It is worth the extra effort to find the trail since bushwhacking up the canyon is very difficult. Follow the cairned trail northeast to a former camp area [23-XX, 0.4] that is now overgrown with catclaw. Prospectors used a long metal cable strung between a metal post (N33° 28′ 31.0″, W111° 21′ 38.8″) and a large boulder

Greg Davis viewing La Barge Canyon from the cliffs of Peters Mesa. Malapais Mountain is the high point on the horizon. Triangle Cave is in the cliff below Malapais Mountain. March 2007 photo.

at this camp as a pack-animal picket line. From the picket line, the route crosses Squaw Canyon Wash to the south side. No defined trail crosses the wash, and misplaced rock cairns can lead you astray.

On the south side of the wash, a faint trail heads up the steep slope. If you don't find the cairned trail within 100 feet up the slope, go back to the wash, and try another route. It is worth the extra effort to establish the location of the cairned trail. The multi-armed saguaro cactus skeleton[272] that we used as a landmark has fallen on the trail. Just beyond the fallen cactus, the trail makes a right turn on a rocky point (N33° 28' 36.0", W111° 21' 30.4").

The faint trail disappears, and the route goes to the left (N33° 28' 37.4", W111° 21' 28.7") as it crosses the large ravine of Squaw Canyon. Near the top, we found the tread of a trail (N33° 28' 42.7", W111° 21' 30.2"), which will guide you up closer to the cliff area.

A hiker can get through the cliff at the top of the steep hill in two ways—up the smooth bedrock ravine on the left side of the cliff or up a slot broken through the cliff face. Neither route requires technical climbing.

Taking the ravine on the left, scramble up and under some smooth rocks in the ravine to get above the cliff. Then head to the right and go up a steep ramp where you top out on the flat (N33° 28' 45.5", W111° 21' 27.7") near Jake's Camp area [23-Q]. Another route through the cliffs goes up a broken slot just below Jake's Camp [23-Q] and leads to the top (N33° 28'

43.8″, W111° 21′ 27.3″). We estimate the location of his former camp [23-Q,).8] to be near the GPS coordinates of (N33° 28′ 43.5″, W111° 21′ 26.7″).

HISTORY AND LEGENDS

In the 1960s, Brian Lickman was part of a crew of young men working for Robert "Crazy Jake" Jacob. He said they built a horse trail up Squaw Canyon to reach Jake's diggings that overlooked Deering Canyon.[273] Our Squaw Canyon route probably follows most of the trail they built, except we took a hiking route through the cliffs below Jake's Camp [23-Q] instead of following the horse trail all the way to the top. Jake's men were working out of the camp [23-NN] at the junction of Deering and La Barge Canyons. The second [23-V] and third [23-Q] camps had not yet been established.

Tom Kollenborn's map on the inside back cover of *Superstition Mountain: In the Footsteps of the Dutchman* shows a trail up Squaw Canyon. That trail goes through the cliffs near the "y" in the word Canyon.[274] We did not check this route and did not add it to our maps, but on one field trip we did get to the top of the mesa above Triangle Cave by going up the ravine on the left (north) side of Triangle Cave. Greg Davis and others said that Crazy Jake dynamited the trail going through the last part of the cliff so that no one else could use the trail.[275]

A photo of Jake's Camp [23-Q] in the January 23, 1980, issue of the *Apache Sentinel* shows tents on Peters Mesa where we observed camp remnants on the ground. The aerial photo shows the slots in the cliff where a hiker can approach the camp from below.[276]

From 1963 to 1986, Crazy Jake used Squaw Canyon (aka Squaw Box Canyon)[277] as a shortcut between two camps in La Barge Canyon, [23-NN] and [23-V], and one camp on Peters Mesa [23-Q]. Don Van Driel and Greg Hansen of the Mesa Ranger District referred to the Squaw Canyon route as the "Z" trail. Van Driel recalled the steel cable [23-XX] that was used to tie up the horses at the bottom of the steep section near a camp. He also remembered riderless horses being driven down Squaw Canyon from Peters Mesa and then being rounded up at the bottom of the cliffs. Tom Kollenborn has always known the trail up Squaw Box Canyon as "Jake's Trail."

The Squaw Canyon route may have been used by the cattlemen in the early 1900s since rancher Tex Barkley is reported to have found a Spanish saddle and spurs at the bottom of the cliffs here. Walter Gassler wrote about his concerns of possible conflicts with Robert "Crazy Jake" Jacob when Gassler was exploring the top of Peters Mesa in 1983, but he encountered no problems. Although Gassler searched for the Lost Dutchman Mine from 1936 to 1984 and wrote about Tex Barkley's discoveries, he never mentioned the route up Squaw Canyon.[278]

Trip 61

SPANISH TRAIL AND MALAPAIS MOUNTAIN

A little-used former trail takes you from the Peters Trail on Peters Mesa, over Malapais Mountain and down to Tortilla Flat on SR88. This historic high-country route will challenge the best experienced trekkers.

ITINERARY

From Peters Trail on top of Peters Mesa, go northwest, skirt the east side of Malapais Mountain, then cross over the north end of Malapais Mountain. Continue northwest staying east of Geronimo Head to a break in the cliffs above Tortilla Flat.

DIFFICULTY

Very difficult hike. Not doable by horses except as noted. Elevation change is +1,220 and -2,910 feet.

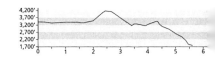

LENGTH and TIME

5.6 miles, 7.5 hours one way.

MAPS

Arizona USGS topo maps NAD27: Horse Mesa Dam, Mormon Flat Dam, Weavers Needle, and Goldfield. Superstition Wilderness Beartooth map, grid H11 to F10. Maps 27 and 28.

FINDING THE TRAIL

Use map 28. The route starts at the 90-degree turn in the Peters Trail on top of Peters Mesa (N33° 28' 21.8", W111° 20' 31.6").

THE TRIP

Start on Map 28 on page 333. From the Peters Trail (105) at the 90-degree turn on Peters Mesa [28-T, 0], head northwest and look for a faint trail sometimes marked by cairns. At the start of the trip, the route finding is easiest, so if you are having trouble here, you can expect to have a lot of trouble following the route after the first mile or so. This was a former horse trail, so you will not encounter any cliffs or major obstacles except as noted for the washed-out and missing trail sections.

Staying on the route as it crosses the head of Pistol Canyon [27-QQ 1.1] may be difficult since the grass obscures the path. Your objective is to get into Deering Canyon at Roy Bradford's Camp [27-Z, 1.5] (N33° 29' 08.1", W111° 21' 33.7") just southwest of Hill 3661 and follow it north to near its end. We have found pothole water in Deering Canyon at Bradford's Camp. Horse riders may find it difficult to proceed up Deering Canyon due to the dense vegetation. We found that the overgrown trail stayed on the left (west) side of the Deering Canyon although traveling in the wash might be easier.

Follow Deering Canyon as it curves west and heads to the top of Malapais Mountain, topping out just east of Hill 4159. Skirt Hill 4159 on the right (east) side, and drop down to the flat where the remnants of a switch-back trail go off the edge of the mesa [27-J, 2.7] (N33° 29' 50.0", W111° 22' 00.6"). Heading down the short length of the switchbacks is more of a historic tour than a practical route, since the switchbacks are washed out, and you end up in the steep, vegetation-choked ravine. A more practical (but less interesting) route off the mesa for hikers is to go down the boulder field [27-D] to the west. Horse riders will not be able to negotiate the descent off the mesa using either the washed-out trail or the boulder field.

Follow the description for Trip 59 (Peters Canyon Loop) on page 329, which takes you near Hill 3509 [27-R, 4.1] and down the slot [27-S, 4.8]— impassable to horses. The trip ends at SR88 near Tortilla Flat [27-A, 5.6].

Roy Bradford with pet cat Pinkey at his camp [27-Z] in Deering Canyon at the southeast end of Malapais Mountain. Photograph by George Snell and copied by Al Reser, circa 1940s-1950s. Courtesy Superstition Mountain Historical Society, Al Reser Collection.

HISTORY AND LEGENDS

In 2003, Greg Davis told us about the trail going north in Deering Canyon from Roy Bradford's former camp [27-Z]. We were able to trace it on the ground that same year. Following the "Old Trail" shown on J. Alan Stirrat's 1948 map proved more time consuming than going cross-country through the wash or going over the top of Malapais Mountain. His map is one of the few that shows Pistol Canyon [27-QQ] by name.[279]

The switchbacks [27-J] on the trail off of Malapais Mountain indicate that this was a major horse trail at one time. Our hiking route through the cliff breaks [27-S] above Tortilla Flat might not have been the continuation of the packhorse trail because the cliff break is narrow and rugged, and it is not suitable for stock animals now.

A more plausible pack-trail route below the switchbacks [27-J] could have gone north and east, eventually dropping into Peters Canyon near the potholes [27-G]. We have not investigated that route thoroughly, but Bob Corbin told us to look for cairns and signs of a trail going west, out of Peters Canyon, from the pothole area. Corbin has ridden into Peters Canyon to the pothole area from Tortilla Creek, so that part of the route is doable on a horse.

In 1873, the army may have used the route described in the paragraph above by going down the switchback trail [27-J], contouring below Hill 3509 [27-R], continuing northeasterly, and dropping down into Peters Canyon for their January 8, 1873, camp on the creek [27-G]. See Trip 45 (Garden Valley Loop) on page 256 for more of the army's march in the mountains.

Donnelly's D-Spur wranglers Hank Jones (left) and Bruce Kinney (right) ride into the parking lot at Tortilla Trailhead [29-T] on a pack trip returning from Peters Mesa. The saddle-sore dudes rode the last 3.3 miles from Tortilla Well [29-B] on FR213 in a jeep. April 2005 photo.

TORTILLA TRAILHEAD

From Apache Junction, go 22 miles northeast on SR88 to milepost 221, and turn south into the signed Tortilla Trailhead parking area. If you have four-wheel drive, you can continue 3.3 miles on FR213 to the end of the road near Tortilla Well. From Roosevelt Lake Dam, the distance is 20 miles southwest on SR88 to FR213.

FINDING THE TRAILHEAD

Leave your vehicle at the parking lot [29-T] on SR88 if the four-wheel-drive

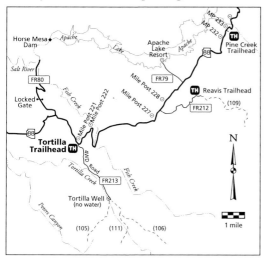

FR213 is too rugged for your vehicle—the first 0.1 mile is the roughest. From SR88 [29-T] to the decommissioned Tortilla Well and water tank [29-B] at the end of FR213 (N33° 29' 33.2", W111° 17' 41.2"), the 1.25-hour walk or 3.3-mile horse ride is easy.

FACILITIES

No facilities exist at the trailhead on SR88, but you will find a rest area about a mile east on SR88 at milepost 222. Bring your own water. Theft and vandalism are common, so don't leave valuables in your vehicle.

THE TRAILS

Three trails start near the south end of FR213. Signed Peters Trail (105) begins at the Tortilla Well windmill and water tank [29-B]. The Peters Trail heads southwest up the bed of Tortilla Creek, follows Peters Canyon, goes over Peters Mesa, and ends near Charlebois Spring in 6.6 miles.

The unsigned JF Trail (106) [29-A], 0.1 mile east of Tortilla Well windmill, goes southeast, up the hill, across the ridge to Tortilla Pass in 5.9 miles, and ends at Woodbury Trailhead in 9.1 miles.

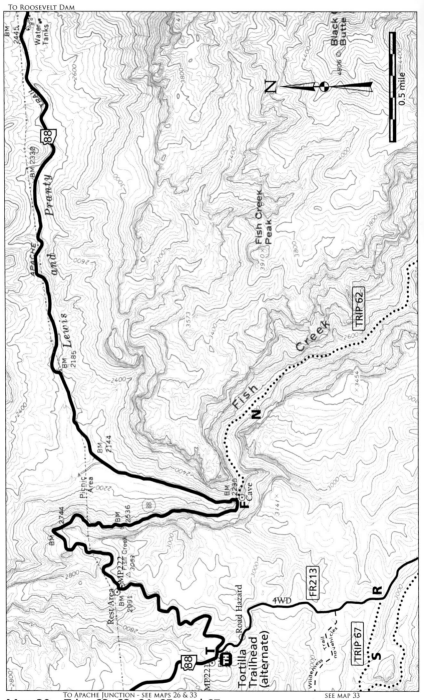

Map 29 – Trips 62, 63, 64, 65, and 67.

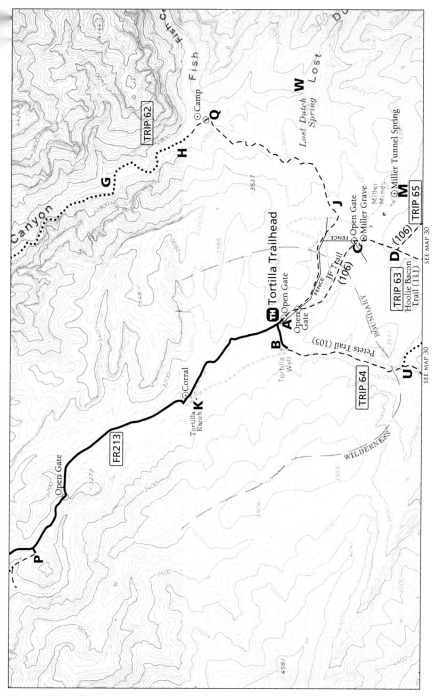

Map 29 continued – Trips 62, 63, 64, 65, and 67.

In 0.8 mile from the Tortilla Trailhead, the Hoolie Bacon Trail (111) branches off the JF Trail at the top of the first hill [29-D] and proceeds south through Night Hawk Spring Basin and Horse Camp Basin. It connects with the Red Tanks Trail (107) [4-B] in La Barge Canyon for a total of 5.1 miles.

Tortilla Well windmill [29-B] is not in operation, and it does not produce water. Even when there is water in Tortilla Creek at Tortilla Flat on SR88, the creek at Tortilla Ranch may be dry. Bring your own water.

HISTORY AND LEGENDS

Over the years, the Tortilla Ranch [29-K] was considered part of the Reavis Ranch operation—early owners were Jack Fraser, Clemans Cattle Company, John "Hoolie" Bacon and Charlie Upton, and Floyd Stone. The land at the headquarters site was never homesteaded and remains in federal ownership today. The buildings, wells, and fences were private property—range improvements—on the Tortilla grazing allotment. These improvements and the grazing permit were bought and sold, but not the land. The Tortilla grazing allotment enclosed the area bounded by Fish Creek, Rogers Canyon at Angel Basin, Tortilla Pass, Red Tanks Divide, Trap Canyon, Tortilla Mountain, Hells Hole Spring on Tortilla Creek, and part of the Horse Mesa Dam road.

View of Tortilla Ranch [29-K] looking toward the east. The small building in the bottom right corner is the bunkhouse. Tortilla Creek is on the bottom edge of the photo. Photograph by Al Reser, March 1974. Courtesy Superstition Mountain Historical Society, Al Reser Collection.

Little remains of the Tortilla Ranch site [29-K]. The old barn was torn down in the late 1970s, and all that remains is the concrete-slab floor. The ruins of other ranch improvements are still here—the stone water tank near the well (the windmill is gone), a concrete slab for the bunkhouse, a concrete water trough, and T-shaped poles that held material for shade. Several big netleaf hackberry trees grow here next to the large parking area.

The JF Trail starts down the road at a small turnaround area [29-A]. The ruins of more concrete water troughs dated June 12, 1959, are nearby. About 0.1 mile west of the vehicle turnaround is the abandoned Tortilla Well windmill and metal water tank [29-B], which mark the start of the Peters Trail.

The Hoolie Bacon Trail (111) is named for John Bacon, who was nicknamed "Hoolie." John was not related to Vance Bacon, the geologist who worked for Celeste Maria Jones and died in a fall from Weavers Needle. John Bacon's daughter Lucille married Floyd Stone, and they were owners of Reavis Ranch from 1955 to 1966. The Stones later ran cattle from their IV Ranch just east of Fish Creek.[280]

Although, for many years, Weavers Needle was the focus of the Lost Dutchman Mine searches, the Tortilla region of the Wilderness also received considerable activity. An area [30-I] west of Horse Camp Basin near the Peters Trail (105) is considered to be the site of one Mexican mining camp and the source of cut timber for their mines. The diggings at the Miller mines [30-C] and the drift [30-F] discovered by Estee Conatser about a mile and a half to the southeast of Tortilla Trailhead are evidence of more recent searches for mineral wealth. Before he died at Tortilla Flat on November 11, 1910,[281] John Chuning made extensive searches for the Lost Dutchman Mine in the Tortilla area using ladders to climb the sheer cliffs, but along with the others, he failed to find the Lost Dutchman Mine.[282]

Without divulging names, author Estee Conatser, in *The Sterling Legend*, writes that two men, in the early 1950s, located a sizable cache of gold south of Tortilla Ranch. She believes this discovery may be connected to stories about Indians with buried gold in that region. She also recounts the story of large a cache of gold supposedly guarded by a band of Apache known as the Black Legion. This gold is presumed to be in the Black Cross Butte area, but the clues and treasure map are rather vague.[283]

Tortilla Creek cuts northwest across the Wilderness some 16 miles, starting from Tortilla Pass in the south, draining to the north into Canyon Lake near Tortilla Flat. Barry Storm and Estee Conatser considered the possibility that Tortilla Creek could be the Cañon Fresco marked on the Gonzales treasure map. Both authors refer to early prospectors finding placer gold in Tortilla Creek—above and below the waterfalls and in an unnamed section of the creek during the mid-1960s. Russel Perkins, an early postmaster of Tortilla Flat, described the remains of a large encampment near the falls on Tortilla Creek, which were still visible in the 1940s. In that same area, Carl Clark reported finding the remains of a Spanish hexagon drill bit.[284]

Alignments of mountain peaks, cacti, and canyons have all been proposed as clues leading to the Lost Dutchman Mine. Estee Conatser reported that seven giant saguaros were growing in a straight line "a mile or so east of Tortilla Mountain."[285] We have not seen this group of seven cacti, but it is not uncommon to see alignments of four or five saguaro cacti. George "Brownie" Holmes, in his 1944 manuscript *Story of the Lost Dutchman*, wrote an account of another clue involving the alignment of Weavers Needle with Four Peaks, when Four Peaks is viewed as one peak. The unnamed location of this alignment was through a saddle to a low ridge, with Four Peaks to the north and a high needle rising in the south. The Dutchman's camp was reputed to be in the canyon below the ridge.[286] While these clues are rather vague and probably not that useful for the serious mine seeker, they pique the imagination of many trekkers and give ample reason to scan the landscape for these and other fascinating features.

See History and Legends in Trip 62 (Fish Creek Loop) on page 350 for the U.S. Army's march through the Tortilla Ranch area in May of 1873.

Cowboy Mickey Plemens at the Tortilla Ranch bunkhouse [29-K]. Photograph by Al Reser, February 1965. Courtesy Superstition Mountain Historical Society, Al Reser Collection.

SUPERSTITION WILDERNESS TRAILS WEST

FISH CREEK LOOP

Although Fish Creek is easily accessible from SR88, the narrow boulder-choked canyon deters many casual hikers. You will enjoy the solitude, seasonal pools of water, and dense canopy of trees.

ITINERARY

Park your vehicle at the Tortilla Trailhead on SR88. Walk east on dirt SR88 down to the bottom of Fish Creek Hill. Hike up (south) Fish Creek, head over to the old Tortilla Ranch site, and follow dirt FR213 back to SR88.

DIFFICULTY

Difficult day hike. Moderate over-night trip. Not doable by horses. Elevation change is ±1,230 feet.

LENGTH and TIME

10.2 miles, 9 hours round-trip.

MAPS

Arizona USGS topo maps NAD27: Horse Mesa Dam and Weavers Needle. Superstition Wilderness Beartooth map, grids I9 to J11. Map 29.

FINDING THE TRAIL

See the trailhead map on page 341. The hike starts at a Tortilla Trailhead parking area on SR88 [29-T, 0] (N33° 31′ 33.6″, W111° 19′ 05.8″).

THE TRIP

Start on Map 29 on page 342. It is possible to park a vehicle at the Fish Creek Bridge [29-F], but space along the side of the road is very limited. Tortilla Trailhead on SR88 [29-T] is usually a better choice for parking. If you just want to take a short, easy hike up Fish Creek [29-N, 0.6] and return the same way, then it is more convenient to park at the Fish Creek Bridge. With an extra vehicle, you can set up a shuttle so you don't have to walk on the roads.

    The trip starts from the Tortilla Trailhead parking area [29-T, 0]. Walk east on the Apache Trail, SR88, 2.2 miles to the Fish Creek Bridge [29-F, 2.2] at the bottom of Fish Creek Hill. From the north end of the bridge abutment, drop down into the creek bed and head east. To avoid walking through the proverbial pool of water under the bridge, you can take the trail at the south end of the bridge to the big cave. From the cave, another steep trail takes you down to the normally dry bed of Fish Creek.

Hiking is pleasant under the canopy of Arizona sycamores and Fremont cottonwoods, with intermittent water forming large clear pools. House-sized boulders slow your progress, so 0.5 mile per hour is a good estimate for hiking speed. Following the footprints of others will help you negotiate the routes around the major obstacles. The narrow canyon hinders reliable GPS measurements, so keeping track of the side canyons is the best bet for marking your progress through the canyon.

At a ravine entering from the east [29-G, 4.8], author Jack Carlson made a loop trip over Fish Creek Mountain and down Mud Spring Canyon. He was really surprised when he found a black bear in the thicket at Mud Spring. Luckily, the bear decided to leave the thicket.

Eventually Fish Creek Canyon opens up [29-H, 5.3], making the walking easier, but the shade and seasonal water disappear. At the cotton-wood trees upstream from Lost Dutch Canyon, you may find water again.

The good trail [29-Q, 5.5] (N33° 29' 53.8", W111° 16' 34.8") from Fish Creek Canyon to the top of the ridge [29-J] is marked with rock cairns. Nearby Lost Dutch Spring is often dry. Head up to the low ridge [29-J, 6.4],

Dick Walp hiking up Fish Creek on a bypass around some large boulders. June 2010 photo.

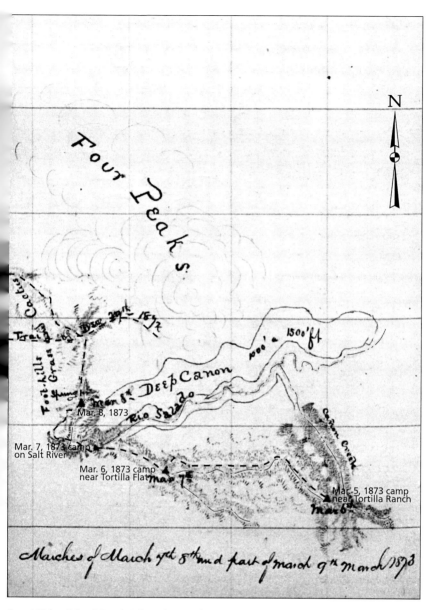

Page 126 from John G. Bourke's diary showing the army's marches from March 5 to 9, 1873. Place names on the map helped identify the locations: Rio Salado (Salt River) and Cañon Creek (Fish Creek), but Tortilla Creek was not named. We overlaid dashed lines for the trail and streams. We also added typeset dates for his camps and the north arrow. Bourke's scout into Cañon Creek (Fish Creek) was not marked as a trail on the above map. March 5 camp was near Tortilla Ranch. March 6 camp was near Tortilla Flat. March 7 camp was at the Salt River near Canyon Lake. Bourke's notation on the above map is labeled incorrectly—March 6 camp should be March 5 camp, and March 7 camp should be March 6 camp. The original color map is from USMA Library, West Point, New York.[287]

follow the faint track of an old road down to the JF Trail by keeping the fence on your left (south), turn right (north) to meet FR213 [29-A, 7.0], and return on FR213 going north to SR88 [29-T, 10.2], where the trip description ends.

HISTORY AND LEGENDS

Hacksaw Tom was a notorious road agent along the Apache Trail from 1905 to 1910. He was known for robbing wagons and stagecoaches at the bottom of Fish Creek Hill with a sawed-off shotgun and then disappearing up Fish Creek Canyon. Hacksaw Tom's last robbery may have been in 1910, when the only automobile robbery on the Apache Trail occurred.[288]

A 1978 discovery of items in a carpetbag was identified with Hacksaw Tom. The carpetbag containing locks, a flour-sack mask with eyeholes, and a twelve-gauge double-barreled shotgun was unearthed in a cave near Apache Gap. After seeing the shotgun, Larry Hedrick, former Director of the Superstition Mountain Museum, concluded that Hacksaw Tom acquired his name from the appearance of his weapon—a shotgun with sawed-off barrel and stock. Previously it was assumed he was named for hacksawing the locks from the strong boxes. All of Hacksaw Tom's memorabilia is on display at the Superstition Mountain Museum in Apache Junction.[289]

The U.S. Army Fifth Cavalry made camp in the Tortilla Ranch area [29-A] on March 5, 1873. The scout under the command of Major William H. Brown left Camp McDowell on January 6, 1873, and was returning to McDowell after searching the Superstition, Pinal, and Graham Mountains for Apaches. On the morning of March 6, Second Lieutenant John Bourke, aide-de-camp to General Crook, and several others rode northeast over the mountain pass [29-J] near the former Miller Mines [29-C] and down into Fish Creek, which they referred to as Cañon Creek. They rode upstream, going east for a mile, then returned and rode north-northwest downstream [29-H] for a mile until they were stopped by "huge boulders and deep pools of water."[290] See Bourke's map on page 349.

After scouting Cañon (Fish) Creek, Bourke and his party caught up with the main column, which was headed westerly in what looked like a direct route to the Tortilla Flat area [27-A] for the March 6, 1873, camp. The next day they made a short march of 4 miles to the Rio Salado (Salt River) and camped on the north side of present-day Canyon Lake—their previous camp on January 7, at the start of the expedition nearly two months earlier.[291]

From the Salt River, the command headed up Cottonwood Creek on March 8, went over to Sycamore Creek, marched down Sycamore Creek, and crossed the Verde River at Camp McDowell to end the scout on March 11, 1873.[292] The military march from Rogers Trough to Tortilla Ranch on March 5, 1873, is described in the Woodbury Trailhead on page 49.

HOOLIE BACON TRAIL—PETERS TRAIL LOOP

This enjoyable trip crosses a lesser-traveled region of the Wilderness. The trip passes the Miller Mines, follows Tortilla Creek for a short stretch, and goes over Horse Ridge to Horse Camp Basin. Some nasty cross-country travel through catclaw is balanced by especially nice views of Music Mountain and Tortilla Mountain. The return on the Peters Trail goes by Kane Spring.

ITINERARY

From Tortilla Trailhead at the end of FR213, follow JF Trail (106) and Hoolie Bacon Trail (111) to Horse Camp Basin. Go cross-country to Peters Trail (105) and return via Tortilla Well.

DIFFICULTY

Difficult hike and ride. Elevation change is ±1,460 feet.

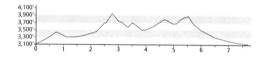

LENGTH and TIME

7.7 miles, 8 hours round-trip.

MAPS

Arizona USGS topo maps NAD27: Horse Mesa Dam and Weavers Needle. Superstition Wilderness Beartooth map, grids I11 to I12. Map 30.

FINDING THE TRAIL

See the trailhead map on page 341. The JF Trail begins at the end of FR213 (N33° 29' 34.1", W111° 17' 31.7")—0.1 mile east of Tortilla Well windmill.

THE TRIP

Start on Map 30 on page 354. Start at the end of FR213 [30-A, 0]. The JF Trail begins at the road barricade. See Trip 65 (JF Trail to Woodbury Trailhead) on page 360 for the description of the Miller Mines and the JF Trail from the trailhead [30-A, 0] to the junction with the Hoolie Bacon Trail [30-D, 0.8].

At the wooden trail sign [30-D], take the Hoolie Bacon Trail across the grassy hillside—dotted with prickly pear, honey mesquite, and catclaw acacia.

The trail soon drops down to Tortilla Creek where one-seed juniper, netleaf hackberry, redberry buckthorn, and mesquite grow along the creek.

When the trail crosses to the south side of Tortilla Creek [30-X, 1.4], you have the option of going down canyon (northwest) for a return via Tortilla Well [30-B] to Tortilla Trailhead [30-A, 3.3], for a total trip loop of about 3 hours. This is a really nice section of Tortilla Creek. This part of the trip is considered only moderately difficult for hikers, but riders may have problems negotiating the trailless streambed.

The trail continues south, heading upstream, along Tortilla Creek. From the pictures in her book, we think the small flat [30-Y, 1.8] was Estee Conatser's camp when she explored the Lost Dutchman Mine Jr. on the rocky peak [30-F] to the east.[293] From her camp area, the Hoolie Bacon Trail leaves Tortilla Creek, takes a right turn to the southwest, and crosses a major wash coming down from Cedar Basin Canyon on a well-defined horse trail marked by large rock cairns.

Two out-of-service concrete water troughs for Night Hawk Spring sit on the left (east) side of the trail. One is inscribed with the date "7/30/37." Farther up the wash, only a drip of water comes out of the pipe at Night Hawk Spring (N33° 28' 15.8", W111° 17' 02.7"), so don't count on it for water.[294] The trail heads up to Horse Ridge passing through an area with abundant one-seed juniper trees, for which Cedar Basin Canyon to the east is named. Many people refer to these juniper trees as cedar because the aroma and appearance of the wood are similar to cedar.

The trail reaches a low saddle [30-Z, 2.5], where a lone Arizona rosewood tree grows. Continuing higher through manzanita, sugar sumac, and redberry buckthorn, the pass on Horse Ridge [30-BB, 2.8] is marked by a lone mesquite tree. A trail-of-use goes east across the ridge, but we have not field checked it beyond the trail marked on our Map 30.

Horse Camp Spring is a few yards right (west) of the trail. Here you may find water in the bedrock near a cottonwood tree. The spur trail [30-V, 3.2] (N33° 27' 34.4", W111° 17' 41.2") to the corral has disappeared, so just before you cross an unnamed ravine, you need to head cross-country less than 0.1 mile toward the abandoned Horse Camp Corral [30-TT] (N33° 27' 33.0", W111° 17' 44.9"). To make the loop trip shorter, you can go cross-county on the route of a former trail from the corral [30-TT] to the ridge [30-OO]—saving about 0.6 mile.

Back on the Hoolie Bacon Trail [18-V, 3.2], the trip continues over a low hill and drops down to a wide valley—where the trail heads south. At an unsigned trail junction [30-N, 3.8] (N33° 27' 07.6", W111° 17' 53.6") marked by a small rock cairn, this trip leaves the Hoolie Bacon Trail.

View to the west to Music Mountain [30-W] from the Hoolie Bacon Trail [30-BB]. Horse Camp Spring is at the small cottonwood tree in the center of the photograph. May 2011 photo.

If you plan to continue on the Hoolie Bacon Trail, the trip mileages are 4.2 miles at the Trap Canyon camp area [30-E] and 5.1 miles at the end of the trail in La Barge Canyon at the junction with the Red Tanks Trail [4-B]. See Trip 5 (Red Tanks Divide Loop) on page 68 and Trip 18 (Upper La Barge Box Loop) on page 131 if you plan to spend time in the Upper La Barge area.

Continuing on this trip from [30-N, 3.8], take the unsigned trail-of-use going northwest up the valley. The trail-of-use follows a flat bench on the right side of the valley. When the trail-of-use enters a wash, go right (north) following the wash upstream—easy walking and mostly free of catclaw—to a point below a small hill [30-H, 3.9].

The abandoned section of Peters Trail [30-N to QQ] in this valley, which is shown on the 1966 Weavers Needle USGS topo map, is no longer usable—not generally visible on the ground and overgrown with catclaw. So, your strategy is to find a route free of catclaw on your trek to connect with the present-day Peters Trail [30-QQ]. Traveling through the catclaw is easier if you wear leather gloves to push the catclaw out of the way.

From the wash [30-H, 3.9], you need to make a decision either to stay in the wash and go around the east side of the small hill, or to go up on the bench and around the hill on the west side. In both cases you reach the ridge [30-OO] overlooking Peters Canyon valley. The westerly route is shorter,

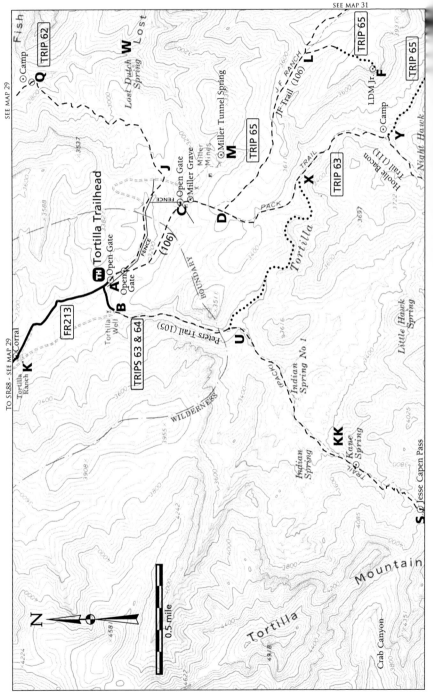

Map 30 – Trips 63, 64, 65, and 66.

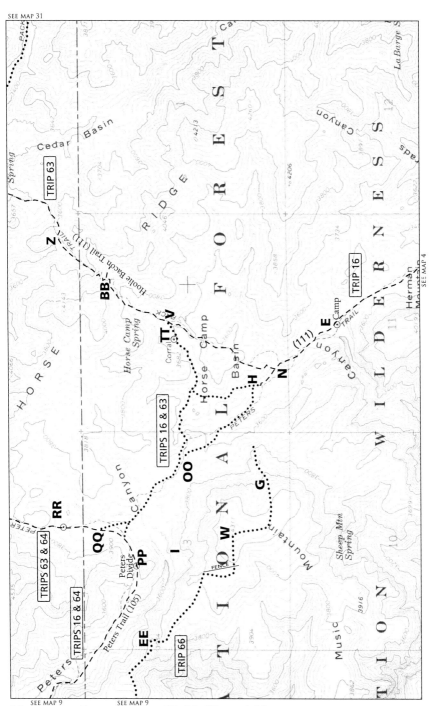

SEE MAP 4

TRIP 63

TRIP 16

TRIPS 16 & 63

TRIPS 63 & 64

TRIPS 16 & 64

TRIP 66

Cedar Basin

Horse Camp Spring

Horse Camp Basin

Peters Divide

La Barge

Herman Mountain

Sheep Mtn. Spring

Music

FENCE

FENCE

Hoolie Bacon Trail (111)

Peters Trail (105)

(111)

SEE MAP 9   SEE MAP 9

Map 30 continued – Trips 63, 64, 65, and 66.

but it has more catclaw, although if you zigzag around a lot, you can find a reasonably clear route.

From the ridge [30-OO, 4.5] overlooking Peters Canyon, you can see the soldier camp and cut timber area to the west [30-I] and the cliffs of Tortilla Mountain to the north. Peters Trail (105) heading to Charlebois Spring goes west over the large knob on the horizon [30-PP], but our trip heads east. From the ridge [30-OO, 4.5], pick the easiest route down the slope, cross Peters Canyon wash, and head up the bench until you intersect the Peters Trail [30-QQ, 5.1] (N33° 27' 52.6", W111° 18' 40.0"). After the bushwhacking episode, Peters Trail will seem like a superhighway.

Follow Peters Trail north up to a low pass [30-RR, 5.4], then down and up to the high pass [30-S, 5.6], which we named Jesse Capen Pass.[295] The steep rocky trail descends the spine of a ridge with steep drop-offs on either side, so watch your footing on the loose rocks. Horse riders and packhorses often have difficulty on this section of trail. Kane Spring [30-KK, 6.0] (N33° 28' 32.6", W111° 18' 23.8") is to the right (east) of the trail and is identified only by the spur trail. In 2011, we observed that our landmark cottonwood tree was uprooted. Kane Spring usually has water. The concrete water trough near the spring is filled with dirt and is not visible anymore.

From Kane Spring [30-KK], the trip continues downhill (southeast), and the trail surface changes from rock to soft dirt. Indian Spring and Indian Spring No. 1 do not have water—they may only have been concrete water troughs that have been removed. Tortilla Creek crossing [30-U, 7.0] is well marked by large rock cairns. From here [30-U], the trail goes north following either bank of the creek and sometimes down the center of the creek bed. This section of trail would be impassable when Tortilla Creek is at flood stage.

Tortilla Creek is very scenic here with a thick growth of netleaf hackberry, mountain mahogany, lemonade berry, one-seed juniper, scrub oak, and a canopy dominated by large Arizona Sycamore trees. The pale-red cliffs are covered with green lichen. Even when Tortilla Creek is dry, this is a pretty area. When the steep cliff to the east recedes, the end of Peters Trail approaches the abandoned Tortilla Well windmill [30-B, 7.6]. A short distance up the road, the trip ends at Tortilla Trailhead [30-A, 7.7].

HISTORY AND LEGENDS

For Sims Ely's stories about the soldier and Mexican camps, cut mine timber, and Spanish Trails, see Trip 64 (Peters Trail to Charlebois Spring) on page 357. For Estee Conatser's story about the Lost Dutchman Mine Jr. along Tortilla Creek, see Trip 65 (JF Trail to Woodbury Trailhead) on page 360.

Peters Trail to Charlebois Spring

This is the shortest route to Charlebois Spring through a lesser-traveled region of the Wilderness. The trip takes you by Kane Spring, which usually has water. Historic Peters Mesa offers a place to relive the accounts of many Lost Dutchman stories. Short excursions are possible from centrally located Charlebois Spring to Music Canyon, La Barge Canyon, and Marsh Valley.

ITINERARY

From Tortilla Trailhead, follow Peters Trail (105) into Peters Canyon, up to Peters Mesa, and down to La Barge Canyon. A short distance on the Dutchman's Trail (104) brings you to Charlebois Spring.

DIFFICULTY

Difficult day hike. Moderate backpack. Very difficult ride. Elevation
change is +1,340 and -1,880 feet.

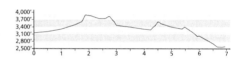

LENGTH and TIME

6.9 miles, 5 hours one way.

MAPS

Arizona USGS topo maps NAD27: Horse Mesa Dam and Weavers Needle. Superstition Wilderness Beartooth map, grids I11 to G112. Maps 30 and 32.

FINDING THE TRAIL

See the trailhead map on page 341. The trail starts at the Tortilla Well wind-mill [30-B] (N33° 29′ 33.2″, W111° 17′ 41.2″) at the Peters Trail wooden trail sign and heads south along Tortilla Creek.

THE TRIP

Start on Map 30 on page 354. The trip to Charlebois Spring can be a long day hike or part of a longer overnight trip. From Tortilla Well windmill [30-B, 0], Peters Trail (105) follows Tortilla Creek and makes many crossings that are well marked by rock cairns. Tortilla Creek is very scenic with a thick growth of netleaf hackberry, mountain mahogany, juniper, and scrub oak, but the narrow canyon is dominated by the canopy of large Arizona sycamore trees.

The remains of the windmill and tank [30-B] at Tortilla Well in 1993. The windmill blades and gearbox have since fallen off the tower and vandals more recently have pulled the tower down. The storage tank is still here. The well is out of service and does not provide water.

In the fall, the golden leaves of the sycamore trees and the pale-red cliffs covered with green lichen add a splash of color to this narrow canyon. For a much easier trip, you can turn around where the trail leaves Tortilla Creek and goes up the large wash on the right (south) [30-U, 0.6].

The trail leaves Tortilla Creek [30-U], heads southwest on the south side of a large wash, and continues across a wide valley. Indian Spring and Indian Spring No. 1 do not have water. Kane Spring [30-KK, 1.6] (N33° 28′ 32.6″, W111° 18′ 23.8″), on the left (east) side of the trail, usually has water. The wood and metal spring box has deteriorated and only a pool of clear water is here. The sugar sumac (laurel) tree above the spring drops its leaves in the pool. The large cottonwood tree has been uprooted and no longer acts as a landmark for the spring.

From Kane Spring [30-KK], Peters Trail goes up a steep hill, which is very difficult for riders and packhorses. From Jesse Capen Pass [30-S, 2.0], the trail drops into a small ravine, goes over a lower pass [30-RR, 2.2], and descends into Peters Canyon drainage. The cliffs of Tortilla Mountain rise in the west, while the rolling hills of the horse country open to the southeast.

At the bottom of the descent [30-QQ, 2.5], a cross-country route—and sometimes a bushwhack—goes left (southeast) to Horse Camp Basin. Trip 63

Hoolie Bacon Trail—Peters Trail Loop) on page 352 describes this area. Our rip continues on the Peters Trail, goes up to a saddle [30-PP, 2.8], named Peters Divide, just north of a big knob on the horizon, and then drops to the bed of Peters Canyon. The detailed description for the rest of the trip is given in Trip 16 (Charlebois Spring—Loop 3) on page 123.

A summary of the important mileages is: Peters Trail leaves Peters Canyon [32-O 4.2], Salt Flat area on Peters Mesa [32-T, 4.7], junction with Dutchman's Trail [32-M, 6.6], and Charlebois Spring [32-BB, 6.9]. Trip 14 (Charlebois Spring—Loop 1) on page 113 describes the Charlebois Spring area. Return the same way to Tortilla Well [30-B, 13.8], or plan an extended trip from this central location in the Wilderness.

HISTORY AND LEGENDS

In the early 1900s, Tortilla Mountain was renamed Kit Carson Mountain, but the Tortilla name was soon restored when historians learned Kit Carson never explored this region.[296]

Sims Ely, in his 1953 book *The Lost Dutchman Mine*, describes the horse country and the possibility that a soldier camp on the western end was the site of a Mexican camp. The horse country that Ely recounts is the area shown on the Weavers Needle topographic map in Sections 2 and 3 where the landmarks are named Horse Ridge, Horse Camp Spring, and Horse Camp Basin. Rancher Jim Bark and Ely considered this area important because the camp was the site of cut wood (covering about forty acres), which they believed was used as timber in the Mexican mines.[297]

We looked around one possible area where there might be cut timber [18-I], but only found one cut stump and two larger stumps that may have rotted. West of that location is a dense thicket that is impossible to penetrate, but it looks as if it once contained large mesquite trees.

Ely reasoned that they could determine the direction of the Mexican mines by tracing the route that the timber was carried. He speculated that it could have been taken over two routes. The first was the old alignment of the Peters Trail that went south past Trap Canyon, connecting with the Hoolie Bacon Trail and over to the mouth of La Barge Canyon at Upper La Barge Box. Trip 16 (Charlebois Spring—Loop 3) on page 121 uses this cross-country route that is now mostly overgrown with catclaw. In 1910, Ely said he saw sections of this trail that were three feet wide and cut into the rock. The other possible route went northwest on the Peters Trail, past Kane Spring, down toward Tortilla Creek. Many authors refer to this section of the Peters Trail along the base of Tortilla Mountain as the Spanish Trail.

JF TRAIL TO WOODBURY TRAILHEAD

This enjoyable trip crosses a lesser-traveled region of the Wilderness. The Miller Mines near the Tortilla Trailhead are easy to find (although not much remains there). The Lost Dutchman Mine Jr. will take some extra effort to locate. A side trip from Tortilla Pass to the cliff dwellings in Rogers Canyon is worthwhile if you have time on an extended trip.

ITINERARY

From Tortilla Trailhead follow JF Trail (106) over Tortilla Pass to Woodbury Trailhead.

DIFFICULTY

Moderate hike. Difficult ride. Elevation change is +2,210 and -1,830 feet.

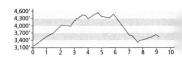

LENGTH and TIME

9.1 miles, 6 hours one way.

MAPS

Arizona USGS topo maps NAD27: Horse Mesa Dam, Iron Mountain, and Weavers Needle. Superstition Wilderness Beartooth map, grids I11 to L14. Maps 1, 30, and 31.

FINDING THE TRAIL

See the trailhead map on page 341. The JF Trail begins at the end of FR213 (N33° 29′ 34.1″, W111° 17′ 31.7″)—0.1 mile east of Tortilla Well windmill.

THE TRIP

Start on Map 30 on page 354. This trip can be done as a 9.1-mile-trans wilderness trek to Woodbury Trailhead [1-A] requiring a 58-mile vehicle shuttle, or a round-trip 11.8-mile day trip to Tortilla Pass [31-J] and back [30-A]. Some hardy day hikers may prefer to return from Tortilla Pass by boulder hopping down Tortilla Creek to Tortilla Well [30-B].

The trip starts at the end of FR213 [30-A, 0] where the unsigned JF Trail begins at an open gate in the fence and road barricade. The JF Trail

Miller Mine operation in 1920. George Drakulick (aka George Miller) is second from the right. Dr. Aiton is third from left.[298] From The Lost Dutchman Mining Corporation, Inc. prospectus by Dr. Robert A. Aiton. Photograph by McCulloch Bros. Courtesy of Gregory Davis, Mining and General Promotional Prospectuses Collection.

follows the single track uphill to an open gate with posts made of railroad ties [30-C, 0.6]. This is the Miller Mines area.

If you have time, three places in the Miller Mines area may be of interest. First, George Miller's gravesite [south of 30-C] (N33° 29' 14.6", W111° 17' 09.4") is 5 feet to the left (east) side of the JF Trail—about 61 yards south of the railroad-tie gate. The grave is marked with a metal ore-cart rail, about a foot long, sticking out of the ground. Second, the concrete engine-hoist foundation [southeast of 30-C] (N33° 29' 12.9", W111° 17' 06.0") for the main Miller Mine shaft is still visible—the 1920s photo of the operation is shown above. The old trail has disappeared due to lack of use, so you will have to bushwhack through the catclaw on the hillside to look for the foundation. Third, Miller Tunnel Spring [30-M] (N33° 29' 06.8", W111° 16' 56.3") is located over the ridge to the south in a small niche that was dug into the south bank of the ravine.[299]

Back on the JF Trail, from the open gate [30-C], head up the ridge (south) to the top of the hill [30-D, 0.8] where the JF Trail meets the Hoolie Bacon Trail (111) at a wooden trail sign. The vegetation is very sparse here with prickly pear, mesquite, and catclaw growing among the grasses.

Bear left (southeast) on the JF Trail. As the JF Trail begins a gentle climb along the crest of some small hills, the vegetation is more abundant and

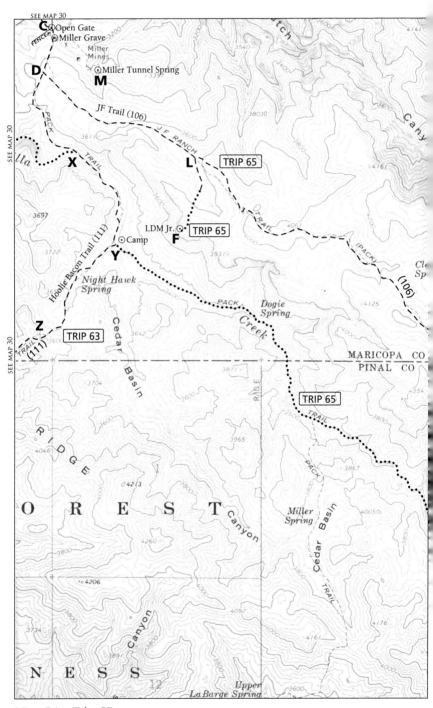

Map 31 – Trip 65.

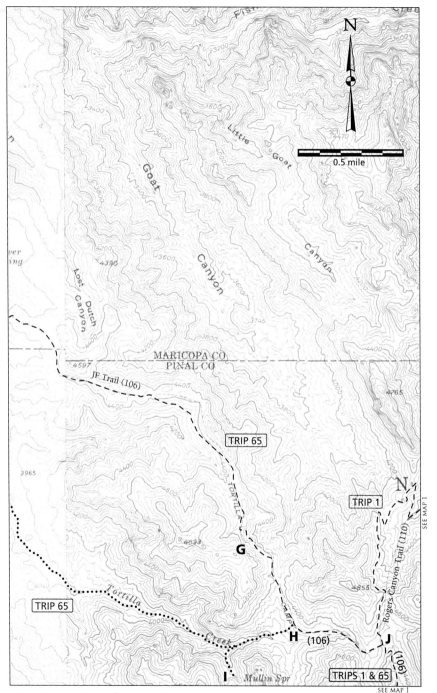

Map 31 continued – Trip 65.

varied—mountain mahogany, juniper, mesquite, manzanita, catclaw acacia and mimosa, Arizona rosewood, shrub oak, sugar sumac, and yucca. The horizon is broken with the towering stalks of the century plant and sotol, and the rocks are covered with green lichen. The trail-of-use to LDM Jr. [31-L, 1.6] branches to the right and is described in a following section.

You may find water in the potholes where the JF Trail crosses Clover Spring Wash at mile 2.8. The trail weaves around the tops of the ridges, crosses many saddles, and makes a steep descent on a switchback [31-G, 4.9] into the upper drainage of Goat Canyon.

The trail then crosses a low saddle into the Tortilla Creek drainage where it passes the abandoned trail junction [31-H, 5.4] (N33° 26′ 50.7″, W111° 13′ 50.8″) to Mullin Spring [31-I]. For a difficult side trip to Mullin Spring, go cross-country from this trail junction down to Tortilla Creek. Enter the bed of Mullin Spring Wash where it meets Tortilla Creek (N33° 26′ 45.0″, W111° 14′ 10.9″). When the bushwhacking becomes easier, work your way over to a game trail on the left (east) hillside. Up the wash just past the spring, cross from the east to the west side of the wash to the concrete trough at Mullin Spring [31-I] (N33° 26′ 36.4″, W111° 14′ 07.9″), which is at the base of a small cliff. Mullin Spring is south of the location shown on the topo map. We consider this a reliable source of water in the winter months.[300]

From the junction [31-H, 5.4], the trail crossings may have pothole water in winter. It is a short distance up to Tortilla Pass [31-J, 5.9], where the Rogers Canyon Trail (110) comes in from the (left) north.

La Barge Mountain is the high mountain to the west, rising to 5,077 feet—twenty feet higher than Superstition Mountain. On a trip to Tortilla Pass in November 1993, we were greeted with snow blanketing all the trees and bushes, but in subsequent years the pass was a pleasant rest stop. Except for the lack of a nearby water source, the pass might make a good camp.

You have several trip choices from Tortilla Pass [31-J]. First, continuing south on the JF Trail takes you to the Woodbury Trailhead [1-A] for the completion of this trip. Second, a side trip to the cliff dwellings [1-G] in Rogers Canyon is 2.5 miles down the Rogers Canyon Trail. You can find good camping places in the grassy flat in Angel Basin [1-F] where Trail 110 enters Rogers Canyon. See Trip 1 (Rogers Canyon Cliff Dwellings) on page 50. And finally, day trippers can return to Tortilla Trailhead via the same way (JF Trail 106), or they can take the slower, boulder-hopping route through Tortilla Creek, which ends at Tortilla Well [30-B]. On the map, we drew the dotted line over the old trail along Tortilla Creek, but we found it easier to walk down the dry bed of the creek.

Continuing toward our Woodbury [1-A] destination, the JF Trail follows the west ridge of Woodbury Gulch going south from Tortilla Pass

[1-J] into Randolph Canyon. After the trail passes though some green thickets of mountain mahogany, juniper, tomatillo, sugar sumac, and shrub oak, you have good views across the valley to the south and west. The trail crosses Randolph Canyon [1-N, 7.6], which may have potholes of water, then goes uphill and follows the west bank of Randolph Canyon. The trail crosses the wash twice, passes the Wilderness Boundary sign, and reaches the water storatge tanks and dirt tank near Woodbury windmill [1-C, 8.5], which produces water according to the needs of the Martin Ranch. Woodbury is cow country and you will likely see some cows lazing under the mesquite trees here.

Since the trail does not go next to the Woodbury windmill, use the dirt tank as your landmark to follow the trail. Keep the dirt tank on your right and the storage tanks on your left as the trail curves around the dirt tank and begins to head south toward the signed junction [1-B, 8.6] with Woodbury Trail (114). The JF Trail, now a dirt road, continues south as it goes over a small hill to the Woodbury Trailhead parking lot, where the trip ends [1-A, 9.1]. See Woodbury Trailhead on page 47 and Trip 1 (Rogers Canyon Cliff Dwellings) on page 50 for information on the south end of the JF Trail.

SIDE TRIP TO LOST DUTCHMAN MINE JR.

Estee Conatser, author of *The Sterling Legend*, searched the Superstition Mountains for the Lost Dutchman Mine (LDM) and found a mine that at first seemed to fit the description of the LDM. She named it the Lost Dutchman

The windmill [1-C] near the site of the Woodbury cabin in 1993. The junction of the JF Trail and Rogers Canyon Trail at Tortilla Pass [1-J] is hidden to the right of the highest peaks on the horizon.

Mine Jr. The mine [31-F] is located on a rocky cliff 0.3 mile northwest of Hill 3931. Only seasoned hikers with climbing experience should attempt this side trip.[301] Estee is a *nom de plume* derived from her initials "S. T." Her full name is Shirley T. Conatser.

Since the side trip from the JF Trail over to the cliff [31-F] (N33° 28' 28.9", W111° 16' 32.1") may take some time and energy, it is best to make it on a separate trip or on the return from Tortilla Pass. Getting from the JF Trail [31-L] over to the site [31-F] requires crossing a wide ravine. Leave the JF Trail going westerly [31-L, 3750] (N33° 28' 44.8", W111° 16' 26.9") at a bend in the JF Trail where a flat area accommodates a trail-of-use. A lone juniper tree stands on the slope to the right (northwest). Follow the faint trail down and back up the ravine, and aim for the unnamed peak [31-F].

From below the cliffs—using a photo from Conatser's book—we identified the round, black hole of the cave and the shape of the rock fin that points the way down to the mine and cave. On another trip, back on top of the cliffs where the highest point looks like a stack of broken rocks [31-F], we headed north a few feet until we saw the hole in the mine ceiling. It is a sheer drop off the Tortilla Creek side of the cliff, so be careful. From the ceiling hole, it is a steep scramble in the ravine to the mine entrance, which faces northwest. To us, the mine looked like a natural opening in the rock, although some cuts on the walls could be pick marks. We will let you decide. The approach to the cave below looked too steep, so we did not attempt it.

The view from the cliff near the mine into Tortilla Creek and the Night Hawk Spring Basin is spectacular, and these areas would make a good destination for a day hike or overnight trip using the Hoolie Bacon Trail. See Trip 63 (Hoolie Bacon Trail—Peters Trail Loop) on page 351.

HISTORY AND LEGENDS

In 1920, Dr. Robert Aiton, Secretary-Treasurer of the Lost Dutchman Mining Corporation, Inc., published a pamphlet describing the history of the Miller Mines [30-C] and promoting stock for sale in the corporation. George Von Drakulick, aka George Miller, was the president, and John Hluper was the vice-president. The promising assay report of 20.42 ounces of gold per ton is suspect because the mine apparently was not successful.[302] Several local landmarks are named for George Miller—Miller Mines, Miller Tunnel Spring, and Miller Spring.

Miller died of a heart attack at his mining operation in 1936 when he was showing the area to some friends. Following his wishes, he was buried [30-C] near the mines—his grave was blasted out of solid rock. A partner, Earnest Martin, died in 1927 and is also buried on a hill near the diggings. Dr. Aiton died in 1928 and is buried in Superior, Arizona.[303]

Music Mountain

This loop trip takes the Peters Trail up to Peters Mesa and then returns on a cross-country route over the top of Music Mountain. Occupying a central position in the eastern Superstition Mountain range, Music Mountain offers spectacular views in all directions.

ITINERARY

From Tortilla Well, follow Peters Trail (105) into Peters Canyon and up to Peters Mesa. Go south on the ridges from Peters Mesa to Music Mountain. Drop into Horse Camp Basin, and return to Tortilla Well.

DIFFICULTY

Difficult hike. Not recommended for horses except as noted. Elevation change is ±2,380 feet.

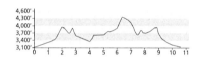

LENGTH and TIME

10.6 miles, 9 hours round-trip

MAPS

Arizona USGS topo maps NAD27: Horse Mesa Dam and Weavers Needle. Superstition Wilderness Beartooth map, grids I11 to H12. Maps 30 and 32.

FINDING THE TRAIL

See the trailhead map on page 341. Start at the wooden Peters Trail sign [30-B] (N33° 29′ 33.2″, W111° 17′ 41.2″), which is a few yards west of the abandoned Tortilla Well windmill and silver water tank.

THE TRIP

Start on Map 30 on page 354. See Trip 64 (Peters Trail to Charlebois Spring) on page 357 for the trail description from Tortilla Well [30-B, 0] to Peters Canyon [32-O, 4.2]. The last creek crossing [32-O] in Peters Canyon makes a pleasant lunch stop—especially with seasonal water in the potholes.

Continue on Peters Trail as it climbs out of Peters Canyon, heading west up to Peters Mesa. At the pass [32-SSS, 4.5], leave Peters Trail going left (southeast), and begin the cross-country trek heading across the mostly flat ridges toward the top of Music Mountain.

The wide ridge ends at a narrow hogback [32-EE, 5.9] that forms the divide between Music Canyon and Peters Canyon. This is the turnaround point for horse riders, since the next 0.3 mile is fairly rough and brushy. Begin the route across the hogback on the left (north) side, and look for game trails or open space between the boulders. There is no correct way to negotiate this rocky outcrop. On the south end of the hogback, we saw a game trail that might go down to Peters Creek, but we did not try to follow it.

From the south end of the hogback, pick a line-of-sight route to the small saddle about 0.1 mile ahead. You'll see a small knob on the left (north) side of the saddle. Look for narrow benches beneath the vegetation, running across the steep slope. We are not sure if these benches are remnants of a former trail or just natural, but they are a great help in getting across the overgrown hillside.

At the small saddle, go right and stay high for a few hundred feet. When you see a reasonable route across the rocks, continue south where the open country and flat ridges resume.

Tortilla Mountain, with its small knob on top, is in view to the north for most of the trip. Weavers Needle and Bluff Spring Mountain come into view from several saddles as you gain elevation. When you cross a barbed-wire fence—the Tortilla/Superstition grazing allotment boundary—at the base of the last uphill section, you are getting close to the top.

Music Mountain [32-W, 6.7, 4311] has a flat top, so getting around up here is easy. Continue south from the top, and descend the wide, flat ridge of the mountain to the southeast rim where you get a view out to the rugged landscape of Trap Canyon, La Barge Canyon, and Coffee Flat Mountain.

Proceed off the edge of the mountain [32-G, 7.1] to the east. Plan your route carefully as you descend the cliffs so as not to "cliff-out" and have to climb back up the hill. Looking east across Horse Camp Basin, pick a line-of-sight route—try to avoid areas of thick catclaw—to meet the cross-country route that connects with Peters Trail [32-QQ, 8.1]. Go north on Peters Trail (105), and return to Tortilla Well [30-B, 10.6]. It is another 3.3 miles on FR213 to the Apache Trail (SR88) from Tortilla Well.

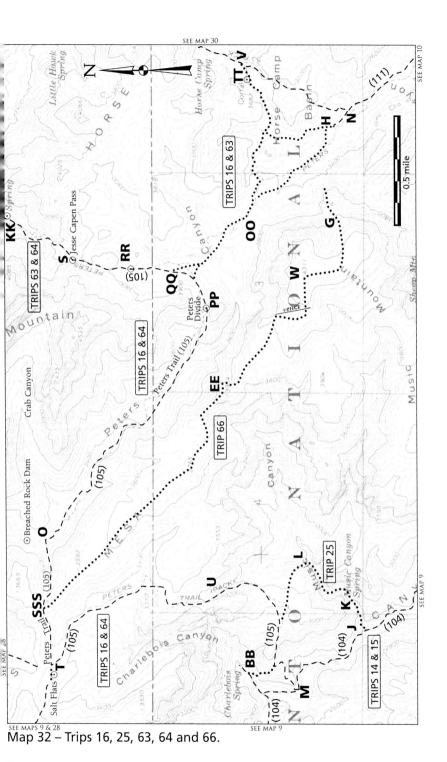

Map 32 – Trips 16, 25, 63, 64 and 66.

TORTILLA CREEK WATERFALL

The waterfall in the Upper Box of Tortilla Creek may be the waterfall that detoured the soldiers while on their trip from Fort McDowell to the Silver King Mine, resulting in the Two Soldiers Lost Mine story.[304] It is rough hiking in a pretty canyon that often has pools of water.

ITINERARY

From Tortilla Trailhead, drive about 1.4 miles south on FR213. Park in a pullout, take a trail down to Tortilla Creek, then go cross-country, mostly in Tortilla Creek, to the waterfall. Return the same way.

DIFFICULTY

Difficult hike. Not recommended for horses except as noted. Elevation change is -430 feet.

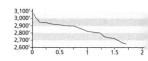

LENGTH and TIME

1.7 miles, 3.5 hours one way.

MAPS

Arizona USGS topo map NAD27: Horse Mesa Dam. Superstition Wilderness Beartooth map, grid H10. Map 33.

FINDING THE TRAIL

See the trailhead Map on page 341. From Tortilla Trailhead on SR88 [33-T], drive about 1.4 miles on FR213, which is always four-wheel drive. Park on the right (west) side of FR213 at a turnaround area in the saddle of the ridge [33-P] (N33° 30′ 36.8″, W111° 18′ 38.4″). The unsigned trail is on the northwest side of the saddle.

THE TRIP

Start on Map 33 on page 371. The unsigned trail [33-P, 0] is well defined on the ground and goes down the left (west) slope of the drainage. When the trail reaches the bench, it turns left toward Tortilla Creek and ends at the creek. Just as the trail makes that left turn, head straight, going northwest on any game trail that you can find. Going across the bench can be a real

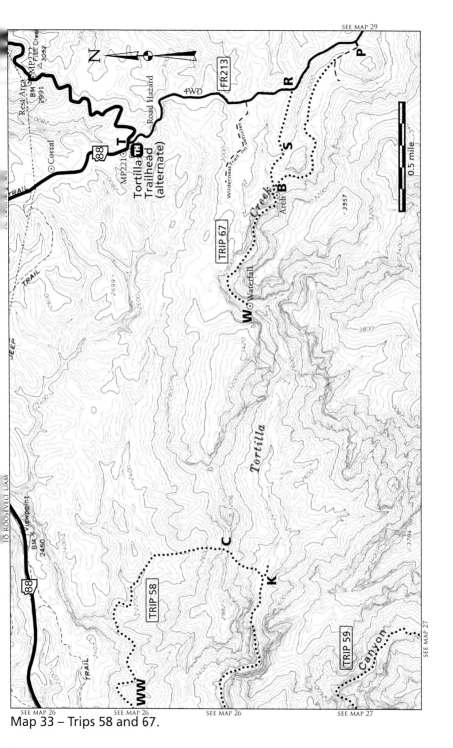

Map 33 – Trips 58 and 67.

bushwhack unless you are good at recognizing the game trails. Exit the bench when you have had enough bushwhacking, and enter the creek bed, which is often dry and may be easier walking. This is as far as horse riders should go.

Follow Tortilla Creek downstream to the waterfall [33-W, 1.7] (N33° 31' 04.4", W111° 19' 52.8"). It is slow hiking due to the large boulders, pools of seasonal water, and streamside vegetation. You sometimes need to crawl under and over boulders. The route finding is often laborious, but interesting.

At the waterfall [33-W] in January 2011, we could go down the right (north) side about halfway, but not to the bottom, so this was the turnaround point. A climbing sling attached to a nearby hackberry tree may indicate that some people rappelled to the bottom of the estimated 50-foot drop. When we hiked here about 1982, we were able to go to the bottom of the waterfall on a trail along the north cliff—the trail has since disappeared. We did not recall, on that same 1982 trip, seeing the large, vertical, dacite slab that is now blocking the pour-off of the waterfall.

Return the same way to your vehicle [33-P, 3.4]. Or, you could leave Tortilla Creek at the top of the Upper Box [33-B, 2.4] (N33° 30' 57.8", W111° 19' 17.7"), head up to the saddle [33-S, 2.6], connect with FR213 on the ridge [33-R, 2.9], and walk back to your vehicle [33-P, 3.2].

Tortilla Creek near the beginning of the trip to the waterfall [33-W]. January 2011 photo.

Superstition Wilderness Trails West

REAVIS TRAILHEAD

The Reavis Trailhead is off SR88, between mileposts 227 and 228, about 28 miles northeast of Apache Junction and 14 miles southwest of Roosevelt Dam. From SR88, turn east on FR212. Drive uphill 2.8 miles to the end of FR212.

FINDING THE TRAILHEAD

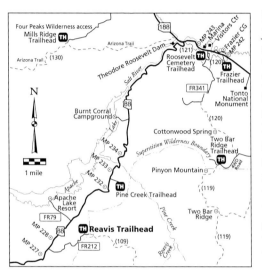

From the town of Apache Junction on SR88, travel another 12 miles past Tortilla Flat to FR212. From Roosevelt Lake on SR88, look for FR212 about 1.6 miles southwest of the Apache Lake Resort Road. FR212 is a one lane, dirt road with several eroded sections that require a high-clearance vehicle. The 3,700-foot trailhead elevation provides a panoramic view of the Salt River Canyon and Apache Lake to the northwest.

FACILITIES

The trailhead has a hitching rail for horses and a small parking lot. Bring your own water. Nearby Apache Lake Marina and Resort has full facilities—motel, restaurant, bar, boat launch, and boat rental.

THE TRAILS

The Reavis Ranch Trail (109) begins at the end of FR212 at the road barricade (N33° 33' 23.8", W111° 13' 38.6"). This good trail follows the abandoned road to Reavis Ranch in 9.3 miles. The popular Reavis Falls Trail branches off the Reavis Ranch Trail at an unsigned junction in 3.2 miles (N33° 32' 45.5", W111° 11' 24.6") and continues to Reavis Falls for a total of 6.1 miles.

Complete trip descriptions, maps, and history for Reavis Trailhead are in our companion book, *Superstition Wilderness Trails East*.

PINE CREEK TRAILHEAD

Pine Creek Trailhead is east of SR88, between mileposts 232 and 233, about 33 miles northeast of Apache Junction and 9 miles southwest of Roosevelt Lake Dam. Go east on FR665 and drive 0.6 mile over the hill to the first water trough. FR665 is 1.1 miles southwest of the Pine Creek Bridge on SR88.

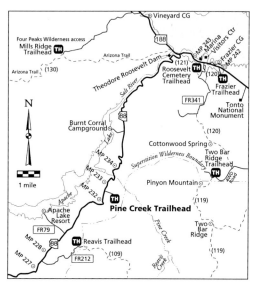

FINDING THE TRAILHEAD

Go north on SR88 about 2.5 miles past the Apache Lake Marina Road. Or, from Roosevelt Lake, go south on SR88 for 9 miles. When you turn east on the signed FR665, between mileposts 232 and 233, you will see a metal corral ahead. Continue through the gate on the left side of the metal corral. FR665 goes 0.6 mile up and over a hill to a concrete water trough and the unsigned trailhead area (N33° 35′ 01.8″, W111° 12′ 18.5″). FR665 is a one lane, dirt road with eroded sections requiring a high-clearance vehicle and possibly four-wheel drive if the road is not maintained. Park at the metal corral (near N33° 35′ 22″, W111° 12′ 32″) if your vehicle or trailer can't negotiate FR665. Don't block access to the corral.

For a short walk up Pine Creek from the bridge, it might be okay to park along the road for a while. For any day trip or overnight trip, it is best to park on FR665, where you can avoid the traffic and have plenty of room to unload stock animals.

FINDING THE TRAIL

The route heads northeast from the concrete water trough (N33° 35′ 01.8″, W111° 12′ 18.5″) near the end of FR665 and shortly turns east.

Complete trip descriptions, maps, and history for Pine Creek Trailhead are in our companion book, *Superstition Wilderness Trails East*.

ROOSEVELT CEMETERY TRAILHEAD

Roosevelt Cemetery Trailhead is off of SR188 about 27 miles northwest of Globe. Turn left (south) into the Lakeview Park between mileposts 242 and 243. Within 100 feet, turn right into the Roosevelt Cemetery Trailhead parking lot.

FINDING THE TRAILHEAD

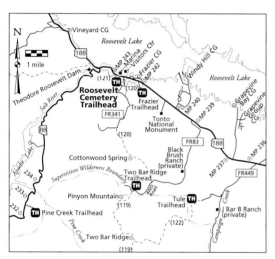

Drive about two miles north of the Tonto National Monument entrance on SR188, and turn left into the Lakeview Park mobile home park. Turn right on the first road, within 100 feet of the highway, and park in the Roosevelt Cemetery parking lot. The Lakeview Park is directly across the highway from the entrance to the Roosevelt Lake Visitors Center.

FACILITIES

The Roosevelt Cemetery Trailhead has no facilities except for parking. Roosevelt Lake Visitors Center is nearby. Bring your own water.

THE TRAIL

Only one trail begins at this trailhead, Roosevelt Cemetery Trail (255). The paved trail begins on the southwest side of the parking area (N33° 40' 2.0", W111° 08' 5.6") and heads up a small hill to the Roosevelt Cemetery. The paved trail ends at the cemetery entrance. A dirt trail continues uphill to the Thompson Trail (121), which is part of the Arizona Trail system. At the Thompson Trail, a pedestrian gate blocks stock animals from entering or exiting the Roosevelt Cemetery Trail.

Complete trip descriptions, maps, and history for Roosevelt Cemetery Trailhead are in our companion book, *Superstition Wilderness Trails East*.

FRAZIER TRAILHEAD

The Frazier Trailhead is off SR188, between mileposts 242 and 243, 26 miles northwest of Globe—1.2 miles north of Tonto National Monument and 0.7 mile south of Roosevelt Lake Visitors Center. Turn southwest onto FR221, and drive about 0.1 mile to the parking area.

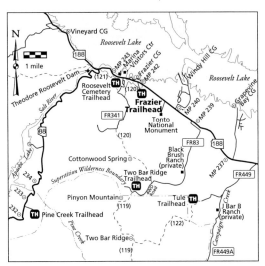

FINDING THE TRAILHEAD

Drive about 1.2 miles north of the Tonto National Monument entrance on SR188, and turn left onto FR221. The dirt road takes you around the right side of the Frazier Power Station and a wooden corral. The road ends at the trailhead parking lot. From the Frazier Horse Campground, you can reach the Frazier Trailhead by a horse trail and tunnel that go under SR188.

FACILITIES

No facilities exist at the trailhead except for pull-through parking. Camping, water, restrooms, and equestrian facilities are available on the north side of SR188 at the Frazier Recreational Site, 0.4 mile away by horse trail.

THE TRAIL

Lower Cottonwood Trail (120) begins on the southwest side of the parking area (N33° 39' 43.6", W111° 07' 23.3") and heads west toward Cottonwood Creek. Within a few yards, near the wooden trail sign, a trail branches to the left (east) and goes to the Frazier Recreation Site in 0.4 mile where you can camp with your horses. Trail 120 continues south along Cottonwood Creek and joins FR341 at Thompson Spring in 1.2 miles.

Complete trip descriptions, maps, and history for Frazier Trailhead are in our companion book, *Superstition Wilderness Trails East.*

TWO BAR RIDGE TRAILHEAD

Two Bar Ridge Trailhead is off SR188, between mileposts 239 and 240, 23 miles northwest of Globe—about 2 miles south of Tonto National Monument. Turn southwest onto FR83, and drive about 5.2 miles to the parking area. The last 3 miles of the dirt road requires four-wheel drive.

FINDING THE TRAILHEAD

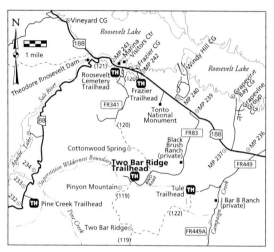

Drive southwest on FR83 about 1.9 miles to the junction with the Black Brush Ranch (aka Two Bar Ranch), which is private. Bear left on FR83, and continue uphill for 3.3 miles on FR83. As the road becomes steep and rough, four-wheel drive is required.

FACILITIES

No facilities exist at the trailhead except for parking. Bring your own water. See Roosevelt Lake Area in our companion book, *Superstition Wilderness Trails East,* for visitor facilities along SR188.

THE TRAILS

Two Bar Ridge Trail (119), which is part of the Arizona Trail, begins on the south side of the parking area (N33° 35' 51.2", W111° 07' 40.2"). It takes you south to meet the Tule Trail (122) in 3.4 miles, Walnut Spring in 6.8 miles, and Reavis Gap Trail in 7.3 miles at Reavis Gap. Cottonwood Trail (120) branches off FR83 in a flat area about 1.3 miles back down FR83 from the trailhead—just west of the metal water-storage tank. The Cottonwood Trail, also part of the Arizona Trail, takes you to Cottonwood Spring in 1.2 miles and on to Frazier Trailhead in 5.9 miles.

Complete trip descriptions, maps, and history for the Roosevelt Lake area are in our companion book, *Superstition Wilderness Trails East.*

TULE TRAILHEAD

From Apache Junction at Idaho Road, drive east on US60 for 49 miles to SR188, on the west side of Globe. From Globe, go north on SR188 for 20 miles to FR449 (J Bar B Road) between mileposts 235 and 236. FR449 is 2 miles north on SR188 from the Spring Creek Store. Drive west on FR449 for 2 miles to its junction with FR449A. Stay right on FR449 for 1.2 miles to the end of the road. Tule is pronounced "Two-lee."

FINDING THE TRAILHEAD

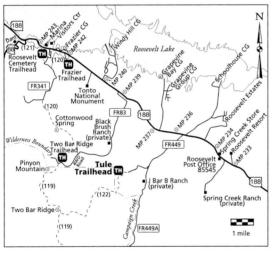

FR449 is well marked and easy to follow. Bear right at the junction with FR449A, go up and over a steep, small hill, and follow the dirt road with a gravel overlay. FR449 ends at a turnaround and small parking area posted with information and trailhead signs.

FACILITIES

No facilities are located at the Tule Trailhead except for a small parking area. Bring your own water. See the section titled Roosevelt Lake Area in our companion book, *Superstition Wilderness Trails East,* for visitor facilities along nearby SR188.

THE TRAIL

Tule Canyon Trail (122) begins from the south side of the parking area (N33° 35' 35.9", W111° 04' 32.5") and is marked with a wooden trail sign. From the trailhead, you have a clear view of Two Bar Mountain across the open desert.

Complete trip descriptions, maps, and history for Tule Trailhead are in our companion book, *Superstition Wilderness Trails East.*

CAMPAIGN TRAILHEAD

From Apache Junction at Idaho Road, drive east on US60 for 49 miles to SR188, on the west side of Globe. In Globe, go north on SR188 for 20 miles to FR449 (J Bar B Road) between mileposts 235 and 236. FR449 is 2 miles north on SR188 from the Spring Creek Store. Drive west on FR449 for 2 miles to the junction with FR449A. Take FR449A left for 5.1 miles to Campaign Trailhead near Reevis Mountain School.

FINDING THE TRAILHEAD

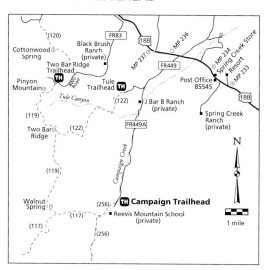

FR449 is well marked to the junction with FR449A. FR449A is a four-wheel-drive road that follows the bed of Campaign Creek. FR449A may be impassable during periods of heavy rain. In the dry season, a high-clearance vehicle will work in ideal weather and road conditions. Avoid the deep, soft sand. Following the signs to Reevis Mountain School will keep you on FR449A to Campaign Trailhead.

FACILITIES

The Campaign Trailhead (former Upper Horrell Trailhead) has no facilities. Purify drinking water from the creek and springs, or bring your own water.

THE TRAILS

Campaign Trail (256) begins at the parking area (N33° 31' 54.3", W111° 04' 42.8"), goes south on FR449A, and leaves FR449A at a wooden sign. Do not use the trail through Reevis Mountain School (private property). The Campaign Trail meets the Reevis Gap Trail (117) in about 1.1 mile.

Complete trip descriptions, maps, and history for Campaign Trailhead are in our companion book, *Superstition Wilderness Trails East*.

PINTO CREEK TRAILHEAD

From Apache Junction at Idaho Road, drive 29 miles on US60 to Superior. Continue east toward Miami and Globe on US60 for 12 more miles. One mile east of the Pinto Creek highway bridge, turn left (north) on paved FR287 (Pinto Valley Mine Road) between mileposts 239 and 240. If you are coming from Miami, drive west on US60 for 4 miles to the Pinto Valley Mine Road. Follow public road FR287 (paved and dirt) across Pinto Valley Mine property to the Pinto Creek Trailhead near the Iron Bridge on Pinto Creek.

FINDING THE TRAILHEAD

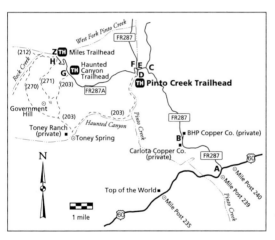

Do not drive on any roads marked *Active Mining Area*. From US60 [A, 0], drive north on paved FR287 for 2.8 miles to the Pinto Valley Mine entrance [B, 2.8], and bear left on dirt FR287. Follow the *Public Access, Haunted Canyon*, and *JH6 Ranch* signs across the mine property. Turn left at the JH6 Ranch locked gate [C, 6.7]. Before you cross the Iron Bridge [E, 7.2], turn left (south), look for the Haunted Canyon Trail (203) sign, and continue to the locked gate (N33° 25′ 31.4″, W111° 00′ 9.7″) [D, 7.4]. Park near the gate, but don't block the gate or the road. A medium-clearance vehicle is required.

FACILITIES

The Pinto Creek Trailhead does not have any facilities. Bring your own water.

THE TRAIL

From the locked gate, Trail 203 follows the road to a small corral in 1.5 miles. At the corral, go right through a barbed-wire gate on the unsigned Trail 203.

Complete trip descriptions, maps, and history for Pinto Creek Trailhead are in our companion book, *Superstition Wilderness Trails East*.

Haunted Canyon Trailhead

From Apache Junction at Idaho Road, drive 29 miles on US60 to Superior. Continue east toward Miami and Globe on US60 for 12 more miles. One mile east of the Pinto Creek highway bridge, turn left (north) on paved FR287 (Pinto Valley Mine Road) between mileposts 239 and 240. Follow FR287 (paved) and FR287A (dirt) to the trailhead. If you are coming from Miami, drive 4 miles west on US60 to the Pinto Valley Mine Road.

FINDING THE TRAILHEAD

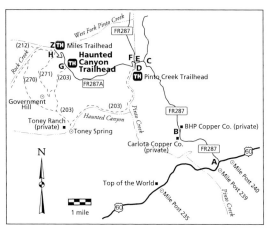

Do not drive on any roads marked *Active Mining Area*. Follow the directions in Pinto Creek Trailhead to the Iron Bridge [E, 7.2]. Cross the Iron Bridge over Pinto Creek. At the signed intersection with FR287A [F, 7.3], take FR287A west to the Haunted Canyon Trailhead on FR287A [G, 11.1]. If you go too far and miss the trailhead, backtrack from Miles Trailhead about 1.9 miles on FR287A. A medium-clearance vehicle is required. Allow extra driving time for getting lost on the first section of the road through the mine operations [B, 2.8 to C, 6.7].

FACILITIES

The Haunted Canyon Trailhead has no facilities. Bring your own water.

THE TRAILS

The sign, *Trail 203*, for the Haunted Canyon Trailhead parking lot (N33° 25′ 33.0″, W111° 03′ 17.3″) is on the right (east) side of FR287A. The Haunted Canyon Trail (203) begins across the road from the parking area.

Complete trip descriptions, maps, and history for Haunted Canyon Trailhead are in our companion book, *Superstition Wilderness Trails East*.

MILES TRAILHEAD

From Apache Junction at Idaho Road, drive 29 miles on US60 to Superior. Continue east toward Miami and Globe on US60 for 12 more miles. One mile east of the Pinto Creek highway bridge, turn left (north) on paved FR287 (Pinto Valley Mine Road) between mileposts 239 and 240. Follow FR287 (paved) and FR287A (dirt) to the trailhead. If you are coming from Miami, drive 4 miles west on US60 to the Pinto Valley Mine Road.

FINDING THE TRAILHEAD

Do not drive on any roads marked *Active Mining Area*. Follow the directions in Haunted Canyon Trailhead to the Haunted Canyon Trailhead [G, 11.1]. Continue to the end of FR287A and the Miles Trailhead [Z, 13.0] (N33° 26' 14.3", W111° 04' 01.9"). Park or set up camp wherever you like. A medium-clearance vehicle is required.

FACILITIES

The Miles Trailhead has corrals, a barn, plenty of room for parking, and space for group camping under the tall sycamore trees. Bring your own water.

THE TRAILS

The West Pinto Trail (212) (N33° 26' 14.3", W111° 04' 01.9") starts near the Superstition Wilderness sign. The West Pinto Trail meets the Bull Basin Trail (270) in 0.5 mile. Paradise Trail (271) (N33° 26' 09.1", W111° 03' 46.3") is 0.2 mile back down FR287A from the Miles Trailhead at the *Trail 271* sign.

Complete trip descriptions, maps, and history for Miles Trailhead are in our companion book, *Superstition Wilderness Trails East*.

ROGERS TROUGH TRAILHEAD

From Apache Junction at Idaho Road, go east 15 miles on US60 to Florence Junction. Two miles east of Florence Junction on US60, between mileposts 214 and 215, turn north on Queen Valley Road for 1.8 miles to FR357 (Hewitt Station Road). Go right 3 miles to FR172. From Superior, go west to Queen Valley Road and follow the above directions. Locked gates on FR357 block access to FR172 from the east. Go north on FR172 for 9 miles to the junction of FR172A and go right 4 miles on four-wheel-drive FR172A to the end of the road. A high-clearance vehicle is required on FR172.

FINDING THE TRAILHEAD

Nine miles on FR172 brings you to the junction of FR172A where you go

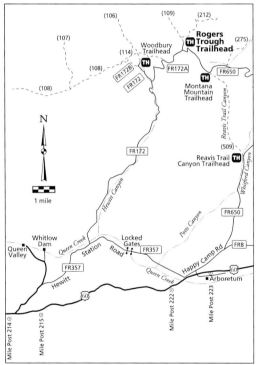

right (east) for 4 miles to Rogers Trough Trailhead. After heavy rains, FR172A sometimes requires four-wheel drive.

FACILITIES

Rogers Trough Trailhead has hitching posts for stock. Bring your own water.

THE TRAILS

Reavis Ranch Trail (109) (N33° 25' 19.9", W111° 10' 21.7") goes north from the Rogers Trough parking lot to Reavis Valley in 6.5 miles. A short distance from the Rogers Trough parking lot, the West Pinto Trail (212) branches off to the northeast and ends at Miles Trailhead in 8.8 miles.

Complete trip descriptions, maps, and history for Rogers Trough Trailhead are in our companion book, *Superstition Wilderness Trails East.*

MONTANA MOUNTAIN TRAILHEAD

Follow directions in Rogers Trough Trailhead to the junction of FR172 and FR172A. Go right about 3.6 miles on four-wheel-drive FR172A to the signed junction with FR650. Take FR650 for 2 miles to the Montana Mountain Trailhead. A high-clearance vehicle is required on FR172, and FR172A sometimes requires four-wheel drive. FR650 is always four-wheel drive.

FINDING THE TRAILHEAD

Montana Mountain Trailhead is about 2.4 miles southeast of Rogers Trough Trailhead on FR172A and FR650. Montana Mountain Trailhead (N33° 24' 19.6", W111° 09' 22.3") is marked by a small rock cairn and a fallen-down trail sign that reads *Trail 509*.

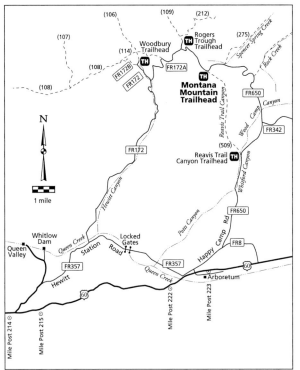

FACILITIES

Montana Mountain Trailhead does not have any facilities. Bring your own water.

THE TRAILS

From the vehicle pullout at the Montana Mountain Trailhead, Reavis Canyon Trail takes you 5.1 miles down the mountain to Reavis Trail Canyon Trailhead, where the Reavis Canyon Trail meets FR650 again. This is part of the Arizona Trail.

Complete trip descriptions, maps, and history for Montana Mountain Trailhead are in our companion book, *Superstition Wilderness Trails East*.

TRANS-WILDERNESS TRIPS

We selected several long hikes and horse rides that connect one trailhead to another. More possibilities exist. All the trips can be traveled in either direction. You can enhance the quality of the treks by including side trips. The one-way shuttle distance is rounded to the nearest mile. Roads are suitable for passenger cars, except as noted. The individual trip descriptions note trail hazards that may block your stock animals. Some trips are described more fully in our companion book, *Superstition Wilderness Trails East*.

Trip 68. Peralta Trailhead to First Water Trailhead

Follow Peralta Trail (102) to Fremont Saddle, connect with Dutchman's Trail (104) in East Boulder Canyon, and go over Parker Pass to First Water Trailhead. See Peralta Trailhead and First Water Trailhead. The trail distance is 10.9 miles. Vehicle shuttle distance is 25 miles.

Trip 69. Peralta Trailhead to Canyon Lake Trailhead

Follow Peralta Trail (102) to Fremont Saddle, connect with Dutchman's Trail (104) in East Boulder Canyon, and go down Boulder Canyon taking Boulder Canyon Trail (103) to Canyon Lake Trailhead. See Peralta Trailhead and Canyon Lake Trailhead. The trail distance is 12.7 miles. Vehicle shuttle distance is 31 miles.

Trip 70. Peralta Trailhead to Tortilla Trailhead

Follow Dutchman's Trail (104) to Bluff Spring, La Barge Spring, and Charlebois Spring. Take Peters Trail (105) to Tortilla Trailhead. See Peralta Trailhead and Tortilla Trailhead. The trail distance is 15.4 miles. Vehicle shuttle distance is 42 miles. Four-wheel drive is required for Tortilla Trailhead, or add 3.3 miles to the trail distance if you walk on FR213.

Trip 71. Carney Springs Trailhead to Lost Dutchman State Park

Take the Carney Springs Trail and West Boulder Trail to Boulder Saddle. Take Superstition Mountain Ridgeline Trail across Superstition Mountain to Siphon Draw. Follow Siphon Draw Trail (53) to Siphon Draw Trailhead inside the Lost Dutchman State Park. Trip 28 (Superstition Mountain Ridgeline) describes this trip. The distance, mostly cross-country, is 10.5 miles. Vehicle shuttle distance is 21 miles. Not doable by horses.

Trip 72. Dons Camp Trailhead to Broadway Trailhead

Follow Lost Goldmine Trail to Broadway Trailhead. See Trip 26 (Lost Goldmine Trail from Dons Camp Trailhead). The trail distance is 9.7 miles. Vehicle shuttle distance is 15 miles.

Trip 73. Broadway Trailhead to Crosscut Trailhead

Follow Jacob's Crosscut Trail to Crosscut Trailhead. See Trip 34 (Jacob's Crosscut Trail from Broadway Trailhead). The trail distance is 5.8 miles. Vehicle shuttle distance is 7 miles.

Trip 74. First Water Trailhead to Canyon Lake Trailhead

Follow Dutchman's Trail (104) and Second Water Trail (236) to Boulder Canyon. Connect with Boulder Canyon Trail (103), which ends at Canyon Lake Trailhead. See First Water Trailhead and Canyon Lake Trailhead. The trail distance is 7.4 miles. Vehicle shuttle distance is 12 miles.

Trip 75. First Water Trailhead to Reavis Trailhead

This is Tom Kollenborn's well-known *Ride Through Time.* From First Water Trailhead, follow Dutchman's Trail (104) to Charlebois Spring. Take Peters Trail (105) to Tortilla Ranch. Connect with JF Trail (106), Rogers Canyon Trail (110), and Reavis Ranch Trail (109) to reach Reavis Ranch. Continue on Reavis Ranch Trail to Reavis Trailhead. See First Water Trailhead and Reavis Trailhead. The trail distance is 36.9 miles. Vehicle shuttle distance is 29 miles. A section of Rogers Canyon Trail [1-NN] is dangerous for horses.

Trip 76. Tortilla Trailhead to Woodbury Trailhead

Take FR213 to Tortilla Trailhead. Pick up the JF Trail (106), and follow the trail to Woodbury Trailhead. See Trip 65 (JF Trail to Woodbury Trailhead). The trail distance is 9.1 miles. Vehicle shuttle distance is 57 miles. A four-wheel-drive vehicle is required if you drive to the Tortilla Trailhead at the end of FR213. Add 3.3 miles to trail distance if you cannot drive on FR213.

Trip 77. Woodbury Trailhead to Rogers Trough Trailhead

Follow JF Trail (106) to Tortilla Pass. Continue on Rogers Canyon Trail (110) and Reavis Ranch Trail (109) to Rogers Trough Trailhead. See Woodbury Trailhead, Rogers Trough Trailhead, and Trip 1 (Rogers Canyon Cliff Dwellings). The trail distance is 9.4 miles. Vehicle shuttle distance is 5.3 miles. A four-wheel drive vehicle is sometimes required for Rogers Trough Trailhead on FR172A. If you cannot drive on FR172A, add 3.7 miles to the trail distance to make a loop back to the start at Woodbury Trailhead using FR172A, Woodbury Trail (114), and JF Trail (106).

Trip 78. Reavis Trailhead to Peralta Trailhead

From Reavis Trailhead, follow Reavis Ranch Trail (109) to Reavis Ranch, then continue to Rogers Canyon where you connect with Rogers Canyon Trail (110). At Tortilla Pass, where the Rogers Canyon Trail ends, pick up the JF Trail (106) and go south. Take Woodbury Trail (114), Coffee Flat Trail (108), and Dutchman's Trail (104) to end at Peralta Trailhead. See Reavis and Peralta Trailheads. See Trip 1 (Rogers Canyon Cliff Dwellings), Trip 2 (Dripping Spring), and Trip 17 (Reeds Water). The trail distance is 31.9 miles. Vehicle shuttle distance is 45 miles. Map 1 shows a section of Rogers Canyon Trail [1-NN] that is dangerous for horses.

Trip 79. Miles Trailhead to First Water Trailhead

Hikers from www.hikearizona.com first made this trek in November 2007. Follow West Pinto Trail (212) to Oak Flat. Take Campaign Trail (256) to Fire Line Trail (118). A side trip to Circlestone adds 1.6 miles. Camp in Reavis Valley. Take Reavis Ranch Trail (109) north, Frog Tanks Trail (112) west, Rogers Canyon Trail (110) south, JF Trail (106) south to Woodbury Trailhead for camping and a water cache. Take Coffee Flat Trail (108) southwest, Red Tanks Trail (107) north and west, and camp at La Barge Spring. Take Dutchman's Trail (104) to First Water Trailhead, ending the 47-mile trek. Vehicle shuttle distance is 64 miles. See Miles Trailhead, Woodbury Trailhead, and First Water Trailhead.

Trip 80. Arizona Trail. Rogers Trough Trailhead to Frazier Trailhead

Traveling south to north, start at Rogers Trough Trailhead, and follow Reavis Ranch Trail (109) to Reavis Valley. Take Reavis Gap Trail (117) and Two Bar Ridge Trail (119), which connects with FR83. Continue on Cottonwood Trail (120) to Frazier Trailhead and the Frazier Equestrian Campground. See Rogers Trough Trailhead, Two Bar Ridge Trailhead, and Frazier Trailhead. The trail distance is 24.9 miles. Vehicle shuttle distance is 68 miles.

Trip 81. Tule Trailhead to Frazier Trailhead

From Tule Trailhead, take Tule Trail (122) to Two Bar Ridge Trail (119). Go north on Two Bar Ridge Trail to FR83 and connect with Cottonwood Trail (120), which ends at Frazier Trailhead, for a total of 15.4 miles. Vehicle shuttle distance is 9 miles.

Trip 82. Campaign Trailhead to Reavis Trailhead

From Campaign Trailhead, take Campaign Trail (256) and Reavis Gap Trail (117) to Reavis Valley. Continue on Reavis Ranch Trail (109) to Reavis Trailhead for a total of 15.7 miles. Vehicle shuttle distance is 32 miles.

REFERENCE NOTES

1. Jack Carlson and Elizabeth Stewart, "Summary of Quarter Circle U Ranch Bill of Sale History, 1876-1981," unpublished compilation, February 21, 2003. James Swanson and Tom Kollenborn, *Superstition Mountain: A Ride Through Time* (Phoenix: Arrowhead Press, 1981), pp. 112, 188, 191.

2. Ibid.

3. BLM land patents for T1N R8E S1 on website www.glorecords.blm.gov/. Serial Patent file No. 1139014, Charles Weekes, April 30, 1953; Serial Patent file No. 1064034, Joseph Miller, May 12, 1933; both from Tucson Land Office, BLM, RG49, National Archives Building, Washington, DC. Pinal County Recorder, Joseph Miller to William King, Book of Deeds 53, p. 38; King to Haymore, Book of Deeds 65, p. 35; Nichols to Weekes, Books of Deeds 69, p. 420; Weekes to USA, Docket 91, p. 246. Weekes Family Collection, Superstition Mountain Historical Society. Richard G. Schaus, "Frederick Charles Weekes 1865-1949," *Arizona Cattlelog*, July 1974, pp. back cover, 32.

4. BLM land patents for T1N R8E S20 on website www.glorecords.blm.gov/. James Swanson, Thomas Kollenborn, *The History of Apache Junction, AZ* (Apache Junction, Arizona: Goldfield Press, 1990), p.31.

5. Serial Patent file No. 1073049, William Van Horn, November 7, 1934; Serial Patent file No. 1064034, Joseph Miller, May 12, 1933; both from Tucson Land Office, BLM, RG49, National Archives Building, Washington, DC. Pinal County Recorder, Joseph Miller to William King, Book of Deeds 53, p. 38.

6. Serial Patent file No. 1085913, Wayne E. Barnard, October 1, 1936; Tucson Land Office, BLM, RG49, National Archives Building, Washington, DC.

7. Serial Patent file No. 1129133, Wayne E. Barnard, May 23, 1950; Tucson Land Office, BLM, RG49, National Archives Building, Washington, DC. Pinal County Recorder, Index to Deeds, Grantor 1940-1980, "B," Docket 101 lists small parcel sales by Barnard. Barney Barnard, *The True Story of Jacob Walzer, Superstition Mountain and his Famous Dutchman's Lost Mine* (Apache Junction, Arizona: Rancho del Superstition, 1956). Earlier editions of Barnard's book, with slightly different titles, were coauthored with Charles Frederick Higham, who wrote the first version of the book in 1946.

8. Serial Patent file No. 1110275, George Woodard, January 29, 1941; Serial Patent file No. 1125804, Julian King, May 12, 1949; both from Tucson Land Office, BLM, RG49, National Archives Building, Washington, DC. Julian M. King, *Sand in Our Shoes*, ed. Rosemary Shearer (Gold Canyon, Arizona: Terra Rosa Books, 2007). Pinal County Recorder, USA to William Woodard, Book of Deeds 76, p. 31; George Woodard to Julian King, Book of Deeds 76, p. 32 and Book of Deeds 77, p. 237.

9. Arizona State Land Department, patent #3389, 6-26-1945 (3R Ranch, 588 acres); patent #3895, 1-20-1947 (Dons Tank, 40 acres); patent #3894, 1-20-1947, (Quarter Circle U Ranch, 140 acres). Also see Note 1.

10. BLM land patents for T1S R11E, T2S R11E, T2S R12E on website www.glorecords.blm. gov/. Mineral Patent file No. 6257 and 6258, Charles Hastings, July 31, 1882; Tucson Land Office, BLM, RG49, National Archives Building, Washington, DC.

11. BLM land patents for T1S R10E, T2S R10E on website www.glorecords.blm.gov/. Arizona State Land Department, patent #5184, 1-27-1961 (Allen).

12. Tom Kollenborn, "Kollenborn's Chronicles, Florence Junction . . . The Other Junction," *Apache Junction News*, April 20-26, 2009, p. A4. Tom Kollenborn, "Florence Junction: The Other Junction," *Superstition Mountain Entertainment and Historical Guide*, Winter 1998-99, p. 23. Arizona State Land Department, patent #1567, 4-8-1930 (Willoughby); patent #2061, 1-19-1939 (Caldwell); patent #3681, 3-20-1946 (Boskon); patent #3817, 3818, 3819, 10-14-1946 (Swaney).

13. Thomas E. Glover, *The Lost Dutchman Mine of Jacob Waltz, Part 1: The Golden Dream* (Phoenix: Cowboy Miner Productions, 1998), chapter 21.

14. Robert Sikorsky, *Quest for the Dutchman's Gold, the 100-year Mystery* (Phoenix: Golden West Publishers, 1983-1993), pp. 73-75.

15. Clay Worst, "The Lost Dutchman Mine," *Fact & Fiction of the Dutchman's Lost Mine* (Apache Junction, Arizona: Superstition Mountain Historical Society, 2006), p. 18. Clay Worst, speaker at the Superstition Mountain Historical Society annual meeting (Apache Junction, Arizona, Superstition Mountain Museum, February 15, 1994).

16. John Wilburn, *Dutchman's Lost Ledge of Gold, and the Superstition Gold Mining District* (Mesa, Arizona: Publications Press, 1990, 1993).

17. Jay Fraser, *Lost Dutchman Mine Discoveries* (Tempe, Arizona: Affiliated Writers of America, 1988).

18. Robert Blair, *Tales of the Superstitions* (Tempe, Arizona: Arizona Historical Foundation, 1975), pp. 104-111.

19. Swanson, *Superstition Mountain: A Ride Through Time*, p. 176.

20. Helen Corbin, *The Curse of the Dutchman's Gold* (Phoenix: Foxwest Publishing, 1990), p. 87. Swanson, *Superstition Mountain: A Ride Through Time*, p. 43.

21. Sims Ely, *The Lost Dutchman Mine* (New York, New York: William Morrow, 1953), p. 17.

22. Corbin, *The Curse*, pp. 231-234.

23. Clay Worst, communication on April 11, 1994.

24. Swanson, *Superstition Mountain: A Ride Through Time*, p. 182. Ely, pp. 134-145.

25 Thomas Kollenborn, "Superstition Mountain Place Names," *Superstition Mountain Journal*, v11, 1992, p. 38. Carlson, "Summary of Quarter Circle U Ranch Bill of Sale . . ."

26. Kollenborn, "Superstition Mountain Place Names," p. 37.

27. Glover, *The Lost Dutchman Mine of Jacob Waltz, Part 1 . . .*, pp. 334-345, location map on page 338. Robert Garman, *Mystery Gold of the Superstitions* (Mesa, Arizona: Lane Printing, 1975, 1977, 1980), p. 74. Robert Garman, "More about the Peralta Stone Maps," *Superstition Mountain Journal*, v3, 1984, p. 41-44. Travis Marlowe, *Superstition Treasures* (Phoenix: Tyler Printing Co., 1965), pp. 23-51.

28. John D. Wilburn, *Dutchman's Lost Ledge of Gold* (Apache Junction, Arizona, 1995), p. 4. "Bright Yellow Gold, Rich Mines of the Superstition District," *Arizona Daily Gazette*, November 27, 1894, p. 1, col. 1-2. From the Newspaper Collection of Gregory E. Davis.

29. Maricopa County Recorder, Record of Mines #1, p. 70 (Wild Cat Mine), p. 88 (Big Chief Mine), Arizona Department of Library and Archives.

30. BLM land patents for T1N R8E S1 on website www.glorecords.blm.gov/. Mineral Patent file No. 27344, Joseph R. Morse (Old Wasp Mine), August 6, 1896, Tucson Land Office, BLM, RG49, National Archives Building, Washington, DC.

31. Wilburn, (1995), p. 19-27.

32. Jack San Felice, *When Silver Was King* (Mesa, Arizona: Millsite Canyon Publishing, 2006).

33. Maricopa County Recorder, Record of Mines #7, p. 238 (Defender Gold Mine, November 19, 1895), p. 384 (Shooting Star Mine, August 15, 1896), Arizona Department of Library and Archives. Bark's Mine is shown just upstream from Fish Creek on the Salt River

on the map titled "U.S.G.S. Reconnaissance Map of Country between Salt River Reservoir and Phoenix," by A. P. Davis, July 1903.

34. Jack Carlson and Elizabeth Stewart, *Superstition Wilderness Trails East* (Tempe, Arizona: Clear Creek Publishing, 2010), p. 279.

35. John G. Bourke, *Field Notes, Scouts in Arizona Territory, Nov. 18th 1872 to April 8th 1873*, pp. 141-143. Microfilm copied from Arizona State University, Hayden Library, Special Collections. Also, John G. Bourke, *The Diaries of John Gregory Bourke, Volume One, November 20, 1872 – July 28, 1876*, ed. Charles M. Robinson III (Denton, Texas: University of North Texas Press, 2003), pp. 55-71.

36. Ibid. Bourke did not draw a separate map for the March 5, 1873, march. On the Map page 126, he referenced the map on page 101, but Map page 101 does not correspond to the text of his diary, so we only used the diary text to determine Bourke's route from Rogers Trough to Tortilla Ranch.

37. Gregory E. Davis, conversation on June 15, 2010. Tom Kollenborn told Davis that Billy Martin used the names Woodbury Canyon and Woodbury Gulch for the name of the ravine going up to Tortilla Pass.

38. On June 4, 2010, we found that Dripping Spring was only flowing at 10 drips per minute, which is not a useful flow of water. The cliff face was wet, but we could not coax more water to drip. A trickle of water was flowing in Randolph Canyon, so it was surprising that Dripping Spring did not have more water.

39. John Dahlmann, *A Tiny Bit of God's Creation: Our Majestic Superstitions* (Tempe, Arizona: Reliable Reproductions, 1979), pp. 122.

40. Dahlmann, p. 39.

41. Nyle Leatham, cover photograph of cave in Fraser Canyon, *Superstition Mountain Journal*, v2:3, July 1982. Gregory E. Davis, conversation on February 18, 1994.

41. Bob Ward, "Apache J. J. Polka and His Gold," *Superstition Mountain Journal*, v3, 1984, pp. 35-36. Val Paris (Bob Ward), "Maybe, just maybe, I've found the Lost Dutchman," *Superstition Mountain Journal*, v3, 1984, pp. 37-38.

42. Swanson, *Superstition Mountain: A Ride Through Time*, p. 22.

43. Chuck Backus and Howard Horinek, conversations during cattle roundups at the Quarter Circle U Ranch from 2000 through 2009.

44. The 2009 Tonto National Forest Travel Management Rule proposed that FR1928 be closed to vehicles.

45. Dahlmann, pp. 122-126. Steve Bowser, e-mail (forwarded by Jack San Felice) on December 3, 2008. Mr. Bowser sent us a trip report for the Whetrock Canyon Loop, which included

a map and the location of Dahlmann's cave that we had not been able to find on previous trips. Dick Walp gave the Teapot name to the locator rock.

46. Garman, *Mystery Gold . . .*, James Whetlach story on pp. 39-44, treasure map on p. 76. Kris Johnson, "Superstition Gold," *Apacheland Arrow*, August 1978, p. 5, col. 2 (published by Apacheland Movie Ranch). Arizona Bureau of Vital Statistics, Jesse Mullins, http://genealogy.az.gov.

47. Pinal County Recorder: Mines Book 50, pp. 26, 32 1/2; Mines Book 56, pp. 370, 403-A, 408-412; Docket 102, pp. 50-51; Docket 389, pp. 442-462. The names of the mining claims vary, and we have spelled them as shown in the recorded documents. We have not found any mining records for James Whetlach or for Whetrock Canyon between 1893 and 1937. The 1882 Pioneer Mining District map by Gustavus Cox does not name the Whetlach mines, which may have been on the Cole District part of the map.

48. Garman, *Mystery Gold . . .*, photo of ore chute on p. 84.

49. Thomas Kollenborn, conversations on October 28, 1993, and March 8, 1994. Arizona Bureau of Vital Statistics, John J. Fraser, http://genealogy.az.gov. See the section titled "Frazier Trailhead" for Thad Frazier and "Trip 1, Reavis Ranch from Reavis Trailhead" for John Fraser in Jack Carlson and Elizabeth Stewart, *Superstition Wilderness Trails East* (Tempe, Arizona: Clear Creek Publishing, 2010). Research assistance on July 13, 2010, by Nancy Sawyer and Melanie Sturgeon at the Arizona State Archives helped us determine that Fraser was a U.S. citizen. J. J. Fraser, 1906 Great Register of Maricopa County, Arizona. U.S. Passport Applications, U.S. District Court, Phoenix, Arizona, for John James Fraser on March 8, 1918, and November 22, 1920.

50. National Archives, College Park, Maryland, RG59, General Records of the Department of State, Passport Applications, Entry A1 534, Box 694, Year 3-19-1918, John James Fraser, #9799.

51. Many older maps show the Red Tanks Trail continuing north in Red Tanks Canyon—going all the way to Red Tanks Divide beyond our turn [3-BB]. In April 2008, we checked the area north of [3-BB] in Red Tanks Canyon and could not find evidence of a former trail going up that direction. In April 2011, we checked for that older map trail on the north side of Red Tanks Divide and could not find it. So, we are not sure why the older maps show that trail alignment. Our maps show the correct trail—verified by GPS field measurements.

52. Tom Kollenborn and James Swanson, *Superstition Mountain: In the Footsteps of the Dutchman* (Apache Junction, Arizona: Ray's Printing, 2008), color map on inside of back cover, "Eye on the Trail" rock formation.

53. Superstition Mountain Museum, display map.

54. Milton Rose, "The Story of the First and Second Hunts for the Mine of Jacob Waltz," *Superstition Mountain Journal*, v2:3, July 1982, p. 7.

55. James Swanson and Thomas Kollenborn, *In the Shadow of the Superstitions; The History of Apache Junction* (Apache Junction, Arizona: Goldfield Press, 1990), p. 9.

56. Jim Byrkit and Bruce Hooper, *The Story of Pauline Weaver; Arizona's Foremost Mountain Man, Trapper, Gold-Seeker, Scout, Pioneer* (Sierra Azul Productions, 1993), pp. 1-62. Edwin Corle, *The Gila River of the Southwest* (Lincoln, Nebraska: University of Nebraska Press, 1951), pp. 33, 34, 145. Estee Conatser, *The Sterling Legend, The Facts Behind the Lost Dutchman Mine* (Pico Rivera, California: Gem Guides Book Co., 1972), p. 42.

57. Jim Waugh, *Phoenix Rock, a Guide to Central Arizona Crags* (Glendale, Arizona: Polar Designs Publications, 1987), p. 318.

58. Tyler Williams, *Arizona Summits, South, A guide to mountains, peaks and high points* (Flagstaff, Arizona: Funhog Press, 2009), pp. 149-151.

59. Swanson, *Superstition Mountain: A Ride Through Time*, pp. 84-91.

60. Waugh, p. 320.

61. Gregory E. Davis, Edwin Green, Fred Guirey, Art Weber, "History of the Dons Trek," *Superstition Mountain Journal*, v2:4, October 1982, pp. 7-23. Gregory E. Davis, communication in April 2010.

62. Gregory E. Davis, communication in April 2010.

63. James E. Bark, "The Bark Notes," unpublished manuscript edited and annotated by Thomas Probert, no date, pp. 48-49.

64. Several authors have written about the Two Soldiers Lost Mine; Ely, pp. 51-73; Conatser, pp. 35-41; and San Felice, pp. 223-244. We used the dates that Jack San Felice researched for his *When Silver Was King* book.

65. Ibid.

66. Benjamin J. Butler, *Q. E. D. Lost Dutchman File*, Q. E. D. Incorporated, "Two Ex-Soldiers Incident," by Abe Reid, April 21, 1957, courtesy of Gregory E. Davis. The source and sequence of obtaining Butler's original papers was—Tom Kollenborn, Ron Eagle, and sister of Benjamin Butler. Joe Ribado's e-mail of 12-3-2010 directed us to many of the sources for this story. The discussion on the former TheLostDutchman.net during October 2007 between Kraig Roberts and Peter Espinosa was very insightful. Tom Kollenborn, "Kollenborn Chronicles, Two Soldiers' Lost Mine," *Apache Junction News*, February 23–March 1, 2009, p. A4. Gregory

E. Davis and others located the soldier's grave during the October 2006 Dutchman Rendezvous.

67. Dahlmann, pp. 97-99.

68. Gregory E. Davis, conversation on June 3, 2011. He showed us his copy of the 1969 printing with Bluff and Crystal Springs interchanged.

69. Thomas Kollenborn, "Celeste Jones' Search for Jesuit Gold," *Superstition Mountain Journal*, v1:4, October 1981, pp. 15-16.

70. Art Christiansen gave us two 1956 Goldfield 7.5 minute topo maps (printed in 1973 and 1982) that show the Quarter Circle U Trail, which ended in Boulder Basin on the Charlebois Trail (now named the Dutchman's Trail). Maps printed in 1986 replaced the Quarter Circle U Trail name with Peralta Trail, which also went to Boulder Basin. The Peralta Trail now ends in East Boulder Canyon, but we do not have a date for that realignment.

71. Brian Lickman, conversation in November 2010 about Al Morrow and the area around his camp. Lickman camped with Morrow for about two years in the mid 1960s.

72. Corbin, *The Curse*, Kollenborn centerfold map.

73. Kollenborn, "Celeste Jones' Search . . ., pp. 15-16.

74. Ibid., p. 14.

75. Harry Black, *The Lost Dutchman Mine, A Short Story of a Tall Tale* (Boston: Branden Press, 1975), p. 117. Tonto National Forest Trail Survey Report, Mesa District Office, November 3, 1970.

76. Dahlmann, pp. 66-67.

77. Erle Stanley Gardner, *Hunting Lost Mines by Helicopter* (New York: William Morrow, 1965), p. 54.

78. Swanson, *Superstition Mountain: A Ride Through Time*, p. 83.

79. Sikorsky, pp. 66-67.

80. Ibid., pp. 7, 119.

81. Helen Brooks, "Ed Piper Buried in Pauper's Grave," *Apache Sentinel*, August 17, 1962, p. 1, col. 6-7. From the Newspaper Collection of Gregory E. Davis.

82. Black, p. 65.

83. Barry Storm, *Thunder God's Gold,* ed. Robert Schoose (Apache Junction, Arizona: Schoose Publishing, 1986 reprint), pp. 40-41.

84. Corbin, *The Curse*, Tom Kollenborn centerfold map.

85. Swanson, *Superstition Mountain: A Ride Through Time*, pp. 187, 192.

86. Louis Ruiz, conversation on December 7, 1993.

87. Brian Lickman, conversation on July 16, 2010.

88. Al Morrow to Al Reser, January 14, 1968. Superstition Mountain Historical Society, Al Reser Collection, Al Morrow folder.

89. Al Morrow to George Sherman, November 2, 1968, courtesy of Superstition Mountain Historical Society, George Sherman, George Abbott, and Wayne Ranney. In the letter

Morrow wrote, "Water is scarce up here now, and rain has been even scarcer. In Needle Canyon, I mean. However the big waterhole up near the head of the canyon has lots of fresh water in it."

90. Albert Morrow, *Famous Lost Gold Mines of Arizona's Superstition Mountains* (Apache Junction, Arizona: Superstition Mountain Historical Society, 1990, original manuscript 1957), p. vi.

91. Gregory E. Davis, "The Weiser-Walker Map," *Superstition Mountain Journal*, v18, 2000, pp. 7-23.

92. Ibid., p. 21.

93. Ibid.

94. Bark, pp. 18-19. Clay Worst, *Fact & Fiction of the Dutchman's Lost Mine*, "The Lost Dutchman Mine," (Apache Junction, Arizona: Superstition Mountain Historical Society, 2006), pp. 13.

95. Gregory E. Davis, conversations on November 13, 2004, and June 4, 2011. Tom Kollenborn told Davis that he could still ride a horse on the Middle Trail in the 1950s and it was the fastest way to get to Bluff Spring from the Quarter Circle U Ranch.

96. Davis, "The Weiser-Walker Map," p. 13.

97. Gregory E. Davis, conversation during a hike on 9-25-2004 on the Barks Canyon Trail. Davis said that Tom Kollenborn told him the Barkley Cattle Company had a salt lick here in the 1950s.

98. Waugh, pp. 296-327.

99. Bill Sewrey, conversation on April 15, 1993. Story first told to us by Jan Holdeman in early 1993.

100. Kollenborn, "Superstition Mountain Place Names," pp. 35-39.

101. Arizona State Department of Health, Division of Vital Statistics, Certificate of Death, Martin N. Charlebois, December 24, 1948, http://genealogy.az.gov. "Martin Charlebois Dies In Glendale," *The Arizona Republic*, December 25, 1948, p. 15. Pinal County Recorder, Marks and Brands Book #1, February 13, 1885, p. 155, Joe Charlebois recorded the Diamond J brand. Pinal County Recorder, Marks and Brands Book #1, August 8, 1891, p. 427, Martin Charlebois (a minor) recorded the Circle 5 brand. WWI Draft Registration Cards, 1917-1918, Martin Napoleon Charlebois, ancestry.com.

102. Black, p. 64. Conatser, pp. 66-68.

103. Arizona State Department of Health, Division of Vital Statistics, Certificate of Death, Rhinehart Petrasch, Rhinehart Petrasch, and Herman Petrasch, http://genealogy.az.gov.

104. Gregory E. Davis, conversation on April 5, 2011, and copies of his 1993 trip photos to Brads Water. Arizona State Department of Health, Division of Vital Statistics, Certificate of Death, Roy Bradford, http://genealogy.az.gov.

105. Chuck Crawford, conversation on October 13, 2001. Jack San Felice, "Dutch Hunters of the 21st Century," *Apache Junction Independent, Lost Dutchman Days 2004*, February 2004, pp.4-8. Jill Jones, "Former Sheriff Candidate Dies," *Apache Junction News*, September 24-30, 2007, p. A-2. Lanie Bethka, "Vanderpool Wins Sheriff's Race," *Apache Junction News*, November 14-20, 2000, p. 1.

106. Jack San Felice, conversation and hike to Abe Reid's mine on December 7, 2001.

107. Billy Martin Jr., conversations on many occasions. "Abe Reid," *The Arizona Republic*, October 8, 1958, p. 34, col 2. Arizona State Department of Health, Division of Vital Statistics, Certificate of Death, Abe L. Reid, October 1, 1958, http://genealogy.az.gov.

108. Tom Kollenborn, e-mail on March 30, 2003.

109. F. P. Trott, "That Globe Road," *Phoenix Daily Herald*, December 19, 1891, p. 2, col. 3.

110. Howard Horinek, conversation during work on the Coffee Flat Spring on March 30, 2005. Some maps label the Coffee Flat Spring [11-D] as Deerhorn Spring, but the ranchers refer to it as Coffee Flat Spring. Likewise, some maps label the Coffee Flat Corral [11-W] as the Whitlow Corral.

111. Judith Backus, e-mail on December 16, 2009 of wildlife photos at the Quarter Circle U Ranch water troughs—big horn sheep, deer, mountain lion, bobcat, javelina, and coyote. Bobby Beeman, e-mails of motion-activated photos in 2009 through 2011. Howard Horinek, conversation in 2009 indicated they have also photographed fox and coatimundi.

112. James "Jimmy" Anderson was the brother of Gertrude Mae Anderson who married William Augustus Barkley. James Anderson was born in North Dakota in 1877. He died on February 18, 1930, in Mesa, Arizona. Sources: www.ancestry.com and http://genealogy.az.gov.

113. Ely, pp. 123-128.

114. Walter Gassler, *The Lost Peralta-Dutchman Mine* (Apache Junction, Arizona: Superstition Mountain Historical Society, 1990, original manuscript 1983), p. 46.

115. Curt Gentry, *The Killer Mountains, A Search for the Legendary Lost Dutchman Mine* (New York: The New American Library, 1968), p. 164. Swanson, *Superstition Mountain: A Ride Through Time*, p. 191.

116. Gentry, p. 174.

117. Corbin, *The Curse*, p. 227.

118. Gentry, pp. 146-147.

119. Gentry, pp. 162-169, 182-184, 193.

120. Al Morrow to Al Reser, August, 16, 1966, Superstition Mountain Historical Society, Al Reser Collection, Al Morrow folder.

121. Corbin, *The Curse*, Tom Kollenborn centerfold map.

122. Ely, p. 124.

123. Ely, pp. 123-128.

124. Gentry, centerfold Map D.

125. Gentry, pp. 135, 136, 167, 169, 186, 193.

126. Corbin, *The Curse*, p. 145.

127. Al Reser Collection, Mining Claims folder, Superstition Mountain Historical Society. Clay Worst, "Dedication, In Memory of Alva B. 'Al' Reser, 1908-2000," *Superstition Mountain Journal*, v18, 2000, p. 5.

128. Dave Cameron told us about this route to the saddle just east of Hill 3502 in 2003. He checked the route going south, up the ravine, starting from La Barge Canyon (near N33° 27' 37", W111° 21' 35") and mostly stayed in the bottom of the ravine, going around the west side of a waterfall near the top. His hiking time was one hour and twenty minutes up and one hour on the return.

129. Gregory E. Davis said he first hiked through this break in the cliff with brother Frank in February 1976. He verified the route for us and gave us a photo of the break from below.

130. J. Alan Stirrat, *Map of Lost Dutchman and Other Legendary Mine Areas in the Superstition Mountains of Arizona* (Anaheim, California, 1948), (reprinted El Paso, Texas, 1959).

131. George Martin, conversation, no date.

132. *Pinal Drill* newspaper, October 7, 1882. Courtesy of Jack San Felice.

133. Barbara Baldwin Salyer, *Arizona 1890 Great Registers* (Mesa, Arizona: Arizona Genealogical Advisory Board, 2001), p. 188.

134. Ninth District Court, First Judicial District, Arizona Territory, Pinal County, Alfred Charlebois vs. George Marlow, May 1, 1883, #407. Copy from Gregory E. Davis and Arizona State Archives.

135. Bark, pp. 129-130. Bark used the spelling of La Barge and Marlowe, whereas we used Lebarge and Marlow.

136. Pinal County Recorder, Misc. Book 4, Water Location, pp. 200-201, May 22-23, 1891.

137. Pinal County Recorder, Marks and Brands Book #1, p. 283.

138. Albert T. Bolton, *Township Exteriors Plat Map of Salt and Gila River Baseline survey* (Tucson: U.S. Survey Generals Office, April 18, 1899). Courtesy of BLM, Phoenix Office.

139. Pinal County Treasurer, Tax and Sales Record Book, Collections Office, Pinal County, AT 1881 [sic 1890], p. 46. These records are now at the Arizona State Archives.

140. Territorial Brand Book of Arizona, April 30, 1897, p. 77, Arizona State Archives. Shows new filing in 1897, and under "Remarks" it reads "John Lebarge to Bark and Criswell, by bill of sale dated June 10, 1983."

141. Marriage Licenses, Book A1, p. 33, Maricopa County Superior Court. Maricopa County Probate Court No. 256, September 20, 1893. Maricopa County Probate Court No. 259, October 21, 1893. *Tempe News*, June 10,

1893, p. 2, col. 3, "A very difficult surgical operation—the removing of a cancer from the breast of Mrs. John Le Barge of this place was successful [sic] performed by Dr. Chas. H. Jones, Thursday. The doctor was assisted by Dr. S. C. Heineman, of Tempe, and Drs. M. W. Ward and Aneil Martin, of Phoenix."

142. Storm Schoose reprint, p. 19. Barry Storm, *The Mountains that were God, Thunder Gods' Gold* (Chiriaco Summit, California: Stormjade Books, 1967), p. 45. Kollenborn, "Superstition Mountain Place Names," pp. 35-39.

143. Michael Sheridan and Jan Sheridan, *Recreational Guide to the Superstition Mountains and the Salt River Lakes* (Phoenix: Impression Makers, 1984), p. 7.

144. Caption from photo of La Barge Spring taken on 1-12-1957 by Jerry Carr (Dan Hopper's stepfather), courtesy of Gregory E. Davis from his La Barge Canyon photo and map book.

145. Ray Ruiz and Louis Ruiz, conversation on July 4, 1994. Ray Ruiz died on August 26, 2010, at age 97.

146. Thomas Kollenborn, "Mountains Yield Skeleton of Biplane," *Superstition Mountain Journal*, v2:3, July 1982, pp. 10-11; and "Old Superstition Crash," v1:1, January 1981, p. 17.

147. Fred Mullins was probably Frederick William Mullins, the father of Jesse and Hart Mullins. Arizona State Department of Health, Division of Vital Statistics, Certificates of Birth and Death for the Mullins family members, http://genealogy.az.gov.

148. Conatser, p. 87. Barry Storm, *Thunder Gods' Gold* (Quincy, Illinois: Storm-Mollet Publishing, revised enlarged edition, Oct. 1953), pp. 70-72 and map p. 87. *Barry Storm, Bonanza of the Lost Dutchman* by B. Storm, a collection of *Desert Magazine* articles reprinted by Allied Services, Orange, CA, no date, pp. 3-5. Wagoner Map, *Superstition Mountain Journal*, v2:1, January 1982, pp. 20-21.

149. Gregory E. Davis, communication on April 12, 1994. Lori DelSecco, conversation on July 14, 2010. Lori said that she and two other hikers—Dean Barney and Steve Hovanec—made a loop trip through Trap Canyon from the SR88 Tortilla Trailhead. They rode bikes to the start of the JF Trail, hiked Hoolie Bacon Trail, bushwhacked down Trap Canyon, came up La Barge Box on the Red Tanks Trail, and returned on the Hoolie Bacon Trail and JF Trail to their bikes. It was a 13 hour trip. They are all MCSO search and rescue team members.

150. Gregory E. Davis, communication in April 2010.

151. Gregory E. Davis, "The Origin of the Dons Club," *Superstition Mountain Journal*, v2:3, July 1982, pp. 21-23. Gregory Davis, communication on April 12, 1994.

152. Tom Kollenborn, "Camp Bowers: Pete Carney's Legacy," *Apache Junction News*, March 5-11, 2007, p. A4. *Arizona Republican*, "Mesa: To Develop Mining Property," June 20, 1907, p. 8, col. 3. *Arizona Republican*, "Camp Bowers Scene of Mining Activity . . .," August 5, 1908, p. 8, col. 5. *Arizona Gazette*, "Carney Mines Development," August 10, 1911, sec. 2, p. 3, col. 4. The Carney Mines newspaper articles for this note and the following Carney notes were found in the Newspaper Collection of Gregory E. Davis with the help of Tom Kollenborn's newspaper index.

153. *Arizona Republican*, "Building a New Road to the Superstitions . . .," November 21, 1908, p. 12, col. 3.

154. *Arizona Blade Tribune*, "P. G. Carney," September 24, 1910, p. 2, col. 4. *Arizona Gazette*, "Camp Carney is Coming to the Front," February 27, 1912, p. 9, col 3-4. *Arizona Gazette*, "Preparing to Ship Ore," November 9, 1912, p. 13, col. 6.

155. *Arizona Republican*, "Trip to Carney," October 4, 1913, p. 11, col. 4. *Arizona Gazette*, "Wreck and Ruin Tale from Mystery Camp," February 4, 1914, p. 1, col. 6-7. *Arizona Blade Tribune*, "Carney Mine Wrecked . . .," February 7, 1914, p. 1, col. 5. *Mesa Daily Tribune*, "$250.00 Reward . . .," February 19, 1914, p. 2, col. 7.

156. *Arizona Blade Tribune*, "No. 2648 Sheriff's Sale," June 23, 1917, p. 2, col. 3-4.

157. Arizona State Department of Health, Division of Vital Statistics, Certificate of Death for Peter Grannan Carney, http://genealogy.az.gov. U.S. Veterans Gravesites, Peter Granan [sic] Carney, ancestry.com.

158. Matt Cavaness, *Memoirs of Matt Cavaness*, typed by Joseph Miller, Arizona State Library and Archives, Phoenix, #58531, manuscript p. 57.

159. Pinal County Recorder, Misc. Book 4, p. 204.

160. Pinal County Recorder, Misc. Book 13, p. 294.

161. Jimmie E. Jinks, *Mineral Investigation of the Superstition Wilderness . . .*, USGS Open-File Report 83-885, MLA 136-82, 1982, pp. 24, 61, 62, 75.

162. Kollenborn, "Superstition Mountain Place Names," p. 38. Bill Burger, Arizona Game and Fish Department (AZGFD), e-mails in February 2006. AZGFD, "Comprehensive Historical Perspective," no date. Kelly Kessler, USFS, e-mails in October 2016. "Environmental Assessment for Dacite Cliffs Mine Project," September 2008. John D'Anna, *Arizona Republic*, "Officials seek killer of 89 bats," 4-16-2009, p. B3, c. 1.

163. Gregory E. Davis, communication on April 12, 1994.

164. Thomas Kollenborn, *Al Senner's Lost Gold of Superstition Mountain* (Apache Junction, Arizona: Superstition Mountain Historical Society, 1990, original manuscript date 1982).

165. Bruce Grubbs, *Hiking Arizona's Superstition & Mazatzal Country* (Helena, Montana: Falcon Publishing, 2000), pp. 95-97, map on p. 94. Chris Coleman helped us find Irv Kanode's GPS route of 2-22-2008 titled "Old West Boulder Canyon Ridge" on www.hikearizona.com.

166. On February 13, 2010, Chris Coleman and Jesse Perlmutter hiked up the north side of Superstition Mountain and intersected the Ridgeline Trail east of Peak 5024 [19-C]. Chris Coleman followed the Joe Bartels GPS route of 10-15-2007 titled "Reverse Flatiron" on www.hikearizona.com Joe came up the north side of Superstition Mountain from the Massacre Grounds to the area near [19-C].

167. *Arizona Daily Herald*, "Jim Bark's Find," October 5, 1899, p. 1, col. 4, reprinted in *Superstition Mountain Journal*, v2:3, July 1982, p. 20.

168. John Annerino, *Outdoors in Arizona, A Guide to Hiking and Backpacking* (Phoenix: Arizona Highways, 1989), pp. 57-61.

169. We used the Robber's Roost and Dacite Mesa trip reports from the following people: Irv Kanode, Joe Bartels, and Sredfield on www.hikearizona.com; and Ted Tenny and Eileen Root on www.azhikers.com.

170. Jack San Felice, conversations and field trip led by San Felice on January 18, 2005. Jack San Felice, "The Apache Kid's Cave," *The Museum Messenger* (Apache Junction, Arizona: Superstition Mountain Historical Society, v26:2, April-May-June, 2008), pp. 16-17. *Saturday-Evening Press*, "Exploring the Retreat of Apache Kid," October 9, 1897, p. 1. *Arizona Republican*, "The Kid's Cave," June 10, 1897, p. 4, col. 2-3. The newspaper articles are from the Newspaper Collection of Gregory E. Davis.

171. Don Wells, e-mail on October 30, 2004. Don gave us the name for Indian Rock.

172. Rosemary Shearer, communication on July 26, 1994. Kollenborn, "Superstition Mountain Place Names," pp. 35-39. Dahlmann, p. 37. Julian M. King, *Sand in Our Shoes*, ed. Rosemary Shearer (Gold Canyon, Arizona: Terra Rosa Books, 2007).

173. Stephen K. Hansen, BLM Phoenix, conversation on December 4, 2010. He told us how to find the benchmark data on www.ngs.noaa.gov, -Surveys, -Survey Mark Datasheets, -Datasheets, -USGS Quad, -Goldfield, -Superstition.

174. Dave Hughes, e-mail on February 9, 2011 and field notes from February 15, 1981.

175. Larry Shearer, conversation in December 2000.

176. Chris Coleman, conversations, e-mails, and trip reports in February and March 2007. His hiking partner was Will McNeillie. On the first trip up the ridge to Peak 5057, they followed veteran hikers Mack, Jack, and Jerry (last names unknown), who showed them the route through the cliffs. Chris suggested that we use the speckled rock to identify the start of the route.

177. Ron Lorenz, "Superstition Wash, Civilian Conservation Corps," *Superstition Mountain Journal*, v3, 1984, pp. 22-23. Tom Kollenborn, "Superstition Wash Camp," *Apache Junction News*, August 26-September 26, 1997, p. A6. Tom Kollenborn, "A CCC Camp In Apache Junction," *Apache Junction News*, August 20-26, 2001, p. A4. Ron Lorenz, "Camp Superstition Wash," *Geology, Historical Events, Legends and Lore of Superstition Mountain* (Apache Junction, Arizona: Superstition Mountain Historical Society, 2007), p. 121-122. Tom Kollenborn, "The CCC Camp In Apache Junction," *Apache Junction News*, August 22-28, 2011, p. A4. Superstition Mountain Historical Society, CCC Collection. National Archives, College Park, Maryland,

178. Tom Kollenborn, e-mail on July 14, 2005. Kollenborn wrote that a man named Hallberg worked the tunnel in the back of the cave at one time. Around 1939, two unnamed men were working in the cave. No gold was found there as has been rumored.

179. Betty Swanson, "Newly Built Trail Provides Path to Tonto Gate," *Apache Junction News*, December 6-12, 2010, p. 1. Swanson reported that Bryan Martyn, Pinal County District 2 Supervisor, resolved the lack of access to the Tonto National Forest by working with local residents, Tonto National Forest, and the Lost Dutchman State Park. The access trail and gates were opened to the public in November 2010.

180. Wilburn, p. 20.

181. *Mesa Free Press*, November 15, 1895, p.3, col. 2. *Phoenix Daily Herald*, November 25, 1895, p. 8, col. 1. Both newspaper articles are from the Newspaper Collection of Gregory E. Davis. Louis Ruiz and John Wilburn, conversations from 1993 through 2011.

182. Jesse Feldman, e-mail May 30, 2011. Feldman photographed the exposed drifts of the Bull Dog Mine that the Treasure Chest bulldozer operator uncovered on May 4, 2007, then the drifts were filled in and destroyed. The hill where the main shaft entrance was located had been removed about a year or more before.

183. Wilburn, pp. 12-31.

184. John Wilburn, conversation on December 7, 1993.

185. Thomas Kollenborn, "Dr. Ralph Palmer, Arizona Pioneer," *Superstition Mountain Journal*, v1:1, pp. 14-15. Wilburn, p. 26. Swanson, *Superstition Mountain: A Ride Through Time*, pp. 93-97.

186. Nancy and Ken McCollough, conversations in February 2004, January 25, 2006, and November 8, 2009. Ken passed away on 6-19-2010 and Nancy on 4-16-2017.

187. Waugh, p. 307.

188. Waugh, p. 296.

189. Chris Coleman helped us field check the Joe Bartels GPS route of October 15, 2007 titled "Reverse Flatiron" on www.hikearizona.com. Joe came up the north side of Superstition Mountain from the Massacre Grounds [18-U] to the top near [14-C]. On February 13, 2010, Chris Coleman and Jesse Perlmutter hiked up the north side of Superstition Mountain and intersected the Ridgeline Trail east of Peak 5024 near [14-C]. Chris started at the Crosscut Trailhead and used the Jacob's Crosscut Trail and Treasure Loop Trail to access the trail that goes by The Hand [18-T] rock climb.

190. Requests to the Forest Service for the FR28 road closure Forest Order were not fulfilled. We estimate that the FR28 was abandoned in March 2009.

191. Ken and Nancy McCollough conversation, no date.

192. Thomas E. Glover, *Treasure Tales of the Superstitions* (Prescott, Arizona: Granite Creek Publishing, 2015), chapter 4. Glover, *The Lost Dutchman Mine of Jacob Waltz, Part 1*, chapter 7.

193. Gregory E. Davis, "Silverlock and Goldleaf, A story of Carl A. Silverlock and Carl J. Malm," *Superstition Mountain Journal*, v15, 1997, pp. 6-27.

194. Ely, p. 135. Barry Storm seems to be the first author to mention $18,000. Barry Storm, *Trail of the Lost Dutchman* (Phoenix: Goldwaters, 1939), p. 37. Storm, *Thunder Gods Gold* (Treasure Trail Edition), p. 36.

195. Arizona State Department of Health, Division of Vital Statistics, Certificates of Death, Carl A. Silverlock July 18, 1929, Carl J. Malm, April 25, 1947, http://genealogy.az.gov. Charles Silverlock (aka Carl Silverlock), Arizona Department of Library, Archives and Public Records, RG 107, Maricopa County SG 8, Superior Court, Insanity, 1908-1909, Box 5.

196. Gregory E. Davis, conversation on November 20, 2009. Davis identified this canyon as West Fork First Water Creek.

197. Members of a Mesa hiking club told us about this route on November 23, 2009. We were able to follow the route from the rock cairns they established at each road intersection.

198. Ted Tenny, author of *Goldfield Mountain Hikes*, e-mail on March 20, 2011, described this route.

199. Ely, pp. 134-145. Bark, pp. 57-63.

200. Garman, *Mystery Gold . . .*, pp. 7-16.

201. Gregory E. Davis, communication on April 12, 1994.

202. George "Brownie" Holmes, *Story of the Lost Dutchman* (Apache Junction, Arizona: Superstition Mountain Historical Society, 1990, original manuscript 1944, Phoenix), p. 31. "A Mammoth Stone House in the Superstitions," *Arizona Daily Gazette*, August 16, 1893, p. 2, col. 1, reprinted in *Superstition Mountain Journal*, v2:2, April 1982, p. 19.

203. Harvey L. Mott, "Home of Ancients Discovered in Superstition Mountains," *Arizona Republic*, December 15, 1931. From the Newspaper Collection of Gregory E. Davis

204. Superstition Mountain Museum, Apache Junction, Arizona, map display. Gregory E. Davis, conversation and field trip on January 27, 2007.

205. Bourke, *Field Notes . . .*, pp. 101-107. Bourke, *The Diaries . . .*, pp. 55-58.

206. Ibid. Also, see the companion book *Superstition Wilderness Trails East*, "Lower Pine Creek," by Carlson and Stewart, for an earlier scout in Pine Creek and the photo and drawings of "Weavers Needle" (Bourkes Butte).

207. Ibid. Also, see the companion book *Superstition Wilderness Trails East*, "Spencer Spring Creek," by Carlson and Stewart, for the scouts near the West Fork Pinto Creek area.

208. Bourke, *Field Notes . . .*, pp. 99-107. Bourke, *The Diaries . . .*, pp. 55-58.

209. Mary Bond, letter in February 1995. Ms. Bond, a winter visitor from Alberta, Canada, hiked the Upper First Water Creek and she suggested that we use the rectangular butte and Cross Butte as landmarks for getting over to the top of O'Grady Canyon.

210. Dick Nelson and Sharon Nelson, *Hiker's Guide to the Superstition Mountains* (Glenwood, New Mexico: Tecolote Press, 1978), p. 65.

211. Thomas Kollenborn, "Superstition Mountain Car," *Superstition Mountain Journal*, v1:3, July 1981, p. 7; and "Potpourri," v2:3, July 1982, p. 21. Kollenborn, conversation and horse ride on January 21, 1996. Kollenborn said the vehicle was east of Transmission Pass near a single pole saguaro cactus, along the former road to the Pearce Mine.

212. Joan Baeza, "Arizona's Wilderness Rangers," *Arizona Highways*, November 1981, pp. 33-34.

213. Corbin, *The Curse*, pp. 192, 200-206. Swanson, *Superstition Mountain: A Ride Through Time*, pp. 47-64. James Kearney, "Death in the Superstitions: The Fate of Adolph Ruth," *The Journal of Arizona History*, v33:2,

Summer 1992, pp. 117-152. Gary Cundiff, "The Adolph Ruth Story," http://freepages. genealogy.rootsweb.ancestry.com/~gcundiff/LostD is a comprehensive collection of information on Adolph Ruth.

214. Harvey L. Mott, "Home of Ancients Discovered in Superstition Mountains," *Arizona Republic*, December 15, 1931. Harvey L. Mott, no title, *Arizona Republic*, December 16, 1931. Harvey L. Mott, "Great Stone God Rules Superstitions' Prehistoric City," *Arizona Republic*, December 17, 1931. Harvey L. Mott, "Ashes of Prehistoric Hearth Found in Superstitions," *Arizona Republic*, December 18, 1931. From the Newspaper Collection of Gregory E. Davis. Harvey Mott, "Harvey Mott's first hand account of finding Ruth's Skull," *Superstition Mountain Journal*, v20, 2002, pp. 14-19.

215. Jack San Felice, conversation on October 11, 2005. San Felice brought the missing "vici" to our attention. Adolph Ruth's "veni vidi" note is from the files of Gregory E. Davis. Davis obtained it from Tom Kollenborn who obtained it from the Barkley family.

216. Gregory E. Davis, "Ruth's Skull: The Left and Right Sides," *Superstition Mountain Journal*, v20, 2002, p. 10.

217. Second Water Spring is officially located below Obie Stoker's Camp [20-OO] as shown on the topo map, but most people refer to the dense vegetation along Second Water Trail as Second Water Spring [20-KK].

218. Dahlmann, p. 35.

219. Michael J. Wintch, conversation on January 27, 2004 at the USFS Mesa District Office. Mike said one cow had a Pima Indian brand, one had an ear tag, and another had an ear crop. He considered the names of the wranglers confidential, so we have not been able to interview them. Ross Hecox, "Wild Cow Catchers," *Western Horseman*, October 2010, pp. 93-98, shows how the Ericsson brothers rounded up wild cattle in Arizona. We don't know if they performed the roundup at Second Water, but from the article, they seem to have the expertise to do the job.

220. Joe Ribado, conversations and e-mails in 2010. Joe is the grandson of Obie Stoker. Tom Kollenborn, "Obie Stoker: Fool's Gold," *Apache Junction News*, March 27-April 2, 2006, p. A4. Notice of Mining Location, Maricopa County, October 17, 1975, Docket 11378, p. 893, courtesy of Gregory E. Davis, Obie Stoker Collection.

221. In June 2010, Dick Walp and Jack Carlson field checked the mines and found bear scat at the entrance and inside the lower mine. A smooth area in the soft dirt looked like it was made by the bear for a bed. They also observed bear scat near Stoker's Camp and on the Second Water Trail just east of the dirt tank in Garden Valley.

222. Christina Fuoco-Karasinski, "Two Bodies Found In Supers, Believed to be 2 of 3 men missing from Utah," *Apache Junction News*, January 17-23, 2011, p. A-1. Rick Gwynne found the skeletons of two Utah men—Malcolm Meeks and Ardean Charles—on the northeast slope of Yellow Peak on January 5, 2011. They had been missing since July 6, 2010. Christina Fuoco-Karasinski, "Third Body Found In Superstitions," *Apache Junction News*, January 24-30, 2011, p. A-2. Superstition Search and Rescue (SSAR) found the third man, Curtis Merworth, on Black Mesa on January 15, 2011. Tom Kollenborn, "Kollenborn's Chronicles, A Deadly Vision," *Apache Junction News*, February 28–March 6, 2011, p. A-4. Kollenborn summarizes the rescue effort in this article.

223. Clay Worst, "The Hill of the Horse's Head," *Superstition Mountain Journal*, v11, 1992, p. 40. Clay Worst, conversation at Canyon Lake MCSO station on January 2, 2010.

224. Swanson, *History of Apache Junction*, p. 20.

225. Peggy Aylor to Al and Martha Reser, June 6, 1967, Superstition Mountain Historical Society, Al Reser Collection, Aylor folder. Swanson, *Superstition Mountain: A Ride Through Time*, pp. 123-126, 186. *The Arizona Republic*, January 7, 1968, p. D20, obituary for Charles Edgar Aylor, died January 4, 1968 in Florence, Arizona, his body was sent to the University of Arizona College of Medicine for medical research. Martha A. Aylor died on May 15, 1970, at the age of 69, SSDI from ancestry.com.

226. Holmes, *Story of the Lost Dutchman*, p. 40. George Holmes, compiled and annotated by T. E. Glover, *The Lost Dutchman Mine of Jacob Waltz, Part 2, The Holmes Manuscript* (Phoenix: Cowboy Miner Productions, 2000), p. 158.

227. Superstition Mountain Museum, museum display and description, Apache Junction, Arizona. Clay Worst, communication on May 18, 1994.

228. Storm, *Thunder Gods Gold* (Treasure Trail Edition), pp. 22, 115.

229. Corbin, *The Curse*, Tom Kollenborn centerfold map. Kollenborn, *Superstition Mountain: In the Footsteps of the Dutchman*, color map on inside of back cover. Don Van Driel, conversation on July 22, 1993. Tom Kollenborn, conversation on October 28, 1993.

230. Swanson, *Superstition Mountain: A Ride Through Time*, p. 185.

231. Corbin, *The Curse*, Kollenborn centerfold map.

232. Dennis Wagner, "The Great Gold Chase," *Superstition Mountain Journal*, v5, 1986, p. 36, reprint from the *Phoenix Gazette*, six-part series from March 17 to 22, 1986.

233. Brian Lickman, conversation in Apache Junction on May 19, 2010.

234. Robert E. Lee's book *The Lost Dutchman Mine* shows a color photograph of this camp [23-V]. The page in the color signature is unnumbered, but the photo caption reads, "Top: Robert S. 'Crazy Jake' Jacobs campsite in the mountains."

235. Corbin, *The Curse*, Tom Kollenborn centerfold map. Kollenborn, *Superstition Mountain: In the Footsteps of the Dutchman*, color map on inside of back cover. Don Van Driel, conversation on July 22, 1993. Gregory E. Davis took Jack Carlson to Crazy Jake's Camp on Peters Mesa on February 28, 2007.

236. Don Van Driel, conversation on July 22, 1993. Tom Kollenborn, conversation on October 28, 1993.

237. Wagner, pp. 31-41.

238. Don Van Driel, conversation on July 22, 1993.

239. Clay Worst, "The Salazar Survey," *Superstition Mountain Journal*, 1985, v4, pp. 27-35. Clay Worst, communication on May 18, 1994. Steven Creager, "The Salazar Re-survey; a Re-calculation of the Salazar Data," unpublished manuscript dated 8-9-2002, courtesy of the Superstition Mountain Historical Society, Steven Creager Collection.

240. Larry Hedrick, conversation on August 27, 1993. *The Arizona Republic*, February 22, 1989, B3, and February 7, 1989, B1. Thomas Kollenborn, "In Search of the Lost Bronze," *Superstition Mountain Journal*, 1988, v7, pp. 5-6. Betty Swanson, "A Special Treasure, Whiskey cache finder Hedrick participates in 'CC Hide-a-Case' revival," *Apache Junction News*, May 31–June 6, 2010, p. A1.

241. Bark, p. 173. Corbin, *The Curse*, pp. 103, 176. Swanson, *Superstition Mountain: A Ride Through Time*, p. 57.

242. Nelson, pp. 53-54, Paint Mine Saddle is identified by name here.

243. Gregory E. Davis, conversation on February 18, 1994.

244. Davis, "Silverlock and Goldleaf . . ., p. 16.

245. Gregory Davis, communication on April 12, 1994.

246. Storm, Schoose reprint, p. 9. Storm, *The Mountains that were God . . .*, p. 33.

247. Nelson, pp. 53-54.

248. Corbin, *The Curse*, p. 157. Bark, pp. 106-107.

249. Gregory Davis, communication on April 12, 1994.

250. Storm, Schoose reprint, p. 50-53.

251. "Crash Injures Three Seriously On Apache Trail Today," *Apache Sentinel*, August 21, 1959, p. 1, col. 1-3.

252. Dick Walp, conversations on June 1, 2002; February 16, 2003; September 18, 2004; November 26, 2005; May 19, 2011; and May 31, 2011.

253. Mary Leonhard, "The Site's the House," *The Arizona Republic*, April 26, 1964, Section E.

254. Dick Walp, conversation on May 19, 2011.

255. "Charles E. Aylor" obituary, *The Arizona Republic*, January 7, 1968, p. D20, col. 2. "Charles Edgar Aylor" obituary, *Apache Sentinel*, January 4, 1968, p. 7, col. 1-2.

256. Stirrat, *Map of Lost Dutchman . . .* The Stirrat map is the only place we have seen Box Spring identified.

257. L. L. Lombardi, *Tortilla Flat Arizona, Then and Now* (Tortilla Flat, Arizona: Sunshower Corporation, May 1996).

258. Storm, Schoose reprint, pp. 32-35. Storm, *Thunder Gods Gold* (Treasure Trail Edition), pp. 75-81. "Gonzales' Mexican Mine Map," *Superstition Mountain Journal*, January 1982, v2:1, pp. 24-25. For a detailed analysis, see Gregory E. Davis, "Empty Canyon Lake Reveals Site of Old Mexican Arrastres," *Superstition Mountain Journal*, 2008, v26, pp. 50-57.

259. "Gonzales' Mexican Mine Map," *Superstition Mountain Journal*, January 1982, v2:1, pp. 24-25.

260. Superstition Mountain Museum, Apache Junction, Arizona, map display.

261. Milton Rose, "The Story of the First and Second Hunts for the Mine of Jacob Waltz," *Superstition Mountain Journal*, July 1982, v2:3, pp. 6-7. Conatser, p. 56. Swanson, *Superstition Mountain: A Ride . . .*, p. 43. Ely, pp. 115-116. Wilburn, p. 8. Arizona State Department of Health, Division of Vital Statistics, Certificate of Death for Gottfried Petrasch, Rhinehart Petrasch, and Herman Petrasch, http://genealogy.az.gov.

262. Conatser, pp. 45-46.

263. Gassler, pp. 1-3. Corbin, *The Curse*, p. 212.

264. Gassler, p. 17.

265. Gassler, pp. 1-3.

266. Ely, pp. 137-145. Our former book editor, Gerry Benninger, noted an inconsistency in Sims Ely's account of Scholey's story. The symptoms of arsenic and strychnine poisoning are very different. See Serita Deborah Stevens, *Deadly Doses, A Writer's Guide to Poisons*, (Cincinnati, Ohio, Writer's Digest Books, 1990), pp. 10-20.

267. Gassler, pp. 1-16.

268. Gassler, p. 16.

269. Corbin, *The Curse*, pp. 226-229. "Obituaries, Walter Gassler," *The Tribune*, May 9, 1984, p. C3, col. 1-2. "Gassler," *The Phoenix Gazette*, May 9, 1984, p. D4, col. 12. Both newspapers are from the Newspaper Collection of Gregory E. Davis. Gassler died on May 3, 1984.

270. Clay Worst, conversation on February 15, 1994.

271. Gassler, pp. 10-11.

272. A photo of this saguaro cactus skeleton is shown in *Hiker's Guide to the Superstition Wilderness* by Jack Carlson and Elizabeth Stewart (Tempe, Arizona: Clear Creek Publishing, 1995), p. 175. In 2010, the trunk of the cactus was lying lengthwise

on the trail. Going around the cactus was difficult on the steep slope, but at least we knew we were on the obscure trail.

273. Brian Lickman, conversations in 2010. Jesse Feldman told us that Brian may have worked on the Squaw Canyon Trail when Brian and his father, Ron Feldman, worked for Crazy Jake.

274. Kollenborn, *Superstition Mountain: In the Footsteps of the Dutchman*, color map on inside of back cover.

275. Gregory E. Davis, conversation on July 11, 2010, in Tempe, Arizona.

276. Doris J. Mathews, editor and photographer, "Robert Jacobs Camp," *Apache Sentinel*, January 23, 1980, p. B20, col. 1-3. From Gregory E. Davis files, "Photos of Prospector Camps in the Superstition Mountains," and "1980 Newspaper Collection."

277. Tom Kollenborn, conversation on March 8, 1994.

278. Gassler, p. 5.

279. Stirrat, *Map of Lost Dutchman . . .*

280. Swanson, *Superstition Mountain: A Ride Through Time*, pp. 26, 111. U.S. Patent 02-67-0035 for the IV Ranch, from USA to Floyd and Lucille Stone, January 23, 1967.

281. Tom Kollenborn, conversations on March 8 and March 28, 1994. Arizona Bureau of Vital Statistics, Certificate of Death, John Chuning, http://genealogy.az.gov. Chuning died on November 11, 1910 at age 65 at Tortilla Flat—occupation listed as miner. Chuning's physician was R. Palmer.

282. Holmes, *Story of the Lost Dutchman*, p. 30. Holmes, *The Lost Dutchman Mine of Jacob Waltz, Part 2 . . .*, p. 117.

283. Conatser, pp. 89-91.

284. Conatser, pp. 39, 40, 87. Storm, Schoose reprint, p. 35. Storm, *Thunder Gods Gold* (Treasure Trail Edition), pp. 79-80.

285. Conatser, p. 74.

286. Holmes, *Story of the Lost Dutchman*, pp. 15, 34.

287. Bourke, *Field Notes . . .*, map on p. 126. Color copy of map was made for us by Susan Lintelmann, USMA Library, Special Collections and Archives, Department of the Army, United States Military Academy, West Point, New York.

288. Jim Files, "Superstition Mountain Museum," *Superstition Mountain Journal*, 1989, v8, pp. 5-6.

289. Ibid. Larry Hedrick, "Hacksaw Tom," unpublished manuscript. James Colton, "Hacksaw Tom," *Superstition Mountain Journal*, v2:2, p. 21-22. Hank Brown, "What We Found," *Superstition Mountain Journal*, 1989 v8, pp. 27-28. Swanson, *Superstition Mountain: A Ride Through Time*, pp. 148-149.

290. Bourke, *Field Notes . . .*, pp. 143-147. Bourke, *The Diaries . . .*, pp. 55-71.

291. Ibid.

292. Ibid.

293. Conatser, photographs, no page number.

294. Dick Walp, Greg Davis, and Jack Carlson traced the Night Hawk Spring water pipes from the concrete water troughs up the wash to the spring box. A vertical vent pipe about 50 feet down the wash from the spring was designed to prevent air locks from forming in the pipe. They looked in the spring box and could see water, but they figured the water was not flowing because the outlet pipe was clogged or the spring box was damaged.

295. Steve Bower and Jack Carlson named this pass for Jesse Capen who died in a fall from Tortilla Mountain on 12-4-2009. His camp was in the area just southeast of this pass.

296. Kollenborn, "Superstition Mountain Place Names," pp. 35-39.

297. Ely, pp. 129-133.

298. The men in the photo were identified by Gregory E. Davis and Tom Kollenborn.

299. Gregory E. Davis, conversation and field trip on 12-31-2010. Davis showed us his 1983 field notes and photographs, which we used with his help to locate the various diggings at the Miller Mine area. We thought Miller Spring was in the same ravine as the main Miller Mine, but Davis showed us the correct location [30-M].

300. In May 2010, we looked for Mullin Spring, but could not find it. The trails had been overgrown since our 1980s visit. Dave Cameron and Rogil Schroeter, knowing of our interest in the spring, e-mailed their Jan. 2, 2011 trip report to us. They found Mullin Spring "very well camouflaged by overgrowth" with murky water. With Dave's gps location, we found the spring in good condition with clear water in Nov. 2015 and May 2016.

301. Conatser, pp. 82-84. For Conatser's background, see Gregory E. Davis, "Dedication, Shirley T. Wood Conatser," *Superstition Mountain Journal*, v20, 2002, pp. 5-9.

302. "The Lost Dutchman Mining Corporation, Inc." prospectus by Dr. Robert A. Aiton, 1920. Courtesy of Gregory E. Davis.

303. James Colten, "Miller Springs," *Superstition Mountain Journal*, v1:4, October 1981, p. 19. Tom Kollenborn, "The Lost Dutchman Mine, Inc. Part I," *Apache Junction News*, July 18, 2000, p. A4. Tom Kollenborn, "The Lost Dutchman Mine, Inc. Part II," *Apache Junction News*, July 25, 2000, p. A4. "Death Balks Prospector's Search for Hidden Wealth," *The Arizona Republic*, April 7, 1936, pp. 1, 7. From the Newspaper Collection of Gregory E. Davis.

304. See the Two Soldiers Lost Mine story in Jack San Felice, *When Silver Was King* (Mesa, Arizona: Millsite Canyon Publishing, 2006), pp. 223-244. Also see Ely, pp. 51-73. Conatser, pp. 35-41.

Selected Bibliography

Additional research sources can be found in the Reference Notes.

Altshuler, Constance Wynn. *Cavalry Yellow & Infantry Blue*. Tucson: The Arizona Historical Society, 1991.

Altshuler, Constance Wynn. *Chains of Command*. Tucson: The Arizona Historical Society, 1981.

Arizona Brand Book and Supplement, State of Arizona. Phoenix: Live Stock Sanitary Board, 1943, 1953, 1963.

Bark, James E. "The Bark Notes." Unpublished manuscript edited and annotated by Thomas Probert, no date.

Blair, Robert. *Tales of the Superstitions*. Tempe, Arizona: Arizona Historical Foundation, 1975.

Bourke, John. *The Diaries of John Gregory Bourke, Volume One*. Edited by Charles M. Robinson III. Denton, Texas: University of North Texas Press, 2003.

Bourke, John. *Field Notes, Scouts in Arizona Territory, Nov. 18, 1872 to April 28, 1873*. Arizona State University, Special Collections, microfilm of diary, 973.8 B667. Color copies of Bourke's maps from United States Military Academy Library, Special Collections, West Point, New York.

Brown, Wynne. *Trail Riding Arizona*. Guilford, Connecticut: The Globe Pequot Press, 2006.

Conatser, Estee. *The Sterling Legend*. Baldwin Park, California: Gem Guides Book Company, 1972.

Corbin, Helen. *The Curse of the Dutchman's Gold*. Phoenix: Foxwest Publishing, 1990.

Dahlmann, John. *A Tiny Bit of God's Creation*. Tempe, Arizona: Reliable Reproductions, no date.

Dean, Jeffrey, S. *Salado*. Albuquerque: University of New Mexico Press, 2000.

Ely, Sims. *The Lost Dutchman Mine*. New York: William Morrow and Company, 1953.

Feldman, Jesse. *Jacob's Trail*. Apache Junction, Arizona: Jesse Feldman, 2009.

Garman, Robert. *Mystery Gold of the Superstitions*. Mesa, Arizona: Lane Printing and Publishing, 1975.

Garrido, Betty (editor). *Superior, Arizona, 1882-1982 Centennial*. Superior, Arizona: Superior Centennial Celebration Committee, 1982.

Gassler, Walter. "The Lost Peralta-Dutchman Mine." Unpublished manuscript 1983, Rare Book Reprint by the Superstition Mountain Historical Society, Apache Junction, Arizona, 1990.

Gentry, Curt. *The Killer Mountains*. New York: The New American Library, 1968.

Glover, Thomas E. *The Lost Dutchman Mine of Jacob Waltz: Part 1, The Golden Dream*. Phoenix: Cowboy Miner Productions, 1998.

Glover, Thomas E. *The Lost Dutchman Mine of Jacob Waltz: Part 2, The Holmes Manuscript*. Phoenix: Cowboy Miner Productions, 2000.

Grubbs, Bruce. *Hiking Arizona*. Guilford, Connecticut: The Globe Pequot Press, 2008.

Hancock, Jan. *Horse Trails in Arizona*. Phoenix: Golden West Publishers, Inc., 1994.

Holmes, George "Brownie." "Story of the Lost Dutchman." Unpublished manuscript 1944, Rare Book Reprint by the Superstition Mountain Historical Society, Apache Junction, Arizona, 1990.

Kollenborn, Thomas. *The Chronological History of the Superstition Wilderness Area . . .*, Apache Junction, Arizona: Thomas Kollenborn, 1st edition 1988, 2nd edition 2000, 3rd edition 2011.

Kollenborn, Tom, and James Swanson. *Superstition Mountain: In the Footsteps of the Dutchman*. Apache Junction, Arizona: Ray's Printing, 2008.

Liu, Charles. *60 Hikes within 60 Miles, Phoenix, including Tempe, Scottsdale, and Glendale*. Birmingham, Alabama: Menasha Ridge Press, 2006 and 2007.

Marlowe, Travis. *Superstition Treasures*. Phoenix: Tyler Printing Company, 1965.

Nelson, Dick, and Sharon Nelson. *Hiker's Guide to the Superstition Mountains*. Glenwood, New Mexico: Tecolote Press, 1978.

Rose, Milton F. "Rainbows End, Story of the Lost Dutchman Gold Mine." Unpublished manuscript, no date, reprint by the Superstition Mountain Historical Society, Apache Junction, Arizona, no date.

San Felice, Jack. *Superstition Cowboys*. Mesa, Arizona: Millsite Canyon Publishing, 2011.

San Felice, Jack. *Lost El Dorado of Jacob Waltz*. Mesa, Arizona: Millsite Canyon Publishing, 2015.

San Felice, Jack. *When Silver Was King*. Mesa, Arizona: Millsite Canyon Publishing, 2006.

Schoose, Robert. *Goldfield Boom to Bust*. Apache Junction, Arizona: Robert "Mayor Bob" Schoose, 2008.

Sikorsky, Robert. *Quest for the Dutchman's Gold*. Phoenix: Golden West Publishers, 1994.

Storm, Barry. *Thunder God's Gold*. Edited by R. Schoose. Apache Junction, Arizona: Schoose Publishing, 1986.

Storm, Barry. *Thunder Gods Gold*. Phoenix: Southwest Publishing, 1946.

Swanson, James, and Tom Kollenborn. *Superstition Mountain: A Ride . . .*, Phoenix: Arrowhead Press, 1981.

Wilburn, John. *Dutchman's Lost Ledge of Gold*. Apache Junction, Arizona: GBI Printing, 2006.

Wood, Scott, Martin McAllister, and Michael Sullivan. *10,000 Years on Tonto National Forest*. Albuquerque: Southwest Natural and Cultural Heritage Association, no date.

Useful Addresses

EMERGENCY TELEPHONE NUMBERS

Dial 911 from any telephone for emergency help. For non-emergency problems see the listings under *Government Agencies, Parks*, and the comments below.

Pinal County Sheriff's Department has jurisdiction in the southern part of the Superstition Wilderness. Contact them at 971 North Jason Lopez Circle, Building C, Florence, AZ 85132, (520) 866-5111, www.pinalcountyaz.gov/sheriff.

Maricopa County Sheriff's Department has jurisdiction in the northern portion of the Superstition Wilderness. Contact them at Mesa District, 1   840 S. Lewis, Mesa, AZ 85210, (602) 876-1853, www.mcso.org.

Gila County Sheriff's Department has jurisdiction on the eastern end of the Superstition Wilderness near Roosevelt Lake. Contact them at 1100 South Street, Globe, AZ 85502, (928) 425-4449, www.gilacountyaz.gov/government/sheriff.

GOVERNMENT AGENCIES

Arizona State Land Department, 1616 W. Adams St., Phoenix, AZ 85007, permits and general information (602) 542-4631, www.azland.gov.

Forest Supervisors Office, Tonto National Forest, 2324 E. McDowell Road, Phoenix, AZ 85006, (602) 225-5200, www.fs.fed.us/r3/tonto.

Globe Ranger District, Tonto National Forest, 7680 S. Six Shooter Canyon Road, Globe, AZ 85501, (928) 402-6200, www.fs.fed.us/r3/tonto.

Mesa Ranger District, Tonto National Forest, 5140 E. Ingram Street, Mesa, AZ 85205, (480) 610-3300, www.fs.fed.us/r3/tonto.

Tonto Basin Ranger District, Tonto National Forest, 28079 N. SR188, Roosevelt, AZ 85545, (602) 225-5395, located at Roosevelt Lake Visitors Center, www.fs.fed.us/r3/tonto.

MUSEUMS AND COLLECTIONS

Blue Bird Mine Gift Shop, 5405 N. Apache Trail, Apache Junction, AZ 85119, (480) 982-2653, 4.5 miles northeast of Apache Junction on State Route 88.

Bob Jones Museum and Superior Historical Society, 300 Main Street, Superior, AZ 85173.

Buckboard Restaurant and Museum, 1111 W. Highway 60, Superior, AZ, 85173, museum and cafe (520) 689-5800, www.worldssmallestmuseum.com.

Bullion Plaza Cultural Center & Museum, Bullion Plaza, 150 N. Plaza Circle, Miami, AZ 85539, (928) 473-3700, www.bullionplazamuseum.org.

Gila County Historical Museum and Society, 1330 N. Broad Street, Globe, AZ 85501, (928) 425-7385, www.gilahistorical.com.

Goldfield Ghost Town, 4650 N. Mammoth Mine Road, Apache Junction, AZ 85119, (480) 983-0333, www.goldfieldghosttown.com. On SR88 north of Apache Junction.

Pinal County Historical Museum and Society, 715 S. Main St., Florence, AZ 85132, (520) 868-4382, www.pinalcountyhistoricalmuseum.org.

Roosevelt Lake Visitors Center, (Tonto Basin Ranger Station), 28079 N. SR188, Roosevelt, AZ 85545, (602) 225-5395, www.fs.fed.us/r3/tonto.

Superstition Mountain Museum and Historical Society, 4087 N. Apache Trail, Apache Junction, AZ 85119, (480) 983-4888, www.SuperstitionMountainMuseum.org. On State Route 88, northeast of Apache Junction.

Tortilla Flat Restaurant, 1 Main Street, Tortilla Flat, AZ 85190, (480) 984-1776, www.tortillaflataz.com, 17 miles northeast of Apache Junction on State Route 88.

ORGANIZATIONS

Apache Junction Chamber of Commerce, 567 West Apache Trail, Apache Junction, AZ 85120, (480) 982-3141, www.ajchamber.com.

Arizona Mountaineering Club, 4340 E. Indian School Road, Ste. 21-164, Phoenix, AZ 85018, www.arizonamountaineeringclub.net.

Arizona Trail Association, mailing P.O. Box 36736, Phoenix, AZ 85067, office 534 N. Stone, Tucson, AZ 85705, (602) 252-4794, www.aztrail.org.

The Dons of Arizona, P.O. Box 44740, Phoenix, AZ 85064, (602) 258-6016, www.donsofarizona.com.

Globe-Miami Chamber of Commerce, 1360 North Broad Street (Route 60), Globe, AZ 85501 (928) 425-4495, 1-800-804-5623, www.globemiamichamber.com.

Reevis Mountain School of Self Reliance, 7448 South J–B Ranch Road, Roosevelt, AZ 85545, (928) 257-1544, info@reevismountain.org, www.reevismountain.org.

Superior Chamber of Commerce, 165 Main Street, Superior, AZ 85173, (520) 689-0200, www.superiorarizonachamber.org.

Superstition Area Land Trust (SALT), P.O. Box 582, Apache Junction, AZ 85117, (480) 983-3454, www.azsalt.org.

Superstition Mountain Treasure Hunters, 10702 East Apache Trail, Apache Junction, AZ 85120, (480) 983-3484, www.smth-gold.com.

Superstition Search and Rescue, P.O. Box 1123, Apache Junction, AZ 85117, (520) 333-7727, www.superstitionsar.org, Emergency Only (480) 898-4265.

PARKS

Besh-Ba-Gowah Archaeological Park, 1324 S. Jesse Hayes Road, Globe, AZ 85501, (928) 425-0320, www.globeaz.gov/visitors/besh-ba-gowah.

Boyce Thompson Arboretum, 37615 East Arboretum Way, Superior, AZ 85173, near milepost 223 on US60 west of Superior, (602) 827-3000, www.btarboretum.org.

Lost Dutchman State Park, 6109 N. Apache Trail, Apache Junction, AZ 85119, SR88 northeast of Apache Junction, (480) 982-4485, www.azstateparks.com/lost-dutchman/.

Tonto National Monument, 26260 N. SR188 #2, Roosevelt, AZ 85545, (928) 467-2241, on State Route 188 across from Roosevelt Lake, www.nps.gov/tont/.

RIDING STABLES

Apache Lake Ranch, P.O. Box 15693, Tortilla Flat, AZ 85190, (928) 467-2822, 2 miles west of Apache Lake at milepost 227 on State Route 88.

Don Donnelly's D-Spur Ranch Riding Stables, 15371 East Ojo Road, Gold Canyon, AZ 85118, (off of Peralta Road), (602) 810-7029, www.dondonnellyd-spur.com.

O.K. Corral Stables, 5470 E. Apache Trail, Apache Junction, AZ 85119, (480) 982-4040, www.okcorrals.com.

INDEX

Bold indicates map or photo caption.

veni, vidi, vici, 273
Vic (last name unknown), 311

W

Waggoner. *See* Wagoner
Wagner, O. E., 156, **156**
Wagoner (first name unknown), 157
Wagoner Map. *See* treasure maps
Walker, Dr. John D., 106
walls (stone and rock), 126, **136**, 139, 140,
 288, **290**, 291, 308, 312, 315
Walp, Richard "Dick," **183**, **296**, 311-312, **348**
Waltz, Jacob, 32, 34, 35, 60, 106, 126, 204,
 294, 330
Ward, Bob (Val Paris), 60
Ward, Huse, 90
water, 38. *See also* springs
waterfalls
 Bluff Spring Mountain, **148**, 151
 Lower First Water Creek, 301
 Massacre Grounds, 239
 Peters Canyon, 326, 327, 330
 Siphon Draw, 218
 Tortilla Creek, 321, 345, 346, 370, 372
 Upper First Water Creek, 178, 267
Waugh, Jim, 80
Wave Cave, 172, 185
Weaver, Pauline, 21, 80
Weavers Needle, 80, **86**, **91**, 109, 110, **136**,
 140, 141, **309**
Weavers Needle (rock climb), 80, 110, 111
Weavers Needle Crosscut Trail, 94, 96, 108,
 109, 110
Weber, Arthur "Art," **91**
Weeden, Thomas, 106
Weekes, Charles F. II, 30, **219**
Weekes, Charles F. III, 30, 31, **31**, **219**, **222**
Weekes, Charles F. IV, **222**
Weekes, Felton, **222**
Weekes, Margaret, **219**
Weekes, Merle (Peterson), **219**
Weekes, Violet, **222**
Weekes Station, **232**
Weiser, Jacob, 106
Weiser-Waker Map. *See* treasure maps
West Boulder Canyon, 270, **270**
West Boulder Saddle, 170, 172
West Boulder Trail, 170–172, **171**
West Fork First Water Creek, 264
Whetlach, James, 63
Whetrock Canyon, 61
Whiskey Spring Canyon, 157
Whiskey Spring Trail, 155
Whitlow, Charles, 32, 90

Whitlow Canyon, 128, 130, **145**
Whitlow Corral. *See* corrals
Whitlow Dam, 32
Whitlow Ranch. *See* ranches
Wickenburg, Arizona, 34
Wilburn, John, 34, 37
Wilderness Act, 37, 137
Wilderness ethics. *See* ethics
wildflowers, 221, 222
wildfires, 11, 54, 72, 128, 253, 270
wildlife
 bats, 169
 bear, **66**, 67, 276, 277, 348
 bighorn sheep, 130
 coatimundi, 130
 fox, 130
 javelina, 67, 130
 lion, 67, 130
 mule deer, 86, 130, 176
 ringtail cat, 130
Wildoner, Dewey, **265**, 311, 312
Williams, Tyler, 80
Williams Camp, 87, 91, **91**, 94
Willoughby, Harold J., **33**
Willoughby, J. R., 32, **33**
Willow Canyon, 80
Willow Creek, 272
windmills
 Cottonwood, 72, 128, 130, 134
 First Water Creek, 246, 247
 JF Headquarters, **48**
 Lower Reids Water, 130
 Reeds Water, 72, 128, 129, **129**, 130, 134
 Tortilla Well, 341, 345, 356, 357, **358**
 Upper Reids Water, 130
 Woodbury, 51, 67, 365, **365**
Wiser, Jacob, 34
Woodard, George, 31, **31**
Woodbury cabin (site), 47, **365**
Woodbury Gulch, 51, 364, 389n37
Woodbury Mill, 60
Woodbury Trail, 55, 58
Woodbury Trailhead, 41, 47
Worst, Clay, 34, 282, 292, **293**, 334

Y

Yavapai Trail, 318
Yellow Peak, 279
Yellow Peak Canyon, 279, 286
YMCA (Phoenix), 164
Young, Harland, 294

Z

Z Trail, 288, 292, 337

About the Authors

Jack Carlson and Elizabeth Stewart are the authors of the award winning books *Superstition Wilderness Trails East* (a companion volume to this book) and *Hiker's Guide to the Superstition Wilderness*.

Jack has been hiking and exploring the Superstition Mountains since 1974. He is a native of Harrisburg, Pennsylvania, and graduated from Pennsylvania State University with a B.S.E.E. degree in 1965. He received an M.B.A. degree in 1974 from Northern Arizona University.

In Chicago, Jack was employed with the steel industry and worked on computer automated industrial equipment. In Arizona, he worked as an electrical engineer in semiconductor manufacturing.

Jack resides in Tempe, Arizona, where he is the owner and publisher of Clear Creek Publishing.

Elizabeth has always loved the outdoors. As a child she traveled with her parents on many family vacations to the National Parks where she experienced the freedom of hiking and camping.

Elizabeth was born in San Francisco, California, and spent two of her high school years in London, England. She graduated from the University of California, Berkeley with an A.B. degree and from the University of Arizona with a J.D. degree. She worked for the Maricopa County Attorney in the Juvenile, Criminal, and Civil Divisions and as an Assistant Attorney General for the State of Arizona in the Civil Division.

Elizabeth served a six-year term on the Arizona State Parks Board, including a year as chairman. She is a member of the Arizona History Convention Board, The Anza Trail Foundation Board, and the Partnership for the National Trails System Board. She resides in Tempe, Arizona.

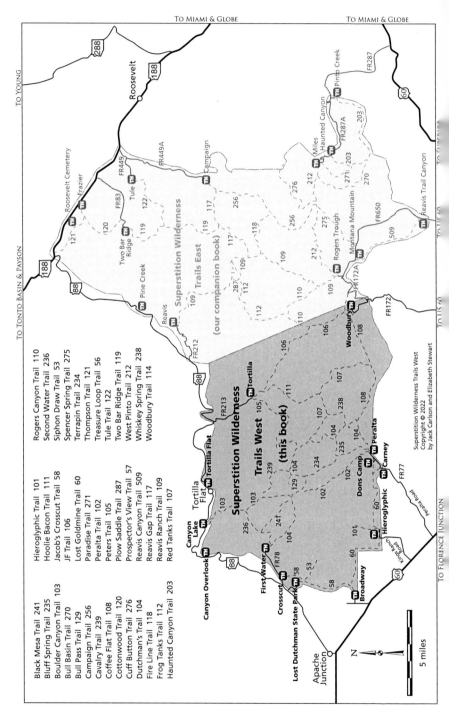

Trailheads and Trails in and near the Superstition Wilderness